Risk Communication and Community Resilience

T0384147

Risk communication is crucial to building community resilience and reducing risk from extreme events.

True community resilience involves accurate and timely dissemination of risk information to stakeholders. This book examines the policy and science of risk communication in the digital era. Themes include public awareness of risk and public participation in risk communication and resilience building. The first half of the book focuses on conceptual frameworks, components, and the role of citizens in risk communication. The second half examines the role of risk communication in resilience building and provides an overview of some of its challenges in the era of social media. This book looks at the effectiveness of risk communication in socially and culturally diverse communities in the developed and developing world.

The interdisciplinary approach bridges academic research and applied policy action. Contributions from Latin America and Asia provide insight into global risk communication at a time when digital technologies have rapidly transformed conventional communication approaches. This book will be of critical interest to policy makers, academicians, and researchers, and will be a valuable reference source for university courses that focus on emergency management, risk communication, and resilience.

Bandana Kar is a Research Scientist in the National Security Emerging Technologies Division at Oak Ridge National Laboratory, Oak Ridge, Tennessee, USA.

David M. Cochran, Jr. is a Professor of Geography in the School of Biological, Environmental and Earth Sciences at the University of Southern Mississippi in Hattiesburg, Mississippi, USA.

Routledge Studies in Hazards, Disaster Risk and Climate Change
Series Editor: Ilan Kelman
Reader in Risk, Resilience and Global Health at the Institute for Risk and
Disaster Reduction (IRDR) and the Institute for Global Health (IGH),
University College London (UCL)

This series provides a forum for original and vibrant research. It offers contributions from each of these communities as well as innovative titles that examine the links between hazards, disasters and climate change, to bring these schools of thought closer together. This series promotes interdisciplinary scholarly work that is empirically and theoretically informed, with titles reflecting the wealth of research being undertaken in these diverse and exciting fields.

Community Engagement in Post-Disaster Recovery
Edited by Graham Marsh, Iftekhar Ahmed, Martin Mulligan, Jenny Donovan
and Steve Barton

Climate, Environmental Hazards and Migration in Bangladesh
Max Martin

Governance of Risk, Hazards and Disasters
Trends in Theory and Practice
Edited by Giuseppe Forino, Sara Bonati and Lina Maria Calandra

Disasters, Vulnerability, and Narratives
Writing Haiti's Futures
Kasia Mika

Climate Change Impacts and Women's Livelihood
Vulnerability in Developing Countries
Salim Momtaz and Muhammad Asaduzzaman

Risk Communication and Community Resilience
Edited by Bandana Kar and David M. Cochran, Jr.

For more information about this series, please visit: www.routledge.com/Routledge-Studies-in-Hazards-Disaster-Risk-and-Climate-Change/book-series/HDC

Risk Communication and Community Resilience

**Edited by Bandana Kar and
David M. Cochran, Jr.**

Routledge
Taylor & Francis Group

LONDON AND NEW YORK

First published 2019
by Routledge
2 Park Square, Milton Park, Abingdon, Oxon OX14 4RN

and by Routledge
605 Third Avenue, New York, NY 10017

First issued in paperback 2020

Routledge is an imprint of the Taylor & Francis Group, an informa business

British Library Cataloguing-in-Publication Data
A catalogue record for this book is available from the British Library

Library of Congress Cataloging-in-Publication Data
A catalog record for this book has been requested

ISBN 13: 978-0-367-72813-7 (pbk)
ISBN 13: 978-1-138-08821-4 (hbk)

Typeset in Times New Roman
by Apex CoVantage, LLC

Contents

Acknowledgments

The publication of this book has involved the dedication, inspiration, and hard work of many people over the last few years. We greatly appreciate our colleagues at Routledge who believed in this project from the beginning even when it was little more than an idea. We are thankful to Faye Leerink for approaching us about editing this book and guiding us through the proposal stage. We are also deeply indebted to Ruth Anderson, who has been remarkably patient and supportive of this project as we progressed from original proposal to published volume. This book is part of the series, *Routledge Studies in Hazards, Disaster Risk and Climate Change*, which, since 2015, has produced an impressive number of insightful and cutting-edge studies. We great appreciate Dr. Ilan Kelman, the editor of this series, for his support of our proposal and for his valuable feedback in the early stages of the project. We are honored to have our book be part of this distinguished series.

We also thank our 32 authors and co-authors who contributed their valuable time and research results to the success of this volume. The fifteen chapters in this book represent a wide range of themes that speak to the vitality and diversity of the risk communication and resilience literature. We are grateful to the authors for their patience and timely response to our requests.

For the past five years, we have organized paper sessions on Risk Communication and Resilience at the annual American Association of Geographers (AAG) meetings. We are grateful to our presenters over the years and their thoughtful comments that have contributed to how we have approached this book. We look forward to sharing ideas and learning from other researchers on this topic of risk communication and resilience at future AAG meetings.

We would like to thank the National Science Foundation (CMMI-1335187) and the United States Department of Homeland Security (HSHQDC-12-C-00057) for funding our work on risk communication and resilience on the Mississippi Gulf Coast over several years. Their support provided the foundation for hiring a dynamic team of researchers, including Dr. J. O. "Joby" Bass, and research assistants, including Nicole E. Callais, James Dickens, Haley Feather, Lamar Gillespie, William Kinkead, Cody Knuth, Xiaohui Liu, Abigail Smith, Matt Sumrall, and Joslyn Zale.

Lastly, we thank the readers of this book and hope they find inspiration in these chapters to pursue new research pathways in risk communication and community resilience.

Bandana Kar,
Oak Ridge National Laboratory
David M. Cochran, Jr.,
University of Southern Mississippi

Figures

Tables

Contributors

Kathryn E. Anthony, Ph.D., is an Assistant Professor in the School of Communication at the University of Southern Mississippi. Her research interests are medical decision-making, risk and crisis communication, disaster communication, and patient-provider communication. She has served as a research consultant for the March of Dimes and the National Center for Food Protection and Defense.

DeeDee Bennett, Ph.D., is an Assistant Professor in the College of Emergency Preparedness, Homeland Security, and Cyber Security at the University at Albany – SUNY. She was Assistant Professor and Director of the Emergency Management and Disaster Science program at the University of Nebraska at Omaha. Her primary research areas include emergency management, socially vulnerable populations during disasters, emergency communications, disaster policy, and mobile wireless communications. Dr. Bennett has received funding from the National Science Foundation and the Department of Homeland Security for her research, and has published on topics related to emergency management, disability, and wireless technology.

Brandon C. Boatwright is a doctoral student in the School of Advertising and Public Relations at the University of Tennessee, Knoxville.

Nicole E. Callais, M.S., is a Ph.D. student in the Department of Geography at the University of Tennessee in Knoxville, Tennessee.

Ava M. Christie, Ph.D., is a Project Manager for West Star Development, a commercial real estate investment and management firm. Ava's research focuses on Local Emergency Planning Committees in Kansas. Ava is a member of the American Institute of Architects (AIA), and has served on the Kansas Assessment Team training and activating professionals to assess buildings for re-entry safety after disasters. She is a committee member of the AIA's National Disaster Assistance Committee, and is also serving on the planning committee for the EPA's Region 7 Local Emergency Planning Committee Educational and Training Conference.

David M. Cochran, Jr., Ph.D., is a Professor of Geography in the School of Biological, Environmental and Earth Sciences at the University of Southern Mississippi in Hattiesburg, Mississippi. His research focuses on risk perceptions, resilience, and sustainability of coastal populations in the Gulf of Mexico and Caribbean Sea. His research has been funded by IIE-Fulbright, National Science Foundation, Department of Homeland Security, and the Gulf Region Health Outreach Program. His current work examines household resilience among ethnic minorities, immigrants, and disadvantaged communities of the Mississippi Gulf Coast.

Christopher A. Craig, Ph.D., is an Assistant Professor of Management at the Arthur J. Bauernfeind College of Business at Murray State University in Murray, Kentucky. His research explores the complex interactions among businesses, the natural environment, and society.

Frances L. Edwards, M.U.P., Ph.D., CEM, is Deputy Director of the National Transportation Security Center at Mineta Transportation Institute, professor of political science, and director of the MPA program at San Jose State University. She is the author or co-author of three books, twelve monographs for MTI, more than 20 chapters in professional books and over 30 articles. She has consulted with DHS, FEMA, National Academy of Sciences, NATO, the European Union, and agencies in Japan and Turkey. She is a certified emergency manager with 20 years' experience as a director of emergency services in California, and a term on the Seismic Safety Commission.

Michael Egnoto, Ph.D., is an Assistant Clinical Professor at the University of Maryland and an Affiliated Researcher at the National Consortium for the Study of Terrorism and Responses to Terrorism (START).

Song Feng, Ph.D., is an Associate Professor of Climatology in the Department of Geosciences at the University of Arkansas in Fayetteville, Arkansas. His research interests encompass past, present, and future climate changes and impacts using global and regional climate models and advanced statistical methods.

Matthew L. Fahrenbruch is a Doctoral Candidate in Geography at the University of Kansas. He is a broad-based field geographer with interest in nature-society topics in Latin America and the American West. Of specific interest are rural political ecologies of tourism and resource production. His research has focused on tourism development and vulnerability in San Juan del Sur, Nicaragua, and the political ecology of jellyfish fisheries on the Miskitu Coast of Nicaragua. Mathew also served as a Research Assistant on a federally funded project, 'Central America Indigena' that studied indigenous land tenure and the impact resource use in Central America.

Suzanne L. Frew is the President and Founder of The Frew Group, a consulting firm that helps public and private sectors bridge cultural divides and create risk resilient communities. She uses innovative strategies such as games and design thinking to include diversity, equity and inclusion in the development of culturally-competent policies, programs and cross-cultural communication strategies. She is an adjunct instructor in the University of Hawaii's National Disaster Preparedness Center, a contributing author of professional articles and book chapters, a member of the International Association of Emergency Managers' Emerging Technology Caucus and the Diversity Committee, and the Gender and Disaster Network.

Daniel C. Goodrich, MPA, CEM, MEP, is the Senior Transportation Security Scientist at the Mineta Transportation Institute at San Jose State University, and a lecturer in the MSTM and MPA programs. He is co-author of eight monographs for MTI, research report for NCHRP, and five chapters in professional books. He has consulted with Transportation Research Board, NATO, the European Union, and agencies in Austria and Turkey. He is a Certified Emergency Manager with over twenty years' experience in the fields of security and emergency management, including the US Marine Corps Security Forces, county public health emergency management, and Lockheed Martin Space Systems. He is a Master Exercise Practitioner.

Margaret Hellweg, Dr. rer. nat., has been the Operations Manager at the University of California Berkeley Seismological Laboratory (BSL) since 2005. She completed her Diploma from the Universität Göttingen (Masters) in Physics. She has worked in broadband seismology at the Bundesanstalt für Geowissenschaften und Rohstoffe, in strong motion seismology at the United States Geological Survey in Menlo Park, and in volcano seismology for her doctoral thesis at the Universität Stuttgart. Dr Hellweg joined the BSL in 2001 as a postdoc working on regional moment tensors for nuclear monitoring.

Andrew M. Hilburn, Ph.D., is an Assistant Professor of Geography in the Department of Social Sciences at Texas A&M International University in Laredo, TX. His research focuses on diverse themes ranging from energy geographies, waste management, rural property and territorial regimes, and community development in Mexico and the US. As a stand-alone geographer, he teaches an even more expansive range of courses while promoting geographic education in Laredo. Dr. Hilburn holds degrees in Geography from the University of South Alabama (B.S.), University of Southern Mississippi (M.S.), and University of Kansas (Ph.D.).

Bandana Kar, Ph.D., is a Research Scientist in the National Security Emerging Technologies Division at Oak Ridge National Laboratory. She was an Associate Professor in the Department of Geography and Geology at the University of Southern Mississippi. Her continuing research focuses on integrating geospatial and computational sciences to understand urban dynamics and human dimensions of global change for building resilient infrastructures and cities in the digital era. Her research interests are in geospatial intelligence, crisis informatics and knowledge discovery, urban and infrastructure resilience, emergency management and humanitarian responses, and risk communication. She has been funded by the Department of Homeland Security, National

Science Foundation, Department of Defense, and National Aeronautics and Space Administration.

Salimah LaForce is Senior Policy Analyst at the Georgia Institute of Technology's Center for Advanced Communications Policy (CACP). She has 14 years of experience conducting policy and industry research for CACP's emergency communications initiative, as well as user needs research, utilizing study results to inform policy recommendations in several domains, including technology access, generally, and the benefit of said access to educational, employment, and social opportunities, specifically. Salimah is the project director for the Wireless RERC project, Policy and Outreach Initiatives to Accelerate Adoption of Wireless Technologies. She has co-authored more than 78 federal regulatory filings, papers, presentations, and journal articles.

Brooke Fisher Liu, Ph.D., conducts research on how government messages, media, and interpersonal communication motivate people to successfully prepare for, respond to, and recover from natural and anthropogenic disasters and disease outbreaks. Her current research focuses on the role of social and mobile media in building community resilience along with factors such as demographics, emotions, hazard knowledge, religiosity, and risk perception. Liu is an Associate Professor of Communication at the University of Maryland, and leads the Risk Communication & Resilience Research Program at the National Consortium for the Study of Terrorism and Responses to Terrorism (START), a U.S. Department of Homeland Security Center of Excellence.

Xiaohui Liu, Ph.D., is a post-doctoral researcher in Social Work and International Studies at Dalhousie University in Halifax, Nova Scotia, Canada.

Lauren L. Morris, Ph.D., holds a B.S. in Environmental Science and Policy from the University of Maryland and an M.S. in Oceanography and Coastal Science and a Ph.D. in Geography from Louisiana State University. In 2011, she participated in the Knauss Marine Policy Fellowship in Washington, D.C. From 2012 to 2016, she worked as the sustainability coordinator for Louisiana Sea Grant, where she participated in and led projects on hazard resilience and community sustainability. At the time of this writing, she is an independent researcher living in Tennessee.

Oluponmile Olonilua, Ph.D., is an Associate Professor in the Political Science Department at Texas Southern University. Her research focuses on emergency management, risk and crisis, public policy, etc. She is a board member of the Natural Hazards Mitigation Association and a member of the Texas Floodplain Managers Association. She is also a certified floodplain manager and a hazard mitigation/floodplain management plan reviewer for Community Rating System credits with the Insurance Services Office (ISO). She was the 2009 recipient of the Mary Fran Myers Scholarship award and is the Continuing Education Credit Coordinator for the Natural Hazards Workshop.

Tyler G. Page, Ph.D., examines the effects of crisis communication, both from a reputation perspective and from a safety perspective. He has a background in public relations and marketing in the technology sector, including work as the first marketing/public relations person at Qualtrics. His dissertation research developed a new model for examining the relationship between crisis response messages and postcrisis reputation. Dr. Page is an Assistant Professor at Mississippi State University and resides with his wife and son in Starkville.

Elizabeth L. Petrun Sayers, Ph.D., is a full behavioral and social scientist at the RAND Corporation with over ten years of experience researching risk-related topics. Petrun Sayers studies how traditional and new media shape risk perceptions, decision making, and behaviors. Her current research focuses on understanding how individuals respond to health, security, and environmental risks. Petrun Sayers' research has been supported by grants and contracts from multiple federal agencies, including the Department of Homeland Security, Department of Defense, Centers for Disease Control and Prevention, and the National Science Foundation, among others.

Andrew S. Pyle, Ph.D., is an Assistant Professor in the Department of Communication at Clemson University. He has a Ph.D. in communication from George Mason University. His research focuses on the intersection of crisis communication and intercultural communication. His research interests are in the ways that organizations employ social media to manage crisis communication. Dr. Pyle is teaching courses in the areas of public relations and crisis communication. He is an active member of the Southern States Communication Association and the Public Relations Society of America.

Carrie E. Reif-Stice, Ph.D., is an Assistant Professor in the Department of Communication at Columbus State University in Columbus, Georgia.

Jason D. Rivera, Ph.D., is an Assistant Professor at SUNY Buffalo State within the Public Administration and Nonprofit Management Program. He earned his Ph.D. at Rutgers University–Camden in public affairs with a concentration in community development. His research interests include disaster response and recovery processes, representative bureaucracy, social capital, governance, and social justice.

Holly Ann Roberts, M.A., is a Program Manager and Researcher in the Risk Communication and Resilience Program at the National Consortium for the Study of Terrorism and Responses to Terrorism (START). Her research interests include organizational communication, risk and crisis communication, social media, natural disasters, reputation management, and health crises.

Tracie Sempier, Ph.D., is the Coastal Storms Outreach Coordinator for the Mississippi-Alabama Sea Grant Consortium in Ocean Springs, Mississippi.

Amber Silver, Ph.D., is an Assistant Professor for the College of Emergency Preparedness, Homeland Security and Cybersecurity. Her primary research interests focus on how individuals and groups make decisions before, during, and after high-impact weather. More specifically, she is interested in the roles that public attention, risk perception, and communication play in protective action decision making during extreme events. Her most recent research has focused on the ways that new technologies, including social media, influence how individuals obtain, interpret, and respond to official and unofficial warning information.

Jennifer A. Strauss, Ph.D., is the External Relations Officer, Berkeley Seismological Laboratory, serving as the head of the Berkeley Seismological Laboratory's Earthquake Research Affiliate Program, including earthquake early warning (EEW) and novel technologies for geophysical research. She is a physicist with a research history in powder diffraction, X-ray crystallography, computer modelling, and ice sheet dynamics and radar altimetry studies on the West Antarctic Ice Sheet. She was a co-chair of the inaugural Postdoctoral Society of Argonne National Laboratory. She received a bachelor of science degree in physics from the University of Texas at Austin in 2001 and a Ph.D. from Stony Brook University in May 2007.

Steven J. Venette, Ph.D., is a Professor in the Department of Communication Studies at University of Southern Mississippi. His research focuses on risk and crisis communication, organization, and argumentation of communication components.

Haorui Wu, Ph.D., is a Postdoctoral Research Associate in the Natural Hazards Center at University of Colorado Boulder. With the interdisciplinary training in the fields of engineering and applied sciences (architecture, community and regional planning, landscape architecture, and urban design) and social sciences (social work), Dr. Wu's research focus is on global climate change, disaster, and other world crises. He has been actively examining the dynamic human-place interplay in the post-disaster reconstruction, recovery, and rehabilitation initiatives through the lens of environmental and social justice, especially from the perspective of supporting and empowering vulnerable and marginalized individuals, families, and communities.

Joslyn Zale, Ph.D., is a Technical Writer and Compliance Coordinator at the National Center for Spectator Sport Safety and Security (NCS4) at the University of Southern Mississippi in Hattiesburg, Mississippi.

Thomas T. Zawisza, Ph.D., is an Assistant Professor of Justice Studies at Lasell College in Newton, Massachusetts. His primary research interest is using eye tracking technology to examine the role environmental stimuli have on the decision to burgle. He is also interested in the journey-to-crime which includes investigating reference points of victims and offenders, the distance victims and offenders travel, and the direction victims and offenders travel. Dr. Zawisza holds a bachelor's degree from Kent State University, a master's from Eastern Tennessee State University, and a doctorate from the University of Arkansas at Little Rock, all in criminal justice.

Abbreviations

ANSS	United States Advanced National Seismic System
CANTUR	National Chamber of Tourism of Nicaragua
CGS	California Geological Survey
CIA	United States Central Intelligence Agency
CISN	California Integrated Seismic Network
CMAS	Commercial Mobile Alert System
CMSAAC	Commercial Mobile Service Alert Advisory Committee
CSMIP	California Strong Motion Instrumentation Program
DHS	United States Department of Homeland Security
DMA	Disaster Mitigation Act (United States)
EAS	Emergency Alert System
ED	United States Department of Education
EPA	United States Environmental Protection Agency
EPCRA	United States Emergency Planning and Community Right to Know Act
FCC	Federal Communication Commission
FEMA	Federal Emergency Management Agency
FEWS	Famine Early Warning System
GFDRR	Global Facility for Disaster Reduction and Recovery
GSN	Global Seismographic Network
INTUR	Nicaraguan Institute of Tourism
IPAWS	Integrated Public Alert and Warning System
IRIS	Incorporated Research Institutions for Seismology
JICA	Japan International Cooperation Agency
KDEM	Kansas Division of Emergency Management
LEPC	Local Emergency Planning Committee
NASA	National Aeronautics and Space Administration
NCEI	National Centers for Environmental Information (part of the National Oceanic and Atmospheric Administration)
NEA	National Education Association Health Information Network
NEIC	United States National Earthquake Information Center
NEMA	Nigerian Emergency Management Agency
NERA	Nigerian National Emergency Relief Agency
NGDC	United States National Geophysical Data Center

NIMS	National Incident Management System
NOAA	United States National Oceanic and Atmospheric Administration
NRC	United States National Research Council
NWS	United States National Weather Service
NYSC	Nigerian National Youth Service Corps
ONC	Citizen's National Observatory (Mexico)
OSHA	United States Occupational Safety and Health Administration
PDM	Pre-Disaster Mitigation Program
PRI	Ports Resilience Index
PRM	Participatory Risk Mapping
QCN	Quake Catcher Network
RVIA	Recreational Vehicle Industry Association
SARA	United States Superfund Amendments and Reauthorization Act
SASMEX	Seismic Alert System of Mexico
SINAPRED	Nicaraguan National System for the Prevention, Mitigation, and Awareness of Disasters
UNEP	United Nations Environment Programme
UNDHA	United Nations Department of Humanitarian Affairs
UNISDR	United Nations International Strategy for Disaster Reduction
UNWTO	United Nations World Tourism Organization
UrEDAS	Urgent Earthquake Detection and Alarm System (Japan)
USAID	United States Agency for International Development
USCB	United States Census Bureau
USDOD	United States Department of Defense
USDOE	United States Department of Energy
USDOL	United States Department of Labor
USGS	United States Geological Survey
VAM	Vulnerability Analysis and Mapping
VOAD	Voluntary Organizations Active in Disasters
WARN	United States Warning Alert Response Network Act
WDC	World Data Center
WEA	Wireless Emergency Alerts
WSSN	Worldwide Standardized Seismographic Network
WTTC	World Travel and Tourism Council

Introduction

Bandana Kar and David M. Cochran, Jr.

With record high frequent and intense extreme weather events worldwide in 2017 and 2018, there is an urgent need to advance community resilience through the shared efforts of public and private sector stakeholders. Risk communication, specifically the development of a multi-hazard, multicultural, and people-centered forecasting and early warning systems, is considered an important and necessary component of resilience building efforts by such recent initiatives as the Sendai Framework, the United Nations International Strategy for Disaster Reduction, and the Rockefeller 100 Resilient Cities, among others (UN 2015).

Risk communication, being a dynamic process, requires the exchange of information among stakeholders to aid with preparedness, response, and recovery efforts before, during, and after an extreme event. Traditional risk communication follows a command-and-control approach in which information is disseminated from emergency management agencies to the broader at-risk communities. This approach ensures that accurate alert messages are disseminated from reliable sources using channels such as TV, radio, and cell phones to geotargeted communities impacted by a disaster. This approach, however, can also stifle public participation, prevent messages from being contextualized to meet the needs of diverse communities, fail to effectively integrate local knowledge about impacts in messages, and generally is limited to official – or at least mainstream – languages (e.g., English in the U.S.), thereby creating a barrier for individuals who speak other languages and potentially putting their lives at risk.

Social media and other decentralized, collaborative, and network-based systems have become popular platforms for risk communication because they allow emergency management agencies and the public to share information in near real time (Palen et al. 2009; Vieweg et al. 2010; Young, Flowers, and Ren 2011). Twitter is a good example that is being widely used by the National Weather Service (NWS), Federal Emergency Management Agency (FEMA), and U.S. Geologic Survey (USGS) for alert dissemination as well as the public to provide real-time situational awareness about a variety of different disasters. Social media enables proactive engagement of public and private stakeholders without being constrained by language, message length, or media type (i.e., information as text, audio/video, imagery, or other type) (Wendling, Radisch, and Jacobzone 2013). Social media fosters spontaneous creation of decentralized networks of users united by language, ethnicity, or geographic situation, which enables them to communicate effectively together. Social media-based risk communication also tends to incorporate more local knowledge and to provide more up-to-date information than conventional command-and-control approaches (Wendling, Radisch, and Jacobzone 2013). Nonetheless, this form of grassroots risk communication helps propagation of misinformation, reduces the overall quality of information, and fosters information overloads as a result of the non-refereed participation of numerous stakeholders both within and beyond the areas impacted by an event (Wendling, Radisch, and Jacobzone 2013).

Undoubtedly, risk communication is crucial in building resilience and mobilizing the public to take action. The effectiveness of risk communication in building resilience, however, is influenced by (1) the sociocultural-economic and psychological characteristics of the public as well as their commitment to and levels of participation, (2) the geotargeting ability of the warning systems to ensure elimination of rumors while updating alert messages, and (3) the message content and length (Kar and Cochran 2016). In view of these challenges, this book seeks to shed light on how government authority, technology, and the public can shape and improve risk communication in the 21st century. The case studies contained within these pages collectively provide an overview of risk communication by focusing on its technological, socio-economic-cultural, and political constructs and outcomes. In this regard, the book complements recent other works published by Routledge on global climate change and hazards.

This book is organized into four parts. Part 1 highlights the components of risk communication and their current challenges and limitations. DeeDee Bennett and Salimah LaForce begin this section with an in-depth examination of the Wireless Emergency Alert (WEA), an important component of the Integrated Public Alert and Warnings System (IPAWS), which is directed by the U.S. Federal Emergency Management Agency (FEMA) and other federal bodies. Since its deployment in 2012, the WEA system has become increasingly common in American society, but its long-term effectiveness depends in part on its continued improvement as a risk communications tool. The following chapter, written by Jason D. Rivera, uses bounded rationality to examine the experiences of Hurricane Sandy victims applying for federal disaster relief. Rivera finds that asymmetries in access to information effectively shut out some segments of the impacted population. For future disasters, more decentralized modes of information exchange might be more effective in achieving greater equity with regard to disaster assistance. The final chapter of Part 1, written by Bandana Kar, David M. Cochran, Jr., Joslyn Zale, Nicole E. Callais, and Xiaohui Liu, examines the perceptions and preferences of Mississippi Gulf Coast residents to the WEA system. Their results illustrate the ongoing challenge of risk communication in this diversifying area of the southeastern United States in which a small but growing segment of the population needs both English and non-English warning messages.

Part 2 examines the social constructs of risk communication by presenting the results of a series of case studies that examine the roles of citizens (and noncitizens) in risk communication. Andrew M. Hilburn and Thomas T. Zawisza begin this section with a case study about perception and communication of risk along the U.S.–Mexico border in the twin border cities of Laredo and Nuevo Laredo. Using participatory risk mapping (PRM), the authors shed light on the complex role of undocumented transnational migration, narcotrafficking, and organized crime in this dynamic and divisive international border region. The following chapter by Ava M. Christie evaluates the role of Local Emergency Planning Committees (LEPCs) as risk communication intermediaries between government agencies and the public. Focusing on the state of Kansas in the Great Plains region of the U.S., Christie identifies important urban and rural differences in the long-term effectiveness of LEPCs in communicating risk about hazardous chemical exposure. The third chapter in Part 2, written by Suzanne L. Frew, focuses on the role of social media in risk communication, not only in terms of preparedness, response, and recovery but more importantly as a tool for long-term community resilience. Drawing from a series of case studies, Frew demonstrates how social media has been used to support risk reduction, expand outreach and engagement, and open up mitigation planning to ever broader segments of the public. Oluponmile Olonilua concludes this section with a case study of risk communication and disaster response in Nigeria. Government risk communication in Nigeria remains largely top-down in nature, but widespread use of mobile phone social media apps among the public indicates that more decentralized approaches might prove more effective.

Part 3 highlights current challenges of effectively using risk communication in community resilience building activities. Frances L. Edwards, Daniel C. Goodrich, Margaret Hellweg, and Jennifer A. Strauss begin with an examination of earthquake early warning systems in Japan and California. The rapid onset and potentially widespread impacts of earthquakes make their accurate and timely forecasting extremely important. Technological advancements in sensors over the last half-century have gone far to safeguard public rail transportation, emergency services, and other vital infrastructures from potentially catastrophic impacts of earthquakes. Kathryn E. Anthony, Steven J. Venette, Andrew S. Pyle, Brandon C. Boatwright, and Carrie E. Reif-Stice follow with a chapter that emphasizes the importance of strategic design in risk communication messaging. The authors argue that risk communication policy should focus on the dissemination of consistent information through multiple channels, especially social media, to ensure that appropriate and timely messages reach as diverse a cross-section of society as possible. The third chapter of Part 3, written by Lauren L. Morris and Tracie Sempier, focuses on the U.S. ports in the Gulf of Mexico. Using the Ports Resilience Index (PRI), the authors examine how greater communication between port authorities, tenants, and customers enhances risk communication through greater engagement of stakeholders in disaster preparedness planning. Haorui Wu concludes Part 3 with a study of a reconstruction project following the 2013 Lushan Earthquake in China. Wu draws from a series of qualitative interviews and focus groups to recount how different stakeholders, including government personnel, university researchers, and local residents, used participatory dialogue to rebuild rural communities impacted by the disaster with the goal of maximizing resilience and reducing risk.

Part 4 highlights the challenges still associated with risk communication that need to be addressed in order to reduce risk and build resilience as identified by the Sendai Framework. Christopher A. Craig, Elizabeth L. Petrun Sayers, and Song Feng begin this section with an examination of the role of risk communication and weather in the tourism industry. Focusing on a coastal camping facility in the southeastern U.S., the authors demonstrate how effective risk communication can offset at least some of the economic impacts of climate change and extreme weather to bolster the resilience of tourism businesses. Continuing along the theme of tourism, Matthew L. Fahrenbruch offers a case study of San Juan del Sur, a Pacific coast community in Nicaragua. The community was devastated by a tsunami in 1992, and a burgeoning tourism industry has developed since then. Despite efforts to increase risk communication capacity through a tsunami early warning system, greater attention must be placed on specific vulnerabilities unique to the tourism industry. The third chapter in Part 4, written by Tyler G. Page, Brooke Fisher Liu, Holly Ann Roberts, and Michael Egnoto, examines risk communication in K-12 education in the United States. Drawing from the results of a survey of schools on the East Coast, the authors provide an in-depth view of how teachers, staff, and administrators prepare for crises through risk communication protocol and what needs to be done to improve existing practices. In the concluding chapter of Part 4, Amber Silver explores the potential of social media as a risk communication tool, drawing example from a series of recent events. Silver argues that social media, although not without its weaknesses, has an enormous potential for improving community resilience before, during, and after disasters and crises.

References

Kar, B., and Cochran, D. 2016. Final Report – An Integrated Approach to Geo-Target At-Risk Communities and Deploy Effective Crisis Communication Approaches. *Department of Homeland Security – Science and Technology Directorate (DHS – S&T)*. Accessed on December 20, 2018 at www.dhs.gov/publication/integrated-approach-geo-target-risk-communities-deploy-effective-crisis-communication.

Palen, L., Vieweg, S., Liu, S. and Hughes, A. 2009. Crisis in a Networked World Features of Computer-Mediated Communication in the April 16, 2007, Virginia Tech event. *Social Science Computer Review*, 1–14.

United Nations Office for Disaster Reduction. Sendai Framework for Disaster Risk Reduction 2015–2030. 2015. In *Proceedings of the Third United Nations World Conference; United Nations Office for Disaster Reduction*. Geneva, Switzerland.

Vieweg, S., Hughes, A., Starbird, K., and Palen, L. 2010. *Microblogging During Two Natural Hazard Events: What Twitter May Contribute to Situational Awareness*. CHI 2010. Atlanta, Georgia, April.

Young, C. L., Flowers, A., and Ren, N. 2011. Technology and Crisis Communication: Emerging Themes from a Pilot Study of US Public Relations Practitioners. *Prism*, 8(1): 1–11.

Wendling, C., Radisch, J., and Jacobzone, S. 2013. *The Use of Social Media in Risk and Crisis Communication*. OECD Working Papers on Public Governance, No. 24, OECD Publishing, Paris. Accessed at http://dx.doi.org/10.1787/5k3v01fskp9s-en.

Part 1

Risk communication in the digital era

In the face of increased frequency and severity of disasters worldwide, risk communication is increasingly seen as a precondition of disaster preparedness, response, and recovery. Risk communication involves the exchange of information among stakeholders about an impending hazard and its associated risks, with the intent of helping local populations take appropriate actions to mitigate its impacts. Following a disaster, there is a need to disseminate verifiable, accurate, and updated information to the impacted communities in order to assist with relief and response efforts.

A variety of technologies are used for risk communication, including conventional devices such as TV and radio and advanced digital communication technologies like social media and cell phones. Traditional risk communication follows a command-and-control structure in which information is disseminated hierarchically from authorized agencies or organizations to communities at risk. In the United States, Wireless Emergency Alert (WEA) messages are disseminated over cell phones during hazard events. With the rise of connected devices and widespread use of the Internet, digital communication and social media have become vital to post-disaster risk communication. Specifically, community initiatives at the local level allow using digital communication to provide contextual and situational information needed for shelter, medical assistance, and search and rescue operations, among others. The success of digital communication is dependent on the participation of local actors and organizations to produce local knowledge while identifying conflicts and hoaxes.

The success of risk communication in this digital era is influenced by the availability of applications and devices, the participation of the public, and the capability of using the same technologies for different disasters. On September 19, 2016, WEA alerts were sent to residents of New York City to encourage the public to help apprehend a bombing suspect, which caused public uproar and complicated an already tense situation. The experience demonstrated that WEA messages might be effective in disseminating risk information and mobilizing public response during natural hazards but are less effective or a hindrance during other types of hazardous events. Likewise, social media, while allowing the public to share and generate contextual knowledge, also promotes the dissemination of information that is not validated for useful for humanitarian or emergency management purposes (Liu et al. 2018). Furthermore, social media users sharing information about a hazard event may not even come from the location where the event has occurred. Social-mediated crisis communication models reveal that social media users depend more on broadcast journalists for information during a disaster event than social media itself (Austin, Liu, and Jin 2012; Liu, Fraustino, and Jin 2015). It is also unclear how dependable digital communication technologies are during and after a disaster event. While conventional channels like sirens could be used for communication, cell phones might be temporarily out of order, as was the case during Hurricane Maria in Puerto Rico.

The last – and most important – component of a successful risk communication is the public, who need to receive, understand, and respond to messages. While both hierarchical and nonhierarchical systems of risk communication are widespread, members of the public are ultimately the ones responsible for deciding what information to trust and act on. While the recent increase in character length of WEA messages from 90 to 360 allows for the dissemination of more pertinent information, the language of WEA messages (English) is prohibitive for certain segments of society who are not proficient in English (Kar 2017). By contrast, social media and digital communication allows for information to be disseminated in languages other than English, but might be limited in terms of how to respond to hazard events (Kar 2017). It is critical to understand these pros and cons of contemporary risk communication before exploring what the future of risk communication should be and how it could be integrated in resilience building activities.

The first section of the book provides a look at the conceptual framework of risk communication by highlighting three chapters that explore the components of risk communication. Chapter 1 addresses the issue of technology and its accessibility in the context of disabled population and population with limited English proficiency. This chapter sheds light on the advantages and weaknesses of WEA and current Integrated Public Alert and Warnings System (IPAWS) in meeting the need of impacted communities in the U.S. in disseminating risk information. Chapter 2 explores how public and emergency management agencies (EMA) perceive different channels and technologies used for risk communication. While both traditional and digital communication are used and preferred by the general public and EMA personnel, it is essential to understand which channels are being trusted by these two groups to create a beneficial and successful risk communication environment. Chapter 3 draws from a case study of the Mississippi Gulf Coast and explores how warning messages are perceived and used by the general public. It functions as a conclusion to this first section, but it also lays the foundation for the following three sections of the book.

References

Austin, L., Liu, B., and Jin, Y. 2012. How Audiences Seek Out Crisis Information: Exploring the Social-Mediated Crisis Communication Model. *Journal of Applied Communication Research*, 40: 188–207.

Kar, B. 2017. Results of an Integrated Approach to Geo-Target At-Risk Communities and Deploy Effective Crisis Communication Approaches. In *Emergency Alert and Warning Systems: Current Knowledge and Future Research Directions*. Washington, DC: The National Academies Press, pp. 70–73.

Liu, B., Fraustino, J., and Jin, Y. 2015. How Disaster Information Form, Source, Type, and Prior Disaster Exposure Affect Public Outcomes: Jumping on the Social Media Bandwagon? *Journal of Applied Communication Research*, 43(1): 44–65.

Liu, X., Kar, B., Zhang, C., and Cochran, D. 2018. Assessing Relevance of Tweets for Risk Communication. *International Journal of Digital Earth*, 12. doi:10.1080/17538947.2018.1480670.

1 Text-to-action

Understanding the interaction between accessibility of Wireless Emergency Alerts and behavioral response

DeeDee Bennett and Salimah LaForce

Wireless communications

Disaster warnings are messages sent to inform the public about preparedness and response activities related to an imminent or ongoing event. The public often decides whether or not to take protective action based on the method of dissemination, the content of the message, and individual circumstances (Lindell and Perry 1987, 2003; Mileti 1999; Rogers and Sorensen 1991). Research indicates that clear warning messages that include specific locations regarding the hazard event can increase the likelihood that people take protective action (Latimer 2009; Lindell and Perry 2012). Typically, emergency management agencies (or other alert authorities) are responsible for the dissemination of disaster warnings using a variety of methods, including television, radio, outdoor sirens, social media, and mobile phones. For some individuals, timely receipt of the warnings is dependent on the method used. For example, people indoors may not receive an alert if it is sent only by outdoor sirens. Likewise, those listening to online streaming audio may not receive a warning message if it is sent only through the Emergency Alert System. Focusing on one of the most recently employed methods, WEA, this chapter details messages received on mobile wireless devices. The mobile wireless modality and ubiquity is intended to ensure timely receipt of emergency messaging and ameliorate dependency on legacy messaging systems that may not reach all populations in an impacted area. Studies have indicated that certain populations may experience different impacts following disasters (Fothergill, Maestas, and Darlington 1999; Lindell and Perry 2003; Wisner et al. 2003). In emergency management, these populations are known as those with access and functional needs; in academic terms, these are the populations often most at risk. The most vulnerable populations may vary from country to country, and membership in one group does not guarantee increased risk. Historically, however, vulnerable populations have been disproportionately affected by disasters (Tierney 2006; Wisner et al. 2003). In the U.S., the more vulnerable populations include people with disabilities, certain racial and ethnic minorities, older adults, individuals with low literacy, those for whom English is a second language, and lower income households, among others. Given the increased risk of some vulnerable populations, this chapter focuses on the accessibility of emergency alerts on mobile devices for vulnerable populations emphasizing concerns for people with disabilities. In particular, this chapter describes accessibility considerations across the warning process, notably receiving, factors that impact understanding, and responding (i.e., the decision to take protective action) to alerts and warnings sent via mobile wireless devices. It provides background information on wireless alerting mechanisms and summarizes the results from several studies (Table 1.1) related to WEA. The discussion section identifies and briefly addresses the strengths, weaknesses, opportunities, and threats to emergency messages.

Receiving modalities

As American adults increasingly keep their cell phones near them at all times, emergency messages through cell networks are more likely to reach people than any other alerting channel (e.g., television, radio, NOAA weather radio, sirens). Approximately 70 percent of users never turn their phone off, and 65 percent indicated that they sleep near their phone (Lenhart 2010; Smith 2011). As of November 2016, 95 percent of Americans owned a mobile phone, 77 percent of which were smartphones (Pew Research Center 2017). This technology transition, from fixed to mobile, in the emergency communications context, has unique implications for many different segments of historically underserved populations. For example, wireless-only households are on the rise and research indicates that minorities, the economically disadvantaged, and young adults are pushing the trend (Blumberg and Luke 2009, 2017; Dutwin, Keeter, and Kennedy 2010). For example, nearly 64.8 percent of Hispanic households and 59 percent of Americans living near poverty live in wireless-only households (Blumberg and Luke 2017). Large majorities of people with disabilities use mobile phones, with many members of the deaf population often using mobile phones (and texting) as a primary communication tool (Wireless RERC 2009). As such, sending emergency messages via mobile wireless devices has the potential to reach a diverse and dynamic population. At least three methods of disaster warnings are possible via mobile devices: subscription-based messaging services, mobile applications (apps), and WEAs.

Subscription-based messaging

Local governments and college campuses often use proprietary, subscription-based messaging services to alert their communities of threats to health, life, or property. Public warnings received through this service are only dedicated to the location where the user subscribed. These messages also are sent via short message services (SMS) and are often subject to bandwidth congestion experienced during disasters. Despite this limitation, a 2013 census survey of approved alert authorities found that the majority of local municipalities use a subscription-based messaging service to disseminate disaster warnings (Bennett 2015). Advancements in mobile phone technology, however, may threaten the viability of such

Table 1.1 Summary of study purposes, methods, samples, and key findings

Project	Purpose	Methods	Sample(s)	Key Findings	Citation
2013 WEA Survey Rehabilitation Engineering Research Center for Wireless Technologies (Wireless RERC) Funded by the National Institute on Disability, Independent Living, and Rehabilitation Research (NIDLRR formally NIDRR)	Establish an evidence base regarding WEA and people with disabilities via data collections on the availability, awareness, and accessibility of WEAs.	Study specific survey, online data collection (convenience sample)	$N = 1830$ $n = 321$ (disability)	WEA alerts need additional features to be more effective. Over 70% of respondents like the idea of including icons, graphics or maps in the WEA message, and 67% of respondents like the idea of an Internet link so that they may receive more information. Respondents with disabilities who responded expressed concerns with the receipt of WEA alerts, system consistency, and requests for additional features.	Bennett (2015)
2013 Survey of Integrated Public Alert and Warnings System (IPAWS) approved alert authorities Center for Advanced Communications Policy (CACP) Funded by the Department of Homeland Security, Federal Emergency Management Agency, IPAWS Program Management Office	Collect data on local alerting officials' adoption of WEA as an option to disseminate emergency messages, level of comfort with the system, and frequency of use.	Study specific survey directly emailed to all IPAWS approved alerting authorities (random sample)	$N = 139$ (33% response rate)	The majority of authorities are not using IPAWS for WEA. They indicated a need for (a) additional training and (b) the ability to test the system. Respondents did not consider the needs of people with disabilities for alerting.	Bennett, Benson, and Sharpe (2014)

(Continued)

Table 1.1 (Continued)

Project	Purpose	Methods	Sample(s)	Key Findings	Citation
2014 Focus Groups Center for Advanced Communications Policy (CACP) Funded by the U.S. Department of Homeland Security, Science and Technology Directorate	Explore features needed in mobile devices, including customizable notification signals (vibration strengths, light cadence, sound frequencies) to increase WEA message recognition. Focus group findings informed the development of prototype discussed later.	Five focus groups were conducted using a purposeful sampling of individuals with hearing disabilities.	$N = 35$	The WEA audible signal should incorporate extreme multi-pitch tones. The WEA audible signal should override the phone's volume setting, turning on the volume if necessary. The WEA tactile signal should be detectable through purses and clothing, and users should be able to vary the strength of the tactile signal by changing a setting on their phone. WEAs should enable all visual signals on the phone. Incoming WEA messages should be interoperable with the mobile phone's Bluetooth system so that the alert can be transmitted to other wearable alerting systems.	Mitchell, LaForce, Linden, Bennett, and Touzet (2014)
2014–2015: Public Response to Alerts and Warnings: Optimizing the Ability of Message Receipt by People with Disabilities Center for Advanced Communications Policy (CACP)	Research and development efforts aimed at maximizing message diffusion to deaf and hard-of-hearing citizens by determining the ideal vibration strength for a WEA and assessing	Market analyses to ensure the prototype was based upon the market realities in which WEA operated. Including the accessibility level of WEA-capable devices,	214 WEA-capable cell phones in accessibility review 28 WEA-capable cell phones in vibration strength testing	Vibration strength is a factor in response time to WEA messages, BUT stronger is not always better. User's response time indicated that a vibration strength of 1.4g is most effective. Beyond 1.4g, diminishing value to certain groups (stronger is not always better).	Department of Homeland Security (2015)

Funded by the U.S. Department of Homeland Security, Science and Technology Directorate	the utility of adding a display light to alert people who are deaf or hard-of-hearing of an incoming WEA message. quantifying the vibration strengths of WEA-capable devices on the market. Iterative prototype design and development. Usability testing.	46 usability study participants 20 Deaf or hard-of-hearing 22 blind or low vision 4 deaf-blind	Adding a WEA light cadence can increase response time to WEA messages populations. Simultaneously activating all notification signals – sound, vibration, and light – will increase timely receipt of WEA messages.	Center for Advanced Communications Policy (2015)
2015 WEA Survey Center for Advanced Communications Policy (CACP) Funded by the U.S. Department of Homeland Security, Science and Technology Directorate	Revised the initial 2013 WEA survey and collected data to assess awareness, use, and subsequent protective action after receipt of a WEA message.	$N = 1334$ $n = 713$ (disability)	Respondents without a disability were twice as likely to report having heard of WEA before taking the survey (WEA-aware). Respondents that were WEA-aware were more likely to take immediate protective actions based on the information in the alert. The majority of all respondents all respondents indicated an interest in the inclusion of icons, graphics, maps, or an Internet link in the alert message. 21% indicated an interest in the inclusion of an ASL interpretation of the message.	

services. Mobile phone numbers are increasingly becoming as important as our social security numbers (Petrow 2017). As mobile wireless devices become unique identifiers, an already reluctant public may wish to restrict use further, limiting the reach of these emergency messaging services.

Mobile applications (apps)

Apps are also used as emergency communications tools. Apps may originate through state or local municipalities or through third-party private organizations. Both types require users to install the application on their mobile devices. Many warning-related mobile apps also require users to enable their global positioning service (GPS) or location-based mechanisms and enable push notifications for optimal utility. These requirements may prevent the full functionality of the app regardless of individual ability – for example, users with insufficient storage on their mobile device. Apps, while otherwise convenient, are similar to the subscription-based messaging regarding the location of the potential hazard. Messages received through apps are dedicated to the location of the local municipality, or the app could be dedicated to location(s) manually selected by the user. Again, emergency message receipt via this vehicle is limited.

Wireless Emergency Alerts (WEAs)

WEA messages appear on mobile phones similar to text messages. However, WEA does not use SMS technology to send messages (NRC 2011). Instead, WEA messages are sent via cell broadcast technology. Cell broadcast technology uses cell towers within the immediate impact area and sends messages to mobile phones within reach of the towers (FEMA 2014; NRC 2011) allowing the messages to be geotargeted (NRC 2013). Therefore, only individuals in the impacted area will receive the message directly. The automatic delivery and the use of cell broadcasting are the main features that distinguish WEA messages from other subscription-based third-party emergency message services (Bennett and Laforce 2013; NRC 2011). Also, cell broadcast messages do not rely on the data channel to send WEAs and are therefore not subject to any network congestion during emergencies (NRC 2011).

WEA history

Ever-increasing cell phone use in the United States is cause for concern regarding the modernization of the nation's emergency alerting capabilities and has catalyzed a massive effort to integrate multiple infrastructures and methods used for emergency alerting into a unified system. On June 26, 2006, *Executive Order 13407: Public Alert and Warning System* outlined the "policy of the United States to have an effective, reliable, integrated, flexible, and comprehensive system to alert and warn the American people in situations of war, terrorist attack, natural disaster, or other hazards to public safety and well-being (public alert and warning system)" (EO 13407 2006). The U.S. Department of Homeland Security (DHS) presided over the implementation of the policy outlined in EO 13407. Among the many functions detailed in EO 13407 was the ability to alert people with disabilities and distribute geographically targeted alerts. Function IV states that DHS shall "include in the public alert and warning system the capacity to alert and warn all Americans, including those with disabilities and those without an understanding of the English language." In the fall of 2006, Title VI: Commercial Mobile Service Alerts of the Security and Accountability for Every Port Act of 2006 (Safe Port Act), also known as the Warning Alert Response Network (WARN) Act was signed into law. The WARN Act supported and expanded upon the policy of EO 13407, outlining many requirements of the system. The most germane of these requirements to this discussion and particularly pertinent to shaping the WEA system stipulated that:

- The system have a flexible architecture that transmits alerts across a variety of communications technologies (including wireless)
- Have geotargeting capabilities
- Reach underserved populations
- Include mechanisms to ensure that members of the public with disabilities and older individuals receive alerts and information provided through the system (SAFE Port Act 2006).

The Federal Communications Commission (FCC) was directed to establish a committee to implement the provisions of the WARN Act. In 2007, the FCC formed the Commercial Mobile Service Alert Advisory Committee (CMSAAC) to develop technical standards and protocols to enable wireless providers to transmit emergency alerts. After a year of deliberation, the FCC established rules on the use of mobile phones for public alerts. Based on public comments from industry, government, and advocacy stakeholders, and on the CMSAAC recommendations, the FCC adopted technology neutral rules governing wireless providers who elect to transmit WEAs to their subscribers (FCC 2008). On April 7, 2012, WEA, formerly known as the Commercial Mobile Alert System (CMAS), was deployed to the public.

Description

WEAs are achieved through a public and private partnership between wireless service providers and federal, state, and local governments. Approved alert authorities at federal, state, and local government levels can use FEMA IPAWS to generate and send warning messages to cell phones as WEA messages. WEA messages are text-like alerts that inform the recipient of the location, time of an immediate threat, and the recommended protective actions. WEAs, unlike subscription-based systems, are opt-out (except presidential messages), so one with a WEA-capable device will automatically receive emergency warnings. To encourage public participation, consumers with WEA-capable devices receive the messages free of charge and without enrollment. Devices must be WEA-capable, however, and the wireless carrier must be one of the several voluntary participants in the service. At a hearing before Congress in October 2013, a representative from CTIA – which represents the wireless industry – indicated that the number of wireless carrier participants enables WEA to reach nearly 98 percent of the mobile wireless subscribers (McCabe 2013).

To avoid over-alerting and an opting-out exodus, WEAs were designed to be directly applicable warnings of impending danger. As such, there are currently three alert categories for WEA messages: presidential, imminent threat (natural or human-made hazard), and AMBER (child abduction). Beginning on May 1, 2019, the system will support an Emergency Governmental Information category (information concerning shelter locations, evacuation routes, boil water advisories, and other pertinent life and property saving information that comes in the wake of an initial emergency message). Stakeholders supporting the fourth category suggested that it may encourage the use of WEA for non-weather-related local emergencies.

WEA messages have a prescribed alert sound and vibration cadence to distinguish them from personal text messages. As of the date of this publication, WEAs are limited to 90 characters in length, but a September 2016 FCC Report and Order revised regulations increasing the maximum WEA character length to 360 characters on 4G LTE and later networks, effective May 1, 2019. Additionally, effective November 1, 2017, revised regulations support the use of embedded references such as Uniform Resource Locators (URLs) in the WEA message content. As discussed in later sections, providing additional information via URLs can enhance accessibility and comprehensibility of the content *and* direct the user to official sources for verification, thereby supporting decision-making regarding whether or not to take the recommended protective actions.

Factors that impact emergency messaging on mobile wireless devices

The differences between the use of subscription-based messaging, mobile apps, and WEA for emergency alerts are enough to influence the behavioral responses of citizens. Unlike the difference between warnings through TV, radio, or telephone, the choice to disseminate via mobile devices leads to a host of other considerations. Focus group and survey data have indicated that individuals *may* misunderstand the urgency or location of a disaster-related warning message disseminated to their mobile devices. For example, before the focus group, some participants were unable to distinguish the difference between a WEA message or a subscription-based text message. Many assumed that WEAs were the subscription-based service, and if they were not in their home county, they questioned whether it applied to them, not realizing that WEAs are geotargeted. In a 2013 nationwide survey of 1,830 people, over 40 percent of all respondents first learned of WEA after receiving their first emergency message. Lack of prior knowledge about WEAs before receipt left many people dubious of the sender and the veracity of the message.

Accessibility promises

Historically, some people with sensory disabilities have not had access to emergency information because of lack of technology that best accommodates their communication needs (CACP 2015; Davis and Phillips 2009). This is no longer the case. Advances in technology and trends toward personalization and customization of the user experience make the promise of complete access achievable. Further, WEA is the first national emergency notification system that was proactively inclusive of people with disabilities before development and deployment. As such, federal rulemaking concerning WEA has consistently considered the impact of revised rules on people with disabilities. In the initial rollout of the system, the accessibility provisions were limited to the distinct alerting tone and vibration cadence discussed earlier. Since wireless providers had limited control over cell phone design, many of the accessibility promises concerning WEA relied on cell phone manufacturers enabling customizability of the device for the individual user. As smartphone technology increasingly included built-in accessibility features, people with disabilities could enable features to improve access to WEA messages. Nevertheless, researchers continually reported that people with disabilities were experiencing access barriers (Johnson et al. 2010; LaForce et al. 2016; Touzet 2016).

People with disabilities

Indeed, for many people who are deaf or hard of hearing, text format is an improvement over emergency alert system messages (EAS) sent over television and radio. For some members of the deaf community, however, and specifically for those who primarily communicate in American Sign Language (ASL), messages sent in English text present a language barrier. In the context of life-saving emergency alerts, there remains a need to ensure that all individuals, including those who use ASL, have parity of access to the information necessary to make informed decisions. Implementation of the WEA service necessitated continued research on how people with disabilities use mobile phones during emergencies, identifying the device and user need requirements for effectively alerting this population, and protective actions taken in response to emergency messages. Data collected from both a 2013 nationwide survey on WEA awareness and use among the public and a 2015 WEA survey on WEA awareness, accessibility, trust, and validation of message content provide pertinent information on how the public (especially people with disabilities) view the use of WEA. Specifically, the WEA survey respondents with disabilities expressed concerns with the receipt of WEA alerts, system consistency, and requests for additional features.

WEA awareness and receipt

When publicly launching a new program or campaign, the first step is to build awareness. Awareness campaigns serve to improve buy-in and acceptance.

However, research on the inclusiveness of people with disabilities and those with language difference with regards to WEAs highlight the lack of awareness by both alerting authorities and the general public (Bennett 2015). In 2015, CACP conducted a nationwide survey on WEA awareness and found that a majority of all respondents (60 percent) had heard of WEA before participating in the research. In previous (2013) WEA survey data, 59 percent of all respondents had heard of WEA. These data indicate that despite increased WEA-capable phone penetration, WEA awareness levels had remained flat (see Figure 1.1). Further, respondents without disabilities were twice as likely to report having heard of WEA (69 percent) than respondents with disabilities (53 percent). Chi-square analysis revealed that people who have no difficulty hearing are two times more likely to have prior knowledge of WEA than people who have hearing difficulties ($p < 0.001$).

A majority of total respondents (65 percent) reported receiving WEA messages. The receipt-rate found in 2015 was an increase of 20 percentage points since the 2013–2014 survey data, which showed only 45 percent of respondents had received a WEA message. The increase may be a result of more WEA activations and/or greater diffusion of WEA-capable handsets among the populace. More respondents without disabilities reported they had received WEA messages (72 percent) than those respondents with disabilities (60 percent). This finding was significant based on the chi-square analysis ($p < 0.01$). Among the two respondent groups with sensory disability (vision and hearing), consistent with assertions above regarding insufficient access for the deaf community, more respondents with vision limitations reported receiving WEAs (64 percent) than respondents with hearing limitations (54 percent). As mentioned earlier, awareness of WEA is important because of the several means by which to receive text-like emergency messages.

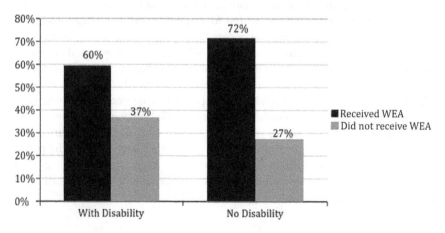

Figure 1.1 2015 Survey findings on receipt of a WEA message – with disability and without disability

Source: CACP 2015

Accessibility of WEA attention signals

A unique feature of WEA is the distinctive signal that distinguishes it from other texts. The use of the distinctive sound impacts awareness, accessibility, and understanding based on the specific device used by the individual, user device habits, and individual ability. The sound attention signal is the primary means by which respondents with and without disabilities are alerted to incoming WEA messages. However, the respondents without disabilities rely on the sound at a greater rate than those with disabilities, 50 percent compared to 32 percent (DHS 2015). Conversely, regarding the vibration signal, respondents with disabilities had a slightly higher dependence than those without, 16 percent compared to 14 percent. Similarly, with the light attention signal (which is not currently a WEA requirement), 7 percent of respondents with disabilities rely on a visual indicator to alert them of incoming WEA messages compared to 5 percent of respondents without disabilities. These data indicate an opportunity to improve the WEA attention signals by incorporating a light option for all WEA-capable handsets and ensuring that the vibration and sound signals are sufficient to alert people with different perceptual abilities. Ideally, the capability to personalize the attention signals would improve utility for all users, as the dampening of signal perception may be constant due to disability or changing due to ambient and/or competing sounds in the surrounding environment.

Responding

When WEAs first launched, there was a poignant lack of public campaigns to introduce this new method of disseminating warning messages. In fact, early research revealed that the number one way people first heard of WEA was by receiving a message for the first time. It was alarming, but not with the intended effect. Consequently, many of these early WEA recipients attributed their apathy toward protective action to their lack of awareness. Some confused the messages for regular text messages. Those who did not subscribe assumed the messages were spam. Others believed the messages did not apply to them because they referred to events elsewhere or because the message did not provide enough information. As shown in Figure 1.2, nearly 35 percent of respondents felt that message was not applicable to them personally, and only 25 percent of respondents took protective action after receiving an alert.

Behavioral response and awareness

Researchers at CACP examined 2015 survey data to determine if there was a relationship between behavioral responses to WEA messages and whether the respondents were aware of WEA before taking the survey. Using findings from a univariate analysis, they closely examined the relationship between two or more variables, such as disability, WEA awareness, and behavioral response to WEA to understand if greater awareness and exposure to WEA alerts increased trust and

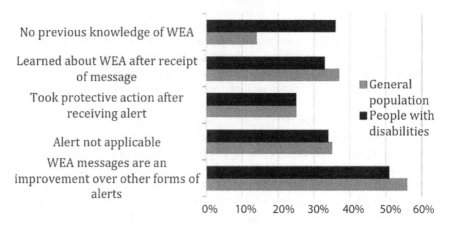

Figure 1.2 2013 survey findings on WEA awareness and use by demographic

appropriateness of individual responses. These relationships were examined using chi-square analyses of the relative distribution of values between and among discrete variables. Given that a model has yet to be generated for how all contributing variables might relate to specific behavioral outcomes, multiple independent testing was used. One survey item asked respondents to rank their agreement with the statement, "*I took action immediately based on the information in the alert.*" Results indicated that those who were previously aware of WEA (WEA-aware) were slightly more likely to take immediate action after receipt of a WEA message than respondents who were unaware of WEA ($p < 0.01$) (WEA-unaware). Fifty-six percent of respondents that were WEA-aware indicated that they agreed or strongly agreed with the above-quoted statement, while 39 percent of respondents who were WEA-unaware agreed or strongly agreed.

Whether respondents believed that the emergency would impact their area varied according to their prior knowledge of WEA. Forty-eight percent of those who were WEA-aware strongly agreed or agreed that they did not take action because the emergency was not near them. This compares to 55 percent of respondents of WEA-unaware respondents. Similarly, 33 percent of respondents who had prior knowledge of WEA disagreed or strongly disagreed with this statement, while only 21 percent who were not aware of WEA did. This is significant because it indicates that individuals rely on their own judgment about a pending emergency when they are unfamiliar with the mechanism that notifies them.

Individuals may make a counterproductive decision regarding the emergency when they are unfamiliar with the alerting tool. In related research, it was found that people were more likely to take protective actions in response to EAS messages than to WEA messages (52 percent and 27 percent, respectively), suggesting that greater familiarity and trust of EAS messages as a result of its legacy, compared with the relatively new WEA (Touzet 2016). As such, greater awareness and exposure to WEA alerts should have a positive relationship with trust

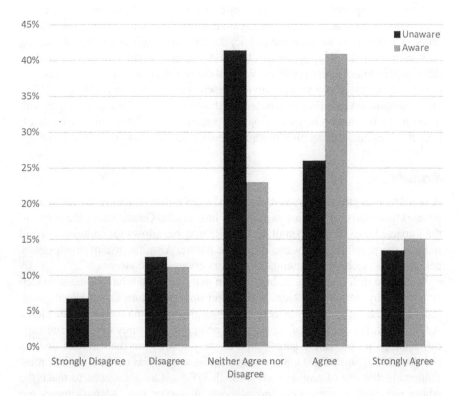

Figure 1.3 2015 findings on immediate action taken
Source: DHS 2015

and appropriateness of individual responses to alerts; as one increases, so does the other. The WEA 2015 survey data supported this assertion. Individuals who were familiar with WEA "were more likely to act immediately, less likely to be unsure of what action to take, and less likely to make judgments about whether the emergency alert applied to them" (LaForce et al. 2016).

Discussion

Typical behavioral response following mobile alerts is based on individual understanding of the capabilities of devices and the type of emergency messaging received. When deciding to take protective action, individuals will seek to understand if they are in immediate threat (Mileti and Peek 2000). However, when individuals receive a message while out of town, they may disregard the message if it is from a subscription-based message or a mobile app from their home location. When individuals are unable to discern that the message is sent via WEA, disregarding the message will make them more vulnerable. Additionally, if WEA is used too frequently to warn the public of non-imminent emergencies, many people might opt-out of the system, again making them more vulnerable. Unlike other channels used to warn the public, the frequency of emergency messaging may increase individual sensitivity to WEA because of the unique role mobile devices play in our everyday lives. While there are many methods to disseminate emergency messages on mobile devices, each one presents its challenges. Wireless Emergency Alerts (WEAs), however, show promise in linking messages with direct protective action behavior from the public. A list of strengths, weaknesses, opportunities, and threats provides a framework for discussion.

Strengths

A primary strength of WEA is its technical capabilities. It can reach millions of people, thousands, or just a few hundred in seconds. Geotargeting the alerts to the impacted area, large or small, as the case may be, allows for containment and reduces the possibility of over-alerting the public. Also, the use of one-to-many cell broadcast technology attenuates network congestion concerns.

WEAs are different from mobile apps in that they do not have to be uploaded or adopted by the user. Instead, WEA is an opt-out feature on mobile devices, reducing the need for individuals to be technically savvy to receive mobile alerts. Additionally, the delivery of messages to cell phones ensures maximal message diffusion, as people rarely leave home or sleep apart from their mobile devices (Lenhart 2010; Smith 2011). Since communities are only as resilient as their most vulnerable, the use of mobile texts through WEAs is advantageous to reach the whole community, specifically populations at greater risk. Manufacturers are increasingly incorporating accessibility features that enhance the utility of WEAs for people with various disabilities. WEAs are also capable of disseminating messages written in multiple languages, designed to reach underserved populations, and including mechanisms that address the information access needs of people with disabilities and older adults.

Weaknesses

Like the heroes in Greek tragedies, the greatest strength of WEA is also its greatest weakness. Unfortunately, the technical capacity of the system has not been fully operationalized. Take geotargeting, for example. Areas with fewer cell towers cannot take full advantage of precision geotargeting that the system allows. In essence, WEA features are being constrained by business efficiencies that determine the number of cell towers in an area based on population density. Another instance when the technical aspects convert from an opportunity to a barrier concerns device accessibility.

While new smartphones have built-in accessibility features, people with disabilities and households with low incomes do not always upgrade their devices at the same rate as higher income households and individuals without disabilities. As such, a portion of the populace still has devices that are not optimized for accessibility, and some may even predate the availability of WEA. Further, the FCC's enhancement to increase the character length of WEA will only apply to devices on 4G LTE and later networks. While 4G coverage is now extensive, not every user owns a 4G-supported device, barring many from receiving the additional information provided in the longer messages. As discussed earlier, accurate, actionable, and sufficient information supports people taking protective actions.

Opportunities

Using WEA presents an opportunity to reach the public more efficiently compared to other wireless emergency messaging methods. Given the three current methods to receive emergency messages on mobile wireless devices, WEA offers the unique ability to reach the populace without extensive effort on the part of the user. As outlined in this chapter, the automatic nature of WEAs are helpful to those who are not technically savvy, people with disabilities, and those disinclined to subscribe to messaging services. For alert authorities, the use of WEA offers a cost-effective solution to reach a wider populace, unlike the per-text, per-recipient model of many third-party subscription-based services.

WEA messages may also provide more opportunities for the public to take the proper protective action, but it is dependent on trust of the message. Other methods that rely on public understanding of GPS, subscription, and current county location could impede their certainty that the message applies to them, reducing the probability that they will take the proper action, regardless of individual ability. Without broader public education regarding WEA, however, people may continue to question the reliability of the message.

Finally, the progression of technology dictates that our capabilities in communication will grow and that our reliance on mobile wireless devices will expand. For some subsets of the population, consumption of information has drastically changed from the previous decade; mobile phones and tablets have taken the place of TV, radio, and desktop computers via Internet streaming. As the population moves toward a one device per person instead of a one device per household society, individuals become uniquely identifiable (Petrow 2017). This can be a great opportunity to inform the public based on their unique needs. Taking advantage of device and network capabilities could allow the user to customize notification signals and message content presentation, thereby improving receipt and message comprehension. With adequate legislation and regulatory review, WEA messages will be able to incorporate more features as the system matures.

Threats

As mentioned in the description, WEAs are provided as a public and private partnership between wireless service providers and federal, state, and local governments. As with any cross-sector collaboration, this partnership is voluntary (Forrer, Kee, and Boyer 2014). If wireless providers decide that this service is no longer in their best interest, the dissemination of emergency messaging via

WEA might be threatened. Even though device manufacturers are not officially members of the partnership, their development activities impact the end goal for all mobile wireless-based messaging.

There are other threats, as well. Device inaccessibility may impede the warning process. Individuals may not properly hear or understand the messaging, which will impact action. Additionally, since WEA is an opt-out system, messaging can be disseminated haphazardly. Frequent incorrect messages to locations not at risk may increase the possibility that large numbers of the population will disable the alerts from their mobile devices, leaving them more vulnerable in the future. Finally, to continuously provide adequate messaging, the use of WEA is at the mercy of policy makers. Legislative and regulatory proceedings will have to keep pace with technological advancements to maintain and improve the effectiveness of this system.

Conclusion

Mobile wireless devices offer a relatively new method to communicate emergency messages to the public. However, there are a few different methods to send and receive wireless emergency messages. Each presents implication for protective action response sought by alert authorities. The latest method, Wireless Emergency Alerts, appears to improve the appropriate behavioral response by individuals receiving the emergency message. The overview presented in this chapter, however, displays implications for practice, policy, and research.

Alert authorities, which include emergency managers, should be aware of the differences between each text (or text-like) messaging they employ to communicate with the public. While costs and ease-of-use should be considered, the behavioral response by all individuals within the potential impact area should also be assessed. The impact of policy, of course, could influence the use of text messaging service. However, in this case, policy has the unique ability to thwart the effectiveness of WEAs if not continuously updated by policy makers or adopted by alert authorities. Without adequate legislation and regulatory review, WEAs may lose relevance as communications capabilities expand.

Going forward, researchers should note how new devices (and technologies) of the public-private partnership may impact the disaster warning process. The ability for individuals to perceive and receive the message may be impaired by the frequency range of the sound notification signal, the strength of vibration cadence, or the participation of the wireless carrier in the public-private partnership. The ability to understand emergency messages may be inhibited by the accessibility features of the devices and the text-only presentation of message content. All affect the ability of the individual to quickly decide to take protective actions in response to alerts and warnings.

References

Bennett, D. 2015. *Gaps in Wireless Emergency Alerts (WEA) Effectiveness*. Atlanta: Center for Advanced Communications Policy.

Bennett, D., and LaForce, S. 2013. FM Radio and RBDS-Based Emergency Alerting: Possibilities and Potholes. *Public Administration Faculty Publications*, 80: 1–11.

Blumberg, S., and Luke, J. 2009. Reevaluating the Need for Concern Regarding Noncoverage Bias in Landline Surveys. *American Journal of Public Health*, 99(10): 1806–1810.

———. 2017. *Wireless Substitution: Early Release of Estimates from the National Health Interview Survey, July – December 2016.* National Center for Health Statistics, National Health Interview Survey Early Release Program. U.S. Department of Health and Human Services, Centers for Disease Control and Prevention, pp. 1–13.

CACP (Center for Advanced Communications Policy). 2015. *American Sign Language and Emergency Alerts: A Primer*. Atlanta: Georgia Institute of Technology.

Davis, E., and Phillips, B. 2009. *Effective Emergency Management: Making Improvements for Communities and People with Disabilities*. Washington, DC: National Council on Disability.

DHS (Department of Homeland Security). 2015. *Final Report: Optimizing Ability of Message Receipt by People with Disabilities: Prototype Findings Report/Vibration Scale*. Washington, DC: Department of Homeland Security, Science and Technology Directorate.

Dutwin, D., Keeter, S., and Kennedy, C. 2010. Bias from Wireless Substitution in Surveys of Hispanics. *Hispanic Journal of Behavioral Sciences*, 32(2): 309–328.

Executive Order 13407. 2006. *Public Alert and Warning System*. Accessed on December 12, 2018 at www.gpo.gov/fdsys/pkg/WCPD-2006-07-03/pdf/WCPD-2006-07-03-Pg1226.pdf.

FCC (Federal Communications Commission). 2008. *Third Report and Order in the Matter of the Commercial Mobile Alert System, Appendix C: Final Rules, Subsections 10.240–10.250*. Washington, DC: Public Safety and Homeland Security Bureau.

FEMA (Federal Emergency Management Agency). 2014. *Wireless Emergency Alerts*. Accessed on December 12, 2018 at www.fema.gov/wireless-emergency-alerts.

Forrer, J., Kee, J., and Boyer, E. 2014. *Governing Cross-Sector Collaboration*. Hoboken: John Wiley and Sons.

Fothergill, A., Maestas, E., and Darlington, J. 1999. Race, Ethnicity and Disasters in the United States: A Review of the Literature. *Disasters*, 23(2): 156–173.

Johnson, J., Mitchell, H., LaForce, S., Price, E., and Lucia, F. 2010. Mobile Emergency Alerting Made Accessible. *International Journal of Emergency Management*, 7(1): 88–99.

LaForce, S., Bennett, D., Linden, M., Touzet, C., and Mitchell, H. 2016. Optimizing Accessibility of Wireless Emergency Alerts: 2015 Survey Findings. *The Journal on Technology and Persons with Disabilities*, 4: 42–54.

Latimer, D. 2009. Deciphering the New Federal Integrated Public Alert and Warning System. *Educause Research Bulletin*, 16: 1–13.

Lenhart, A. 2010. *Cell Phones and American Adults: They Make Just as Many Calls, But Text Less Often Than Teens*. Washington, DC: Pew Research Center. Accessed on December 12, 2018 at http://pewinternet. org/Reports/2010/Cell-Phones-and-American-Adults.aspx.

Lindell, M., and Perry, R. 1987. Warning Mechanisms in Emergency Response System. *International Journal of Mass Emergencies and Disasters*, 5(2): 137–153.

———. 2003. *Communicating Environmental Risk in Multiethnic Communities*. Thousand Oaks, CA: Sage Publications.

———. 2012. The Protective Action Decision Model: Theoretical Modifications and Additional Evidence. *Risk Analysis*, 32(4): 616–632.

McCabe, G. 2013. *FEMA Reauthorization: Ensuring the Nation Is Prepared. In House Committee on Transportation and Infrastructure, Subcommittee on Economic Development,*

Public Buildings, and Emergency Management. Washington, DC: The House Committee on Transportation & Infrastructure.

Mileti, D. 1999. *Disasters by Design: A Reassessment of Natural Hazards in the United States*. Washington, DC: Joseph Henry Press.

Mileti, D., and Peek, L. 2000. The Social Psychology of Public Response to Warnings of a Nuclear Power Plant Accident. *Journal of Hazardous Materials*, 75(2): 181–194.

NRC (National Research Council). 2011. *Public Response to Alerts and Warnings on Mobile Devices: Summary of a Workshop on Current Knowledge and Research Gaps*. Washington, DC: National Academies Press.

———. 2013. *Geotargeted Alerts and Warnings: Report of a Workshop on Current Knowledge and Research Gaps*. Washington, DC: National Academies Press.

Petrow, S. 2017. You're Sharing Your Cell Phone Number Too Frequently. *USA Today Online*. Accessed on December 12, 2018 at www.usatoday.com/story/tech/columnist/ stevenpetrow/2017/06/20/cell-phone-number-scams-identity-theft/102787432/.

Pew Research Center. 2017. *Mobile Fact Sheet*. Washington, DC: Pew Research Center.

Rogers, G., and Sorensen, J. 1991. Diffusion of Emergency Warning: Comparing Empirical and Simulation Results. In *Risk Analysis: Advances in Risk Analysis, Volume 8*. (eds.) C. Zervos, K. Knox, L. Abramson, and R. Coppock. Boston: Springer.

SAFE Port Act. 2006. Title VI of the Security and Accountability for Every Port Act of 2006. *H.R. 4954 Public Law*, 109–347.

Smith, A. 2011. *Why Americans Use Social Media*. Pew Internet and American Life Project. Accessed on December 12, 2018 at www.pewinternet.org/2011/11/15/ why-americans-use-social-media/.

Tierney, K. 2006. Social Inequality, Hazards, and Disasters. In *On Risk and Disaster: Lessons from Hurricane Katrina*. (eds.) R. Daniels, D. Kettl, H. Kunreuther. Philadelphia: University of Pennsylvania Press, pp. 109–128.

Touzet, C. 2016. *Wireless Emergency Alerts (WEA) vs. Emergency Alert System (EAS) National Survey Research Findings*. Accessed on December 12, 2018 at http://cacp. gatech.edu/sites/default/files/docs/weavseashandout.pdf.

Wireless RERC. 2009. *Wireless Emergency Communications: Summary of Initial Findings, October 2006 – September 2009*. Accessed on December 14, 2018 at http:// wirelessrercarchive.gatech.edu/content/publications/wireless-emergency-communica tions-summary-initial-findings-october-2006.

Wisner, B., Blaikie, P., Cannon, T., and Davis, I. 2003. *At Risk: Natural Hazards, People's Vulnerability and Disasters*, Second Edition. London: Routledge.

2 Bounded rationality and federal disaster recovery information

Understanding why access to information matters

Jason D. Rivera

Introduction

Despite the growing literature on how social groups recover from natural disasters, there continues to be a lack of research on the processes whereby individuals decide to apply for individual disaster assistance. No study currently exists that attempts to investigate this decision with any organization, including the Federal Emergency Management Agency (FEMA). The reason for this gap in our understanding potentially lies in how authorities conceptualize individual assistance (IA) in general (McEntire 2015) and how the United States structures the recovery of housing after a disaster. In the United States, housing recovery follows a limited intervention model in which personal insurance is supposed to provide the majority of relief funds, along with some government assistance. As such, when insurance funds are insufficient, government assistance can be acquired (Phillips 2016). Operating under traditional rational choice models, authorities assume that disaster survivors will seek additional governmental assistance due to the alternative choice of fronting the costs of home repairs on their own. Moreover, there is a tendency among the American public to incorrectly assume that when disasters occur, it is FEMA's responsibility to compensate them for their losses, which further motivates survivors to apply for assistance (Schneider 2008). This choice, however, assumes that survivors have knowledge of disaster recovery programs available to them, in addition to the skills required to successfully navigate the bureaucratic application process.

Although the decision to apply for disaster assistance is extremely important in the aftermath of any event, it is even more important in places with low frequencies of disasters. In places that experience disasters on a regular basis, individuals develop conceptual frames that elicit various decisions in reference to how to respond to and recover from an event (Rivera 2014). By contrast, when individuals do not have prior experience with disasters, they must develop decision-making frames in a short period of time if they stand a chance at a successful recovery. Greer (2015) and Rivera (2016) argued that the lived experiences of individuals bound the potential decision alternatives available to an individual attempting to decide whether to apply for aid. The lack of disaster experience within a particular region affects how disasters are interpreted by communities and how and when disaster survivors choose to apply and/or participate in disaster assistance programs (Moore and Bates 1964; Wenger and Weller 1973). As a result, for individuals living in the aftermath of a disaster, decisions are not simply choices of objectively evaluated optimal returns but also the function of asymmetries in information. As such, disaster survivors' decisions are not by-products of maximizing utility from a full range of decision options but rather of bounded rationality (Simon 1955, 2000; Selten 2001).

This chapter explores the decision to apply for federal disaster assistance in the aftermath of Hurricane Sandy. Through the use of focus groups with New Jersey residents and invited interviews with disaster response and recovery entities, I examine how asymmetries in official disaster recovery information influenced an individual's decision to apply for disaster assistance. This chapter also provides policy recommendations on how to reduce asymmetries in disaster recovery information and suggests how future research might enhance our understanding of decision-making after disasters occur.

Decision theory and applying for disaster assistance

Traditional rational choice models assume that when individuals are confronted with a choice, they will choose the alternative that maximizes utility (Simon 1955). According to Simon (1955) this is only possible when: (1) the individual has access to all available information about each decision alternative and the information available is not subject to asymmetric information dynamics; (2) the individual must know what the probability of a successful decision will be to holistically understand the risk associated with any decision; and (3) the individual's interpretation of the costs and benefits associated with each decision is completely objective. Tversky and Kahneman (1981) and Simon (2000) argue that these assumptions are too extravagant to expect from most people because *rational behavior* is determined not only by an objective interpretation of the environment in which one acts but also an individual's *inner environment*, or mental landscape, which is influenced by memories and cognitive reasoning processes. People make decisions within contexts bounded by uncertainty over the outcome of decisions, how they interpret the external environmental conditions, and their cognitive ability to synthesize and understand all of the possible decisions available to them.

Simon (2000) argued that humans tend not to operate in a utility-maximizing manner because of the limitations indicative of human cognitive processes. Specifically,

> the choices people make are determined not only by some consistent overall goal and the properties of the external world, but also the knowledge that decision makers do and don't have of the world, their ability or inability to evoke that knowledge when it is relevant, to work out the consequences of their actions, to conjure up a possible course of action, to cope with uncertainty

(including uncertainty deriving from the possible responses of other actors), and to adjudicate among their many competing [choices].

(Simon 2000)

Moreover, the decision alternatives to which individuals have access are not given, but found. The search for alternative decisions occurs until a satisfactory alternative fulfills an individual's aspiration (Selten 2001). As such, aspirations are not fixed but are dynamically adjusted to each situation and individual. They are raised if satisfactory alternatives are easy to find and lowered if they are not (Selten 2001). Finally, sometimes individuals who know the *most rational decision* deliberately avoid choosing it. In this type of situation, rationality is not necessarily cognitively bound but bound by motivational characteristics (Selten 2001).

When deciding whether or not to apply for FEMA home assistance, individuals should theoretically aspire to gain resources to repair their homes, even if the exact amount of those resources varies. For example, some individuals might be primarily interested in simply making their residences livable so that they can move back in. Others might be more ambitious. According to Rivera (2016), these different levels of aspiration may also be a by-product of damage that was inflicted on individuals' homes. Specifically, the level of damage, or need for resources, biases the individual's evaluation of the benefits a program provides. Those with more severe damage view resource benefits as more satisfying than those with smaller amounts of damage. Finally, if one were to control for aspiration levels and other characteristics, such as the need and knowledge of available programs, some individuals might simply choose not to apply for aid at all. Not applying for aid means an individual refuses assistance not only from FEMA but also from other potential assistance alternatives, such as those provided by state programs and third-sector organizations. In such a situation, an individual's motivation to apply for assistance might be limited by a number of factors that may include cognitive limitations but also subjective notions of program fairness and the individual's past experiences with similar situations (Selten 2001).

Although bounded rationality tends to focus on the psychological processes of the individual, decision-making is also bound by the characteristics of the environment in which the individual acts. According to Simon (1956), the environment is not necessarily the total physically objective world, but only composed of those aspects that have relevance in the context of decision-making. Therefore, the *objective environment* in which an individual acts depends not only on the needs, aspirations, and goals of the individual but also on the subjective way in which the individual perceives the environmental structure (i.e., institutional arrangements). As a result, an individual attains the most satisfaction by gaining access to resources at specific places or through specific institutions, which are typically sparsely located throughout the individual's environment.

When discussing disaster assistance, the physical environment in which the individual is making the decision to apply for aid has finite locations where one can access disaster assistance. Although one may argue that the Internet reduces the limitations of physical access, especially with the rise of e-governance, there are actually several environmental limitations that continue to influence an individual's decision-making. First, dynamics associated with the digital divide still are prevalent amongst communities of color and the poor, which are most vulnerable to disasters and, arguably, in most need of resources after disasters (Murthy 2013). Second, even if individuals are able to access information through the Internet, the institutional environment only provides a limited number of assistance options (Rivera 2014), and the eligibility requirements for each of these options vary in respect to applicant characteristics and geographic location (McEntire 2015). These institutional and environmental limitations limit the availability of potential alternative decisions and reduce the number of options that the individual is able to evaluate.

Finally, in the context of applying for FEMA aid, issues of unfamiliarity and time are important. For individuals who have experienced disasters in the past, similar situations may be familiar to them, thereby making decision-making relatively easier. In situations where the occurrence of disasters is a new phenomenon, however, the individual faces unfamiliar problems. This mandates the decision maker to first devise a method for finding decision alternatives and then evaluate them against one another. With process time constraints associated with FEMA home assistance deadlines and the time it takes an individual to find information and evaluate possible alternatives on top of that, optimizing utility in unfamiliar situations becomes extremely difficult (Simon 1956; Selten 2001). Everything else equal, in situations where time is a limitation on decision-making and a situation is unfamiliar to an individual, time can be the most important variable that influences decisions in which maximum utility is not pursued. As a result of these potential dynamics, this current research project explored the influence that issues of bounded rationality such as time, access to information, and access to resource-providing locations had on individuals' decisions to apply for aid with FEMA among New Jersey disaster survivors in the aftermath of Hurricane Sandy.

Hurricane Sandy and New Jersey

Sandy was the tenth named hurricane during the 2012 hurricane season, developing in the southwestern Caribbean on October 22. Before making landfall, Sandy produced severe flooding along the Atlantic Coast from Florida to Maine as it moved north. The storm affected states as far inland as West Virginia, Ohio, and Indiana. The highest storm surges and greatest inundation on land occurred along the coast of central and northern New Jersey, Staten Island and the southward-facing shores of Long Island, New York, and in Connecticut. On the morning of October 29, the storm's trajectory shifted northeast toward southern New Jersey. By that evening, Sandy made landfall near Brigantine, New Jersey, as a post-tropical cyclone with winds up to 80 miles per hour (Blake et al. 2013).

The damages inflicted on the New Jersey coast were unprecedented in the state's history. According to New Jersey's then-governor, Chris Christie, "I've called this experience New Jersey's Katrina because the damage to our state is nothing that we've experienced ever before" (Drewniak and Roberts 2013).

Although the entire state was affected, the most severe damage was sustained in Monmouth and Ocean Counties. Entire communities were "inundated with water and sand, houses were washed from their foundations, boardwalks were dismantled or destroyed, cars were tossed about, and boats were pushed well inland from the coast" (Blake et al. 2013). Power outages lasted for weeks in some communities and affected about 5 million residents. In February 2013, the governor's office reported that 346,000 housing units had either been damaged or destroyed, with 22,000 of those units classified as uninhabitable. Overall, the governor's office estimated the cost of returning the state to normalcy to be upwards of $36.9 billion (Drewniak and Roberts 2013).

Methods

Theories of rational choice and bounded rationality customarily are tested through the use of econometric models. Although this quantitative method is conducive to explaining the influence of individuals' characteristics on whether they make a particular choice, the method is limited in its ability to explain *why*. As a result, this research utilizes a qualitative approach to data generation. Through the use of focus groups and key informant interviews, data was generated to provide a more holistic understanding of what determines whether an individual applies for disaster home assistance with FEMA beyond what a statistical model is capable of describing.

Focus groups

Two regional focus groups were recruited (Belzile and Oberg 2012; Marková et al. 2007; Morgan 1997), one for northern New Jersey and one for southern New Jersey. To increase the probability of contacting an individual being affected by Sandy, the sampling frame was confined to three municipalities in the north (Long Branch, Asbury Park, and Ocean Township) and three in the south (Atlantic City, Brigantine, and Pleasantville). These cities were chosen because they are located on the coast and they all experienced similar disaster impacts, such as damage from flooding, storm surge, and wind shear. The Eagleton Institute of Politics was hired to help recruit participants for the focus groups. Random digit dial (RDD) samples were developed independently for the northern and southern focus groups, including both cell phone and landline numbers, within the communities that were identified for investigation. Once a household was reached, a random process was used to identify one adult in the household to speak with. After expressing willingness to be interviewed, potential participants were screened for (1) living in the same community when Sandy hit and (2) having experienced damage to owned or rented property during Sandy. This ensured that they would have been motivated to some degree to learn about FEMA assistance in some way. Those meeting both criteria were solicited for participation in a focus group. All those who agreed to participate were asked for detailed contact and demographic information. Calling continued until 25 potential participants were identified for each focus group. A total of 6,239 phone numbers were dialed; 685 of these resulted in respondents willing to begin the screening survey. Among those beginning the screening, 68 were not in an appropriate zip code, 249 reported no Sandy damage, and 186 did not live in the location during Sandy. This left 156 potential participants for focus group recruiting.

In the northern region, 25 individuals expressed interest in participating in the project, and 31 expressed interest in the southern region. Throughout the recruiting process, every effort was made to attract a diverse set of individuals to participate. Along these lines, quota sampling of the population was attempted based on race/ethnicity and informed by statistical information from the U.S. Census (Baker et al. 2013; Lucas 2016). In this regard, the sample was intended to reflect the racial/ethnic breakdown of the geographically sampled regions. To incentivize participation, a $30 cash stipend was offered. Prior to focus group meetings and despite the previously described quota sampling, 11 individuals, six self-identified as white and five as African American, confirmed their attendance in the northern region. In the southern region, 16 confirmed attendance, with ten self-identified as white and six as African American. The northern focus group was held at the Long Branch Free Public Library in Long Branch, New Jersey, and the southern focus group was held at the William J. Hughes Center for Public Policy at Stockton University in Galloway Township, New Jersey. These locations were chosen due to their centrality within each study area and their ease of accessibility by public transportation.

A hybrid of scoping (Belzile and Oberg 2012) and theory-building (Jarrett 1993; Marková et al. 2007; Morgan 2012) focus group administration techniques were utilized. These types of focus groups were chosen over other potential types due to the fact that they allowed the researcher to explore potentially important variables and help inform theory building (Jarrett 1993). Although focus group questions were structured and primed with a survey instrument on individual Hurricane Sandy recovery experiences, once discussion on a topic was initiated, the moderator allowed the conversation to be fluid among participants, only guiding the discussion if the participants strayed too far from the initial topic. Participants were encouraged to express themselves in their own language, as opposed to the language of the researcher. When the moderator was unclear of what a participant meant, the participant was asked to explain and provide examples. This process allowed for the grouping of data within categories that were germane to a particular concept. Each focus group lasted approximately one and a half hours. Both focus groups were audio recorded for future transcription and analysis.

A framework analysis (Spencer and Ritchie 2002) was used to analyze the data generated by the focus groups. Thematic categories were identified within the data based on the statements made by participants, and then indexed. The data was then charted, which entailed moving participants' quotes from their original context and rearranging them under the thematic categories previously developed (Kruger 1994). Because participants were asked to clarify the meaning of their statements within each of the respective focus groups, the verbal data used in the analysis was taken at face value and not reinterpreted by the researcher.

Table 2.1 documents the descriptive statistics of the focus group participants. The day the northern focus group was held, 90 percent of the participants were

Table 2.1 Demographic characteristics and descriptive statistics of focus group participants

Variable	Frequency		% of Sample	
	Northern Group	Southern Group	Northern Group	Southern Group
Race				
White	1	3	10.0%	50.0%
African American	9	3	90.0%	50.0%
Age				
26 to 34 Years Old	0	1	0.0%	16.6%
35 to 44 Years Old	1	1	10.0%	16.6%
45 to 54 Years Old	2	1	20.0%	16.6%
55 to 64 Years Old	2	2	20.0%	33.3%
65+ Years Old	5	1	50.0%	16.6%
Marital Status				
Married	6	3	60.0%	50.0%
Single	1	2	10.0%	33.3%
Divorced/Separated	2	1	20.0%	16.6%
Refused	1	0	10.0%	0.0%
Children in Household				
0	6	4	60.0%	66.6%
1	3	0	30.0%	0.0%
2	1	0	10.0%	0.0%
4	0	1	0.0%	16.6%
5	0	1	0.0%	16.6%
Employment Status				
Unemployed	3	1	30.0%	16.6%
On Medical or Disability Leave	1	0	10.0%	0.0%
Employed Full Time	5	5	50.0%	83.3%
Refused	1	0	10.0%	0.0%
Educational Attainment				
Some High School	1	0	10.0%	0.0%
High School Diploma	1	0	10.0%	0.0%
Some College, No Degree	4	1	40.0%	16.6%
Associate's Degree	2	1	20.0%	16.6%
Bachelor's Degree	1	2	10.0%	33.3%
Master's Degree	0	2	0.0%	33.3%
Refused	1	0	10.0%	0.0%
Household Income				
Less than $25,000	1	0	10.0%	0.0%
$25,000 to $34,999	2	0	20.0%	0.0%
$35,000 to $49,999	2	2	20.0%	33.3%
$50,000 to $74,999	1	2	10.0%	33.3%
$75,000 to $99,999	2	2	20.0%	33.3%
$100,000 to $124,999	2	0	20.0%	0.0%

(*Continued*)

Table 2.1 (Continued)

Variable	Frequency		% of Sample	
	Northern Group	Southern Group	Northern Group	Southern Group
Gender				
Male	6	4	60.0%	66.6%
Female	4	2	40.0%	33.3%
Country of Origin				
United States	10	5	100.0%	83.3%
Other	0	1	0.0%	16.6%
Primary Language				
English	10	6	100.0%	100.0%

African American and only one participant was white. This composition was unexpected based on the individuals who had previously confirmed attendance. In the southern focus group, although 16 individuals had confirmed attendance, only six participated. The southern focus group was more racially balanced than the northern group, with half the group self-identifying as African American and the other half self-identifying as white. Since the topics under discussion were not of a sensitive or controversial nature, the group composition was perceived to minimally skew the generation of data (Morgan 1997).

Key informant interviews

Finally, due to the small sample size of focus group participants, key informant interviews were conducted with various New Jersey county emergency manager coordinators and county-level Voluntary Organizations Active in Disasters (VOADs) (Phillips 2014; Stallings 2007). Interviews have been documented as being extremely useful in disaster research (Oliver-Smith 1996; Phillips 2014; Stallings 2007), especially for gaining access to respondents who are difficult to access through traditional surveying techniques. Moreover, Phillips (2014) maintains that interviews offer an unobtrusive means of triangulating findings. By triangulating the findings of a study's focus groups, a more holistic depiction of what actually occurred in the aftermath a disaster can be discerned (Phillips 2014).

Once individuals were identified as willing to participate in this research, an email was sent to them restating the focus of the study and their rights as a research participant. Respondents were notified that their answers to the researcher's questions would be confidential, and no identifying information about the respondent's exact office of work would be included in the analysis of data. Specifically, respondents were told that although they would be identified as either a New Jersey emergency management coordinator or a New Jersey VOAD (Voluntary Organizations Active in Disaster) coordinator, the county in which they specifically worked would be kept confidential. In all, three county emergency management coordinators and two county VOAD coordinators participated in interviews. The data generated from the interviews were analyzed using a framework analysis similar to the manner in which the focus group data was analyzed.

Analysis

Although statistical analyses of the survey instrument provided to all participants could have potentially highlighted important variables, the analysis would assume that all of the respondents had equal access to knowledge about FEMA's home assistance program and that all that respective information was of the same quality. Therefore, the analyses would not highlight any of the issues raised by bounded rationality for why people decide or nor not decide to apply for disaster home assistance with FEMA, which include access to knowledge about alternative options, timing, and personal experience. The focus group discussions and interviews were instrumental in shedding light on these issues.

Access and quality of information

Within each of the focus groups, participants were asked, "Why did you apply for aid with FEMA, as opposed to or in combination with another type of disaster assistance program?" All of the participants in each of the focus groups had applied to FEMA for assistance and indicated that FEMA was the only organization that they had *initially* thought they could apply for assistance with. This knowledge, however, was typically based on their memories of past national disasters, such as Hurricane Katrina.

The majority of focus group participants related that they had learned about FEMA's assistance programs in several ways. One way was through organized events that were held in respective community centers. One male participant from Atlantic City reported:

> Generally, it's the convention centers. . . . They [FEMA] had at least 30 partners inside the convention center where you would just go in and they would tell you, these are partners of FEMA. Some were not FEMA per se, but because people were looking for different things individuals directed you to different partners. SBA [Small Business Administration] was there. So if you needed to file a claim with SBA someone directed you over there and any other partner or someone.

Additionally, one male participant form Brigantine explained that he had also learned about small assistance grants from the Red Cross at Brigantine's community center:

> And then I was at the community center, and the girl at the community center, I was talking to somebody about what I was going through and she said, "You sound like you need some help. Come on over to my desk." And she was from the Red Cross.

When asked how these individuals learned that these community events were taking place, many related that they had learned about them through their own social networks. For the most part, participants of both races, and varying socio-economic status, emphasized that they had never received *any* information from FEMA directly about the disaster assistance application process. In response to this observation, one county emergency manager whose office is located in one of the most heavily damaged areas by Sandy said:

> Yes, I believe there was some difficulty here [dissemination of disaster resource information]. . . . The biggest issue here was that due to the extensive and duration of power outages, it was difficult to send the word out through electronic means. While the people who were in local shelters received some handouts, those that fled the area had difficulty accessing the information because there was not a central repository to access what was needed. If those impacted registered for assistance [with FEMA] online, they were not provided with the necessary details as to how to proceed . . . I also believe that FEMA did a poor job in communicating or advertising the available programs.

This limitation to information diffusion not only bound individuals' initial knowledge of disaster assistance opportunities in reference to substance/content, but access to the information was also geographically bound to places that FEMA personnel physically visited. As a result, disaster survivors in one location had better access to information than those residing in other counties and/or more heavily devastated areas.

Another way individuals learned about potential sources of aid was through information disseminated over the radio or in newspapers. However, according to most focus group participants, this information seemed to be problematic.

> Last year, it was in the *Asbury Park Press* that there was a grant to assist you with repairing your home. . . . However, the day that [this information was in the paper] was the day after the deadline for the grant had passed. 'Cause of this they extended the deadline, but they only extended the deadline from July 30 to July 31. Now what is that supposed to do for people that have difficulties finding transportation?

In response to this account, another African American participant commented:

> Yeah, and then a lot of the offices where you were supposed to apply to that grant were shut down, and the ones that were left [open] were like in places that you couldn't even get to.

Moreover, accessibility of meeting places also was addressed by a county-level VOAD representative. According to her,

> In the first couple of weeks FEMA . . . set up in office buildings, but they were not easy to reach for those in the impacted areas as they had all lost their

cars in the flooding . . . I think FEMA thought that if they just went to one place people would flock to them. To some degree that's true, but it would have been much better if they had been located in several locations within the impacted area, not outside of it.

The northern focus group specifically highlighted the ineffectiveness of media outlets to provide information of where and when to access disaster assistance. These sentiments were also shared by members of the southern focus group. One verbal exchange between an African American resident of Atlantic City and a white resident of Brigantine documented this dynamic.

[African American participant] By the time you heard that those organizations would be at the [Atlantic City] convention center or at the community center or wherever, on the radio, you had to move heaven and earth to go. They advertised the events publicly at the last minute. It was like they didn't actually want people to show up.
[White participant] Actually, the [Brigantine] community center placed flyers on their doors about a week before they held their events.
[African American participant] OK, yeah, but you had to go there to actually see the advertisement. The public, the actual public wasn't told about when the stuff was happening . . . by the time you found out it was either after the fact or you had to be there later that day.

Interestingly, out of all of the participants in both focus groups, there was only one white woman who learned about FEMA's home assistance program from a FEMA representative. She quickly made it known, however, that it was only due to her personal relationship with the individual prior to Hurricane Sandy that she was able to approach him and ask for information. She admitted that if it had not been for her personal relationship with this individual, she would not have known about the potential programs she could have applied to.

The most common way that individuals gained access to information about disaster assistance was through their own personal networks. Participants provided accounts of how they were able to access information about disaster assistance programs through word of mouth, either through their own family members and/or personal social networks. One white female respondent from Brigantine explained that she had learned about the availability of relief organizations in her respective community center through one of her friend's Facebook posts. One male and one female African American respondent from Long Branch indicated that

[Man] . . . believe it or not, my daughter lives in Pennsylvania, she calls me up and tells me, because she works for the state, that I should apply to FEMA for help. I don't know how she [found] out, but she knew about what was going on in New Jersey better than I did.
[Woman] Yeah, my son was in Ohio, and he gave me more information than anything I was able to get a hold of here.

Similarly, an exchange between two African American participants from the northern focus group continued to illustrate this dynamic:

> [Person 1] Mainly because people that obtained damages and stuff like that, people kind of like got together and talked about their different facets and their different organizations that were helpful and things like that. So it was through word of mouth . . . you know what I mean? And so I heard from this person, I could get in touch with this person and that's the way it went . . . a neighborly thing. . . . Because definitely FEMA certainly didn't tell anybody, "Hey we got help for you."
>
> [Person 2] Yeah like you were saying, our neighbors, all through word of mouth, I found out about water and food rations and whatever . . . so that's how we found out about all that stuff.

Although reliance on these networks sometimes admittedly yielded dated, misinformed, or even questionable information, according to many of the participants, this was the primary way to gain access to information on available resources due to a general trend among the participants that related to a lack of learning about recovery programs from official emergency management organizations, in addition to other formal state and federal agencies. In response to this finding, all county emergency management coordinators related their continued frustration with educating the public on their respective vulnerability to natural disasters and what to do in the aftermath of a disaster. According to one county emergency management coordinator,

> We actively attempt to educate people about preparedness. [Our agency] does numerous speaking events around the county each year. In addition, we do several press releases throughout the year and also post to our website. However, for the most part, people don't believe that they will be impacted [by a natural disaster] and that if they are, believe FEMA will be standing up with everything they need.

As a result, most emergency management coordinators were not surprised that disaster victims heavily relied on social networks for information or to gain access to information about disaster resources. Moreover, they argued that reliance on social networks was more of a by-product of improperly informed *rational ignorance* (Downs 1957; Jankowski 2007), as opposed to a lack of information available to the public in times of normalcy and within the aftermath of the disaster. As such, and according to emergency management coordinators, individuals chose to remain ignorant about FEMA assistance programs because they perceived they were entitled to government assistance. However, this is not the case in a disaster recovery context where authorities adhere to a limited intervention model as opposed to a redevelopment model (Phillips 2016).

Although participants in the focus groups were not asked to comment on how they thought their socioeconomic characteristics may have influenced their decision to apply for disaster assistance with FEMA, key informant interviews highlighted an interesting potential relationship. For example, one county VOAD coordinator stated:

> In many cases, we found that those who were impacted [by Sandy] were of solid moderate income who had never had to reach out for assistance and were very reluctant to do so. It wasn't until much later, sometimes after the closing of programs, that they faced the fact that they needed help.

Unfortunately, his dynamic was not explored within either of the focus groups; however, it raises questions in reference to the influence of social stigma within American society associated with seeking social benefits (Blank and Ruggles 1993; Moffitt 1983; Riphahn 2001) and how that perception translates into disaster contexts.

Personal experiences

In the few cases where information was made available in centralized locations, such as in community or convention centers, those seeking aid were directed to appropriate agencies that would be most helpful to their specific needs. Although service providers were concentrated in specific places, the participants who attended these events said that they had very different experiences. Those who attended events at the Atlantic City Convention Center remembered that many of the individuals there to represent various federal and state government agencies seemed "unsympathetic," "cold," and "overburdened with the number of cases or claims they were dealing with," and in some cases generally gave the impression they "couldn't give a damn" about what those seeking aid were going through. The seemingly unsympathetic and cold individuals who were available to aid resource seeking survivors presented an image of government that although "it was their job to help people [who] were affected [by Hurricane Sandy], they really didn't seem to care if it was beyond their job description." According to participants, these types of experiences were so emotionally draining that they detrimentally impacted their motivation to find alternate programs to apply to. Interestingly, the participants that provided these negative experiential accounts were *all* African American.

Alternately, individuals who had attended events at local community centers related more positive experiences with representatives who seemed to be more sympathetic to their experiences and somewhat sensitive to their potential emotional needs. In these cases, participants were provided with a positive image of government.

> [The] government was there to help and the people they sent made us feel that we would eventually be OK. They told me where I could call for help and where to apply for different types of assistance. Even though they didn't do a great job in A.C. they did show me the government seemed to care

about what I was going through. And yeah, because I had a good experience I think it motivated me to seek aid in other places. . . . Some people had bad experiences with the FEMA people, and then they didn't wanna talk to anybody else. . . . So yeah if it wasn't for those people in the community center I wouldn't have tried to look for help other places.

Although these types of interpersonal interactions yielded different types and quality of information on the availability of resources, according to focus group participants, relatively positive personal experiences with government representatives also positively affected their personal motivation to apply and interact with representatives from other government and third-sector organizations in the pursuit of disaster recovery assistance. Again, it is interesting to note that these more positive experiences were only reported by residents of Brigantine, who were also *all* white. Finally, although not expressed within either the focus groups or through key informant interviews, the level of respective damage indicative to each of these towns may have had an impact on individual experiences, in addition to the manner in which officials interacted with the public.

Discussion and conclusion

Using bounded rationality as a theoretical framework, this chapter has highlighted how access to information on disaster recovery resources influenced Hurricane Sandy survivors' choice to apply for aid with FEMA. Through the use of focus groups and key informant interviews, it was found that various factors identified in the literature as bounding people's ability to make rational decisions were important in the disaster context. Moreover, access to credible and timely information mattered in each individual's decision-making process. Clearly, it is not only important that people have access to important information about disaster recovery but that the information provided to victims is accurate and timely. If not, access does not necessarily unbound an individual's decision-making but further contributes to its limitations. According to Sheppard, Janoske, and Liu (2012), during the disaster recovery phase of an event, risk communication is meant to contribute to decreasing the length of recovery, reduce potential secondary effects, and help ensure that recovery does not create new or replicate vulnerabilities that contributed to risk. Seeger and Padgett (2010) argued that in order for communication to be successful, it must engage a *wide* audience in a collaborative and interactive way. Along these lines, Frank and colleagues (Frank et al. 2006) observed how recovery information was distributed after the 9/11 attacks in New York City to enhance people's potential recovery trajectories. In this situation, recovery information about resources was distributed through the use of a mass media campaign lasting more than a year that included, print, television, radio, and other media (predominately fliers and billboards) that was directly motivated by the notion of educating the city's population on the availability of resources. In this way, large portions of the city's population were provided access to timely and quality information about potential recovery resources that were not subject to asymmetries. As such, future policies should seek to institutionalize media campaigning in the aftermath of disasters as a means of disseminating disaster recovery information to the broadest population possible.

Despite the findings of this current study, this research is limited in its ability to measure not only the effect of traditional demographic variables' influence on decision-making but also how other variables such as individuals' assets/wealth, past experiences with disasters, and public perceptions about FEMA may have influenced decisions (Greer 2015). For example, it was observed that white focus group participants had more positive personal experiences with disaster assistance authorities in comparison to their African American counterparts. Although this seems to anecdotally conform to news stories that have historically illustrated FEMA and other governmental entities as unsympathetic to the needs of minority populations, based on this study's sample size, this is not a confirming observation. Moreover, it is unclear why there were such a disproportionate number of focus group participants who were African American. Although one might hypothesize that this group was more socially vulnerable and/or more severely affected by Sandy, these reasons did not seem to be the case based on statements made within the focus groups. One explanation might relate back to personal experiences. Specifically, because African Americans had experienced more negative interpersonal situations with government, they were more inclined to participate, but this possibility was not confirmed. As such, future research on decision-making in the disaster context should strive to measure the influence of these variables amongst broader and larger samples of disaster survivors.

To this end, the CAUSE model of communication during the recovery phase on disasters attempts to address asymmetries of information that are more a by-product of individual choices and filtering out of information rather than those that result from disaster organizations inadvertently providing information in places and media venues that directly cause asymmetries. This model operates under the notion that in the aftermath of a disaster, members of the public struggle with their own confidence, awareness, and understanding of messages distributed by official sources. Moreover, members of the public also are unsure of their own feelings toward the potential solutions provided by emergency actors and wait for a clear enactment of action by official recovery organizations (Sheppard, Janoske, and Liu 2012). Along these lines, this approach is not only motivated by providing needed information to the public, but also to increase confidence, awareness, and understanding on the behalf of the public to provoke the public into actions that enhance recovery (Rowan et al. 2010), such as applying for aid with disaster relief and recovery agencies. As a result, in locations where sections of the public have had historical experiences that have yielded a lack of confidence in recovery agencies and/or a lack of knowledge on recovery resources available after disasters, CAUSE communication models should be integrated into respective comprehensive disaster/emergency plans as a means to help enhance how information is received by the public as opposed to how it is accessed.

Finally, it was observed that an individual's social network is vital in the process of accessing information. The ever-growing reliance on network-based systems, both online and in traditional social interactions, for accessing information is well documented in the literature (Acemoglu, Bimpikis, and Ozdaglar 2014; Mueller-Frank 2013; Song and Yan 2012). Faas and Jones (2017) maintain that social networks or social capital can facilitate access to resources as well as information on disaster recovery. Quality and amount of information, however, is also tied to the composition of an individual's social network (network diversity). As a result, individuals' social networks have the potential to bound the decision-making choices of individuals if those within the social network are equally ignorant about what to do in the aftermath of a disaster (Faas and Jones 2017). Subsequently, it is not only important for individuals to have social networks that allow them to access and diffuse information to people like themselves (i.e., bonding social capital), but also have diversity within their social networks (i.e., bridging social capital) as a means of connecting victims to various types and sources of information that are not known to everyone (Faas et al. 2017).

Although one policy recommendation would be to create better technological protocols to overcome online network-based operational challenges, this recommendation is not entirely convincing. Situations will always arise when technologies fail to deliver their intended services to the end user. If technology is solely relied on as a means of building community resiliency, then it will only be beneficial when it operates under preconceived operating parameters. Because technology makes it far easier to communicate at higher speeds, its utility is unquestionable. Therefore, in an effort to better disseminate quality information about disaster recovery, FEMA should first attempt to reevaluate the hubs or nodes to which they provide important information (Song and Yan 2012). The reason for this reevaluation of network nodes lies in individuals' sociability or homophily (i.e., the homogeneity of social networks) (McPherson and Smith-Lovin 1987) that has the tendency to reduce the circulation of information from people outside a particular network. In relation to FEMA, and as exemplified by the statements made by study participants here, the nodes through which FEMA has chosen to disseminate information are not performing efficiently. Along these lines, the systems dynamic model of communication in disaster recovery attempt to address how social interaction and feedback loops within networks affect public perceptions and behaviors (Sheppard, Janoske, and Liu 2012). As such, the nodes through which FEMA disseminates information through social networks should be composed predominately of boundary spanners (Kapucu 2006), or individuals that hold a place in several networks concurrently. Ideally, social network nodes should be chosen that exist within a space that occupies both formal and informal relationships with other actors (Kapucu and Hu 2016; Nowell and Steelman 2014) as a means of compensating for feedback loops that may decrease the public's inclination to engage in more optimal decision-making in the aftermath of disasters.

It might be argued that FEMA historically and currently utilizes organizational networks as a means of disseminating information by working with VOADs and other similar broad-based organizations; however, based on the observations identified in this chapter, this approach is not working. Moreover, according to

Rivera and Wood (2016), the extent of involvement of nonprofit organizations that are not typically members of these broad-based large organizations, which also have a more intimate relationship with victims and are profoundly integrated into social networks, is questionable despite federal mandates to do so. As such, offices of emergency management at the state and local levels should be more active in developing relationships with entities such as nonprofits that are not directly related to disaster recovery because they operate in both formal and informal ways with individual community members, other similar organizations, and governments all at the same time. In short, these organizations provide individuals access to network diversity when their own individual social networks are more homogeneous. By finding more appropriate nodes of information dissemination and also better analyzing how networks are utilized in disaster contexts (Varda 2017), FEMA and other disaster recovery entities have the potential of unbounding people's decision-making by providing them access to more alternatives that are also of more credible informational quality. As such, effective communication must account for how different segments of the public perceive and process information (Fischhoff 1995), in addition to how decision-making is bound by the way and through what means information is distributed.

References

Acemoglu, D., Bimpikis, K., and Ozdaglar, A. 2014. Dynamics of Information Exchange in Endogenous Social Networks. *Theoretical Economics*, 9(1): 41–97.

Baker, R., Brick, M., Bates, N., Battaglia, M., Couper, M., Dever, J., Gile, K., and Tourangeau, R. 2013. Summary Report of the AAPOR Task Force on Non-Probability Sampling. *Journal of Survey Statistics and Methodology*, 1(2): 90–143.

Belzile, J., and Öberg, G. 2012. Where to Begin? Grappling with How to Use Participant Interaction in Focus Group Design. *Qualitative Research*, 12(4): 459–472.

Blank, R., and Ruggles, P. 1993. *When Do Women Use AFDC & Food Stamps? The Dynamics of Eligibility vs. Participation*. No. w4429. Washington, DC: National Bureau of Economic Research.

Blake, E., Kimberlain, T., Berg, R., Cangialosi, J., and Beven, J. 2013. *Tropical Cyclone Report: Hurricane Sandy (AL182012), 22–29 October 2012*. Miami: National Hurricane Center.

Downs, A. 1957. An Economic Theory of Political Action in a Democracy. *Journal of Political Economy*, 65(2): 135–150.

Drewniak, M., and Roberts, K. 2013. *Christie Administration Releases Total Hurricane Sandy Damage Assessment of $36.9 Billion*. Office of the Governor, Press Release, November 28, 2012. Trenton, NJ: Office of the Governor, p. 1.

Faas, A., and Jones, E. 2017. Social Network Analysis Focused on Individuals Facing Hazards and Disasters. In *Social Network Analysis of Disaster Response, Recovery, and Adaptation*. (eds.) E. Jones and A. Faas. Cambridge, MA: Elsevier Inc., pp. 11–23.

Faas, A., Velez, A., FitzGerald, C., Nowell, B., and Steelman, T. 2017. Patterns of Preference and Practice: Bridging Actors in Wildfire Response Networks in the American Northwest. *Disasters*, 41(3): 527–548.

Fischhoff, B. 1995. Risk Perception and Communication Unplugged: Twenty Years of Process. *Risk Analysis*, 15(2): 137–145.

Frank, R., Pindyck, T., Donahue, S., Pease, E., Foster, M., Felton, C., and Essock, S. 2006. Impact of a Media Campaign for Disaster Mental Health Counseling in Post-September 11 New York. *Psychiatric Services*, 57(9): 1304–1308.

Greer, A. 2015. *Household Residential Decision-Making in the Wake of Disaster: Cases from Hurricane Sandy*. Doctoral Dissertation. Newark, DE: University of Delaware.

Jankowski, R. 2007. Altruism and the Decision to Vote: Explaining and Testing High Voter Turnout. *Rationality and Society*, 19(1): 5–34.

Jarrett, R. L. 1993. Focus Group Interviewing With Low-Income Minority Populations: A Research Experience. In *Sage Focus Editions, Vol. 156. Successful Focus Groups: Advancing the State of the Art*. (ed.) D. L. Morgan. Thousand Oaks, CA: Sage Publications, Inc, pp. 184–201. http://dx.doi.org/10.4135/9781483349008.n12.

Kapucu, N. 2006. Interagency Communication Networks During Emergencies: Boundary Spanners in Multiagency Coordination. *The American Review of Public Administration*, 36(2): 207–225.

Kapucu, N., and Hu, Q. 2016. Understanding Multiplexity of Collaborative Emergency Management Networks. *The American Review of Public Administration*, 46(4): 399–417.

Kruger, R. 1994. *Focus Group: Practical Guide for Applied Research*. Thousand Oaks, CA: Sage Publications.

Lucas, S. 2016. Where the Rubber Meets the Road: Probability and Nonprobability Moments in Experiment, Interview, Archival, Administrative, and Ethnographic Data Collection. *Socius: Sociological Research for a Dynamic World*, 2: 1–24.

Marková, I., Linell, P., Grossen, M., and Orvig Salazar, A. 2007. *Dialogue in Focus Groups: Exploring Socially Shared Knowledge*. London: Equinox Publishing.

McEntire, D. 2015. *Disaster Response and Recovery: Strategies and Tactics for Resilience*, Second Edition. Hoboken, NJ: John Wiley and Sons.

McPherson, J., and Smith-Lovin, L. 1987. Homophily in Voluntary Organizations: Status Distance and the Composition of Face-to-Face Groups. *American Sociological Review*, 53(3): 370–379.

Moffitt, R. 1983. An Economic Model of Welfare Stigma. *The American Economic Review*, 73(5): 1023–1035.

Moore, H., and Bates, F. 1964. . . . *And the Winds Blew*. Austin, TX: Hogg Foundation for Mental Health.

Morgan, D. 1997. Focus Groups as Qualitative Research. *Qualitative Research Methods Series*, 16(2).

———. 2012. Focus Groups and Social Interaction. In *The Sage Handbook of Interview Research*, Second Edition. Thousand Oaks, CA: Sage Publications, pp. 161–176.

Mueller-Frank, M. 2013. A General Framework for Rational Learning in Social Networks. *Theoretical Economics*, 8(1): 1–40.

Murthy, D. 2013. New Media and Natural Disasters: Blogs and the 2004 Indian Ocean Tsunami. *Information, Communication and Society*, 16(7): 1176–1192.

Nowell, B., and Steelman, T. 2014. Communication Under Fire: The Role of Embeddedness in the Emergence and Efficacy of Disaster Response Communication Networks. *Journal of Public Administration Research and Theory*, 25(3): 929–952.

Oliver-Smith, A. 1996. Anthropological Research on Hazards and Disasters. *Annual Review of Anthropology*, 25(1): 303–328.

Phillips, B. 2014. *Qualitative Disaster Research: Understanding Qualitative Research*. Oxford: Oxford University Press.

———. 2016. *Disaster Recovery*, Second Edition. Boca Raton, FL: CRC Press.

Riphahn, R. 2001. Rational Poverty or Poor Rationality? The Take-Up of Social Assistance Benefits. *Review of Income and Wealth*, 47(3): 379–398.

Rivera, J. 2014. Resistance to Change: Understanding Why Disaster Response and Recovery Institutions Are Set in Their Ways. *Journal of Critical Incident Analysis*, 4(1): 44–65.

———. 2016. *Acquiring Federal Disaster Assistance: Investigating Equitable Resource Distribution Within FEMA's Home Assistance Program*. Doctoral Dissertation. Camden, NJ: Rutgers, The State University of New Jersey.

Rivera, J., and Wood, Z. 2016. Disaster Relief Volunteerism: Evaluating Cities' Planning for the Usage and Management of Spontaneous Volunteers. *Journal of Emergency Management*, 14(2): 127–138.

Rowan, K., Botan, C., Kreps, G., Samoilenko, S., and Farnsworth, K. 2010. Risk Communication Education for Local Emergency Managers: Using the Cause Model for Research, Education, and Outreach. In *Handbook of Risk and Crisis Communication*. (eds.) R. L. Heath, and H. D. O'Hair. New York: Routledge, pp. 168–191.

Schneider, S. 2008. Who's to Blame? (Mis)perceptions of the Intergovernmental Response to Disasters. *Publius: The Journal of Federalism*, 38(4): 715–738.

Seeger, M., and Padgett, D. 2010. From Image Restoration to Renewal: Approaches to Understanding Postcrisis Communication. *The Review of Communication*, 10(2): 127–141.

Selten, R. 2001. What Is Bounded Rationality? In *Bounded Rationality: The Adaptive Toolbox*. (eds.) G. Gigerenzer and R. Selten. Cambridge: MIT Press, pp. 13–36.

Sheppard, B., Janoske, M., and Liu, B. 2012. *Understanding Risk Communication Theory: A Guide for Emergency Managers and Communicators*. Report to Human Factors/Behavioral Sciences Division, Science and Technology Directorate, U.S. Department of Homeland Security.

Simon, H. 1955. A Behavioral Model of Rational Choice. *The Quarterly Journal of Economics*, 69(1): 99–118.

———. 1956. Rational Choice and the Structure of the Environment. *Psychological Review*, 63(2): 129–138.

———. 2000. Bounded Rationality in Social Science: Today and Tomorrow. *Mind and Society*, 1(1): 25–39.

Song, X., and Yan, X. 2012. Influencing Factors of Emergency Information Spreading in Online Social Networks: A Simulation Approach. *Journal of Homeland Security and Emergency Management*, 9(1).

Spencer, L., and Ritchie, J. 2002. Qualitative Data Analysis for Applied Policy Research. In *Analyzing Qualitative Data*. (eds.) A. Bryman and B. Burgess. New York: Routledge, pp. 187–208.

Stallings, R. 2007. Methodological Issues. In *Handbook of Disaster Research*. (eds.) H. Rodriguez, E. Quarantelli, and R. Dynes. New York: Springer, pp. 55–82.

Tversky, A., and Kahneman, D. 1981. The Framing of Decisions and the Psychology of Choice. *Science*, 211(4481): 453–458.

Varda, D. 2017. Strategies for Researching Social Networks in Disaster Response, Recovery, and Mitigation. In *Social Network Analysis of Disaster Response, Recovery, and Adaptation*. (eds.) E. Jones and A. Faas. Cambridge: Elsevier, pp. 41–56.

Wenger, D., and Weller, J. 1973. *Disaster Subcultures: The Cultural Residues of Community Disasters*. Newark, DE: Disaster Research Center.

3 Public expectations of and responses to WEA message content

*Bandana Kar, David M. Cochran, Jr., Joslyn Zale,
Nicole E. Callais, and Xiaohui Liu*

Introduction

With the increase in intense and frequent extreme events, development and maintenance of a multi-hazard, multicultural warning system for risk communication
is crucial to building resilience and increasing preparedness (Fischhoff 2009;
Hooke and Rogers 2005; Mileti and Peek 2000; Morgan et al. 2002; Institute
of Medicine and National Research Council 2015). An effective warning system
must comprise a detection subsystem to predict and monitor the location and time
of a hazard event; an emergency management subsystem to formulate and disseminate alert and warning messages to the public; and a public response subsystem
that focuses on public receipt of and responses to messages (Grabill and Simmons
1998; NRC 2012; Sorensen, Vogt, and Mileti 1987).

Technological advancements and access to real-time data from different
sources have made it possible to predict a hazard and its associated risk with
high accuracy and to formulate and disseminate warning messages with updated
information to at-risk communities using a variety of communication methods
(i.e., voice, electronic signal, text). Risk communication in the 21st century not
only relies on information from traditional sources (hierarchical and vertically
integrated organizations) but also from social media and word-of-mouth sources
(i.e., families and friends) that are typically nonhierarchical and horizontally integrated across society (Liu, Austin, and Jin 2011). Although the dissemination of
information from authoritative sources is a critical part of risk communication, the
conventional hierarchical approach typically fails to incorporate local knowledge
and the viewpoints of at-risk populations. Social media allows creation of Online
Social Networks (OSN) and enables inclusion of local knowledge about risk
information in real time but tends to foster the proliferation of rumors and hoaxes.
Evidently, both hierarchical and network-based risk communication approaches
tend to reduce the quality of the message for different reasons, thereby influencing
public response.

As perceived risk varies across the scientific community, emergency management community, and at-risk populations in general, the message delivery
approach and the channel used to disseminate information as well as the content and style of the messages influence public understanding of and subsequent

response to messages. Likewise, the public is not always aware of the risks associated with a specific hazard event, and their awareness and knowledge might be influenced by prior experience or knowledge gleaned from family and friends that impacts how they respond to alert messages. Studies have shown that the effectiveness of public response to risk communication is influenced by (1) message characteristics – message content and style, source, delivery approaches, and devices (Mileti and Peek 2000; Mileti and Sorensen 1990; NRC 2012) – and (2) message recipient characteristics – social and psychological characteristics of the public (De la Cruz-Reyna and Tilling 2008; Gaillard et al. 2008; Mileti and Peek 2000; Mileti and Sorensen 1990).

In the United States, the Integrated Public Alert and Warning System (IPAWS) was established to "provide integrated services and capabilities to local, state, and federal authorities that enable them to alert and warn their respective communities via multiple communications methods" (FEMA 2012). The goal of IPAWS is to deliver standardized alert messages using multiple communication channels to a broader audience in a timely manner to reduce risk (FEMA 2012). As part of IPAWS, Wireless Emergency Alerts (WEA) messages are sent to the cell phones of individuals, ensuring that alerts reach geotargeted communities in real time. WEA messages, however, are primarily disseminated in English to ethnically and socioeconomically diverse communities across the country whose preferred and primary language may not be English. This not only alienates these communities from responding to alerts due to not understanding the messages but also pushes them to rely more on social media for risk communication. In light of this issue, it is essential to understand how language barriers, along with socioeconomic and cultural diversity, influence public response to alerts so that appropriate steps can be taken by local emergency management agencies to meet the needs of their communities as well as to maximize public response to messages such that risk from hazards can be reduced.

In this chapter, a Protective Action Decision Model (PADM) was used to examine the role of language preference on public response to alerts received from both authoritative sources and social media. A survey of a sample of residents in the three Gulf Coast counties of Mississippi (Hancock, Harrison, and Jackson) was used to answer the following research questions: (1) what is the impact of language on public use of communication channels and (2) to what extent do language and socioeconomic characteristics influence public response to warnings? The next section discusses the Protective Action Decision Model and studies that have explored the effectiveness of risk communication based on message recipient characteristics. Section 3 introduces the study site and describes the methodology and survey instrument used between 2013 and 2016 for this research. Section 4 presents the results of analysis, and Section 5 provides a discussion of the results.

Background

The purpose of risk communication is to deliver clear and concise messages about a hazard event and associated risks to the impacted populations (Krimsky 2007).

Risk communication attempts to promote protective behavior among impacted populations so that they will undertake preparatory actions to reduce risk and exposure to hazard events (Burton, Kates, and White 1993; Reynolds and Seeger 2005). Risk communication must therefore provide information about a hazard event in the form of alert and warning messages using different channels to promote maximum coverage and compliance (Reynolds and Seeger 2005).

At-risk populations, however, are not homogeneous. They constitute diverse groups whose responses to messages are influenced by their risk perception, prior experience with hazard events, and socioeconomic and cultural characteristics (Carter-Pokras et al. 2007; Cronin et al. 2004; Gilk 2007; Kalkstein and Sheridan 2007; Mileti and Peek 2000; NRC 2012; Sorensen 2000; Spence, Lachlan, and Griffin 2007). Successful risk communication must consider the unique needs of these populations as well as enable exchange of information and opinion among stakeholders to contextualize the information to impacted communities to promote compliance with alert and warning messages.

Because public attention changes across the different phases of emergency management, theories have been developed to design messages that will capture public attention and enable positive response to reduce risk and impacts (Sheppard, Janoske, and Liu. 2012). While message design and style is essential to motivate public behavior changes, a variety of models are used to determine how the sociopsychological characteristics of the public might improve compliance.

The Classical Persuasion Model is the predominant model used for persuasive communication (Lindell and Perry 2004). This model primarily focuses on four components to achieve effective risk communication – source, message, channel, and intended effect. The source of disseminating messages must be trustworthy and knowledgeable about the cause and effect of a specific event. Messages must be clear and forceful and should be designed to communicate information about a hazard, its possible impacts, and protective actions to reduce impacts. Given the diversity of the receiver group, emergency managers must use a variety of channels (textual, graphic, sound) to reach out to at-risk populations. Finally, the model requires use of a feedback loop to allow interactive communication between source and receiver in order to clarify messages for better response. A major limitation of this model is that it does not account for the sociopsychological characteristics of receivers that might influence their attention, comprehension, acceptance, and retention and their change in behavior in response to the message.

As receivers are a major component of effective risk communication, several models are used to understand public perception of risk and how that ultimately influences public response. These include mental models; the extended parallel process model; theory of reasoned action; the risk information seeking and processing model, and others (Sheppard, Janoske, and Liu 2012). These models inherently focus on understanding how the public perceives the risk before an event and examining the choices people face and their beliefs to information gaps and misperceptions that need to be addressed. Such knowledge is then used to design messages to change perception of risk and enable positive responses. The purpose of these models, like the classical persuasion model, is to create effective messages by accounting for psychological characteristics of the public.

The Protective Action Decision Model draws from other studies in disasters and provides insight into how individuals respond to risks based on available protective actions and their understanding and evaluation of the risk posed by a hazard event (Lindell and Perry 2004, 2011). According to this model, receivers go through four stages before they heed the warning message and take preparatory actions (Figure 3.1). These stages are: (1) risk identification – identifying the risk associated with a specific event; (2) risk assessment – assessing the risk based on their prior experience and awareness; (3) protective action search – gathering knowledge and information about feasible protective actions based on their prior experience, knowledge, and information provided by source; (4) protective action assessment – evaluating the benefit of each protective action (e.g., evacuating vs. sheltering in place due to extenuating circumstances like having pets or elderly relatives); and (5) protective action implementation – taking steps to implement the best protective action. Unlike other models that focus on message preparation, this model provides insight into the role of sociopsychological characteristics on how the public receives, processes, and responds to messages.

Evidently, risk communication is not a new discipline, and extensive research has been conducted to ensure risk is communicated effectively to the broader

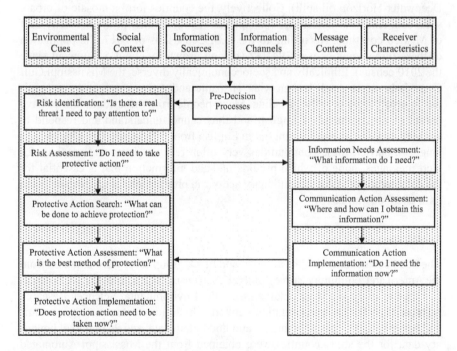

Figure 3.1 Protective Action Decision Model
Source: Lindell and Perry 2004

community to ensure risk is reduced. It is also clear that risk communication is not always effective, and very often individuals' responses are influenced by their own characteristics rather than by the source or message. Most models have also focused on designing messages that clearly disseminate information about hazards, potential risks and consequences, and possible protective actions to individuals using multiple channels to provide accurate and timely information. With increasing dependency on social media, messages are now available from different sources. Furthermore, due to the diversity of recipients, messages also need contextualization. By drawing from PADM, this chapter examines the extent to which the public's social and cultural characteristics, including language, influence their response to WEA messages (authoritative sources) and messages received via social media.

Methodology

Study site

This study was conducted in the three counties of the Mississippi Gulf Coast – Hancock, Harrison, and Jackson (Figure 3.2). These counties are susceptible to coastal hazards, specifically tropical storms during the hurricane season (e.g., Hurricanes Katrina, Rita, Nate) as well as to anthropogenic hazards (e.g., the 2010 Deepwater Horizon oil spill). Collectively, the counties form a mosaic of urban, suburban, and rural landscapes that span a 44 mile stretch of the northern Gulf of Mexico coastline. According to the U.S. Census, as of 2017, the population of these three counties was 394,232 (having grown by about 5.9 percent since the 2010 census). Ethnically and socioeconomically diverse, the Mississippi Gulf Coast is home to small but growing Hispanic and Asian immigrant communities in urban areas near the coastline. Many people from these communities have partial or no command of English and thus cannot understand and respond to warning and alert messages sent out in English from official sources. Due to their language barrier, these communities very often rely on sirens and graphics for alert messages, none of which provide updated information that is essential for the communities to take precautionary actions in preparation for an extreme event (Kar and Cochran 2016).

Spatial data sets

The 2014 socioeconomic data at block and block group level were obtained from the American Community Survey of the U.S. Census. The administrative boundaries for the study site were obtained from the Environmental Sciences Research Institute (ESRI). The transportation networks, hydrology data sets (e.g., streams and water bodies), coastal boundary and flood plain data, and 2014 parcel boundary data for the study counties were obtained from the Mississippi Automated Resource Information System (MARIS), the National Oceanic and Atmospheric Administration (NOAA), and the Federal Emergency Management Agency

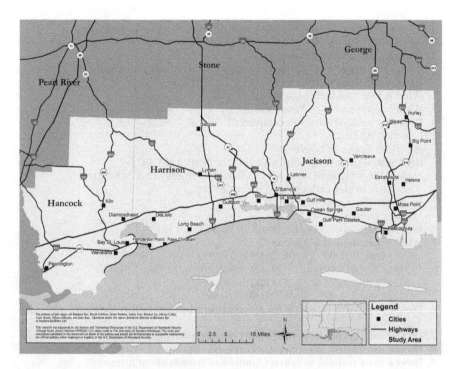

Figure 3.2 Study area along the Mississippi Gulf Coast

(FEMA). The Digital Elevation Model (DEM) data derived from Light Detection and Ranging (LiDAR) data was obtained from the United States Geological Survey (USGS) at 1/9 arc second (3.23 m × 3.23 m) spatial resolution. Data about spatial location and coverage of communication devices (i.e., TV, sirens, radio, and cell phones) were obtained from the local emergency management agencies, Mississippi Emergency Management Agency (MEMA) and the Federal Communication Commission (FCC). All the spatial data sets were projected to North American Datum (NAD 1983), UTM Projection Zone 16N.

Survey data sets

The survey instrument used for this study comprised of a series of yes/no questions, factual questions with multiple choices, and Likert-scale questions to get data about local household perceptions of and responses to alert and warning messages (Table 3.1). Specifically, questions were designed to obtain data for the following variables:

a   Socioeconomic-cultural Characteristics: *Demographic Profiles* (age, gender, ethnicity, education level); *Economic Conditions* (household income, employment status); and *Cultural Traits* (languages spoken fluently).

Table 3.1 Public perceptions of warning and alert messages survey instrument

1. **What is your ethnicity (select one)?**
   White (Not Hispanic)   African American   Native American   Pacific Islander
   Hispanic   Asian   Other
2. **What is your gender?** Male Female
3. **What is your age?** ___ Years Old
4. **How much school have you completed?**
   Less than 9th Grade
   9th – 12th Grade, NO diploma
   High School Graduate (includes alternate route such as GED)
   Some College (Junior/Community College or University, but NO degree)
   Associate's Degree or Technical Degree (2 Year)
   Bachelor's Degree (4 Year)
   Master's Degree
   Professional/Doctoral Degree (Ph.D., E.D., M.D., or J.D.)
5. **What is your household income?**

Less than $10,000	$35,000 to $49,999
$10,000 to $14,999	$50,000 to $74,999
$15,000 to $24,999	$75,000 to $99,999
$25,000 to $34,999	$100,000 and over

6. **Would you like to receive WEA messages in a language other than English?**
   Yes   No
7. **Do you use Facebook to receive alert messages during a disaster?** Yes   No
8. **Do you use Twitter to receive alert messages during a disaster?** Yes   No
9. **Do you use Facebook to contact family and friends about disasters?** Yes   No
10. **Do you use Twitter to contact family and friends about disasters?** Yes   No
11. **Do you use Facebook as a platform to share disaster-related information (for example, images and address information about impacted areas)?** Yes   No
12. **Do you use Twitter as a platform to share disaster-related information (for example, images and address information about impacted areas)?** Yes   No
13. **Would you like your local emergency management agency to use Facebook to deliver alert messages during disasters?** Yes   No
14. **Would you like your local emergency management agency to use Twitter to deliver alert messages during disasters?** Yes   No
15. **Do you think using Facebook or Twitter will allow you to receive alert messages in languages other than English?** Yes   No
16. **Do you believe that the use of social media to deliver alert messages during disasters is a violation of your privacy?** Yes   No
17. **I always trust alert messages I receive from local emergency management agencies (city or county).** Yes   No
18. **I always trust alert messages about severe weather events (such as hurricanes or tornados) if I receive them from the National Weather Service.** Yes   No
19. **If I receive an evacuation notice, I will follow it.** Yes   No
20. **I will follow an evacuation notice only if I receive it from my local emergency management agency (city or county).** Yes   No
21. **I will follow an evacuation notice only if my family and friends are evacuating as well.** Yes   No
22. **I will follow an evacuation notice only if I believe that I am in danger.** Yes   No
23. **I will not follow any evacuation notice.** Yes   No

b   Message Format and Content: *Respondent Preferences* (In what languages do respondents prefer the message to be delivered? Do they use social media to receive messages? What is the level of trust respondents have on messages received from different sources?).

c   Response to Messages: *Message Source* (How does public respond to messages delivered via social media versus traditional media (e.g., TV, radio, sirens) vs. word-of-mouth communication? How does public trust in message source influence their response to messages?); *Respondent Participation* (Do respondents want to participate in message preparation and dissemination? How does their participation influence their response?).

Survey instrument and administration

Following approval by the Institutional Review Board at the University of Southern Mississippi, a 52-item questionnaire-based survey instrument was administered to a sample of residents living in the tri-county area. Three sampling strategies – targeted, snowball, and spatially stratified random sampling – were used for survey administration. In targeted sampling, an online version of the survey (developed using Qualtrics) was disseminated to residents of the study site using social media and social network sites such as Facebook, Twitter, and Reddit, and by posting the survey link through University of Southern Mississippi's (USM) email account to students, staffs, and faculties of USM, many of whom live on the Gulf Coast. The hard copy survey was also used to target immigrant communities in these three counties with help of nonprofit organizations (i.e., Boat People–NAVASA and El Pueblo/Seashore Mission, American Red Cross, and the Gulf of Mexico Alliance) involved in disaster mitigation along the Mississippi Gulf Coast. The participants identified through targeted sampling were encouraged to share the online survey link with others interested and residing along the Gulf Coast, thereby leading to a snowball sampling approach that increased the number of survey respondents.

A spatially stratified random sampling technique was used to identify potential survey participants during in-person administration of the survey. For survey administration, the following steps were implemented to identify 1 percent of households in the study area. First, high-risk areas, susceptible to coastal hazards based on their proximity to the coast and because of their low-lying terrain, were identified. The parcel boundary data was overlaid on the high-risk areas to identify residential parcels that were present south of I-10, the area with dense population in the three study counties. To ensure that vacant lots and blighted properties were eliminated from the final sample of parcels, a supervised photo interpretation was conducted using 1 m × 1 m resolution color infrared imagery.

A random sample was extracted from the final list of residential parcels. In order to get n (100) number of surveys, a total sample of $4n$ (400) was randomly selected. The random sample was increased to account for unoccupied or inaccessible houses and for households that did not wish to participate in the survey. Between May and December of 2015, student workers were hired to administer the survey to identified sample houses through face-to-face visits. Personnel from Boat People–NAVASA and El Pueblo/Seashore Mission were also hired to administer the survey in person to non-English-speaking immigrant residents.

Survey data processing and analysis

The surveyed data were coded for analysis. The ages of respondents (i.e., Question 3 in Table 3.1) were recoded into the following categories, which are used by the U.S. Census Bureau: 18 through 25 years, 26 through 35 years, 36 through 45 years, 46 through 55 years, 56 through 65 years, and 66 or more years old. Other variables were obtained in discrete categories and thus were not recoded.

To get an overview of data distribution, frequency analysis was performed on all questionnaire items including the relevant question – Question 6 (Would you like to receive WEA messages in a language other than English?). One-way analyses of variance (ANOVA) tests were used to examine socioeconomic differences, using age group, ethnicity, education level, and income level as independent variables and language preference as the dependent variable. An independent samples *t*-test was used to examine the role of gender (independent variable) on language preference (dependent variable).

Independent samples *t*-tests were implemented to examine differences among individuals based on their preference (or lack thereof) for WEA messages in languages other than English and on whether they preferred to use of social media to receive hazard-related information. *T*-tests were implemented using Question 6 as the independent variable, and the responses to a variety of other questions as the dependent variables: Questions 7–16 (use of Facebook and/or Twitter to receive alert and warning messages; contact family and friends about disasters and share disaster-related information using social media; would like local EMAs to deliver messages via Facebook and/or Twitter during disasters; belief that Facebook or Twitter allows receiving messages in languages other than English; and belief that using social media to deliver alert messages is a violation of personal privacy).

The socioeconomic characteristics of participants who responded affirmatively to Question 6 (would like to receive WEA messages in a language other than English) were examined to understand their evacuation behavior and trust in warning and alert messages. One-way ANOVAs were performed using age group, ethnicity, education, and income level as independent variables and Questions 17–23 as dependent variables (level of agreement with the following: trust alert and warning messages received from local EMAs and/or the National Weather Service; will follow any evacuation notice received; will follow an evacuation notice only if received from a local EMA, if family and friends are also evacuating, or if belief of danger exists; and will not follow any evacuation notice received). Independent samples *t*-test with gender as independent variable and responses to Questions 17–23 as dependent variables were also conducted.

Linear regression was also used to determine the socioeconomic characteristics that influenced the decision of those individuals who indicated that they would not follow any evacuation notice and wanted to receive WEA messages in non-English languages, using age group and education level as predictor variables. Descriptive statistics were used to further examine the socioeconomic characteristics of individuals who responded neutrality about following an evacuation notice (i.e., primarily ages 36 through 45 years of age).

Results and discussion

The following two sections discuss the results of this study. The first section presents the results obtained from analyzing the entire survey sample, and the second presents the results from the analyses of responses of those of individuals who indicated that they wanted to receive WEA messages in language(s) other than English.

Results (using entire sample population)

The survey sample size was 304, and 275 participants responded to Question 6. Of these 275 respondents, 130 (47.3 percent) indicated that they would like to receive alert and warning messages in a language other than English. Ethnicity of the respondents was found to be statistically significant and was used as a grouping variable for Question 6 (language preference for receiving WEA message). According to Table 3.2 ($F(4, 269) = 77.24$, $p < 0.001$), individuals who indicated Asian or Hispanic ethnicities indicated that they would like to receive alert and warning messages in a language other than English more often than other ethnic groups.

The education level of respondents was also found to be a statistically significant grouping variable for receiving WEA message in preferred languages (Table 3.3: $F(7, 260) = 15.05$, $p < 0.001$). As illustrated, respondents with no high school diploma, those who were high school graduates (even through alternate routes such as the GED), and those whose highest education level was less than ninth grade indicated that they would prefer to receive WEA messages in a language other than English more often than respondents with higher education levels.

Table 3.2 Statistically significant ANOVA pairs based on ethnicity and language preference

Statistically Significant Pair	p value
Caucasian and Hispanic*	< 0.001
Caucasian and Asian*	< 0.001
African American and Hispanic*	< 0.001
African American and Asian*	< 0.001
Hispanic* and Other	< 0.001
Asian* and Other	< 0.001

*Group with more individuals who prefer WEA messages in a non-English language.

Table 3.3 Statistically significant ANOVA pairs based on education level and language preference

Statistically Significant Pair	p value
Less than 9–12th grade* and 9–12th grade but no diploma	0.004
Less than 9–12th grade* and high school graduate	< 0.001
Less than 9–12th grade* and some college	< 0.001
Less than 9–12th grade* and AA/technical degree	< 0.001
Less than 9–12th grade* and bachelor's degree	< 0.001
Less than 9–12th grade* and master's degree	< 0.001
Less than 9–12th grade* and doctorate/professional degree	< 0.001
High school graduate* and some college	0.014
High school graduate* and bachelor's degree	0.047
High school graduate* and doctorate/professional degree	0.040

*Group with more individuals who prefer WEA messages in a non-English language.

Table 3.4 Statistically significant ANOVA pairs based on income level and language preference

Statistically Significant Pair	p value
< $10,000 and $15,000–24,999*	0.028
< $10,000 and $25,000–34,999*	0.025
$10,000–14,999* and $50,000–74,999	0.001
$10,000–14,999* and $75,000–99,999	0.003
$10,000–14,999* and > $100,000	0.016
$15,000–24,999* and $35,000–49,999	0.028
$15,000–24,999* and $50,000–74,999	< 0.001
$15,000–24,999* and $75,000–99,999	< 0.001
$15,000–24,999* and > $100,000	0.001
$25,000–34,999* and $35,000–49,999	0.023
$25,000–34,999* and $50,000–74,999	< 0.001
$25,000–34,999* and $75,000–99,999	< 0.001
$25,000–34,999* and > $100,000	0.001

*Group with more individuals who prefer WEA messages in a non-English language.

The income levels of respondents was also a statistically significant grouping variable with regard to preference for receiving WEA messages in languages other than English (Table 3.4: $F(7, 235) = 9.67, p < 0.001$). Respondents who indicated their income was $34,999 or less were more likely to prefer receiving alert and warning messages in a language other than English as opposed to respondents with higher incomes. Gender and age were found not to be statistically significant variables and did not influence respondents' language preferences with regard to WEA messages.

Respondents who indicated their preference for receiving WEA messages in a language other than English also often indicated that they used Facebook ($t(149.187) = -3.148, p = 0.002$) and Twitter ($t(102.797) = -6.572, p < 0.001$) for alert and warning messages. These respondents indicated that they would contact family ($t(160.046) = -4.249, p < 0.001$) and friends ($t(122.416) = -5.748, p < 0.001$) about hazard events and event-related information. This group also usually indicated that they preferred local emergency management agencies (EMAs) to use Facebook ($t(158.917) = -2.881, p = 0.005$) and Twitter ($t(149.033) = -3.787, p < 0.001$) to disseminate alert messages during hazard events and they believed that social media would allow them to receive such messages in languages other than English ($t(159.145) = -6.004, p < 0.001$).

Results (using responses for participants who prefer non-English messages)

Analysis revealed that respondents in the age range of 18–35 years would evacuate only if their friends and family evacuated (Table 3.5: $F(5, 118) = 6.86, p < 0.001$) or if they believed they needed to evacuate (Table 3.6: $F(5, 116) = 4.022, p = 0.002$) or would not follow any evacuation notice (Table 3.7: $F(5, 116) = 9.154, p < 0.001$).

Table 3.5 Statistically significant ANOVA pairs based on age group and evacuation decision if family/friends decide to evacuate

Statistically Significant Pair	p value
18–25* and 36–45 years	0.010
18–25* and 56–65 years	< 0.001
18–25* and 66+ years	0.001
26–35* and 56–65 years	0.003
26–35* and 66+ years	0.007

*Group with more individuals who will evacuate if friends/family do so.

Table 3.6 Statistically significant ANOVA pairs based on age group and evacuation decision if in danger

Statistically Significant Pair	p value
18–25* and 36–45 years	0.025
18–25* and 56–65 years	0.005
18–25* and 66+ years	0.024

*Group with more individuals who will evacuate if in danger.

Table 3.7 Statistically significant ANOVA pairs based on age group and decision not to follow any evacuation notice

Statistically Significant Pair	p value
18–25* and 46–55 years	0.012
18–25* and 56–65 years	0.001
18–25* and 66+ years	< 0.001
26–35* and 46–55 years	0.009
26–35* and 56–65 years	< 0.001
26–35* and 66+ years	< 0.001

* Group with more individuals who will not follow any evacuation notice.

A comparison of respondents' trust in alert and warning messages and their response to messages (specifically, if they would follow an evacuation notice) revealed that respondents of Asian or Hispanic descent indicated that they trust alert and warning messages if they receive the messages from local EMAs or the National Weather Service (Table 3.8: $F(3, 121) = 9.94, p < 0.001$ and Table 3.9: $F(3, 121) = 7.72, p < 0.001$, respectively). These respondents also indicated that they would always follow evacuation notices (Table 3.10: $F(3, 120) = 11.38, p < 0.001$), specifically, if they received them from local EMAs (Table 3.11: $F(3, 118) = 11.81, p < 0.001$), if their friends and family were evacuating (Table 3.12: $F(3, 120) = 14.12, p < 0.001$), or if they believed they needed to evacuate because they were in danger (Table 3.13: $F(3, 119) = 14.48, p < 0.001$).

Table 3.8 Statistically significant ANOVA pairs based on ethnicity and trust in alert messages received from local emergency management agencies

Statistically Significant Pair	p value
Caucasian and Hispanic*	< 0.001
Caucasian and Asian*	< 0.001
African American and Hispanic*	0.014
African American and Asian*	0.009

*Group with more individuals who trust alert messages from local EMAs

Table 3.9 Statistically significant ANOVA pairs based on ethnicity and trust in alert messages received from the national weather service

Statistically Significant Pair	p value
Caucasian and Hispanic*	< 0.001
Caucasian and Asian*	< 0.001

*Group with more individuals who trust alert messages from the National Weather Service

Table 3.10 Statistically significant ANOVA pairs based on ethnicity and decision to follow any evacuation notice

Statistically Significant Pair	p value
Caucasian and Hispanic*	< 0.001
Caucasian and Asian*	< 0.001

*Group with more individuals who will follow any evacuation notice

Table 3.11 Statistically significant ANOVA pairs based on ethnicity and decision to follow evacuation notice only if received from local emergency management agency

Statistically Significant Pair	p value
Caucasian and Hispanic*	< 0.001
Caucasian and Asian*	0.003

*Group with more individuals who will follow evacuation notices only if they are from a local EMA.

Respondents who identified themselves as white were more likely to claim that they would not follow an evacuation notice (Table 3.14: $F(3, 119) = 41.12$, $p < 0.001$). Respondents whose highest levels of education were less than ninth grade or ninth through 12th grade with no high school diploma indicated that they trusted alert and warning messages from local EMAs (Table 3.15: $F(6, 116) = 4.24$, $p = 0.001$) or the National Weather Service (Table 3.16: $F(6, 117) = 3.94$, $p = 0.001$). This same group of respondents also indicated that generally they would follow evacuation notices (Table 3.17: $F(6, 115) = 2.55$, $p = 0.023$), especially if they received them from local EMAs (Table 3.18: $F(6, 113) = 3.18$, $p = 0.006$).

Table 3.12 Statistically significant ANOVA pairs based on ethnicity and decision to follow evacuation notice only if friends/family evacuate

Statistically Significant Pair	p value
Hispanic* and Asian	< 0.001

*Group with more individuals who will follow evacuation notices only if friends/family do so.

Table 3.13 Statistically significant ANOVA pairs based on ethnicity and decision to follow evacuation notice only if in danger

Statistically Significant Pair	p value
African American and Hispanic*	0.002
Hispanic* and Asian	< 0.001

*Group with more individuals who will follow evacuation notices only if in danger

Table 3.14 Statistically significant ANOVA pairs based on ethnicity and decision to follow evacuation notice only if in danger

Statistically Significant Pair	p value
Caucasian* and Asian	0.002
African American and Hispanic*	< 0.001
Hispanic* and Asian	< 0.001

*Group with more individuals who will not follow any evacuation notice.

Table 3.15 Statistically significant ANOVA pairs based on education level and trust in alert messages received from local EMAs

Statistically Significant Pair	p value
Less than 9th grade* and master's degree	0.046
9–12th grade* and master's degree	0.037

*Group with more individuals who trust alert messages from local EMAs

Table 3.16 Statistically significant ANOVA pairs based on education level and trust in alert messages received from the National Weather Service

Statistically Significant Pair	p value
Less than 9th grade* and some college	0.007
9–12th grade* and some college	0.005

*Group with more individuals who trust alert messages from the National Weather Service

Table 3.17 Statistically significant ANOVA pairs based on education level and decision to follow any evacuation notice

Statistically Significant Pair	p value
Less than 9th grade* and master's degree	0.040

*Group with more individuals who will follow any evacuation notice

Table 3.18 Statistically significant ANOVA pairs based on education level and decision to follow evacuation notice from local EMAs

Statistically Significant Pair	p value
Less than 9th grade* and master's degree	0.024
9–12th grade* and master's degree	0.034

*Group with more individuals who will follow evacuation notices from local EMAs

Gender and income level were not statistically significant predictors of evacuation behavior for individuals who preferred to receive WEA messages in languages other than English. A linear regression was implemented using age group and education level as predictors of response to evacuation notice. The R^2 of this regression was only 0.056, although it was statistically significant ($F(2, 118) = 3.522$, $p = 0.033$). This regression equation found only education to be a statistically significant predictor ($p = 0.009$), which corroborates ANOVA results for education and evacuation notice.

Conclusion

An important finding of this research is that survey respondents of Asian or Hispanic descent tended to prefer receiving WEA messages in non-English languages. This aligns well with the small but growing Vietnamese and Hispanic communities of the Mississippi Gulf Coast. Many members of these communities speak English as a second language, and some do not understand English at all. The generally low levels of education and income among members of these groups suggests they have limited resources with which to attain higher levels of English comprehension. This scenario was corroborated by personnel from two local community organizations – Boat People/NAVASA and the El Pueblo/ Seashore Mission – who communicated with the researchers associated with this project.

Facebook, Twitter, and other social media outlets allow users to communicate in non-English languages, and it is no surprise that large numbers of survey respondents who indicated a preference for receiving WEA messages in languages other than English also noted high levels of social media usage. Based on the results of this research, residents of the Mississippi Gulf Coast who do not understand English tend to rely more on social media for information and communication about hazard events and to receive and share information about preparatory actions. Future research should examine the degree to which minority and immigrant communities rely on social media during hazard events and the type of information they communicate during those events (e.g., type, severity, or temporal or spatial extent of a hazard event; whether they are evacuating; current health status; current location; and current condition of their residences or vehicles).

Another important finding from this research is the convergence of non-English language preference, Asian or Hispanic descent, low educational attainment and income, and youth with trust in evacuation notices from local EMAs. If language is the main barrier preventing these individuals from following official warnings, the introduction of non-English messages might improve public compliance of evacuation notices. It is therefore essential for local EMAs and community organizations, as well as FEMA and the National Weather Service, to issue relevant, up-to-date information to at-risk communities in languages people can understand. Future research should focus on further identifying and implementing effective communication strategies for these and other at-risk communities.

It is critical that local EMAs, as well as state and federal agencies, must ensure that everyone in a potential hazard impact zone, including residents who do not understand English, has access to information that will help reduce their risk and exposure and build their resilience. If alert and warning messages are disseminated only in English, non-English speaking residents might be at a significant disadvantage with regard to taking preparatory actions (e.g., evacuating) without help from family members, friends, or neighbors who understand English.

Another interesting finding of this research is that respondents with lower levels of educational attainment tended be to more agreeable to the idea of complying with evacuation orders than respondents with higher levels of education. This is good, especially for households of non-English speakers and low-income earners, but future research should determine whether this pattern holds true in more affluent and educated coastal regions of the Gulf of Mexico and Atlantic Ocean. For risk communication to contribute to resilience building, it is essential for local EMAs and other disaster management institutions to devise strategies that promote compliance among all residents. There is also considerable need for this type of research in disaster-prone areas of the developing world, especially in culturally diverse regions where a multiple-language approach to risk communication could make significant strides in building the resilience of at-risk communities.

Disclaimer

The findings and conclusions presented in this chapter are those of the authors and do not reflect the policies or opinions of the funding agencies. Dr. Bandana Kar has participated in this project in her own independent capacity and not on behalf of UT-Battelle, LLC, or its affiliates or successors. The views and conclusions expressed in this article are those of the authors and do not reflect the policies or opinions of Oak Ridge National Laboratory, UT-Battelle, the Department of Energy, or the United States government.

References

Burton, I., Kates, R., and White, G.F. 1993. *The Environment as Hazard*, Second Edition. New York: Guildford Press.

Carter-Pokras, O., Zambrana, R. E., Mora, S. E., and Aaby, K. A. 2007. Emergency Preparedness: Knowledge and Perceptions of Latin American Immigrants. *Journal of Health Care for the Poor and Underserved*, 18: 465–481.

Cronin, S. J., Gaylord, D. R., Charley, D., Alloway, B. V., Wallez, S., and Esau, J. W. 2004. Participatory Methods of Incorporating Scientific with Traditional Knowledge for Volcanic Hazard Management on Ambae Island, Vanuatu. *Bulletin of Volcanology*, 66: 652–668.

De la Cruz-Reyna, S., and Tilling, R. I. 2008. Scientific and Public Responses to the Ongoing Volcanic Crisis at Popocatépetl Volcano, Mexico: Importance of an Effective Hazards-Warning System. *Journal of Volcanology and Geothermal Research*, (1–2): 121–134.

Federal Emergency Management Agency (FEMA). 2012. *Wireless Emergency Alerts*. Accessed January 2019 at www.fema.gov/frequently-asked-questions-wireless-emergency-alerts.

Fischhoff, B. 2009. Risk Perception and Communication. In *Oxford Textbook of Public Health*. (eds.) R. Detels, R. Beaglehole, M. Lansang, and M. Gulliford. Oxford: Oxford University Press, pp. 940–952.

Gaillard, J-C., Clavé, E., Vibert, O., Azhari, Dedi, Denian, J-C., and Setiawan, R. 2008. Ethnic Groups' Response to the 26 December 2004 Earthquake and Tsunami in Aceh, Indonesia. *Natural Hazards*, 17–38.

Gilk, D. 2007. Risk Communication for Public Health Emergencies. *The Annual Review of Public Health*, 28: 33–54.

Grabill, J. T., and Simmons, W. M. 1998. Toward a Critical Rhetoric of Risk Communication: Producing Citizens and the Role of Technical Communicators. *Technical Communication Quarterly*, 7(4): 415–441.

Institute of Medicine and National Research Council. 2005. *Public Health Risks of Disasters: Communication, Infrastructure, and Preparedness: Workshop Summary*. Washington, DC: The National Academies Press.

Kalkstein, A. J., and Sheridan, S. C. 2007. The Social Impacts of the Heat – Health Watch/Warning System in Phoenix, Arizona: Assessing the Perceived Risk and Response of the Public. *International Journal of Biometeorology*, 52: 43–55.

Kar, B., and Cochran, D. 2016. Final Report – An Integrated Approach to Geo-Target at-Risk Communities and Deploy Effective Crisis Communication Approaches. *Department of Homeland Security – Science and Technology Directorate (DHS – S&T)*. Accessed on January 2019 at www.dhs.gov/publication/integrated-approach-geo-target-risk-communities-deploy-effective-crisis-communication.

Krimsky, S. 2007. Risk Communication in the Internet Age: The Rise of Disorganized Skepticism. *Environmental Hazards*, 7: 157–164.

Lindell, M. K., and Perry, R. W. 2004. *Communicating Environmental Risk in Multiethnic Communities*. Thousand Oaks, CA: Sage Publications.

———. 2011. The Protective Action Decision Model: Theoretical Modifications and Additional Evidence. *Risk Analysis*, 32(4): 616–632.

Liu, B. F., Austin, L., and Jin, Y. 2011. How Publics Respond to Crisis Communication Strategies: The Interplay of Information Form and Source. *Public Relations Review*, 345–353.

Mileti, D. S., and Peek, L. 2000. The Social Psychology of Public Response to Warnings of a Nuclear Power Plant Accident. *Journal of Hazardous Materials*, 75: 181–194.

Mileti, D. S., and Sorensen, J. H. 1990. *Communication of Emergency Public Warnings: A Social Science Perspective and State-of-the-Art Assessment* (No. ORNL-6609). Oak Ridge, TN: Oak Ridge National Laboratory.

Morgan, M. G., Fischhoff, B., Bostrom, A., and Atman, C. J. 2002. *Risk Communication: A Mental Models Approach*. Cambridge: Cambridge University Press.

National Research Council. 2012. *Disaster Resilience: A National Imperative*. Washington, DC: The National Academies Press.

Reynolds, B., and Seeger, M. W. 2005. Crisis and Emergency Risk Communication as an Integrative Model. *Journal of Health Communication*, 10: 43–55.

Sheppard, B., Janoske, M., and Liu, B. 2012. *Understanding Risk Communication Theory: A Guide for Emergency Managers and Communicators*. Report to Human Factors/ Behavioral Sciences Division, Science and Technology Directorate, U.S. Department of Homeland Security. College Park, MD: START.

Sorensen, J. H. 2000. Hazard Warning Systems: Review of 20 Years of Progress. *Natural Hazards Review*, 1(2): 119–125.

Sorensen, J. H., Vogt, B., and Mileti, D. S. 1987. *Evacuation: An Assessment of Planning and Research* (No. ORNL-6376). Oak Ridge, TN: Oak Ridge National Laboratory.

Spence, P. R., Lachlan, K. A., and Griffin, D. R. 2007. Crisis Communication, Race, and Natural Disasters. *Journal of Black Studies*, 37(4): 539–554.

United Nations Office for Disaster Reduction (UN). 2015. Sendai Framework for Disaster Risk Reduction 2015–2030. In *Proceedings of the Third United Nations World Conference; United Nations Office for Disaster Reduction*. Geneva, Switzerland.

Part 2

Citizen participation in risk communication and resilience

Risk communication is defined as "any purposeful exchange of scientific information between interested parties regarding health or environmental risks" (Covello, von Winterfeldt, and Slovic 1987: 222). Put another way, risk communication can be seen as an ongoing process of multidirectional dialogue about a hazard event and its associated risks among affected stakeholders (Plough and Krimsky 1987; NRC 1989). The purpose of risk communication is to (1) provide accurate information about a hazard and its potential risks, possible consequences and required mitigation steps and (2) contextualize the communication message with regard to the socio-economic-cultural characteristics of the exposed population so that messages are more effective in addressing the specific needs and sensibilities of culturally diverse populations.

Studies have revealed that effective risk communication should account for (1) perceived risk of scientific community, emergency responders, and at-risk population; (2) social, economic, cultural, and political factors of an impacted population; (3) prior experience of the impacted population; and (4) the inclination of an impacted population to seek out information from other sources (Cronin et al. 2004; Carter-Pokras et al. 2007; Kalkstein and Sheridan 2007; Spence, Lachlan, and Griffin 2007; Taylor et al. 2007; De la Cruz-Reyna and Tilling 2008; Gaillard et al. 2008). In light of these factors, Mileti and Peek (2000), Sorensen (2000), and Gladwin et al. (2007) have pointed out that risk communication should explore how risk perception, prior experience, and the sociocultural diversity of the impacted population, as well as public participation in message preparation, influence the reception of risk information from authoritative sources by individuals, as well as the willingness of the public to enhance their own resilience.

The current practice of top-down, linear dissemination of risk information from transmitters (authorities) to receivers (impacted population) works against effective risk communication because it fails to mobilize the public to share local, up-to-date information about a hazardous event. Although a top-down approach eliminates false information and rumors, the stifling of public participation can make the information it produces generic and ill-suited for local conditions. As a result, social media has become a popular risk communication channel in that it uses a decentralized, collaborative, and networked communication approach that allows both impacted and interested populations to share information at any stage of an emergency situation (Shklovski, Palen, and Sutton 2008; Sutton, Palen, and Shklovski 2008; Palen et al. 2009; Vieweg et al. 2010; Young, Flowers, and Ren 2011). Social media also allows the creation of a virtual community that has the freedom to share information, unlike the hierarchical approach, which promotes a dependent relationship between information producers and receivers in which community response and iterative exchanges of information are discouraged (Wenger, Quarantelli, and Dynes 1990; Sorensen 2000; Gladwin et al. 2007). It is important to note that while conventional hierarchical risk communication approaches provide accurate information but fail to incorporate the views and experiences of at-risk populations, decentralized risk communication through social media elevates public participation while opening up the possibility of the dissemination of hoaxes and rumors. Effective risk communication clearly must incorporate elements of both approaches.

Given this dilemma that exists in contemporary risk communication, it is crucial to understand to what extent community participation can be enabled such that the advantages of social media and top-down approach are leveraged to maximize the resilience and preparedness of impacted populations. This section highlights four chapters that examine the path forward in this process. Chapter 4 highlights how the geographical context of risk perception that varies across time and population. Knowledge of this variation requires implementation of participatory approaches to capture risk such that unique perspectives of impacted populations can be used to devise strategies for reducing risk, maximizing effective communication, and building resilience. Chapter 5 discusses the role of Local Emergency Planning Committees in enabling citizen participation in communicating risk associated with hazardous chemicals. Chapters 6 and 7 discuss the role of social media in risk communication and risk reduction in the U.S. and in Nigeria. Collectively, these chapters provide foundational information that might be used to make strategic changes to existing policies to maximize the effectiveness of both hierarchical, centralized policies and decentralized strategies that more effectively incorporate social media as a risk communication tool.

References

Carter-Pokras, O., Zambrana, R., Mora, S., and Aaby, K. 2007. Emergency Preparedness: Knowledge and Perceptions of Latin American Immigrants. *Journal of Health Care for the Poor and Underserved*, 18: 465–481.

Covello, V., von Winterfeldt, D., and Slovic, P. 1987. Communicating Scientific Information About Health and Environmental Risks: Problems and Opportunities from a Social and Behavioral Perspective. In *Uncertainty in Risk Assessment, Risk Management, and Decision Making*. (eds.) V. Covello, L. Lave, A. Moghissi, and V. Uppuluri. London: Plenum Press, pp. 221–239.

Cronin, S., Gaylord, D., Charely, D., Alloway, B., Wallez, S., and Esau, J. 2004. Participatory Methods of Incorporating Scientific with Traditional Knowledge for Volcanic Hazard Management on Ambae Island, Vanuatu. *Bulletin of Volcanology*, 66(7): 652–668.

De la Cruz-Reyna, S., and Tilling, R. 2008. Scientific and Public Responses to the Ongoing Volcanic Crisis at Popocatépetl Volcano, Mexico: Importance of an Effective

Hazards-Warning System. *Journal of Volcanology and Geothermal Research*, 170(1–2): 121–134.

Gaillard, J., Clavé, E., Vibert, O., Dedi, A., Denain, J., Efendi, Y., Grancher, D., Liamzon, C., Sari, D., and Setiawan, R. 2008. Ethnic Groups' Response to the 26 December 2004 Earthquake and Tsunami in Aceh, Indonesia. *Natural Hazards*, 47: 17–38.

Gladwin, H., Lazo, J., Morrow, B., Peacock, W., and Willoughby, H. 2007. Social Science Research Needs for the Hurricane Forecast and Warning System. *Natural Hazards Review*, 8(3): 87–95.

Kalkstein, A., and Sheridan, S. 2007. The Social Impacts of the Heat – Health Watch/Warning System in Phoenix, Arizona: Assessing the Perceived Risk and Response of the Public. *International Journal of Biometeorology*, 43–55.

Mileti, D., and Peek, L. 2000. The Social Psychology of Public Response to Warnings of a Nuclear Power Plant Accident. *Journal of Hazardous Materials*, 181–194.

National Research Council (NRC). 1989. *Improving Risk Communication*. Washington, DC: National Academies Press.

Palen, L., Vieweg, S., Liu, S., and Hughes, A. 2009. Crisis in a Networked World Features of Computer-Mediated Communication in the April 16, 2007, Virginia Tech Event. *Social Science Computer Review*, 1–14.

Plough, A., and Krimsky, S. 1987. The Emergence of Risk Communication Studies: Social and Political Context. *Science, Technology, and Human Values*, 12(1): 4–10.

Shklovski, I., Palen, L., and Sutton, J. 2008. Finding Community Through Information and Communication Technology During Disaster Events. *CSCW'08*. San Diego, CA.

Sorensen, J. 2000. Hazard Warning Systems: Review of 20 Years of Progress. *Natural Hazards Review*, 1(2): 119–125.

Spence, P., Lachlan, K., and Griffin, D. 2007. Crisis Communication, Race, and Natural Disasters. *Journal of Black Studies*, 37(4): 539–554.

Sutton, J., Palen, L., and Shklovski, I. 2008. Backchannels on the Front Lines: Emergent Uses of Social Media in the 2007 Southern California Wildfires. In *Proceedings of the 5th International ISCRAM Conference*. Washington, DC.

Taylor, J., Gillette, S., Hodgson, R., Downing, J., Burns, M., Chavez, D., and Hogan, J. 2007. Informing the Network: Improving Communication with Interface Communities During Wildland Fire. *Human Ecology Review*, 14(2): 198–211.

Vieweg, S., Hughes, A., Starbird, K., and Palen, L. 2010. *Microblogging During Two Natural Hazard Events: What Twitter May Contribute to Situational Awareness*. CHI 2010. Atlanta, Georgia, April.

Wenger, D. E., Quarantelli, E., and Dynes, R. R. 1990. *Is the Incident Command System a Plan for All Seasons and Emergency Situations?* University of Delaware, Disaster Research Center. Preliminary Paper Number 215.

Young, C. L., Flowers, A., and Ren, N. 2011. Technology and Crisis Communication: Emerging Themes from a Pilot Study of US Public Relations Practitioners. *Prism*, 8(1): 1–11.

4 River of difference

Using participatory risk mapping to assess perceived risks in Laredo, Texas, U.S.A., and Nuevo Laredo, Tamaulipas, Mexico

Andrew M. Hilburn and Thomas T. Zawisza

Introduction

Risk communication plays a vitally important role in mitigating human and environmental disasters and hazards. In the more than a half-century of concerted, systematic efforts to develop risk communication, diverse communication models have been applied in the United States and across the globe (Krimsky 2007). These have ranged from linear, top-down, expert-public hierarchical models (Covello and Allen 1988; Kasperson 1992) to mental models (Morgan et al. 2002) and to participatory models (Rayner 1992; Krimsky 2007), the latter of which are the focus of this chapter. One key element of participatory approaches in risk communication is ascertaining how groups of people define risk, or rather, how they construct it. This can be a vital component to risk communication given that participatory risk constructions, by definition, incorporate a diverse array of stakeholders, spanning the public and private sectors, to assess risk. These assessments can then be used to more precisely target and deliver key information to populations following a disaster or, in the case of a known, predictable hazard, provide preemptory and appropriate public education. Participatory approaches are not just *de rigueur* for academics and government agencies; rather, the inclusion of more horizontal and positionality-aware methods upend researcher-researched and expert-amateur power dynamics that can potentially inhibit the efficacy of actionable knowledge of risks and best practices following a disaster (Yeich and Levine 1992).

The use of new communications platforms such as social media carry the potential for more such participatory risk communication by providing portable, user-friendly, and flexible forums for stakeholders from all sides to communicate before, during, and after a disaster (Veil, Buehner, and Palenchar 2011). Additionally, social media has given voice to grassroots, local, and lateral constructions of risk. However, as social media platforms have other, mostly commercial uses besides risk communication, there is difficulty in systematically accessing and assessing data from sites such as Facebook, Yik Yak, Snapchat, and Whatsapp, to name but a few examples. Thus, how stakeholders construct and experience risk via such platforms is difficult to quantitatively gauge. This chapter offers one such method of engaging the public in risk construction through online platforms.

Besides highlighting newer participatory approaches to risk communication, this volume's epistemological orientation toward geography also assumes that risk, and thus risk communication, is both geographically and demographically situated. Risks and risk perception, be they geological-meteorological or civil, are produced by geographical factors operating at global, regional, and local scales. Furthermore, as risks are constructed and experienced across space differently, so they are as well across segments of populations. With the momentum of more participatory approaches taking hold in risk communication, methods to assess the construction or perception of risk and its place and population boundedness are needed. This chapter addresses these needs by highlighting a method to systematically assess how populations construct risk while also providing a case study that illustrates how risks are geographically and demographically contingent. Using Participatory Risk Mapping (PRM), a rapid assessment method that gauges the ubiquity and severity of risks as perceived by a population, this study shows how place and population categories matter regarding perceived risks along the U.S.–Mexico border between the cities of Laredo, Texas, and Nuevo Laredo, Tamaulipas. By allowing participants to construct risk as they experience it, the PRM methodology featured here allows researchers to analyze how risk perceptions match actual place and demographically specific risks. Understanding the gulf between perception and reality about risks according to target populations is key to providing more precise and audience-specific messaging in risk communication.

Background

Participatory approaches in risk communication

Risk communication is a well-developed area of interest among scholars from diverse disciplinary backgrounds (Cho, Reimer, and McComas 2015), including communication (Wogalter, DeJoy, and Laughery 2005), psychology (Morgan et al. 2002), public health (Bennett et al. 2010), and public administration (Lundgren and McMakin 2013), as well as geography and allied environmental sciences (Demeritt and Langdon 2004; Demeritt and Nobert 2014; Porter and Demeritt 2012). The use of public feedback and participation is a smaller subset of this interest (Fiorino 1990; Kasperson 1986). Participatory research in the social sciences is a popular methodological paradigm that decenters the researcher and allows more self-representation of the study population as it sees fit (Yeich and Levine 1992). A more horizontal, participatory approach in social science research notes the situated, positional nature of all knowledge production (Park 1993). Participatory approaches offer methodologies that counteract researcher-researched, expert-amateur power dynamics inherent in mainstream social science research (Herlihy and Knapp 2003: 304). Risk communication requires input as to what constitutes risk. Participatory methods, like the one featured in this study, thus have the potential to produce more accurate, demographically situated, and place-specific constructions of risk that provide potentially more effective risk communication.

Risk perception geography has a deep epistemological history in geography through the human-cultural-political ecology subfields. Gilbert White, along with his students Robert Kates and Ian Burton, began to examine the strategies and responses of individuals to natural hazards, essentially starting a subfield of human-environmental research on environmental hazards that persists today (White 1945; Kates 1962, 1971; Lowenthal 1967; Saarinen 1984). While the *natural hazards* school of research gave too much agency to human behavior, more current risk perception research considers the socioeconomic and historical circumstances as well as behaviors behind risk aversion (Zimmerer 1996; Liverman 1990; Watts 1983). Additionally, more participatory and horizontal research methodologies have added to an enhanced and participant-centered picture of risk perception. This study seeks to contribute to linkages between participatory approaches in risk perception to risk communication. In the following case study, the results point to a particular genre of risk, that of crime, as a significant concern for the participant sample.

Study area

The study area for this chapter is the international metropolitan area of Laredo, Texas, U.S.A., and Nuevo Laredo, Tamaulipas, Mexico (Figure 4.1). These two cities and their adjacent communities are divided by the U.S.–Mexico border as defined by the Río Grande (or Río Bravo del Norte, as it is known in Mexico). The 2015 combined population for the study area is estimated at 631,903, with 248,855 on the Laredo, Webb County, Texas, side and a larger 383,048 people on the side of Nuevo Laredo, Tamaulipas, and the surrounding area (US Census 2015; INEGI 2015). This study area, while divided by an international border, has operated as and remains in some ways a relatively unified metropolitan area. Three automobile-truck bridges, one train bridge, and one pedestrian bridge connect both sides. In fact, Laredo-Nuevo Laredo is considered to be the largest inland port on the U.S.–Mexico border, with over $200 billion U.S. dollars' worth of trade passing through it each year (Texas Comptroller 2015). Many families in the area are binational. Daily commerce and traffic flow relatively freely in both directions. In the past decade, more stringent border controls stemming from the post-9/11 geopolitical landscape and stricter immigration enforcement have served to harden the border and slow crossings. Additionally, the threat and fear of the internecine violence between rival organized crime/drug cartel syndicates and their war with Mexican armed forces and law enforcement has stifled the crossings of people and commerce from Laredo to Nuevo Laredo. An effect of potential spillover violence perhaps contributes to the looming sense among participants that crime is ubiquitous and abnormally high across the border.

This study's participants were asked to reflect on their perceptions of risk that are specific to Laredo and those specific to Nuevo Laredo. Thus, the study area embodies both a physical place-definition and also a perceptual one. Participants were, in a sense, asked to define their own view of the study area with regard to risks or sources of risk. This internationally bifurcated study area provides an

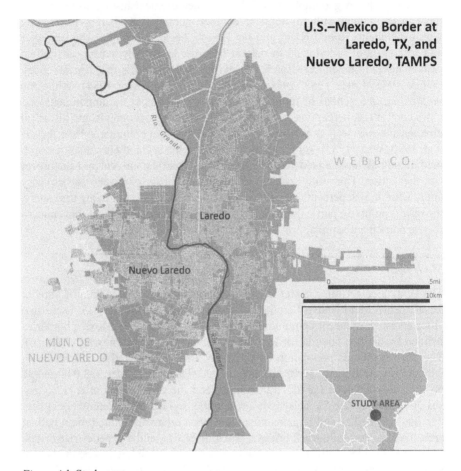

Figure 4.1 Study area

ideal opportunity to test potentially different risk perceptions based in a relatively small area and divided by a politically charged international boundary.

Sample population

The sample population was solicited through an online survey website (survey-monkey.com). The only requirement for participation was that eligible participants had to be at least 18 years of age. Additionally, the link to the survey was distributed through an online research tracking module (sona-systems.com) hosted by Texas A&M International University (TAMIU), the authors' home university. As such, most of the participants are affiliated with TAMIU as students, staff, or some relation to either. Research credit was given to student participants; thus, participation for some was incentivized. While the sample population represents

Table 4.1 Relevant sample characteristics

PRM assessment	Sex		Age	Residency	
	F	M	Mean age	Resident TX	Resident MX
Laredo	115	54	21.5	162	7
Nuevo Laredo	105	47	21.7	145	7

mostly local college students and staff who represent but a sliver of the populations of Laredo and Nuevo Laredo with regard to socioeconomic backgrounds or age cohorts, enough demographic diversity exists to fully exhibit the usefulness of the PRM methodology for risk communication studies. Important to note in the following case study is the fact that the sample was drawn from an overwhelmingly high bilingual (English and Spanish) population. As such, the survey was offered in both English and Spanish to accommodate participant preference.

For this study, 209 eligible participants participated in some part of the online survey. Each participant was asked to list and rank-order perceived risks for both Laredo and Nuevo Laredo. Thus, there are two independent populations for analysis. Some participants were unable to complete one, the other, or both list-rank-order exercises and were omitted from that analysis. As a result, there were 169 participants in the "Laredo risk" sample and 152 participants in the "Nuevo Laredo risk" sample. The demographic characteristics of the sample populations are listed in Table 4.1.

Methods

Participatory risk mapping

To allow participants to construct risk as they experience it while pointing to the place-and-population rootedness of those constructions, this study used participatory risk mapping (PRM). This methodological approach is a rapid but effective way to identify and rank-order risks or sources of risk as perceived by a sample of respondents. Developed by Smith, Barrett and Box (2000, 2001) to study the nature of perceived risks in traditional agrarian communities of the Rift Valley, it has been used to assess perceived risks in East Africa (Quinn et al. 2003; Doss, McPeak, and Barrett 2008; Baird 2009; Webber and Hill 2014), Bangladesh (Inskip et al. 2013), and Mexico (Hilburn 2015, 2016). Risk is defined as "exposure to uncertain and potentially unfavourable consequences" but could potentially be used synonymously with "hazard" (Smith, Barrett, and Box 2001: 3).

Practically, data collection in PRM is a two-stage process. At the onset, participants are asked to provide a list of perceived risks. Participants are then asked to rank-order those risks according to their relative severity from most severe (1) to least severe (2, 3, 4. . .), with ties allowed (Baird, Leslie, and McCabe 2009: 467). Such data have the potential to illustrate the heterogeneity of perceived risk within a sample while also noting the perceived severity or intensity of a particular risk. Thus, PRM shows both the breadth (incidence of a risk being mentioned) and depth (severity) of risks across and within sample populations stratified by demographic and spatial variables. While the PRM methodology was originally designed for person-to-person or person-to-group deployment, its conversion to an online format was carefully considered and tested prior to data collection. The online survey module presented here has notable attributes that enhance the participatory aspect of PRM and other methods for gauging risk. For one, the anonymity provided by being online establishes a digital wall between researcher and participants. Such a divide can possibly foment greater freedom of expression outside the positionality and physical presence of the researcher. Secondly, the greater anonymity of online delivery may attract seemingly more introverted people, allowing them a voice and thus providing a more broadly participatory sample (Stephens-Davidowitz 2012). Thirdly, the online module's potential to allow greater numbers to respond with increased speed transcends the fixed time and space barriers of the front door, focus group room, or town hall, augmenting greater participation for spatially bound and pressed-for-time populations (Yun and Trumbo 2000). Regarding concerns over the validity of gauging the online self, Adams (2015) posits that one must consider political actors, in this case, study participants, as hybrid in that they are both embedded and corporeal while also being networked and virtual. This is especially true today with widespread self-representation on social media platforms. The survey model presented here sought to optimize such advantages through its online delivery module.

The online survey was constructed to allow participants to enter demographic data as one would in a typical online survey (clickable options, enterable fields, and similar functions) on Survey Monkey. Participants were then instructed to list all notable risks on one particular side of the border on a separate sheet of paper or digital notepad; then they were asked to rank these risks from most severe to least severe in a designated open entry field on the survey. They repeated this part for the risks on the other side of the border. To minimize bias, the presentation of each Laredo and Nuevo Laredo risk entries was alternated between participants.

The data can then be *mapped* on two axes by incidence from 0 (no mentions of a risk) to 1 (mentioned by all participants) and a normalized index of severity. While the first metric (incidence or frequency) is simply the proportion of the participants that noted a risk, the normalized index of severity requires a more complex calculation represented by $R_{ij} = 1 - (r_{ij} - 1/n_i)$, meaning the severity factor, R, is the rank or r of the issue j in the context of the group of n issues noted by i participants (Smith, Barrett, and Box 2001; Baird 2009). The mean is taken for each risk's severity index values across the sample or subsample, permitting it to be plotted with incidence/frequency values on a two-dimensional grid.

Lastly, demographic information (Table 4.1) is collected to stratify the risk perception results according to demographic or place-defined group. To test whether there was a relationship between perception risk severity and ancillary variables, logistic regression analysis was conducted for perceptions of both sides of the border, where the dependent variable represented nonviolent and violent perceived risks. This test was conducted after preliminary results indicated a particular relationship between risk and crime. Following the methodology set out by Baird, Barrett, and Box (2009), the top-ranked risks (most severe) for each participant were dichotomized according to whether they were violent or nonviolent. Two independent variables were selected to predict the odds of a nonviolent or violent risks. Gender and frequency of visit to the participants' nonresidency side of the border were recorded in the survey. Frequency of visit was dichotomized so that visit frequency that was monthly, weekly, or daily was coded as "frequent" and annually or never was coded as "non-frequent." Since the dependent variable (risk) was dichotomized, logistic regression was the most appropriate analysis for understanding the relationship between perceived risk and the spatial demographic characteristics of the sample population.

Results

Summary

The interpretation of the incidence-severity graphs merits some explanation. The *x*-axis represents the incidence or proportion of participants that listed a particular risk. The *y*-axis or *severity* factor represents a normalized rank of the severity of that issue across participants who mentioned it. The range of values run from 2 (least severe) to 1 (most severe); thus, the severity runs from up to down in the graph. If one divides the map into quadrants, the bottom-right quadrant encapsulates those risks that are both noted across a sizable portion of the participant sample as well as maintain a notable rank in terms of severity as a perceived risk. Conversely, the top left quadrant represents risks that are neither widespread nor are of high relative severity. The graph allows one to effectively map the differences or similarities in risk perception on either side of the border. Such a visualization permits the discovery of perhaps yet-unrecorded risks as well as in-depth contextualization of issues that are more formally recognized.

Considering the results of both analyses, a total of 47 risks were identified by participants. Participatory risk mapping allows a notable amount of researcher discretion in categorizing risks. While participants list and then rank risks, the researcher must ultimately decide how a response represents a particular risk in order to code it. Thus, a tension exists along a spectrum between a broader, more exclusive, and participant reflexive approach with lower frequencies and one that conflates and summarizes similar risks to provide simpler, perhaps more understandable categories of risk that feature higher frequency values and more completely normalized severity values. Due to the exploratory nature of this particular study, the former, more diverse risk categorization approach was taken in order to allow for the participants to *speak for themselves*.

For both risk perception assessments (Laredo and Nuevo Laredo), an apparent unifying concept among the vast majority of risks was a relationship between crime and risk. Nearly all could easily be considered crimes. One aspect of the researcher-participant disconnect that exists in an online survey is that there is little to no insinuation of what constitutes risk, which makes this overwhelming construction of risk as crime an interesting finding. It should be noted, however, that informing participants about the diverse nature of risk could produce more useful results for applying the results of PRM research in risk communication.

Risks on the Laredo side

Out of the 209 total participants, 169 or 81 percent reported one or more risks for the Laredo side of the border. The most frequently noted risks and their respective severity are listed in Figure 4.2 and Table 4.2. Out of the 42 risks noted for the Laredo side of the U.S.–Mexico border, the most frequently noted risk by participants was drugs/drug use, with 24.2 percent of the sample mentioning it. This risk also featured moderate-high severity, with an index value of 1.4 indicating both the breadth (incidence) and depth (severity) of this perceived risk endemic to Laredo. The second most frequently mentioned risk by participants was some perceived risk concerning the Mexican drug cartels and drug trafficking. This risk, which could be considered more of a perceived risk than a real one on the U.S. side of the border, had an incidence of 23.7 percent, which was less than a percentage point under the previously mentioned drug use/abuse risk. The high incidence of two drug-related risks points to deep concerns about Laredo's location within

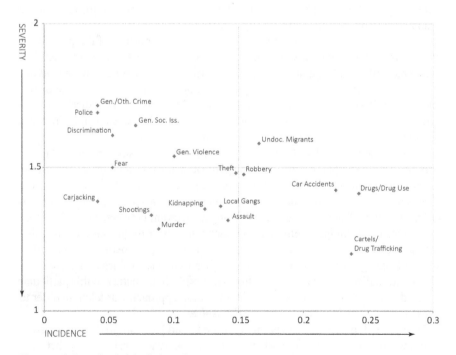

Figure 4.2 Perceived risks in Laredo

Table 4.2 Most frequent perceived risks in Nuevo Laredo and Laredo

Nuevo Laredo			Laredo		
Risk	Incidence	Severity	Risk	Incidence	Severity
Kidnapping	0.38	1.3	Drugs/drug use	0.24	1.4
Shooting	0.28	1.3	Cartels	0.24	1.2
Robbery	0.20	1.8	Car accident	0.23	1.4
Cartels	0.19	1.3	Undoc. migrants	0.17	1.6
Gen. violence	0.16	1.3	Robbery	0.15	1.5
Theft	0.14	1.5	Theft	0.15	1.5
Drugs/drug use	0.14	1.5	Assault	0.14	1.3
Assault	0.13	1.5	Local gangs	0.14	1.4
Murder	0.13	1.0	Kidnapping	0.12	1.4
Gen. fear	0.12	1.6	Gen. violence	0.10	1.5

the production and consumption ends of the drug trade. The relative severity of the cartel/drug trafficking risk (1.2) was even higher than that of drugs/drug use (1.4), indicating the latent violence of drug cartels and drug trafficking. In fact, the cartel/drug trafficking risk had the highest severity value of all Laredo risks, with frequencies over 4 percent. Just under the cartel risk was the risk of a car accident, with 22.5 percent noting it with a moderate-high severity index value of 1.4. Laredo is the sixth-busiest inland dry port in the U.S. (Tomer and Kane 2015), and 51 percent of all commercial truck traffic between Texas and Mexico passes through its roads and highways (Texas Comptroller 2015). A considerable gap in incidence exists between the top three risks mentioned and other risks with undocumented migrants ($i = 16.6$, $r = 1.6$), robbery ($i = 15.4$, $r = 1.5$), theft ($i = 14.8$, $r = 1.5$), assault ($i = 14.2$, $r = 1.3$), local gangs ($i = 13.6$, $r = 1.4$), and kidnapping ($i = 12.4$, $r = 1.4$) and others (Table 4.2).

Risks on the Nuevo Laredo side

For the Nuevo Laredo side, 152 participants (72 percent) out of the entire 209 participant population listed at least one risk. The most frequently noted risks and their severity indices are listed in Figure 4.3 and Table 4.2. The perception of violence, likely due to the increase in real violence in Nuevo Laredo in the past ten years, defined the most frequent risks here. Out of the 39 noted risks for the Nuevo Laredo side of the border, the risk of kidnapping had the highest incidence, with 37.7 percent mentioning it with a high normalized severity score of 1.3. Shootings were second, with an incidence of 28.3 percent and severity score of 1.3. Robbery ($i = 20.1$, $r = 1.8$), cartel/drug trafficking ($i = 18.9$, $r = 1.3$), and risks that were categorized as *general violence* ($i = 16.4$, $r = 1.3$) round out the top five. Notably higher incidences for risks on the Mexican side than the U.S. side were police ($i = 6.9$, $r = 1.5$), becoming lost ($i = 5.0$, $r = 1.7$), and corruption ($i = 4.4$, $r = 1.6$),

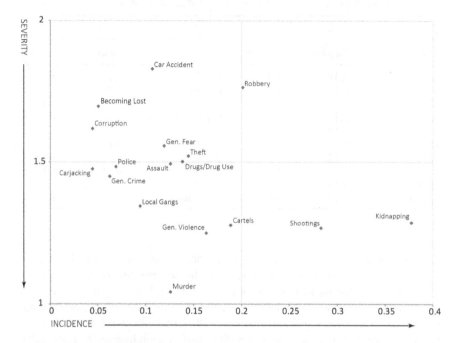

Figure 4.3 Perceived risks in Nuevo Laredo

which comment to perceived governance problems and lack of familiarity with Nuevo Laredo, as most participants (~95 percent) resided in Laredo.

Inferential statistics results

The inferential statistical tests indicate a relationship between experience and knowledge of a place with the perception of risk. Specifically, logistic regression was used with demographic variables to predict the likelihood of participants selecting a violent or nonviolent crime as their primary risk, (i.e. Risk A). For all but one variable, the frequency of visiting the other side of the border from one's residence, there was no significant relationship between mentioning a violent or nonviolent risk. From the one statistically significant logistic regression model, we find that frequency of visit was a strong, significant predictor of participants' perceptions of violent risks in Nuevo Laredo. Those participants who traveled to Nuevo Laredo at least once a month had four times greater odds of reporting a violent crime as a primary risk in Nuevo Laredo, than those participants who never travel to Nuevo Laredo. In other words, participants who had never or rarely visited Nuevo Laredo were much more likely to report a nonviolent crime or some other social, environmental, or economic issue as the primary risk associated with Nuevo Laredo. Analysis metrics are provided in Table 4.3.

Table 4.3 Logistic regression results: sex and frequency regressed on perception of risk

Laredo					Nuevo Laredo				
Variable	B	Std. Error	Sig	exp(B)	Variable	B	Std. Error	Sig	exp(B)
Intercept	1.038	0.341	0.002	2.823	Intercept	1.501	0.497	0.003	4.487
Sex	−0.009	0.397	0.983	0.991	Sex	−0.471	0.569	0.408	0.624
Visit	−0.184	0.387	0.634	0.832	Visit	1.483	0.593	0.001	4.404

Discussion and conclusion

Advantages and limitations for online PRM in risk communication

Like all survey instruments, both in person and online, the format and administration of the survey presented here have some complications and limitations. Nevertheless, the employment of the PRM methodology in an online format was largely successful for this case study and offers promise for further participatory and online risk assessment studies to be used to enhance risk communication. The foremost of these limitations reference the consistency and delivery of the research instrument stemming from participant misunderstanding of the instructions and the subsequent entry of unusable, nonsensical responses to the PRM inquiries. Such issues are commonly reported in the literature (Andrews, Nonnecke, and Preece 2003). Additionally, access to and competence with online resources limits study populations to people with both access to the Internet, as well as the ability to understand online content design and adequately interact with the survey. Such delivery concerns have been noted in a seminal meta-analysis by Wright (2005). Lastly, issues concerning the rigor and honesty with which a participant responds and the inability for the researcher to contextually validate those dynamics is more difficult with an online format. With that noted, the advantages can mitigate these limitations. The first is that a passive, *always-ready* online format expands and extends the potential sample population. Relatedly, the distribution of the instrument can be done without time and financially costly field research. Also, the increasing affordability and ubiquity of Internet access through low-cost smartphones and more expansive networks does minimize, but not correct, access and competence biases of online surveys. Issues with participant consistency can be addressed by the fact that the online survey, if properly tested and designed, is at least delivered to the participant in a more consistent manner than it would in a person-to-person setting. Lastly, the doubts concerning honest self-reporting can also be countered with the idea that online delivery offers participants greater anonymity and may more accurately reflect the internal discourses of the researched, as recent studies on big data and latent desires have shown (Chae et al. 2015; Stephens-Davidowitz 2012). In sum, the results presented here point to statistically significant differences with regard to place- and population-specific risk perceptions in the study area.

Crime as risk in Laredo-Nuevo Laredo

The results of this study indicate a deep association of risk with crime. In the survey, the definition of risk was purposefully left open to participants in order to potentially receive a broad definition of the fundamental risks that affect most everyone's lives. These would include economic risks, health risks, natural hazards, and also social risks such as crime and victimization. However, it was almost exclusively this latter field of risks, of crime and victimization, that people perceived to be both prevalent and severe. There are many processes that influence one's perception of crime and risk of victimization. Physical decay of a city/ neighborhood, disorder, actual and media reported crime, and social incivilities are just a few environmental characteristics associated with perception of crime and risk of victimization. In addition to age, other variables such as race, sex, and prior victimization are some of the individual level characteristics related to the perception of crime and risk of victimization.

Knowledge of and familiarity with a place also contributes to construction of fear and perceived risks. Previous studies distinguish between fear, an emotion, and risk, a more intellectual construct that refers to a known probability of a hazard or threat (Meier and Short 1985; Hollway and Jefferson 1997). Our findings suggest that demographic characteristics such as sex are not significant predictors of risk, which is consistent with previous studies (Rountree and Land 1996). This finding is in contrast to the fear of crime literature, where sex tends to be a determinant of type of fear; females report higher fear of crime than males. In this case, experience and *insiderness* with the *other* side of the border proved to be the only significant predictor regarding the most severe risk being violent or nonviolent. As mentioned earlier, perceptions of risks in Nuevo Laredo were violent.

More interestingly, no logistic regression results were significant for perceived risks on the Laredo side of the border, which was home to an overwhelming majority of study participants. The aforementioned association with experience and the prediction of a violent or non-violent risk did not occur for the side most participants call home. Very narrowly defined, this result indicates perceived violence by those with greater experience in Nuevo Laredo. Conversely, there does not appear to be any attribution of crime as being violent or non-violent by any demographic, such as by gender or experience in Laredo, pointing to a less specific presumption of crime as risk.

How perception stacks up to reality

The perception of risk can both intersect reality and also be incongruent with the incidence of real risk. As noted previously, the fields of risks, in Laredo and Nuevo Laredo, as defined by participants in this study, could almost completely be grouped together as *crime*. Inferences from such a relationship between perceived risk and crime would initially suggest that Laredo and Nuevo Laredo are crime-ridden communities. While the perceived crime-as-risk association transcends the international border, the reality of criminal activity, that is, one defined by crime statistics and reports, is undoubtedly bifurcated by it. Since 2006, crime and violence has escalated across Mexico and especially the Mexican side of the U.S.–Mexico border, when the Mexican government took an active role in combating Transnational Criminal Organizations (TCOs). Experts estimate that approximately 80,000 organized crime-related deaths occurred in Mexico between 2006 and 2015 (Bonner 2012; Beittel 2015). Today, the U.S. State Department classifies Nuevo Laredo as having a *critical* crime risk for Americans abroad there, especially for crimes such as murder, robbery, and kidnapping (OSAC 2016). Statistics from the nonprofit *Observatorio Nacional Ciudadano* (Citizen's National Observatory), which were compiled from both state and municipal sources, also point to the post-2006 uptick and persistence of high incidences of violent crime in the state of Tamaulipas (Tables 4.4 and 4.5) (ONC 2014). Thus, participants' perceptions of violent crime risks on the Nuevo Laredo side are validated to a degree by these external assessments. Additionally, the logistic modelling results that indicate that more *expert* assessment by participants with greater experience in Nuevo Laredo reaffirm the statistics and reporting.

Table 4.4 Crime statistics for the state of Tamaulipas: 2000–2013

Year	Manslaughter	Murder	Kidnapping	Extortion	Robbery	Auto theft
Avg. 2000–2005	378	239	5	8	1,478	3,695
2006	381	346	17	23	2,175	5,274
2007	468	265	20	55	2,542	5,418
2008	556	308	21	88	2,556	5,822
2009	597	288	52	153	3,045	5,837
2010	567	721	47	107	5,043	10,897
2011	517	855	129	157	8,231	10,848
2012	493	1,016	123	154	7,711	8,967
2013	488	555	211	225	6,121	6,140

Source: Observatorio Nacional Ciudadano

Table 4.5 Crime statistics for Laredo, Texas, and the United States: 2000–2014

	2005	2006	2007	2008	2009	2010	2011	2012	2013	2014	% Change
Violent crime rate											
Laredo, TX	510	558	579	609	570	484	465	422	415	389	−24
Texas	528	517	510	508	491	448	409	409	410	406	−23
U.S.	3,432	3,347	3,276	3,215	3,041	2,946	2,905	2,868	2,733	2,596	−24
Property crime rate											
Laredo, TX	6,033	5,828	6,305	6,434	6,048	4,856	4,322	4,351	4,238	3,860	−36
Texas	4,319	4,083	4,122	3,987	4,015	3,767	3,483	3,363	3,253	3,019	−30
U.S.	3,432	3,347	3,276	3,215	3,041	2,946	2,905	2,868	2,733	2,596	−24

Source: FBI UCR Database

The attribution of crime to risk is strong on the other side of the border in Laredo, as well. The connection of participants' perceptions of Laredo-based risk to reality, however, is not as congruent as they are for those in Nuevo Laredo. The U.S.–Mexico border, like many international borders, is an arbitrary line in space, but it is one that does delineate different systems of laws, governance, and societies. Specifically, the hyper-enforced U.S.–Mexico border acts as a check against the most direct effects of the violence and crime related to the aforementioned "war on drugs." In fact, Laredo has markedly lower crime rates than the state of Texas and the United States as a whole. Additionally, crime rates have been falling in Laredo, across Texas, and across the U.S. as crime has risen in Tamaulipas over roughly the same time period. Thus, it appears that while the reality of crime frequency is divided geographically by a border, its perception is not. Perceived risk, in this case, fear of crime, transcends and spills over borders. Lastly, we find that the logistic regression challenged our assumption that fear is a driving force for avoidance. We had an expectation that participants who list violent victimization as a primary risk are also not likely to visit Nuevo Laredo out of fear. Yet, at least for this sample of individuals, we find the opposite to be true. It may be that the need to travel Nuevo Laredo because of medical, financial, familial, or some other reason overrides fear and avoidance. We believe that this finding warrants future research.

Conclusion: How can PRM inform risk communication

This study points to the utility of systematic participatory approaches to gauge public perception of risk. Participatory risk mapping (PRM) is one such approach. PRM allows for a more open, horizontal, and participant-centered construction of risk perception within and between places and demographic groups. Our study provided a nuanced analysis of risk perception in the Nuevo Laredo-Laredo international metropolitan region that identified crime as risk then further contextualized it regarding its attachment to place and how perception matched reality. Lastly, this research contributed a successful example of PRM's successful online deployment, which offers a more flexible and rapid platform to locate risk perception that ultimately can be used to enhance risk communication.

References

Adams, P. 2015. Social Media. In *The Wiley Blackwell Companion to Political Geography*. (eds.) J. Agnew, V. Mamadouh, A. Secor, and J. Sharp. New York: Wiley Blackwell.

Andrews, D., Nonnecke, B., and Preece, J. 2003. Electronic Survey Methodology: A Case Study in Reaching Hard-to-Involve Internet Users. *International Journal of Human-Computer Interaction*, 16(2): 185–210.

Baird, T., Leslie, P., and McCabe, J.T. 2009. The Effect of Wildlife Conservation on Local Perceptions of Risk and Behavioral Response. *Human Ecology*, 37: 463–474.

Beittel, J. 2015. Mexico: Organized Crime and Drug Trafficking Organizations. *Congressional Research Service*, Report 41576.

River of difference 83

Bennett, P., Calman, K., Curtis, S., and Fischbacher-Smith, D. 2010. *Risk Communication and Public Health*. London: Oxford University Press.

Bonner, R. 2012. The Cartel Crackdown: Winning the Drug War and Rebuilding Mexico in the Process. *Foreign Affairs*, 91(3): 12.

Chae, D., Clousto, S., Hatzenbuehler, M., Kramer, M., Cooper, H., Wilson, S. et al. 2015. Association Between an Internet-Based Measure of Area Racism and Black Mortality. *PLoS One*, 10(4): e0122963.

Cho, H., Reimer, T., and McComas, K. 2015. *The Sage Handbook of Risk Communication*. London: Sage Publications.

Covello, V., and Allen, F. 1988. *Seven Cardinal Rules of Risk Communication*. Washington, DC: U.S. Environmental Protection Agency.

Demeritt, D., and Langdon, D. 2004. The UK Climate Change Programme and Communication with Local Authorities. *Global Environmental Change*, 14: 325–336.

Demeritt, D., and Nobert, S. 2014. Models of Best Practice in Flood Risk Communication and Management. *Environmental Hazards*, 4: 313–328.

Doss, C., McPeak, J., and Barrett, C. B. 2008. Interpersonal, Intertemporal and Spatial Variation in Risk Perceptions: Evidence from East Africa. *World Development*, 36: 81453–1468.

Fiorino, D. 1990. Citizen Participation and Environmental Risk: A Survey of Institutional Mechanisms. *Science, Technology, and Human Values*, 15(2): 226–243.

Herlihy, P., and Knapp, G. 2003. Maps of, by, and for the Peoples of Latin America. *Human Organization*, 62(4): 303–314.

Hilburn, A. 2015. Participatory Risk Mapping of Garbage-Related Issues in a Rural Mexican Municipality. *Geographical Review*, 105(1): 42–60.

———. 2016. Gauging the Material Magnitude, Public Perception, and Governance of Roadside Litter in a Rural Mexican Municipio. *Human Ecology*, 44: 479–491.

Hollway, W., and Jefferson, T. 1997. The Risk Society in an Age of Anxiety: Situating Fear of Crime. *British Journal of Sociology*, 48(2): 255–266.

INEGI. 2015. *Encuesta Intercensal 2015*. Aguascaliente, MX: INEGI.

Inskip, C., Ridout, M., Fahad, Z., Tully, R., and Barlow, A. 2013. Human-Tiger Conflict in Context: Risks to Lives and Livelihoods in the Bangladesh Sundarbans. *Human Ecology*, 41: 169–186.

Kasperson, R. 1986. Six Propositions on Public Participation and Their Relevance for Risk Communication. *Risk Analysis*, 6(3): 275–281.

———. 1992. The Social Amplification of Risk: Progress in Developing an Integrative Framework. In *Social Theories of Risk*. (eds.) Sheldon Krimsky and Dominic Golding. Westport, CT: Praeger.

Kates, R. 1962. *Hazard and Choice Perception in Flood Plain Management*. University of Chicago, Department of Geography Research, Paper No. 78.

———. 1971. Natural Hazard in Human Ecological Perspective: Hypotheses and Models. *Economic Geography*, 47: 438–451.

Krimsky, S. 2007. Risk Communication in the Internet Age: The Rise of Disorganized Skepticism. *Environmental Hazards*, 7: 157–164.

Liverman, D. 1990. Drought Impacts in Mexico: Climate, Agriculture, Technology, and Land Tenure in Sonora and Puebla. *Annals of the Association of American Geographers*, 80(1): 49–72.

Lowenthal, D. 1967. *Environmental Perception and Behavior*. Chicago: University of Chicago, Department of Geography Research Paper No. 109.

Lundgren, R., and McMakin, A. 2013. *Risk Communication: A Handbook for Communicating Environmental, Safety, and Health Risks*. New York: Wiley.

Meier, R., and Short, J. 1985. Crime as Hazard: Perceptions of Risk and Seriousness. *Criminology*, 23(3): 389–400.

Morgan, M., Fischoff, B., Bostrom, A., and Atman, C. 2002. *Risk Communication: A Mental Models Approach*. Cambridge: Cambridge University Press.

Observatorio Nacional Ciudadano (ONC). 2014. *Tendencia por entidad federativa – Tamaulipas*. Accessed on February 21, 2017 at http://onc.org.mx/tendencia-por-entidad-federativa/tamaulipas/.

Office of Security Advisory Council (OSAC). 2016. *Mexico 2016 Crime and Safety Report: Nuevo Laredo*. Washington, DC: US State Department.

Park, P. 1993. What Is Participatory Research? A Theoretical and Methodological Perspective. In *Voices of Change: Participatory Research in the United States and Canada*. (eds.) Peter Park, Mary Brydon-Miller, Budd Hall, and Ted Jackson. Westport, CT: Bergin and Garvey, pp. 1–19.

Porter, J., and Demeritt, D. 2012. Flood-Risk Management, Mapping, and Planning: The Institutional Politics of Decision Support in England. *Environment and Planning A*, 44(10): 2359–2378.

Quinn, C., Huby, M., Kiwasila, H., and Lovett, J. C. 2003. Local Perceptions of Risk to Livelihood in Semi-Arid Tanzania. *Journal of Environmental Management*, 68: 1111–1119.

Rayner, S., 1992. Cultural Theory and Risk Analysis. In *Social Theories of Risk*. (eds.) S. Krimsky, and D. Golding. Westport, CT: Praeger Press, pp. 83–115.

Rountree, P., and Land, K. 1996. Perceived Risk Versus Fear of Crime: Empirical Evidence of Conceptually Distinct Reactions in Survey Data. *Social Forces*, 74(4): 1353–1376.

Saarinen, T. 1984. *Environmental Planning: Perception and Behavior*. Longrove, IL: Waveland Press.

Smith, K., Barrett, C. B., and Box, P. W. 2000. Participatory Risk Mapping for Targeting Research and Assistance: With an Example from East African Pastoralists. *World Development*, 28: 1945–1959.

———. 2001. Not Necessarily in the Same Boat: Heterogeneous Risk Assessment Among East African Pastoralists. *The Journal of Development Studies*, 37: 51–30.

Stephens-Davidowitz, S. 2012. How Racist Are We? Ask Google. *New York Times*, June 9.

Texas Comptroller. 2015. Port of Entry: Laredo. *Economic Impact 2015*. Accessed on February 21, 2017 at https://comptroller.texas.gov/economy/economic-data/ports/laredo.php

Tomer, A., and Kane, J. 2015. The Top 10 Metropolitan Port Complexes in the U.S. *Brookings*, July 15. Accessed on January 3, 2018 at www.brookings.edu/blog/the-avenue/2015/07/01/the-top-10-metropolitan-port-complexes-in-the-u-s/.

US Census Bureau. 2015. *US Census American Community Survey*.

Veil, S., Buehner, T., and Palenchar, M. 2011. A Work-in-Process Literature Review: Incorporating Social Media in Risk and Crisis Communication. *Journal of Contingencies and Crisis Management*, 19(2): 110–122.

Watts, M. 1983. On the Poverty of Theory: Natural Hazards Research in Context. In *Interpretations of Calamity*. (ed.) K. Hewitt. Boston, MA: Allen and Unwin, pp. 231–262.

Webber, A., and Hill, C. 2014. Using Participatory Risk Mapping (PRM) to Identify and Understand People's Perceptions of Crop Loss to Animals in Uganda. *PLoS One*, 9(7): e102912.

White, G. 1945. *Human Adjustment to Floods*. Department of Geography Research Paper No. 29. Chicago: University of Chicago Press.

Wogalter, M., DeJoy, D., and Laughery, K. 2005. *Warnings and Risk Communications*. Boca Raton, FL: CRC Press.

Wright, K. 2005. Researching Internet-Based Populations: Advantages and Disadvantages of Online Survey Research, Online Questionnaire Authoring Software Packages, and Web Survey Services. *Journal of Computer-Mediated Communication*, 10(3). doi: 10.1111/j.1083-6101.2005.tb00259.x.

Yeich, S., and Levine, R. 1992. Participatory Research's Contribution to a Conceptualization of Empowerment. *Journal of Applied Social Psychology*, 22: 1894–1908.

Yun, G., and Trumbo, C. 2000. Comparative Response to a Survey Executed by Post, Email, and Web Form. *Journal of Computer-Mediated Communication*, 6(1): 1–26.

Zimmerer, K. 1996. Ecology as Cornerstone and Chimera in Human Geography. In *Concepts in Human Geography*. (eds.) C. Earle, K. Mathewson, and M. Kenzer. Lanham, MD: Rowman and Littlefield Publishers, pp. 161–188.

5 Local Emergency Planning Committees (LEPCs)

30 years as cross-sector forums for community risk communication

Ava M. Christie

LEPC 30-year history

A chemical accident at a Union Carbide plant in Bhopal, India, in 1984 caused thousands of deaths and injuries, and resulting concern among U.S. citizens that led to enactment of the Emergency Planning and Community Right to Know Act (EPCRA 1986a). This act was passed in 1986 as Title III of the Superfund Amendments and Reauthorization Act (SARA). Among various provisions, Subtitle A, Section 301 of the EPCRA introduced Local Emergency Planning Committees (LEPCs) (EPCRA 1986b). While a State-level Emergency Response Commission (SERC) was prescribed to administer them, LEPCs were required to work at the county or planning-district levels of every state, where they partner with community stakeholders to raise awareness and work with public sector agencies to address hazards (Arlikatti, Lindell, and Prater 2007).

The LEPCs were expected to enable preparedness actions by communities where designated industries operated (United States Environmental Protection Agency (USEPA) (USEPA 2015). The work by LEPCs was intended to promote awareness of hazards and related preparedness using emergency planning, hazardous chemical reporting, and emergency chemical release actions in order to reduce threats from "extremely hazardous substances" (Schierow 2010).

Given the all-volunteer membership of LEPCs, leaders work as chairs, but the composition of the members and their roles vary according to the need of the community or county (Drabek 2007). Committee members are required to act on behalf of their community as representatives from local organizations and industries or to have other relevant expertise or roles in public sector emergency management (EPCRA 1986b). The work performed by LEPCs is intended to inform and involve local communities and their representatives with private industry and public service agency representatives (Hahn 2010). As described by EPCRA, the work of LEPCs is to communicate about hazards that could pose risks to communities (Figure 5.1).

As a strategy for risk communication, LEPC oversight of chemical use and presence within assigned districts provides an interface between community members that are part of LEPCs and area facilities where specific chemicals above certain

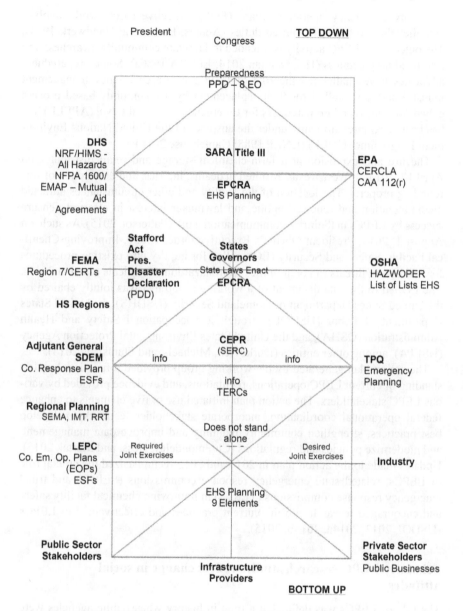

Figure 5.1 A state LEPC risk communication network

amounts are held. To remain in compliance with the EPCRA, LEPCs are required to perform emergency planning within their planning district or county, make information available about hazardous chemical inventory, and prepare actions and disseminate information related to emergency chemical releases. While LEPC compliance actions include chemical tracking and use of a planning district or county emergency operations plans (EOP), proactive LEPC work involves activities that go beyond required duties (Adams, Burns, and Handwerk 1994). The outcome of LEPC activity is intended to facilitate community awareness and improved preparedness (Heintzelman 2014; EPCRA 1986a). Some preparedness advocates have challenged the role of LEPCs in the emergency management industry and have called for their replacement by a community-based process called Awareness and Preparedness for Emergencies at Local Level (APELL) that has been used internationally under the auspices of the United Nations Environment Programme (UNEP) (UNEP 1988; Gablehouse 2016).

The fire and explosion at a farm-chemical storage and retail distributor on April 17, 2013, in West, Texas, resulted in deaths, injuries, and destruction of surrounding property. The location of the facility and other circumstances attracted media attention and renewed public and lawmaker interest in efforts to ensure success by LEPCs in their risk communication work (Patterson 2015). As such, on August 1, 2013, President Obama's Executive Order 13650, Improving Chemical Facility Safety and Security (EO), called for inquiry into existing procedures for addressing threats to communities from hazardous chemicals (Obama 2013). The EO led to the establishment of a working group that was jointly chaired by the United States Department of Homeland Security (USDHS), the United States Department of Labor (USDOL) through its Occupational Safety and Health Administration (OSHA), and the United States Environmental Protection Agency (USEPA), among other entities (Durkovich, Michaels, and Stanislaus 2014).

The action plan generated by the working group provided a functional understanding of current LEPC operations, regulations, and evidence provided by various LEPC stakeholders. The action plan initiated use of five elements to enhance federal operational coordination, incorporate stakeholder feedback to develop best practices, strengthen community planning and improve data management, and modernize policies and regulations (Cholmondeley, Hess, and Martak 2015). Updates made to the action plan in 2014 and 2015 reemphasized the crucial role of LEPCs, related state emergency response commissions (SERCs) and tribal emergency response commissions (TERCs) in improving chemical facility safety and encouraged research into the current practices and effectiveness of LEPCs (USDOL 2013, 2014a, 2014b, 2015).

Scholarly LEPC research studies reflect change in social attitudes

The role of LEPCs was defined at a time in history when public agencies were known to act autonomously (National Commission 2004). New attitudes and strategies, however, resulted from Hurricane Katrina in 2005 and the 2013 West, Texas disaster to change awareness and understanding about environmental and emergency management agency capabilities. A gradual reinterpretation of public policy has coincided with the rise of new needs that have drawn attention to the value of collaborations among public and private sector stakeholders. The impact of this longitudinal change in social attitudes regarding LEPCs and their networks was also evident in studies conducted to identify work practices and priorities of LEPCs. While early studies considered the adherence of LEPCs to policy requirements for compliance, recent studies have explored means to facilitate the involvement of LEPCs in proactive tasks. Studies have also explored the use of quantitative and qualitative methods to gain understanding into the functioning of LEPCs using members as the unit of analysis for research (National Institute for Chemical Studies (NICS) 2001; Obama 2013; Yin 2009).

In a study of LEPCs, Blackwood (2003) described hazard reduction as "most important but un-mandated" for LEPCs, and the LEPC role in accident prevention as unclear but relied upon according to EPCRA (1986a: 239–240). Despite an inexact LEPC public policy role delineation (Kartez 1993), the LEPC research record attests to the value of information gathered, organized, and assessed from LEPC members. Various national, regional, and statewide studies have identified and considered successes and challenges of LEPC work as a means to provide guidance, improvement, and support for chemical risk communication and awareness in American communities. In the discussion that follows, results of a study completed for such a purpose are presented (Christie 2017). That study focused on how members of rural and urban Kansas Local Emergency Planning Committees (LEPCs) described their legislated compliance and proactive work to accomplish sustainability using all-hazards, scalability, and a collaborative approach.

Using a questionnaire that was designed and tested by Matheny (2012) and adopted for LEPC survey research in Ohio, the 2017 Christie study collected LEPC member experiences from county planning district LEPCs across the state of Kansas (Kansas Statutes Annotated 2015). Out of the 105 counties solicited, 52 LEPC chairpersons (49.5 percent) responded to the survey, and 17 of those participants also granted face-to-face interviews. During scheduled interviews participants responded to five open-ended questions about each of four research themes. The research themes were derived from social theory; relevant policy themes identified in the Presidential Policy Directive/PPD-8: National Preparedness (Obama 2011); and President Obama's Executive Order 13650 – Improving Chemical Facility Safety and Security (EO). The four research themes focused on location and its resources, membership and alliances, use of tools and planning approaches, and navigation of location-specific threats (Carlsson 2000; Obama 2011; Durkovich, Michaels, and Stanislaus 2014).

Location and its resources

This research theme addressed the EO action plan to improve the coordination of federal operations and to promote greater awareness of hazardous chemical dangers in support of LEPCs. Population has been shown in the LEPC literature to be a determinant of compliance and proactivity (Adams, Burns, and Handwerk 1994). Because the population of Kansas is small in comparison to other studies in states that developed a scale to determine effects of population on LEPC activity

Table 5.1 Population and character of LEPC counties

County type	KS sample (52)	Matheny (2012) (58)	EPA (939)
"Mainly rural"			
< 50,000	48 (92.3%)	23 (39.7%)	62.5%
"Rural/Suburban"			
50,001–100,000	2 (3.9%)	13 (22.4%)	15.8%
100,001–500,000	1 (1.92)	17 (29.3%)	17.2%
"Mainly Urban"			
500,001–1,000,000	1 (1.92%)	3 (5.1%)	2.6%
> 1,000,000	0 (0.0%)	2 (3.5%)	1.90%

Note: "OA" as the abbreviation for "Overall." "<" means "less than," ">" means "greater than." Total number of respondents in three groupings reported shown in parenthesis in column heads. Numbers of respondents reported in each column with percent in that group shown in parenthesis.

Sources: Matheny 2012: 82–83, 2012; USEPA 2008

(Matheny 2012; USEPA 2008), this study used rural or suburban population categories to analyze their impact on LEPC activity (Table 5.1).

Membership and alliances

This research theme addressed the incorporation of elements of the EO action plan pertaining to stakeholder feedback and development of best practices for involving interested parties to advance work by LEPCs. According to requirements in the EPCRA, LEPCs should include representatives from stated groups or organizations. Matheny (2012) included this consideration about LEPC membership in the survey instrument that was used for the 2017 Christie study but did not include it as one of the criteria by which compliance was rated. In their evaluations of compliance and activity, Adams, Burns, and Handwerk (1994) and Blackwood (2003) required representation of more groups. The Matheny instrument provided participants the opportunity to specify other groups represented, but none were identified by the KS LEPC sample group (Table 5.2).

Use of tools and planning approaches

This research theme addressed the elements of the EO action plan that focused on strengthening of community planning and preparedness activities and improving data management in order to identify ways for renewed public sector support and to facilitate chemical facility data access by LEPCs and stakeholders. The tools and planning approaches used by LEPCs to document, track, and manage risk from hazards in communities have changed over the years, and they are an important element for consideration in the EO action plan (Choi and Kim 2007). Resources widely recognized and employed for chemical information, planning,

Table 5.2 Representation of groups on LEPCs

Representation	KS rural (24)/urban (28)	KS OA (52)	Matheny	EPA
Elected officials	20 (83.3%)/25 (89.2%)	45 (86.5%)	51 (91.1%)	
State/local				11.3%/ 83.3%
Law enforcement	24 (100%)/28 (100%)	52 (100%)	58 (100%)	90.7%
Firefighting	24 (100%)/28 (100%)	52 (100%)	58 (100%)	93.2%
Emergency Management	16 (66.7%)/24 (85.7%)	40 (76.9%)	52 (92.9%)	87.1%
Health personnel	24 (100%)/28 (100%)	52 (100%)	58 (100%)	83.7%
Hospital/emergency	23 (95.8%)/27 (96.4%)	50 (96.1)	58 (100%)	83.4%
Media	9 (37.5%)/19 (67.8%)	28 (53.8%)	35 (62.5%)	54.0%
Transportation	2 (8.3%)/5 (17.8%)	7 (13.4%)	7 (12.5%)	52.4%
Environmental	7 (29.1%)/14 (50.0%)	21 (40.3%)	34 (60.7%)	45.5%
Community groups	12 (50.0%)/14 (50.0%)	26 (50.0%)	34 (60.7%)	63.6%
Covered facilities	14 (58.3%)/27 (96.4%)	41 (78.8%)	54 (96.5%)	68.3%

Note. "OA" is the abbreviation for "Overall." Numbers of respondents are reported in columns and/or with percent in that group shown in parenthesis.

Sources: Matheny 2012: 85, Table 11, 2012; USEPA 2008

Table 5.3 Resources used by LEPCs

Resource	KS rural (24)/urban (28)	KS OA (52)
CAMEO	6/13	19 (36.5%)
Risk data	1/3	4 (7.7%)
GIS data	4/8	12 (23.1%)
Tier I/II	21/22	43 (82.7%)
Other	2/2	4 (7.7%)

Note: "OA" is the abbreviation for "Overall." Total number of respondents in groups reported shown in parenthesis in column heads. Numbers of respondents are reported in columns with percent in that group shown in parenthesis. Computer-aided management of emergency operations (CAMEO) software and global systems information (GIS).

drills, and actual emergencies were listed in the Kansas questionnaire, and participants selected all that were used by their LEPC (Table 5.3).

Navigation of threats

This research theme addressed the element of the EO action plan to modernize policies and regulations in order to identify ways to update regulatory programs associated with work of LEPCs. Occurrence of chemical accidents within LEPC planning districts has been shown to have an impact on work by LEPCs (Matheny 2012; USEPA 2008). In order to assess how chemical accidents changed or did not change the work of LEPCs, participants were asked to provide the number of recent chemical accidents in their LEPC county (Table 5.4).

At the time of the 2017 Christie study, the Kansas (State) Division of Emergency Management (KDEM/SDEM) had a stated mission for sustainability that, according

Table 5.4 Number of chemical accidents within the past five years

#	KS rural (24)/ urban (28)	KS OA (52)	Matheny (58)	USEPA (909)
none	7/3	10 (19.2%)	1 (1.9%)	18.8%
1–5	15/18	33 (63.5%)	8 (13.2%)	48.9%
6–10	2/1	3 (5.8%)	11 (18.9%)	12.5%
11–15	0/2	2 (3.8%)	5 (9.4%)	4.6%
> 15	0/4	4 (7.7%)	29 (49.1%)	15.2%

Note. "OA" is the abbreviation for "Overall"; ">" means "greater than." Total number of respondents in groups reported shown in parenthesis in column heads. Numbers of respondents are reported in columns with percent in that group shown in parenthesis.

Sources: Matheny 2012: 94, Table 18 2012; USEPA 2008

to the PPD-8, employed all-hazards, scalability, and whole-community approaches. Study results enabled these policy imperatives to be described relative to compliance and proactive work practices according to firsthand experiences of Kansas LEPC member participants. The recorded experiences of participants provided the data for this study. Analysis of survey responses and transcribed interviews enabled assessment of LEPC work in both urban and rural contexts and identification of specific viewpoints regarding LEPC compliance and proactivity work practices. To identify compliance and proactive items, this study modified two previously published checklists (Adams, Burns, and Handwerk 1994). A ten-item compliance checklist was used to measure LEPC responsibilities according to EPCRA or the SARA Title III as law. A five-item proactivity checklist was used to understand LEPC action beyond requirements to enable community preparedness and safety (Table 5.5).

The activity index

An activity index scale was developed by Adams, Burns, and Handwerk (1994) and later used by Blackwood (2003) that combined information gathered for the compliance and proactivity checklists. The scale is used to determine the success of LEPCs in accomplishing both required and self-imposed work performance goals and overall effectiveness (Lindell and Whitney 1995). According to this index, inactive LEPCs were considered to be nonfunctional. Hence, survey data obtained for inactive LEPCs were removed from analysis. In the 2017 Christie study, the activity index was compiled by using the survey data obtained from participation of Kansas LEPCs who completed the questionnaire online, and use of the same items described in Adams, Burns, and Handwerk (1994) and Blackwood (2003) (Table 5.6.)

According to the activity index, there were nearly twice as many urban as rural Kansas LEPCs that scored as proactive. When counted together, they outnumbered totals described for respective proactive groups overall reported in Adams, Burns, and Handwerk (1994) and Blackwood (2003). Two rural Kansas LEPCs represented the group scored as compliant, and one rural Kansas LEPC represented the

Table 5.5 The compliance and proactivity item checklists

Item #	Compliance item
1	An LEPC chair
2	An emergency coordinator
3	An information coordinator
4	Members representing groups specified in SARA III
5	Formal LEPC meetings
6	Publicly advertised meetings
7	An emergency response plan submitted to SERC
8	A plan incorporating all elements in SARA III
9	A plan that has been reviewed in the past year
10	Published newspaper notice specified in SARA III that the plan and local hazardous substances data are publicly available

Item #	Proactivity item
1	Has practiced the plan in the past 12 months
2	Has updated the plan in the past 12 months
3	Has a plan that takes natural hazards into account
4	Uses its Extremely Hazardous Substances (EHS) data to make hazard reduction or prevention recommendations to local government or to industry
5	Meets at least quarterly

Table 5.6 Activity index of KS LEPCs and findings of Adams, Burns, and Handwerk (1994) and Blackwood (2003)

Checklist score	Rural KS (24)	Urban KS (28)	OA KS (52)	Adams/Blackwood
"Proactive" 9–10 Compliant and 4–5 Proactive Items	5 (20.8%)	11 (39.3%)	16 (30.8%)	(24%)/8 (14.3%)
"Compliant" 9–10 Compliant and 0–3 Proactive Items	2 (8.3%)	0 (0.0%)	2 (3.8%)	(16%)/14 (25.0%)
"Quasi Active" 6–8 Compliant and 0–3 Proactive Items	16 (66.7%)	17 (60.7%)	33 (63.5%)	(39%)/27 (48.3%)
"Inactive" 1–5 Compliant and any Proactive Items	1 (4.2%)	0 (0.0%)	1 (1.9%)	(21%)/7 (12.5%)

Note: "OA" as the abbreviation for "Overall." If total number of respondents in groupings were reported, then shown in parenthesis in column heads. Number of respondents reported in each column with percent in that group shown in parenthesis.

group scored as inactive, which were both considerably smaller than respective groups reported in Adams, Burns, and Handwerk (1994) and Blackwood (2003). Rural and urban groups of LEPCs that were scored as quasi-active and equal in size when combined were larger than the respective group reported in Adams, Burns, and Handwerk (1994) and Blackwood (2003).

Activity index findings

The inactive LEPC in Kansas was found to have an expired EOP, although the LEPC was undertaking efforts to meet compliance requirements, according to the survey response to checklist items. The inactive LEPC also did not have a chairperson or an information coordinator, although both positions are required by EPCRA. The inactive LEPC at least indicated that it held quarterly meetings and had a representative from emergency management services. The remaining rural LEPCs had chairpersons and a representative from emergency management, and they held regular meetings, but only 70 percent of rural LEPCs in Kansas had a designated information coordinator (Table 5.6).

A comparison of urban and rural counties in Kansas showed that inactive and quasi-active LEPCs occurred both in rural and urban counties. While not all urban LEPCs in Kansas confirmed having a chairperson (96.4 percent) or information coordinator (92.9 percent) or held quarterly meetings (96.4 percent), none were assigned the inactive rating according to the activity index also used in LEPC research by Adams, Burns, and Handwerk (1994) and Blackwood (2003). The average time served by chairpersons was reported by rural Kansas LEPCs as six years and by urban Kansas LEPCs as five years.

Participant feedback, current literature, and researcher observations were used as three research measures to evaluate the research themes. Based on the findings, each research theme was found to align with the EO action plan and was relevant to LEPC practices. Given the role of LEPCs in communicating risk information, these findings described not only existing but also changing roles and responsibilities of local and state networks in risk communication.

LEPC work practices of practical interest

According to Adams, Burns, and Handwerk (1994), hazard reduction or prevention should be an important priority for LEPCs but is not a required or compliance work practice. The 2017 Christie study found that LEPCs rated hazard reduction, community hazard reduction, and chemical release prevention to be of low priority in recent years, which was similar to the findings of Matheny (2012). The highest priority in the past year for the Kansas LEPC participants was community emergency preparedness, followed by hazard vulnerability assessments, which was also the case in Matheny (2012). Community emergency preparedness and hazard vulnerability assessments helped the LEPCs accomplish compliance work to enable submission of EOPs and also aided them with the implementation of an all-hazards approach for EOPs as described in Lindell and Perry (1992).

Public records showed all Kansas counties (100 percent) had submitted EOPs at the time of the study. The participants, however, indicated a lower rate for updating the EOPs on a regular basis – about 76.9 percent reported updating the EOP. The LEPCs also indicated a lower rate for exercising the EOP within the past 2 years (71.2 percent) relative to a greater number (98.1 percent) in Matheny

(2012). Urban Kansas LEPCs outperformed rural counterparts in updating EOPs, but rural Kansas LEPCs outperformed urban counterparts in implementing EOPs.

According to the literature, internal and external factors influenced the success of compliance and proactive work practices of LEPCs (Lindell 1994; Lindell and Meier 1994; Lindell and Brandt 2000). Specifically, having a chairperson encouraged membership and participation as well as regular meetings and so was crucial to LEPCs according to the 2017 Christie study and the national LEPC survey (USEPA 2008). Both rural and urban LEPCs in Kansas reported that they attended meetings related to compliance and participation of communities in risk communication.

The compliance checklist results showed that nearly all Kansas LEPCs fulfilled EPCRA compliance. Furthermore, the participants identified the role of chairperson as an essential external component that is valuable in encouraging community support, and greater diversity within the LEPC as a means to engage the entire community in preparedness and risk awareness.

Use and accessibility of risk data

In the context of LEPC work, risk data refers to information required from industries, according to the 1990 Amendments of the Clean Air Act (USEPA 2011), which stipulates on-site chemical accident prevention program information be made available to local LEPCs. These data should be disseminated to first responders and the local public upon request to prepare them for chemical release incidents (Sutton 1989; Rich, Conn, and Owens 1992). According to Rich, Conn, and Owens (1993), community risk communication programs were less effective due to lack of inquiries to LEPCs by the public and unapproachability of LEPC members.

The 2017 Christie study showed that use of newspaper notices was moderate as a means to inform the public annually that risk data was available for review. While both rural and urban LEPCs used newspapers, radio, and other media as resources to encourage whole community involvement, rural LEPCs more frequently used newspapers to reach out to the public. Regular advertised meetings and personal invitations to meetings were often used to encourage participation. Study participant responses showed that 53.8 percent of LEPCs did not advertise meetings, and 38.5 percent did not publish the required newspaper notice about availability of the EOP and the EPCRA for public review.

Overall, risk communication methods described for use by LEPCs according to the EPCRA were less used than previously recorded according to the Kansas study. Security concerns attributed to post 9/11 growth in terrorism explains use of alternative inquiry request procedures and increased use of precautions relative to risk communications than originally envisioned for LEPCs. Practices described by Kansas LEPC participants supported findings in the literature that summarized dedicated risk communication programs between LEPCs and the public as not well developed (Blackwood 2003; Conn, Owens, and Rich 1990; Rest, Krimsky, and Plough 1991). LEPCs that used innovative social media approaches to explain work performed and invite community representation, however, were developing and were awarded recognition at the Region 7 LEPC Conference (Reitz, Personal Communication 2017).

Despite industry efforts to promote use of risk data as planning resources, the 2017 Christie study found that they were least used (7.7 percent) as resources compared to Tier II reports (82.7 percent), which were most often used. Safety data sheets (SDS) and Tier II reports provided to LEPCs each year by industry facilities may also be interpreted as risk data, although according to the question- naire they were a distinct resource. Public briefings about risk data to inform communities were least used, although LEPC participants indicated community emergency preparedness is one of their high priority tasks. While the literature has described experience in handling chemical accidents as useful for LEPCs (Lindell 1994; Lindell and Meier 1994; Lindell and Brandt 2000; Matheny 2012; USEPA 2008; Whitney and Lindell 2000), the Kanas study found that participants paid more attention and assigned greater effort to improved coordination (25.0 per- cent) as opposed to risk or accident prevention (11.5 percent) as a result of chemi- cal accident experience.

Risk management is not an EPCRA requirement for LEPCs (Rest 1990). To support LEPCs undertaking such proactive work, chemical industry organizations (NICS 1995, 2001) have facilitated and promoted use of information provided by regulated chemical facilities, according to the USEPA Facility Risk Management Program (RMP) for industry. According to the literature and the survey responses of Kansas LEPC participants, LEPCs (most often urban LEPCs) tend to use risk data for risk management only when they have a committee involved in the pro- cess (NICS 1995; Lindell and Meier 1994). The use of risk data has been related to the availability of funding from industries and respective districts (NICS 2001), and likewise persists as a challenge for rural LEPCs as well as urban LEPCs. Nonetheless, three times as many urban than rural Kansas LEPC participants indi- cated using risk data as a planning resource.

The integration of RMP information with Kansas' integrated emergency man- agement system (IEMS) electronic database was considered useful in improving efficiency of EOP production for planning, exercise, and related recordkeeping beginning in 2012. In the Kansas study, ease of access and usability of RMP infor- mation by LEPCs were identified as necessary by the KDEM. To ensure LEPC access to risk data, events and conferences were organized to provide instruction on accessibility and usability of RMP information (Ndiaye and Brewer 2016). Because the study showed that risk data was being used differently by rural and urban LEPCs distinct strategies for future presentations and training of these two groups may be useful.

Use of surveys and checklists to assess LEPC work practices

The role described by the EPCRA for LEPCs has been evaluated in studies described in the literature relative to work practices at the national, regional, and state levels. National surveys have been conducted on three occasions to evaluate compliance and related proactive work, but have also described circumstances that were relevant and of interest to LEPC practice at that time. Three checklists that were used for national surveys were modified for regional and state-level surveys (Blackwood 2003; Matheny 2012; Starik et al. 2000). The modifications to the checklists reflect LEPC practices according to developments that occurred in emergency management policy over time.

Two national LEPC surveys (Adams, Burns, and Handwerk 1994; Starik et al. 2000) provided status reports about compliance with the EPCRA and developed use of checklist scoring to describe participant responses and survey results. Based on their 1994 results, Adams, Burns, and Handwerk identified a correlation between compliance and urban LEPC districts. The results of the 2017 Christie study corroborate this earlier finding. The latest national LEPC survey (USEPA 2008) again emphasized the priority placed on compliance with the EPCRA but still recognized occurrence of proactive work. Based on assessment of LEPC activity and practices, the 2008 USEPA survey findings suggested a need for development of operating budgets. It further identified dedicated membership and regular meetings as determinants for LEPC success. Again, the 2017 Christie study supported these earlier findings.

In keeping with research practice, use of a social theory facilitated the identification of all-hazards as a guiding approach for Kansas LEPCs. Study participants described all-hazards preparedness as integral not just to proactive work tasks but also to performance of compliance work tasks. In accord with recommendations by Matheny (2012), findings of the 2017 Christie study provided evidence for amending the list of recognized compliance work practices used by LEPCs (Table 5.5). As such, the significant recommendation was included that a checklist item be added to describe use of an all-hazard approach during future use of either the Matheny (2012) or Blackwood (2003) compliance work checklists for assessment of LEPC practices.

Liberty (2015) affirmed the value and need for a method by which LEPC work could be assessed in the context of their practice. Use of the activity index that was based on the compliance and proactive work checklists in combination with LEPC member interviews in research have been a useful strategy in LEPC research, including the 2017 Christie study. Further LEPC research using the activity index by state or region was also a recommendation of that study to actualize continued efforts according to the EO action plan as a means to enable successful work practices.

Compliance and proactive work

LEPC work practices documented in the 2017 Christie study showed active enlistment of the whole community consistent with the KDEM sustainability public policy referred to in the research question. These practices helped engage needed LEPC support resources and encouraged greater awareness of varied membership, work applications, and training of participants according to the National Incident Management System (NIMS). Work practices described by participants gave evidence of a changed response to public policy by LEPCs that employed an all-hazards approach for achieving compliance and associated proactive work. Practices described by participants used an all-hazards approach that integrated at least public health and weather preparedness into work performed. Incorporation of an all-hazard approach was recognized and encouraged by the KDEM at Kansas LEPC conferences and meetings in various presentations that described successful practices by Kansas LEPCs.

The benefits from presentations and discussions of successful practices may be missed by lagging LEPCs not in attendance at state conferences or other regional group meetings. As the next-best alternative to attendance, successful LEPC practices may be communicated through updates or newsletters to all LEPCs. Case study examples, instructional information, and helpful contacts could be provided statewide, summarizing biannual conference proceedings. Direct delivery of information about grant opportunities and new web-based resource uses may enable or encourage wider use of Hazardous Materials Emergency Preparedness (HMEP) grant support offered by the KDEM (Saha and Whitfill 2016) and use of newly available USEPA Flood Risk Management Plan (FRMP) and Tier II web-based risk communication strategies (Ndiaye and Brewer 2016). Accordingly, wider distribution of meeting or conference presentation materials was planned for the 2017 Region 7 LEPC conference to inform LEPCs across the region and not just those able to be in attendance (Reitz 2016).

Findings of the 2017 Christie study showed that, overall, Kansas LEPC participants have achieved high levels of compliance, consistent with a goal of the EO action plan, as the primary means to enable risk communication and community awareness in keeping with the EPCRA. Research study recommendations described that this achievement may be further enabled by continued emphasis on fulfilling and maintaining more simply achieved compliance checklist items by lagging LEPCs.

Kansas LEPCs that participated in the 2017 Christie study described proactive work practices undertaken by various urban and rural LEPCs in Kansas that extended duties beyond compliance. While these practices were location specific, they resulted from leadership roles in community preparedness planning supported by regional action councils, KDEM regional coordinators, and within the regional LEPC present in a metropolitan area in Kansas.

State region action was recognized as desirable by study participants as it offered immediate, regular, and relevant support to members of the Kansas LEPC network that were not as accessible at the state level. KDEM organization of regional coordinators was a critical means of enabling regional LEPC action that may be augmented to enhance participation by lagging LEPCs to promote compliance and improved statewide proactive work.

Conclusions supported by LEPC research presented

Preparedness for changing threats and resulting hazards has resulted in the development of federal and state policies, as well as presidential executive orders, to organize a top-down emergency management bureaucracy in the United States. Evidence from documented practices in the field has described the necessity for collaboration across all sectors. Such activity has demonstrated successful integration of preparedness capabilities that emanate from bottom-up work effort that starts at the individual, community, and regional levels. LEPC networks represent a longstanding means of risk communication to enable efforts by public and private sector community members with the chemical industry, among others, to advance community awareness, safety, and preparedness.

Management of hazardous chemicals for use in all states remains a responsibility that has necessitated awareness, collaboration, and preparedness by public and private community stakeholders. The need for LEPCs and their required work practices that originally defined compliance were established by Congress in 1986. Open communication within public sector agencies and with industry and community stakeholders was viewed as a means to address new concerns about the occurrence of threats to communities from certain chemicals. Three national LEPC surveys organized ways to understand how compliance and identified proactive work practices were achieved. Early state or regional LEPC survey research studies through the 1990s presented findings about the internal function of LEPCs to inform social science research of behavior in volunteer organizations as much as they provided a means of informing a status report about LEPC practices.

After the terrorist attacks on September 11, 2001, both federal and state initiatives and resources in emergency management began to prioritize homeland security considerations. The 9/11 attacks and ensuing public safety action resulted in heightened concern for security and changed attitudes about desirability of open and public communication pertaining to hazards and associated preparedness actions (National Commission 2004). Studies that followed considered the new advent of information technology and how LEPC work practices were impacted by developing concerns about homeland security, sharing potentially sensitive or dangerous information and, more recently, by enhancing national preparedness. This is consistent with findings of the 2017 Christie study, presented here, that described a low frequency of certain publicly shared chemical hazard information and risk communication work practices by LEPCs.

The latest national LEPC survey, the EO action plan, and statewide or regional LEPC studies that surveyed LEPC work practices identified the importance of demonstrated compliance and related proactive work. Data from those surveys demonstrated how specific considerations had impacted LEPC work outcomes and were presented with findings of the 2017 Christie study to provide context and improved understanding about longitudinal LEPC action. The varied contexts of LEPC studies and the addition of a new research methodology to those in the literature have helped to advance formulation of the long-standing LEPC research study tradition. That tradition has used data gained from inquiry with LEPC members to describe accomplishment of compliance or proactive work as a means of refreshing endurance, understanding, and assurance in accomplishment of risk awareness and preparedness by LEPCs.

In state or regional LEPC studies, the evident research study tradition has included restatement of the compliance checklist because LEPC work has influenced changed response to public policy. In keeping with that tradition, the findings of the 2017 Christie study led to a proposal for inclusion of use of an all-hazard approach as a compliance checklist item in upcoming applications of the historically used LEPC activity index. In conclusion, the findings described advances in work practices for risk communication to accomplish compliance, maintained proactive work effort, and also provided evidence of strong rather than weak effectiveness of Kansas LEPCs.

References

Adams, W. C., Burns, S. D., and Handwerk, P. G. 1994. *Nationwide LEPC Survey: Summary Report*. Washington, DC: The George Washington University. Accessed at www.mapcruzin.com/scruztri/docs/seek5.htm.

Arlikatti, S., Lindell, M. K., and Prater, C. S. 2007. Building Trust Among Community Stakeholders. In *Understanding and Responding to Terrorism*. (eds.) H. Durmaz, B. Sevinc, A. Yayla, S. Ekici. Amsterdam, The Netherlands: IOS Press, pp. 383–391.

Blackwood, M. J. 2003. *Local Emergency Planning Committees: Collaboration, Risk Communication, Information Technology and Homeland Security*. Doctoral Dissertation. ProQuest Dissertations Publishing (Order No. 3077391).

Carlsson, L. 2000. Policy Network as Collective Action. *Policy Studies Journal*, 28(3): 502–520.

Choi, S. O., and Kim, B. 2007. Power and Cognitive Accuracy in Local Emergency Management Networks. *Public Administration Review*, 67: 198–209.

Cholmondeley, J. B., Hess, G., and Martak, D. 2015. *Response to Executive Order 13650: Looking Ahead*. Paper Presented at the 2015 EPA Region 7 LEPC/TERC Emergency Planning and Response Conference, Nebraska City, Nebraska.

Christie, A. M. 2017. *Case Study of Local Emergency Planning Committee (LEPC) compliance and proactivity experiences*. Doctoral Dissertation. ProQuest Dissertations Publishing. (Order No. 10257674).

Conn, D. W., Owens, W. L., and Rich, R. C. 1990. *Communicating with the Public About Hazardous Materials: An Examination of Local Practice* (Report No. EPA-230-4-0-077). Washington, DC: USEPA.

Drabek, T. E. 2007. Community Processes: Coordination. In *Handbook of Disaster Research*. (eds.) H. Rodriguez, H. E. Quarantelli, and R. Dynes. New York: Springer Science+Business Media, LLC, pp. 217–233.

Durkovich, C., Michaels, D., and Stanislaus, M. 2014. *Executive Order 13650, Actions to Improve Chemical Facility Safety and Security-a Shared Commitment*. Report for the President. Accessed at www.osha.gov/chemicalexecutiveorder/final_chemical_eo_status_report.pdf.

Emergency Planning and Community Right-to-Know Act (EPCRA). 1986a. *42 U.S.C. % 110001 et seq*. Accessed at www.govinfo.gov/content/pkg/USCODE-2011-title42/html/USCODE-2011-title42-chap116.htm.

———. 1986b. *42 U.S.C. % 110001–11050*. Accessed at www.govinfo.gov/content/pkg/USCODE-2011-title42/html/USCODE-2011-title42-chap116.htm.

Gablehouse, T. 2016. *Showing Success and Creating a Sustainable LEPC Program*. General Session Keynote Presented at the 2016 Case Study State LEPC Conference. [location deleted for privacy].

Hahn, D. 2010. How to Create a Public-Private Partnership: A Replicable Project Associated with Business Continuity. *Journal of Business Continuity and Emergency Planning*, 4(3): 274–285.

Heintzelman, H. 2014. *LEPC 101*. Paper Presented at the 2014 Kansas LEPC Conference, Junction City, Kansas.

Kansas Statutes Annotated. 2015. *Emergency Planning and Community Right to Know Act*. Kansas Stat. Ann. % 65–5729. Accessed at http://law.justia.com/codes/Kansas/2015/chapter-65/article-57/section-65–5729/.

Kartez, J. 1993. *Roles in Toxic Hazards Reduction: Implementing Title III's Unwritten Goals* (Hazard Reduction and Recovery Center Report No. 39R). College Station, TX: Texas A&M University.

Liberty, A. 2015. *Measuring the Impact of 9/11 on the Functionality of Local Emergency Planning Committees and the Public Disclosure of Hazardous Chemical Information*. Doctoral Dissertation. ProQuest Dissertations and Theses Global. (Order No. 3730738).

Lindell, M. K. 1994. Are LEPCs Effective in Developing Community Disaster Preparedness? *International Journal of Mass Emergencies and Disasters*, 12(2): 159–182.

Lindell, M. K., and Brandt, C. J. 2000. Climate Quality and Climate Consensus as Mediators of the Relationship Between Organizational Antecedents and Outcomes. *Journal of Applied Psychology*, 85(3): 331–348.

Lindell, M. K., and Meier, M. J. 1994. Effectiveness of Community Planning for Toxic Chemical Emergencies. *Journal of the American Planning Association*, 60(2): 222–234.

Lindell, M. K., and Perry, R. W. 1992. *Behavioral Foundations of Community Emergency Planning*. Washington, DC: Hemisphere Publishing Corporation.

Lindell, M. K., and Whitney, D. J. 1995. Effects of Organizational Environment, Internal Structure and Team Climate on the Effectiveness of Local Emergency Planning Committees. *Risk Analysis*, 15(4): 439–447.

Matheny, E. M. 2012. *A Survey of the Structural Determinants of Local Emergency Planning Committee Compliance and Proactivity: Towards an Applied Theory of Precaution in Emergency Management*. Unpublished Ph.D. Dissertation. Cleveland: Cleveland State University.

National Commission on Terrorist Attacks Upon the United States (National Commission). 2004. *The 9/11 Commission Report*. Washington, DC: Government Printing Office. Accessed at www.9-11commission.gov/about/index.htm.

National Institute for Chemical Studies (NICS). 1995. *Focus on the Future of LEPCs*. Charleston, WV: NICS.

———. 2001. *Local Emergency Planning Committees and Risk Management Plans: Encouraging Hazard Reduction*. Charleston, WV: NICS. Accessed at www.nicsinfo.org/docs/LEPCStudyFinalReport.pdf.

Ndiaye, F., and Brewer, L. I. 2016. *USEPA Risk Management Program Process and Tools*. Paper Presented at the 2016 Kansas LEPC Conference, Manhattan, Kansas.

Obama, B. 2011. *Presidential Policy Directive 8/PPD-8: National Preparedness*. Accessed at www.fema.gov/pdf/prepared/npg.pdf.

———. 2013. *Executive Order No. 13,650 – Improving Chemical Facility Safety and Security, 78 C.F.R. 48029 (2014)*.

Patterson, F. 2015. *West, Texas Fertilizer Plant Disaster Response and Recovery*. Paper Presented at the Kansas Emergency Management Association (KEMA) Conference, Junction City, Kansas.

Reitz, P. 2016. Personal Communication. October 24.

———. 2017. Personal Communication. July 22.

Rest, K. M. 1990. *Implementing Public Policy at the Local Level: A Four-Community Study of SARA, Title III-The Emergency Planning and Community Right-to-Know Act.* Unpublished Ph.D. Dissertation. Boston: Boston University.

Rest, K. M., Krimsky, S., and Plough, A. 1991. *Risk Communication and Community Right-to-Know: A Four Community Study of SARA Title III.* Boston: Center for Environmental Management, Tufts University Press.

Rich, R. C., Conn, W. D., and Owens, W. L. 1992. Strategies for Effective Risk Communication Under SARA Title III: Perspectives from Research and Practice. *The Environmental Professional,* 14(1): 220–227.

———. 1993. "Indirect regulation" of Environmental Hazards Through the Provision of Information to the Public: The Case of SARA Title III. *Policy Studies Journal,* 21(1): 16–34.

Saha, S., and Whitfill, D. 2016. *Hazmat Planning and Training Resources: HMEP Grants.* Paper Presented at the 2016 Kansas LEPC Conference, Manhattan, Kansas.

Schierow, L. 2010. *The Emergency Planning and Community Right-to-Know Act (EPCRA): A Summary* (Report No. RL32683). Washington, DC: U.S. Congressional Research Service. Accessed at http://fpc.state.gov/c18185.htm.

Starik, M., Adams, W. C., Berman, P. A., and Sudharsan, K. 2000. *1999 Nationwide LEPC Survey.* Report conducted at the Center for Environmental Policy and Sustainability Management, The George Washington University, Washington, DC. The U.S. Environmental Protection Agency Website. Accessed at www2.epa.gov/epcra/nationwide-survey-local-emergency-planning-committees.

Sutton, V. V. 1989. *Perceptions of Local Emergency Planning Committee Member's Responsibility for Risk Communication and a Proposed Model Risk Communication Program for Local Emergency Planning Committees Under SARA, Title III.* Doctoral Dissertation. ProQuest Dissertations Publishing. (Order No. 8917011).

United Nations Environment Programme (UNEP). 1988. *The Awareness and Preparedness for Emergencies at Local Level (APELL).* Accessed at www.unep.org/apell/.

U.S. Department of Labor (USDOL). 2013. *Executive Order 13650: December 2013 Progress Update.* The Occupational Safety and Health Administration Website. Accessed at www.osha.gov/chemicalexecutiveorder/EO_ProgressUpdate.pdf.

———. 2014a. Federal Working Group on Executive Order 13650. *Actions to Improve Chemical Facility Safety and Security-a Shared Commitment.* The Occupational Safety and Health Administration Website. Accessed at www.osha.gov/chemicalexecutiveorder/EO_Fact_Sheet_060514.pdf.

———. 2014b. *Executive Order 13650: February 2014 Progress Update.* The Occupational Safety and Health Administration Website. Accessed at www.osha.gov/chemicalexecutiveorder/EO_ProgressUpdate022014.pdf.

———. 2015. *Actions to Improve Chemical Facility Safety and Security: 2015 Status Report.* The Occupational Safety and Health Administration. Accessed on January 19, 2019 at www.osha.gov/chemicalexecutiveorder/EO13650FS-ImprovingChemicalFacilitySafety.pdf.

U.S. Environmental Protection Agency (USEPA). 2008. *2008 Nationwide Survey of Local Emergency Planning Committees (LEPCs).* Accessed at www2.epa.gov/sites/production/files/2013–08/documents/2008_lepcsurv.pdf.

———. 2011. *Guidance for Performing Risk Management Performance Inspections Under Clean Air Act Section 112(r)* (Report No. 550-K-11–001). Washington, DC: Office of Solid Waste and Emergency Response.

———. 2015. *Chemical Emergencies: A Guide for State, Tribal and Local Agencies* (Report No. 550-F-15–002). Accessed at www2.epa.gov/epcra.

Whitney, D. J., and Lindell, M. K. 2000. Member Commitment and Participation in Local Emergency Planning Committees. *Policy Studies Journal*, 28(3): 467–484.

Yin, R. 2009. *Case Study Research: Design and Methods*. Los Angeles, CA: Sage Publications.

6   Harnessing the power of social media for disaster risk reduction and the mitigation planning process

Suzanne L. Frew

Introduction

Social media has become an integral part of disaster response in recent years, driving short-term preparedness activities and inspiring communities to rally and provide recovery assistance in the aftermath of disaster. This prolific technology improves disaster response and allows affected populations to take control of their situations while also helping them to feel more empowered. Social media, however, has not yet been widely used in hazard mitigation, despite being the most promising tool available for such efforts. Through social media, individuals are able to connect and communicate across a wide audience with diverse views and experiences, including the most vulnerable populations within society – e.g., people of color, low-income or elderly individuals, and non-native speakers. This chapter strives to expedite the adoption of social media by exploring how it can be used by communities to reduce their long-term risk through the Federal Emergency Management Agency's (FEMA) nine-step mitigation planning process. These nine tasks are applicable outside the U.S. – they provide a basic framework that can be adapted and used by any community or organization anywhere in the world.

Disasters often have long-term consequences on communities' economic, social, and environmental well-being, but disaster response and preparedness activities are usually short term. Social media platforms, such as Facebook and Twitter, have become vital tools driving short-term preparedness activities through which community leaders and agencies forge a direct line of communication for the delivery of life-saving information. Social media also provides opportunities for individuals to play a role post-disaster, either through private efforts or those led by organizations. For example, Facebook allows nonprofit charities to raise money by adding a *Donate Now* button to ads and account pages. On the other hand, people often have an *out-of-sight, out-of-mind* attitude with regard to disasters. Concern is often short-lived and limited to the time during which dramatic events dominate headlines. Trend analysis shows that while the U.S. public showed a greater interest in key terms such as *disaster preparedness* and *sea-level rise* in the immediate aftermath of Hurricane Sandy, interest quickly waned (Kahn 2013). Concern first decreased in areas that weren't physically impacted, but soon after, even people who were impacted also lost interest.

Because of fleeting interest and capricious attitudes, hazard mitigation – the long-term approach to reducing disaster risk – is a hard sell. It is difficult to break through the constant barrage of everyday information to motivate communities and individuals to safeguard for an event that has not yet happened or may never happen in one's lifetime. As the sustainability of a community depends on actions taken now, new approaches that inform and engage the public are needed to build long-term, community-level resilience and sustainability mindsets.

With the sweeping changes of the digital age, a key to getting the word on the street about the value of mitigation and the mitigation planning process is through social media. Social media offers invaluable avenues and tools to engage members of the public in dialogue, explore their concerns, gather ideas, and drive the process of inclusive risk reduction planning. While many communities, agencies, and organizations may focus on using social media to push out general emergency management information updates, these platforms also offer endless creative opportunities to drive home the long-term risk reduction message and support mitigation planning activities.

The power of social media

Social media platforms allow users to share information and create communities through online networks of people. *Social media* is an umbrella term that defines various activities that integrate technology, social interaction, text, picture, video, and audio. In the past decade, social media has become a dominant form of communication. The basic forms of social media include: social networks (e.g., Facebook); blogs (i.e., online journals); photo and video-based platforms (e.g., YouTube, Instagram); and microblogging (e.g., Twitter). Social media provides a wide reach, but it is fragmented, as there are many platforms available and new ones crop up frequently. Even the more popular platforms being used to engage the public, however, including Facebook, Twitter, YouTube, LinkedIn, and Instagram, need to be evaluated regularly as they – and their users – evolve over time.

These key platforms have made the world seem smaller. No matter where users are located, they have the opportunity to connect with others and share information. People who are active on Facebook and Twitter may have hundreds or even thousands of digital connections. But they often lack real-life human contacts in their own neighborhood. In fact, across the Western world, people feel increasingly disconnected from their neighbors (Dunkelman 2014; Pinker 2014). And when people don't know their neighbors, they are less likely to turn to them in cases of emergency (Cheshire 2015). Aware of this need for building local connections, the social media application Nextdoor was launched in 2010. Its mission is to "build safer, stronger, and happier communities, all over the world" (Nextdoor 2017). According to Joseph Porcelli, Senior City Strategist and *professional neighbor*, currently eight out of ten U.S. neighborhoods use Nextdoor to connect, communicate, and be of service to one another. Members receive critical lifesaving communication from many of Nextdoor's government partners (of which there are 2,500) who utilize a free government interface, Nextdoor for Public

Agencies. "During Hurricane Harvey, in the greater Houston Area, 136 of these government partners shared more than 1,200 updates to keep residents informed," explained Porcelli in a telephone conversation with the author on October 12, 2017 (Porcelli 2017). Aside from Nextdoor, other community and neighborhood-based initiatives have grown in use in recent years. One example is Facebook Community Pages, which is dedicated to topics or experiences of interest to the connected community.

These social media platforms allow agencies, organizations, and neighborhoods to get a message in front of the right people in the right places and at the right times. By targeting a specific audience, the sender is able to obtain immediate feedback on planning initiatives, query users on issues and concerns, push out messages, and sustain engagement over time. Social media can also reach a larger audience and an immensely wide geographic range, which is useful for mitigation purposes. Furthermore, using social media has relatively low operating costs, which is an important consideration for cash-strapped community-based organizations and agencies. With constant on-the-go lifestyles, individuals can access information via their mobile devices from anywhere they have a signal. These platforms are instant, highly scalable forms of communication.

The differences between social media and traditional media – e.g., printed newspapers, radio, and television – is most apparent with regard to the speed at which information is disseminated. Users are able to filter information through easy search mechanisms such as the use of a *hashtag*, a word preceded by the hash mark (#) to signify a topic of interest that can be clicked to find related posts or tweets. Hyperlinks to original or additional sources can offer more detailed information for those interested, while shared information can instantly be updated and accessed from anywhere there is Internet access, expanding flexibility and nimbleness for both senders and receivers.

Who is using social media?

According to a recent poll (Pew Research Center 2017), around 70 percent of Americans use social media to connect with others, share information, and engage with news content. Historically, young adults (18–29 years of age) use social media at high rates. Usage by older adults, however, has increased significantly in recent years as well, especially among the 50–64 and 65+ groups. Survey data emphasize that there are no notable differences by racial or ethnic group: 74 percent of Hispanics, 69 percent of whites, and 63 percent of blacks use social media. The same is true in terms of gender: 72 percent of women and 66 percent of men use at least one social media site. Income and education level, however, do matter: 60 percent of adults who have incomes below $30,000 use social media, compared to 78 percent of adults who have incomes above $75,000. The percentages are almost identical for education level: 59 percent of adults with high school or less use social media, compared to 78 percent of college graduates. Those living in rural areas are slightly less likely to use social media than those in urban and suburban areas, although it should be noted that the percentage of rural social media users has grown significantly since 2009.

When social media was born in the late 1990s, its purpose didn't go beyond enabling people to create a profile and make friends online. Social media has since matured, and an ever-increasing number of people rely on these platforms for their daily news. Today, according to the 2017 Pew survey (Bialik and Matsa 2017) of trends in social and digital news media, 67 percent of Americans get at least some news on social media. While this is only a slight increase compared to 62 percent in 2016, the growth was driven by a sharp increase among older Americans (50–64 and 65+). Equally interesting is that 74 percent of non-whites get news on social media sites, a ten-percentage-point jump from 2016. Similarly, social media use also increased from 60 to 69 percent among those whose educational level was less than a bachelor's degree.

One group that lags behind when it comes to social media use – and more generally, digital technology use – are individuals with disabilities. Disabled Americans (more than 56 million people, according to the U.S. Census Bureau) are three times less likely to go online than their peers without a disability, according to a 2016 Pew Research Center survey (Anderson and Perrin 2017). This might partly be due to the fact that the disabled population is disproportionately comprised of seniors, who have much lower levels of digital adoption than the nation as a whole. Still, the gap remains visible among younger disabled Americans. The survey indicates that 67 percent of disabled Americans between the ages of 18 and 64 say that they own a laptop or desktop computer, compared to 84 percent of their peers who do not have a disability.

These statistics emphasize that social media is used widely among groups that are at highest risk and are most vulnerable to the impacts of disasters, such as the elderly, people of color, the poor, undocumented workers, and those less educated. Historically, these groups weren't easy to reach, but social media has changed that. The aforementioned statistics not only indicate that the majority of American adults are using social media, but adults from diverse socioeconomic and racial backgrounds are increasingly using this technology to access news reports and share their thoughts and concerns. Social media has enabled people who were never heard in the past to speak up and get involved. Nevertheless, not everyone has benefitted equally in the digital age. The group most vulnerable to the impact of disasters, the disabled, appears much less likely to go online than those without disabilities. When utilizing social media for disaster mitigation, this must be kept in mind.

Social media strategies

As with all communications outreach, when information is disseminated through a variety of social media platforms, a wider audience is reached, given that not all community members or groups prefer the same social channels. Messages are delivered in different formats, reflecting the social media outlet's unique protocols (e.g., lengthy and sometimes complex narrative dialogues on Facebook as opposed to short message bursts on Twitter or supported by visually captivating imagery on Instagram). The time of day when individuals access their social feeds may also differ, which allows for flexibility in outreach targets. Posted content now often includes rich data, such as interactive maps with extensive data layers. These

108   *Suzanne L. Frew*

unique qualities of social media platforms serve to greatly benefit the sender who utilizes multiple channels – whether for a campaign or single message distribution.

Social platforms are increasingly used to poll attitudes. Nextdoor, for example, describes innovative ways for using community polls as part of local outreach and engagement (Porcelli et al. 2017). The Norfolk Department of Emergency Preparedness and Response asked residents if they had flood insurance. A healthy conversation arose "about the value of having flood insurance from neighbors in high and low flood hazard areas" (Porcelli et al. 2017: 5).

Mitigation planning and the whole community approach

> In 2013, the Washington Post reported that between 2007 and 2013, 243 mil-
> lion Americans were affected by weather disasters. According to NOAA, as of
> July 2017, there have been nine weather and climate disasters, costing over $1 bil-
> lion each. Despite this reality, the Ad Council reports that 69% of Americans do
> not have a family emergency plan in place.
>
> (Porcelli et al. 2017: 2)

After so much disaster loss in recent years, the world is turning new eyes to build-ing long-term resilience – and mitigation is at the core of this movement. While many mitigation actions are focused on an individual's home, business, or com-mercial building, mitigation measures are also designed to protect *systems* of natural and built environments. Community-level mitigation often requires *big picture* thinking, political buy-in, resources, and widespread support.

Long-term risk reduction gained national prominence in the U.S. with a FEMA initiative entitled Project Impact in the late 1990s, which created incentives for communities to think about future risk. This community-driven effort had long-lasting impacts on the community mindset and led to important legislation with the Disaster Mitigation Act of 2000. Subsequently, DMA 2000 established the Pre-Disaster Mitigation Program (PDM), a competitive grant program that funded the planning and implementation of mitigation projects for states and local govern-ments prior to the event of a disaster. The *whole community* approach advocating inclusive community engagement was later introduced by FEMA Administrator Craig Fugate (also a major advocate of social media) under the Obama administra-tion. This approach emphasizing mitigation and resilience encouraged involving all federal, state, local, tribal, and territorial governmental partners, nongovernmental organizations such as faith-based, volunteer and nonprofit groups, the private sec-tor and industry, and most importantly, individuals, families, and communities.

An overall cultural transition is slowly moving from a *reactive* (response) to a *proactive* (planning) focus. In FY2007, reflecting the original intent of the DMA 2000, in order to apply for the competitive PDM funding, local applicant commu-nities were required to develop and maintain a FEMA-approved Hazard Mitiga-tion Plan. This planning process has now become a foundational basis for building resilience at the community and regional level.

Box 6.1   What do hazard mitigation activities look like?

Mitigation activities include:

- Identifying actions for risk reduction agreed upon by stakeholders and the public.
- Focusing resources on the greatest risks and vulnerabilities.
- Building partnerships by involving citizens, organizations, and businesses.
- Increasing education and awareness of threats and hazards, as well as their risks.
- Communicating priorities to state and federal officials.
- Aligning risk reduction with other community objectives.

What do mitigation actions and concepts look like when implemented?

- Outreach programs that increase risk awareness.
- Projects that protect critical facilities.
- Removal of structures from flood hazard areas.
- Land-use plans.
- Building codes that go beyond *life safety* to allow for operation after an event.

Additionally, mitigation can help accomplish other community objectives, such as leveraging capital improvements, infrastructure protection, open space preservation, and economic resiliency.

Integrating social media into mitigation planning activities

Social media has increasingly played a role in engaging widespread target audiences. Given that online platforms enable risk managers to more effectively expand their reach or hyper-localize their target audience, communities, agencies, and organizations are now more readily embracing social platforms to inform, question, monitor, and gain critical feedback that enables them to craft more targeted strategies and plans.

While developing coastal post-disaster reconstruction guidelines for the Maui County (Hawaii) Department of Planning, The Frew Group (risk resilience and communication consultants) used social media to communicate with high-risk populations in remote locations on multiple islands, including outreach to local native Hawaiian populations living on deeded homesteads. Of paramount importance was a need to reflect cultural sensitivity, honor local preferences, and engage with elderly and youth. Facebook, Twitter, and Instagram posts were successfully integrated into the communications strategy.

Box 6.2 International snapshot: Australia and New Zealand

In a private Facebook message to the author on October 12, 2017, crisis consultant Peter Rekers offers insight to how social media has helped Australia and New Zealand, both well-known for their respective disaster vulnerabilities:

> In Australia, the State of Victoria's Emergency Management Victoria is using social media to reach communities vulnerable to bushfire to help them devise local resilience building solutions. Many of these communities learnt the hard way in 2010 when they were devastated by the Black Saturday fires and are now much more focused on resilience building. One of the key strengths of using social media in building resilience in communities is its ability to reach audiences who, too often, don't want to listen. This is particularly valuable in areas of high and complex risk such as New Zealand. The Alpine Fault 8 (AF8) project is planning for an earthquake of a magnitude 8 or greater in the South Island. The AF8 project is communicating specific as well as general advice and case studies through social media, reaching a vast variety of audiences.
>
> (Rekers 2017)

Some industry experts advocate that more needs to be done with agency-led mitigation in order to create richer content that will facilitate more successful social media engagement. During a telephone conversation with the author on October 11, 2017, George Whitney, a former government disaster management official now in the private sector, observed that mitigation planning activities are often not much more than a program designed to complete a local hazard mitigation plan that is "hardly or never implemented, but updated every five years to meet a FEMA requirement" (Whitney 2017). The result is that there is little to share on social media. If emergency managers want to capitalize on the power of *social*, it is imperative to supply ongoing content that is actionable, accessible, and appealing to wide audiences. Doing so will undoubtedly accelerate the quality and success of the programs, plans, and activities.

FEMA offers an excellent nine-step framework for conducting the mitigation planning process (FEMA 2013). U.S. communities are encouraged to follow these steps. This structure is noteworthy because it provides guidance for communities and organizations anywhere in the world wishing to reduce risks and build resilience. The first three tasks focus on the process of mitigation planning, including who needs to be involved and how to involve them. The remaining tasks address what is accomplished during the planning process and how, when, and where social media can fit into planning. This is best explained by identifying each planning step (or task) and considering social media activities that would help drive success.

Determining planning areas and resources (Task 1)

One of the first actions to take in the planning process is to define the planning area, which refers to the geographic area covered by the plan. Geographic Information System (GIS) maps are often created to visualize the planning locales and are especially valuable planning tools when multiple jurisdictions are working together to address similar threats.

A critical action at the outset is to identify a plan's resource needs. Would you need support to inform a community about the planning activities on social media? Consider posting requests on local geotargeted platforms for social media and technology expertise. Resources could include outside technical assistance or local high school or college students who might know the technology or are social influencers on the platforms most actively used by a wide range of users (and by different age groups) in the local jurisdiction.

Building the planning team (Task 2)

Involving various representatives from across the community and other jurisdictions is critical to inclusive planning. The process will greatly benefit by including team members experienced with social media and familiar with the community's demographics and preferences for online engagement. Such support can be found in many places and crafted through varying relationships, for example with formal team members or volunteers, such as digital volunteers assisting a Virtual Operations Support Team that supports local social media activities following a disaster.[1] Social media outreach can be used to further engage planning members, such as GIS specialists who create and analyze map data to communicate complex information that can then be distributed via social platforms.

Creating an outreach strategy (Task 3)

Transparent public dialogue and engagement are necessary for effective mitigation planning – and a good plan at the end of the process. All community members need to understand how resilience decisions are reached and deserve an opportunity to have their voices heard. Mitigation planning outreach strategies identify what a community wants to accomplish through outreach efforts and whom to involve in the process, as well as how to engage the community and when. When integrated into sundry traditional and online outreach methods, online social engagement offers a robust communications solution. The challenge is to keep thinking *out of the box* to find new and unique ways to reflect a community's personality and preferences.

There are numerous ways in which social media can support mitigation planning outreach: distributing links to literature; offering informational tidbits;

serving as a pointer to other online resources (e.g., a website or a main source that hosts mitigation information); soliciting risk reduction solution ideas; promoting planning meetings; educating on vital details for which decisions are being made; soliciting input through surveys; and gaining feedback.

Social engagement can open a door to community members who are passionately involved and committed to their neighborhoods. For those with driving passion, social media offers a steady bullhorn for advocating viewpoints and rallying support behind concerns. For those unable to attend a key event, social feeds offer streaming of real-time discussions and solicit feedback. Key points of contacts can be continually promoted to answer questions or provide comments. Since all communities struggle with dwindling dollars, posted messages offering downloadable resource links to plans, critical updates, public notices, and press releases can ease pressures on staffing responsibilities.

Box 6.3   Snapshot: Clark County, Kansas Emergency Management

Clark County, Kansas, created the Clark County Emergency Management Facebook Page. They posted video clips, interviews with stakeholders, and photos of activities during their mitigation planning process. Innovatively, they held a drawing for an Apple iPod Shuffle 2GB MP3 Player posting that "all those that participate and provide feedback via this Facebook page will be entered in the drawing" (Clark County Emergency Management 2010).

Reviewing community capabilities (Task 4)

The next step is to evaluate the existing authorities, policies, programs, and resources that help mitigate risks in the community. Resilience building is best done when jurisdictions clearly identify and understand local and state capabilities that enable mitigation strategies to succeed. Important questions might be: Does a community have the capabilities it needs to implement a mitigation strategy? Are there opportunities for improving what is already in place? Do local plans increase social vulnerabilities of high-risk community members, such as non-documented workers, LGBTQ, or those with access and function needs?

Social media provides a range of avenues to individually question community capabilities as well as conduct online research through crowdsourcing approaches. As a *push* information mechanism, social media increases the ability of a community to educate on a wide range of local plans and planning efforts that affect resilience, such as transportation, capital improvement, economic development, and policies and laws.

Conducting a risk assessment (Task 5)

Assessing a community's hazards and vulnerabilities sheds light on its risk level. The risk assessment enables a better understanding of the potential impacts of hazards to a community's people, economy, and constructed and natural environments. It empowers planners to prioritize actions. While many plans have traditionally focused on vulnerabilities to physical properties and infrastructure, there is a growing focus on the safety and well-being of the community's high-risk populations, as discussed in various chapters of this book. Social media offers new, creative means for sharing important data as well as gathering through data mining tools and crowdsourcing activities. Key components of risk assessment include:

- Hazard assessment: Describing natural, technological, and human-caused hazards that affect the jurisdiction.
- Community assets identification: Identifying community assets that are at risk, particularly to people, economy, built environment, and natural environment.
- Risk analysis: Evaluating vulnerable assets, describing potential risks, and estimating losses for each hazard.
- Vulnerability analysis: Summarizing the hazards, vulnerable assets, and potential impacts and losses to understand and rank significant risks and vulnerabilities.

Using social media in these activities can be overlooked by planners and may not traditionally be considered, outside of pushing meeting information out to the public. The *hazard assessment*, a baseline of those hazards to which a community may be exposed, depends on informed research requiring extensive data gathering of a wide range of information located in many sources. These elements include state and local plans, historical documentation of disasters, flood insurance rate maps, community policies, and financial data. Social media/online tools can support the assessment. For example, GIS hazard maps provide vivid graphical data visualizations that are easily understood and can be widely and rapidly distributed through social media. Data for the assessment and map development can be crowd-sourced through social media outreach. Maps (see Figure 6.1), building inventories, related reports, community surveys, and other feedback can be gathered and the documents (or hyperlinks to the source documents) distributed through social media.

Community assets identification is built upon data collection and display. Online surveys can be used to better understand the people served and facilities used, as well as to gather community sentiments to such issues as sensitive habitats and use of open space and other quality of life indicators. The *risk analysis* informs the community of their greatest risks. Conducting the analysis requires qualitative and quantitative evaluation of all of the gathered data. While participatory planning is best done in real time, this is not always possible. Online discussion

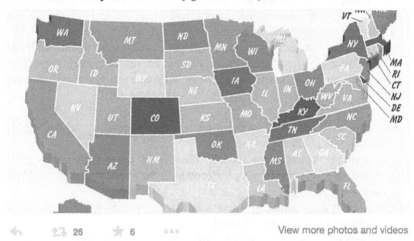

Readygov retweeted

NWS Owlie Skywarn @NWSOwlieSkywarn · Dec 23

Got some free time on break? Check out this @Readygov site & learn about hazards in your state ready.gov/kids/maps

26   6   View more photos and videos

Figure 6.1 The National Weather Service builds state-level hazard risk understanding by posting on its Twitter feed a link to a visually appealing interactive map graphic on FEMA's Readygov's kid's website

threads can support and expand the development of these planning discussions. When a *vulnerability analysis* is conducted, issues of greatest concern can be made accessible and understandable and allow for interactive dialogue through social media.

Developing a mitigation strategy (Task 6)

A completed *risk assessment*, and all of the work leading up to it, crystallizes what a community can lose if and when disaster hits, also paving the road to making informed decisions on what needs to be done to mitigate the risks – the *mitigation strategy*. It reflects the community's goals and risk reduction actions and specifies how it will implement the actions it has chosen.

Online resource links imbedded in social media posts enable followers to learn more about the strategy, specific mitigation measures, planning partners, and tools. Perhaps one of the most important services social media messages can provide is a notice or direct link offering the public an opportunity to review and provide comment on the final draft of a community's mitigation plan prior to its adoption.

Social media is best used in conjunction with whatever traditional mitigation development tools are currently being used. For example, when community meetings are held, public notices, press releases, and informational materials can be sent out online beforehand. During the meetings, active online discussions (e.g. "Tweetchats") enable off-site stakeholders to add their voice to the discussion, asking questions and providing answers in real-time, which underscores the power of timely feedback loops. Media outlets, bloggers, and social influencers can access images and videos of the events underway, potentially encouraging more immediate coverage and furthering an event's social reach. All of these online engagement opportunities can point followers to related websites for more in-depth information and educational opportunities, thus further sustaining engagement.

Social media is a vital element of the plan itself, not just in creating or promoting the plan. Mitigation plans include communication strategies and tactics related to many types of hazard-related information, including time-critical emergency alerts and warnings, availability of flood insurance, and data visualization of floodplains. By both pulling and pushing information, social media increases understanding of community strengths and shortfalls and provides a clear picture of planning efforts.

The most inclusive education and awareness efforts include an integrated strategy that use a variety of educational distribution channels and mechanisms, of which social media platforms, local influencers, and campaign development should be included. Tulsa, Oklahoma, included in its strategy additional measures

---

Box 6.4   Snapshot: Morris County, New Jersey

"During both Hurricane Irene and Superstorm Sandy, Morris County, New Jersey, experienced an astronomical increase in interactions on its social media channels. The public was desperate for information and we were able to provide it because we were embedded in the EOC [Emergency Operations Center]," explained Carol A. Spencer, Digital & Social Media Manager for Morris County at the time, in an email message to the author on June 21, 2013. "After these two events, we reached out to those same people via social media, soliciting input for our 2015 Hazard Mitigation Plan. In late November, we posted on both Twitter and Facebook about mitigation, explaining what mitigation is, why it's important, asking for input via our online survey, and including a link to the survey (Figure 6.2). We wrote about the importance of mitigation on our OEM Public Information blog," she added. Pointing out that there were nearly half a million social media interactions over six days during Hurricane Irene, a number repeated during Superstorm Sandy, Spencer cited the expanded reach for mitigation input using Twitter, Facebook, and OEM's blog (Spencer 2013).

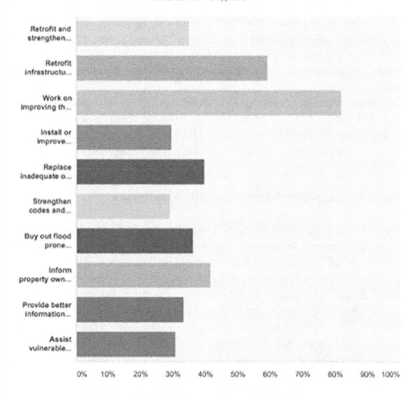

Morris County Hazard Mitigation Plan Update – Citizen Survey

Q22 What types of projects do you believe local, county, state, or federal government agencies could be doing in order to reduce the damage and disruption of natural disasters in Morris County? Select your top three choices

Answered: 186   Skipped: 57

Figure 6.2 Morris County, New Jersey, used Twitter and Facebook to gather public input for assessing community priorities for mitigation investments, according to Carol A. Spencer, former digital and social media manager for Morris County, in an email message to the author on June 21, 2013

for socially vulnerable populations that supported alerts and warnings, evacuations, and medical response, described Bob Roberts, prior emergency manager of Tulsa Public Schools, in a phone conversation with the author on July 14, 2015 (Roberts 2015).

Keep the plan current (Task 7)

At some point, all plans need to be updated to assess goals and activity progress, and make adjustments. FEMA requires a five-year update. Status updates and community feedback on priorities and the level of success of the actions can be driven by social media outreach. The public needs to be involved with monitoring, evaluating, and updating the plan. The online community can be tapped to provide feedback on changes in the conditions due to disaster events, and changes in community needs and resources, potential partners, and capabilities (see Figure 6.3). Through social media posts with questions, links to questionnaires, or driving traffic to a specific website to give feedback, platforms offer a fast, inexpensive way to reach out and learn about what worked and what didn't.

When local policies and ordinances are evaluated or reevaluated, collecting input online can reinforce and/or build wider support for planning decisions. Additionally, social media can target particular neighborhoods for engagement on key issues. Understanding and monitoring online sentiment is paramount for meeting the challenges related to highly political issues. When using tax dollars to protect critical infrastructure or restore and preserve wetlands and wildlife habitats that might not only serve to protect local housing but also support the quality of life of residents, knowing where key stakeholders stand on such issues better prepares one for going into public meetings. Additionally, the public can offer new ideas of resources, potential partnerships, and possible funding sources. Once a plan is developed, obtaining public feedback is critical before finalization, and interested stakeholders can be offered a chance to review and provide input from the comfort of home.

Review and adopt the plan (Task 8)

Once a plan is developed, it needs to be reviewed by key stakeholders. Social media can make the document widely accessible, with information on how to review the plan and provide required public comment. Links to a document open for comment can be located on a community's website. Innovative online communication outreach strategies will penetrate the community across sectors, geographic areas, languages, and cultures more effectively than by only posting on a website or using traditional media. Once a plan is adopted, links to the final community mitigation plan can be widely used, along with language encouraging downloading and printing for public consumption at widely accessible public venues, such as libraries.

 **Utah Mitigation**
@UT_MIT

Via Bronson Smart from @NRCS_Utah -
Video of Huntington Creek Upper Debris
Basin #SHMT #SeeleyFire #HazardMitigation
youtu.be/sRyhzT9dNQs

 YouTube

Huntington Creek upper debris basin
This shows pre-event conditions of the basin as well as video during a storm event in
July 2014 and the results of the event.

View on web

9:36 AM - 26 Aug 2014

Figure 6.3 The state of Utah retweets a partner's YouTube footage to visually document
the impact of flooding on a community's existing structural mitigation measure

---

Box 6.5   Snapshot: City of San Francisco, California

"In San Francisco, we really wanted to make sure we gave the public the
opportunity to weigh-in on our hazard mitigation plan, so we used our
existing outreach mechanisms including social and traditional media, to get

the word out that we wanted to know their thoughts on this important topic [see Figure 6.4]. We encouraged residents to share their feedback with us on Facebook, Nextdoor, and Twitter. We drove home the message that we wanted this plan to incorporate San Francisco's values. Engaging in this dialogue with our stakeholders, which includes the general public, is why our hazard mitigation plan was the first of its kind to cover climate change (sea level rise, temperature rise, and precipitation changes)," said Kristin Hogan, San Francisco Department of Emergency Management, External Affairs, in an email message to the author on October 21, 2014 (Hogan 2014).

 San Francisco Department of Emergency Management
December 4, 2013 · 🌐

We're looking for your feedback on the 2014 Draft San Francisco Hazard Mitigation Plan. The plan describes our City's natural and human-made hazards, identifies actions we can take to reduce their effects, and establishes a process for implementing the plan.

Visit www.sfdem.org/hmp to participate!

👍 Like　　💬 Comment　　↪ Share

Figure 6.4 The city of San Francisco DEM regularly utilizes social media alongside traditional media to engage the public

Create a safe and resilient community (Task 9)

The mitigation strategy and planning effort does not stop at creation, or upon plan implementation. Ongoing, online engagement fosters sustained involvement. It keeps the plan, the planning process, and community interest in resilience alive and moving into the future. It ensures the public stays informed. It helps planners gather additional ideas and provide feedback when needed. Social outreach can keep the conversations active and engaging when the mitigation actions are successfully achieved. Having platforms for celebrating and promoting successes is a perfect use of social media. And after an event occurs, keeping the public informed and connected will set them up to be more prepared and likely to assist in a response and recovery effort.

Box 6.6   Snapshot: Firewise

In a telephone conversation with the author on March 21, 2017 Michele Steinberg, Wildfire Division Director, National Fire Protection Association, stated, "Firewise opened its Twitter account around 2009 and later developed a Facebook page [see Figure 6.5]. We started out simply trying to drive users to our website but found the benefits of social media to be much broader than simply traffic to the site. My observation about one of the great benefits of social, and in this case, I'm thinking about our LinkedIn group in particular, is that it seems to really build trust with our audiences and partners. When an organization like ours can show that we are trustworthy, thoughtful, and transparent by having a proactive presence on social media, it helps us build societal resiliency when we then work to persuade communities to take wildfire safety action" (Steinberg 2017).

Figure 6.5 Firewise retweets an educational graphic and partner appreciation message for a safe, defensible space in urban-wildland interface fire zones

---

Looking toward the future

Social media has *grown up* in its role in emergency management. Long past being simply a fun way to share photos of great meals and socializing with friends and family (though still important for that as well), platforms now serve as vital tools in the disaster risk-reduction toolbox. The dynamic nature of social media's constant changing platforms and new technologies demand users to stay nimble with its use and application and updated with its changes. It is an unpredictable lightening rod that thrusts open the doors of access, breaks down traditional information hierarchy, and sheds light on new pathways to hear a range of voices that have long gone unheard. Just as climate change carves sobering new profiles in the earth's face, physical and cyber-terrorism create ever-growing concerns, and deeply disturbing political shifts pose unforeseen challenges, social media simultaneously gives rise to unexpected strength and opportunity to build resilience.

The roles and character of social media will undoubtedly change the risk communications landscape in the years to come. They will impact how communities engage across the digital divide, break diverse public and private sectors out of insulated silos, encourage innovative partnerships and exchange, and enable cash-strapped agencies and communities to more effectively build community risk resilience. Despite the growing pains inevitable to rapidly changing technologies, these social tools deliver unprecedented opportunity for empowering the whole community to improve their quality of life for *every* member by actively joining in a social movement to reduce their own disaster risks, at a most fundamental and personal level. The social media revolution in resilience building is here to stay, and that is fortunate for us all.

Note

1 For more information about VOSTs please visit https://vosg.us.

References

Anderson, Monica, and Perrin, Andrew. 2017. *Disabled Americans Are Less Likely to Use Technology*. Pew Research Center. Accessed on October 15, 2017 at www.pewresearch.org/fact-tank/2017/04/07/disabled-americans-are-less-likely-to-use-technology/.

Bialik, Kristen, and Matsa, Katerina Eva. 2017. *Key Trends in Social and Digital News Media*. Pew Research Center. Accessed on October 15, 2017 www.pewresearch.org/fact-tank/2017/10/04/key-trends-in-social-and-digital-news-media/.

Cheshire, Lynda. 2015. "Know Your Neighbours": Disaster Resilience and the Normative Practices of Neighboring in an Urban Context. *Environment and Planning A*, 47(5): 1081–1099.

Clark County, Kansas Emergency Management. 2010. Clark County Emergency Management Facebook Page. *Facebook*, May. Accessed at www.facebook.com/pages/Clark-County-Emerg-Mgmt/131526490196112.

Dunkelman, Marc, J. 2014. *The Vanishing Neighbor: The Transformation of American Community*. New York: W.W. Norton & Company, Inc.

Federal Emergency Management Agency (FEMA). 2013. *Local Mitigation Planning Handbook*. Accessed at www.fema.gov/media-library-data/20130726-1910-25045-9160/fema_local_mitigation_handbook.pdf.

Hogan, K. 2014. Personal Communication with the Author. October 21.

Kahn, Brian. 2013. Hurricane Sandy Hasn't Shifted Climate Narrative. *Climate Central*, October 29. Accessed on October 12, 2017 at www.climatecentral.org/news/sandy-didnt-change-a-thing-16669.

Nextdoor. *About Us*. Accessed on October 14, 2017 at https://nextdoor.com/about_us.

Pew Research Center. 2017. *Social Media Fact Sheet*. Accessed on October 14, 2017 at www.pewinternet.org/fact-sheet/social-media.

Pinker, Susan. 2014. *The Village Effect – How Face to Face Contact Can Make Us Healthier and Happier*. Toronto: Vintage Canada.

Porcelli, Joseph. 2017. Personal Communication with the Author. October 12.

Porcelli, Joseph, Flynn, Mary Jo, Starr, Katie, Corona, Joe, and Pyle, Steven. 2017. Increasing Resilience with Nextdoor Polls for Public Agencies. *Nextdoor*. Accessed on October 14, 2017 at http://bit.ly/NextdoorPollsEMA.

Rekers, P. 2017. Personal Communication with the Author. October 12.

Roberts, B. 2015. Personal Communication with the Author. July 14.

Spencer, C. 2013. Personal Communication with the Author. June 21.

Steinberg, M. 2017. Personal Communication with the Author. March 21.

Whitney, G. 2017. Personal Communication with the Author. October 11.

7 Promoting public involvement in disaster risk communication in Nigeria

Oluponmile Olonilua

Introduction

Although there has been considerable progress in Nigeria in communicating disaster risk, the Nigerian Emergency Management Agency has yet to involve the public effectively in all phases of emergency management. There are currently no effective ways to communicate to all those at risk. The agency has focused more on top-down policymaking rather than involving citizens in improving disaster risk communication. Every decision is made at the national level, and control of activities is from the top. Data collection for this research involved telephone interviews with officials and local citizens of major cities with known disasters using semi-structured questionnaires to current and past officials of the Nigerian Emergency Management Agency (NEMA) and to local citizens. Their responses indicate that both agency officials and the public believe that social media are tools that could promote more efficient and more effective public involvement. This chapter defines risk communication, the benefits and challenges of disaster risk communication, risk communication in Nigeria, methods used by the Nigerian Emergency Management Agency, and the use of telephones and social media in disaster risk communication in Nigeria.

Disaster management in Nigeria

Nigeria is the most populous nation in Africa, the tenth-largest country in sub-Saharan Africa by land area and the seventh most populous country in the world (CIA 2017). Nigeria had a population of 186 million in 2016, with over 250 ethnic groups, three major indigenous languages, and English as the official language. According to the CIA Factbook, Nigeria's population will grow to as high as 392 million by 2050 and will become world's fourth most populous country (CIA 2017). Nigeria has a federal system that gives a great deal of autonomy to each of its 36 states. Each state government is led by a governor, with a House of Assembly acting as the legislature. Presidential, gubernatorial, and legislative elections take place every four years. Nigeria has a land area of approximately 356,700 square miles, with a wide range of environmental regions, including coastal swamps, tropical wet forests, tropical dry forests, savanna, and semi-desert (CIA 2017).

Nigeria has the highest rate of mobile phone and Internet use in Africa and the seventh-highest in the world. In July 2015, Nigeria had over 86 million Internet users, which represented 47.4 percent of the population at that time (CIA 2017).

Disaster management in Nigeria dates back to 1906, when the Federal Fire Services was created to manage firefighting and other humanitarian services in emergencies. The devastating drought of the early 1970s led to the establishment of the National Emergency Relief Agency (NERA) in 1976 to provide emergency relief materials to those affected by disasters. The government decided to expand the function of the national agency to cover all phases of disaster management and renamed the agency to be the National Emergency Management (NEMA) Agency in 1999. The Planning, Research, and Forecasting department of NEMA is responsible for coordination of response and mitigation activities with other agencies, prevention, data collection, and public education.

The Nigerian Emergency Management Agency (NEMA) has six zonal offices across the country. Its state equivalents are State Emergency Management Agencies (SEMAs), and local governments are required to have Local Emergency Management Agencies (LEMAs). The agency and its subsidiaries are responsible to prepare for, mitigate, respond to, and recover from disasters. The military, police, and paramilitary are all involved in disaster management. Numerous community-based, faith-based, and nongovernmental organizations also are involved and often serve as first responders.

Large-scale disasters are relatively rare in Nigeria, but human-induced hazards from technological and socioeconomic activities are common. These activities include oil and gas explosions, automobile accidents, collapsed buildings, and airplane accidents. Natural hazards include wildfire, extreme weather, and floods (Soneye 2014; Fasona and Omojola 2005). All states in Nigeria are susceptible to flooding, and floods have caused several deaths and property damage: In 2012 alone, there were 363 deaths and more than 2 million people lost their homes (Fabiyi and Oloukoi 2013).

Flooding in Nigeria has pushed rivers over banks and submerged hundreds of thousands of acres of farmland. As recent as July 2017, floods in the Lagos area claimed at least 20 lives and caused damage to multiple properties. Flooding remains a recurring event in Nigeria (Ologunorisa and Adeyemo 2005). Citizens do not know where to seek help when flooding occurs and are not aware of mitigation measures enacted by the government. There is a lack of public education and involvement of mass media. Vatsa (2004) suggested strengthening community networks in mobilizing assets through participatory programs and suggests the use of information and knowledge through electronic media and the Internet.

Traditionally, developing countries have used the Famine Early Warning System (FEWS) and Vulnerability Analysis and Mapping (VAM) to assess food security in sub-Saharan Africa. This tool is used by decision makers to assess famine threat (Vatsa 2004). The United Nations Development Programme uses a World Vulnerability Report to rank countries based on data from multiple sources in terms of losses due to natural disasters. Their findings show that most developing countries adopted structural mitigation measures that were ineffective in most cases. The nonstructural approach also presented its own problem because it did not take into consideration the social, economic, and cultural aspects of life in these countries. Past research shows that local mitigation plans are difficult to find, if they exist at all, and community projects do not provide resources and information to residents on how to reduce their vulnerability to disasters (Vatsa 2004).

Nigeria is one of the few African countries with legislative successes in disaster risk reduction. The government is a leader in many disaster initiatives and tagged as "leading Africa in political commitment for disaster risk reduction" (van Niekerk 2015: 402). Despite this, factors such as corruption, graft, lack of buy-in from stakeholders, competing interests across government agencies, and others affect the level of success of disaster risk reduction (DRR). NEMA has 22 state level agencies named State Emergency Management Agencies (SEMAs). NEMA has been unable to effectively manage disaster risk due to the size and disaster risk profile in the country, especially since SEMAs and local governments have no formal relationships (van Niekerk 2015). Nigeria conducted a capacity assessment in 2012. The outcome of the assessment was the creation of graduate level courses in DRR at six national universities, DRR training for public school teachers at the local level, and the allocation of one percent of the national budget to mitigation. NEMA has directly implemented grassroots awareness campaigns and the use of local and traditional knowledge. Several states remain reactive to disasters because as many as 14 of the 36 states do not have the appropriate DRR structures and mechanisms. NEMA faces the challenges of limited human resources at the state and local levels (Vatsa 2004).

Past research has found that the agency lacks functional and integrated communication facilities and effective data capturing capabilities (Soneye 2014; Vatsa 2004). The agency is characterized by poor research and data collection and lacking in disaster risk maps that might help to guide future development. Disaster education channels such as campaigns, seminars, workshops, TV/radio talk shows, and conferences have not been effective (Soneye 2014). Its objectives focus mainly on response, research, preventive measures, data collection, public education, and resource coordination. According to Soneye (2014), NEMA's focus remains on occurrences, modelling, warning, and distribution of relief packages. Flood forecasts, preparedness, and recovery are evolving. Additionally, there is little or no attention given to feedback from stakeholders.

Social media is becoming an important mode of communication in Nigeria and can serve as an important tool to facilitate disaster risk communication. The increase in technology and Internet usage has impacted almost all areas of life. Nigeria has the highest density of mobile and Internet networks in Africa, with over 100 million mobile lines. The introduction of Blackberry phones allowed Nigerians much easier access to the Internet compared to citizens of neighboring countries (Ephraim 2013). Internet connectivity through Blackberry devices allowed users, including those in rural areas, to have access to social media even without electricity. Chatting, texting, online activities, Facebook, Twitter, and YouTube all have become very popular. Recent introduction of smartphones and regular mobile phones have increased activities such as chatting, sharing of pictures, and more public engagement. The people use social media to comment on government activities and policies. The telephone companies are using social media to interact more with their subscribers. Churches keep in touch with their converts and church members using livestream, Facebook, Twitter, Live feeds, YouTube, and Whatsapp. Social media are changing and increasing public engagement in various activities in Nigeria (Ephraim 2013).

Risk communication

The concept of vulnerability assessment in risk communication was introduced in the 1970s to refer to critical infrastructure and urban lifelines. Vulnerability assessment allows jurisdictions to determine the impact of hazards on life, safety, critical infrastructure and utilities, buildings, development, populations, the environment, and the economy (Vatsa 2004). Communities can assess their exposure in light of critical facilities and infrastructures, development, redevelopment, and population trends. Through capability assessment, communities can take inventories of existing mitigation activities, policies, plans, and regulations. All of these assessments are linked to the cost of potential damage and how best to reduce that cost by having a pre-disaster mitigation plan and involving the public in the planning process (Olonilua and Ibitayo 2014).

Effective risk communication requires that the government identifies public perception and acknowledges the diversity of the public. The government perceives risk differently than the public, and this is why involving the public in hazard mitigation and preparedness could bridge this difference in risk perception. Effective risk communication should acknowledge the concerns of the public and express empathy for issues raised by the public to enhance risk sharing and vulnerability assessment. For this to work, however, the government must have established and meaningful relationships with members of the public by involving them in advisory panels, committees, focus groups, and government or community projects (Olonilua and Ibitayo 2014).

The public is a large and diverse group. Effective risk communication among the public must take into consideration the interests, concerns, and priorities of its different groups. When stakeholders are involved in issues that affect them, they are more likely to support the implementation of policies and projects (Olonilua and Ibitayo 2011; Olonilua 2016). Another challenge of risk communication is that it can often be interpreted to mean data collection and dissemination and listening to public concerns. The public can be scared of risk and worry more about their immediate needs and comfort. On the other hand, some do not trust government information and have only a limited perception of the disaster threats they face.

Public involvement in disaster management

Public awareness is the extent to which a community is aware of the possibility of a hazard occurrence before and during an actual event and their knowledge of the potential impacts of these events (Cottrell et al. 2001). The public needs to be informed of hazards in their communities but also about the appropriate procedures, such as how and when to evacuate, suitable evacuation routes, hazard warnings, and shelter locations. Public awareness programs serve to enlighten the citizens about hazard preparedness, thereby enhancing their coping mechanisms. Also, public awareness can facilitate the creation of a volunteer force for activities such as evacuation and shelter management, search and rescue, medical, first aid, and sanitation services (Cottrell et al. 2001).

In the pre-disaster phase, public information and awareness help communities and individuals to make informed decisions about where to live and where to purchase property or establish a business, thereby reducing the levels of uncertainty. For example, through public information and awareness campaigns, property owners, real estate agents, potential homebuyers, businesses, and renters become aware of and seek more information about potential hazards and may also facilitate compliance with hazard warnings and emergency preparedness information (Mileti 1999; Perry and Nelson 1991; Mileti and O'Brien 1992). Additionally, increased public awareness may induce the public to push for the integration of natural hazard mitigation with other activities such as land-use planning, housing development, and the need for the protection and preservation of wetlands and other sensitive environments.

Some of the effective ways to keep the public involved in risk communication include the use of maps and outreach projects such as displays in public buildings, radio and TV news broadcasts, social media, fliers, presentations at meetings of relevant local organizations, and the creation of school curricula on hazard mitigation and preparedness. Public awareness emphasizes the importance of public outreach education and increases public knowledge of disasters, keeping them informed before, during, and after a disaster (Perry and Nelson 1991; Driscoll and Salween 1996). According to Perry and Nelson (1991), the dissemination of the risk information of a hazard event to the public enhances the citizens' understanding of the dangers of the hazard event and may facilitate compliance with the hazard warning. The dissemination of public information, including protective strategies, may also enhance the capability of citizens to cope with the effects of a hazard event. Public belief and reaction to risk information about a hazard, however, depends on the perceived credibility of the information source, the clarity of the message, and the persistence of the dissemination of the warning (Mileti and O'Brien 1992). Public information and awareness programs are highly relevant to hazard mitigation because they include actions that inform the public about potential hazards, insurance information, outreach programs designed to promote ways to reduce impact of identified hazards, and the options and resources available to reduce risks to local governments. Through public information and awareness, citizens can make informed decisions on where to live, play, and work.

The mainstream media provide another great opportunity to reach the public when they are involved early in the planning process. They can provide local information such as the history of hazards in the community (Scanlon 1991). Information from the news media has been noted to influence public perceptions and reactions (Driscoll and Salween 1996). The mass media – newspapers, television, and radio – have been identified as the most frequently mentioned sources of information about local environmental hazards (Perry and Nelson 1991). The news media, especially local and regional newspapers, radio, and television collect hazard information from emergency planners or managers and interpret and disseminate risk information to the public. Prater and Lindell (2000) argued that by cultivating media contacts, policy entrepreneurs can facilitate pushing hazard management issues onto the public agenda. Media involvement, however, should focus not only on the mainstream media outlets but should also include local, religious, and ethnic news sources. Emergency planners should include the news media during the planning process and as part of hazard mitigation actions (Kartez 1984). Having a dedicated webpage for citizens to have easy and quick access to hazard information can also improve participation. Survey questionnaires and educational materials can be made available through these dedicated websites. Additionally, each community should use social media and maintain accounts in Facebook, Twitter, Instagram, Snapchat, and other social media channels. Many citizens in Nigeria, young and old, have access to one or more of these accounts and could access hazard mitigation information if it were made available (Olonilua 2016).

Public participation provides an opportunity for people to be involved in decisions that directly affect them. Adoption of mitigation programs can be delayed when stakeholders are not actively involved or when they do not understand the planning process (Godschalk, Brody, and Burby 2003). Public participation seeks to inform, educate, and gather input from the public to enhance the decision-making process and gain support for the implementation of subsequent policies and practices. The extensive involvement of the public in any planning process is pragmatic because public involvement provides an opportunity for people to exchange their knowledge area with the emergency planners themselves. It facilitates a smoother implementation with less opposition. Disaster risk communication must include public participation to ensure that citizens are involved in decisions that directly affect them. It must link expert and local knowledge systems into the planning process so that citizens, who are more knowledgeable about local issues directly affecting them, have input in the dialogue (Fischer 2000). Additionally, emergency managers can facilitate participation by making meeting venues accessible to the public (Young 2000).

Methods of participation include neighborhood meetings, advisory committees, nominal group processes, citizen surveys, voting, letter writing, telephoning, and face-to-face meetings, and more recently, e-government (Glass 1979; Young 2000; Glass 1979). These forums can serve as awareness campaigns to inform and educate the public about the potential risk of hazards. Support for such programs can be enhanced through early involvement of political and environmental groups in the community, churches, schools, and the media dialogue when less technical briefings are used (Scanlon 1991; Brody 2003. The media provide an avenue to educate and disseminate warning information to citizens and should therefore be involved in the hazard mitigation planning process. Early involvement of these stakeholders in the planning process can provide relevant local information, such as a history of hazards in the community (Scanlon 1991). Brody, Godschalk, and Burby (2003) defined participation through the specific actions of stakeholders during the planning process. Such actions included the active roles played in the discussion of policies or alternatives during public hearings, workshops, committee meetings, or informal sessions. Other techniques of citizen participation that the study focused on included hearings, committees and workshops, visioning sessions, forums, and consensus building sessions. In general, forums and consensus building sessions were found to be the most effective participation tools.

Results and findings

Both qualitative and quantitative methods were used in this study. Data were collected through semi-structured interviews emailed to agencies and local citizens. A total of six past and present NEMA officials were interviewed, and questions were posted to a group of 336 citizens. In the next section is a summary of the responses from NEMA officials. On existing government policies on disaster, the officials noted that the enabling Act No. 12 of 1999 as amended by Act No. 50 of 1999 designated and refocused NEMA from being a relief agency to a disaster management agency responsible for all phases of emergency management.

When asked how the agency involves the public in the planning process, the agency reported that it has collaborated with international, regional, and subregional bodies, faith-based organizations (FBOs), community-based organizations (CBOs), grassroots emergency volunteers, states, local government authorities (LGAs), and other relevant bodies for capacity building in disaster management. The agency also collaborates with other relevant stakeholders such as the National Youth Service Corps (NYSC). NYSC members are recent university graduates under the age of 30 and are mandated by the federal government to serve the country in military training for one year after graduation. NEMA has partnered with NYSC to use corps members as vanguards for a standardized proactive disaster management in Nigeria. NYSC members are assigned to all states and rural areas. The rationale behind this is that disasters most often happen in local communities, so it is important to involve the young men and women in disaster management to help at the grassroots level. NEMA calls this initiative the Emergency Management Vanguards, and they are agents of change to advocate safety, serve as disaster risk reduction counselors, civic observers, information gatherers, monitors of risks, and a driving force for public enlightenment within the public setting.

Over the years, the agency has organized several workshops and seminars solely to educate the public. The agency also established the Grassroots Emergency volunteers to train an average of 200 volunteers in all local government areas. The number of volunteers through this program is approximately 6,000 members in 20 states. The agency has also created an Executive Volunteer program for professionals, simulation exercises, and campaigns on periodic disasters, etc. Emergency alerts are sent via the COSPAS-SARSAT system – early warning alerts through signal and media, Journalists against Disasters (JAD), as partners. NEMA is present in the social media via Facebook, Twitter, Instagram, and flicker.

NEMA established a dedicated *call center* at the national office. The call center operates an emergency line which is open to the general public 24 hours a day so people can alert the agency from any part of Nigeria of any disaster occurrence. The agency also partnered with major telephone companies to disseminate information to the public when there is a disaster to avoid panic and stampede. The agency noted that through the various initiatives, the citizens are involved in all the planning stages of preparedness plan for hazards mitigation.

Responses from the local citizens

Questions were posed to a social media group, a cohort of approximately 300 participants. This group was selected because of their diverse educational and financial backgrounds. They all have some college degree and are deemed fit for this study since they understand the importance of phones and are already using social media. The group is active on both WhatsApp and Facebook. Members of the group come from all regions of Nigeria. My decision to use the WhatsApp page is based on the growing usage of WhatsApp in Nigeria and other developing countries for practically everything. Since this research focuses on public engagement using social media, collection of data from WhatsApp seems appropriate and relevant to this research. Nigerians hold meetings and several activities on WhatsApp. This group, which I belong to, has members from all regions of Nigeria. Prior to conducting research, I asked the group for permission to post questions and notified all respondents that their participation was voluntary. Some members were able to direct me to NEMA officials who otherwise would have been difficult to reach.

I asked members of the group if they have experienced flooding. The reason for this question is because all states have experienced flooding and also to avoid confusion with automobile and airplane accidents, which are often represented as disasters by the Nigerian media. About 50 percent of respondents have experienced some type of flooding. Surprisingly, 99 percent of respondents were not aware of any mitigation event by NEMA or its equivalent in the state or local governments, and 96 percent indicated that the state and local governments do not respond to them during floods. Additionally, 96 percent have never received warning about an impending flood and are not aware about NEMA or its presence on social media. Only two members are aware of what NEMA is.

I had met some NEMA officials at the IAEM conference, and one major challenge they noted was educating the public about response. The public responds to these events, not able to provide assistance to the victims but usually to sympathize with them. With the phones, they take pictures of the event and post on social media for entertainment purposes but not to seek help for the victims or to inform public officials. They also mentioned that looting and sharing of obscene pictures are rampant among WhatsApp users.

A review of the NEMA documents, websites, and social media show that the agency uses Facebook to post activities on response and recovery. Such activities include pictures of agency response to spills, automobile accidents, fires, evacuations from bomb attacks, relief assistance, and gun attacks. The agency's Facebook page was created on September 1, 2010, and has over 149,000 likes, with visits from only about 1,800 people.

The agency posts pictures from preventive activities, that is, simulation exercises, and flyers warning citizens to call NEMA and not touch anything on an incident site. There are also flyers and pictures of public education on safety education for drivers, staff training, fire safety warning to traders, and accommodating refugees and pictures of refugees or deportees from other countries. Some of the posts include training of staff on use of social media and meetings with stakeholders such as family physicians. The page also features breaking news on disaster events.

NEMA posts public education video on flood awareness on YouTube in the three major languages in addition to one in English, which is the official language of Nigeria. The video in English was narrated by a popular Nigerian actor. The Disaster Awareness video has over 1,000 views and has social media addresses for NEMA for YouTube, too. The agency also has a video presentation on the 2012 flood on YouTube. NEMA has 54 videos uploaded on YouTube. One of these is a video of a television news report warning residents of an area of possible flooding from a dam break. The other video was an advertisement to alert the public that the agency is on social media.

The agency's website has public education resources such as training for staff and the accomplishments of the agency but contains no real-time warning information for citizens. Additionally, this study finds that the agency's RSS feeds link is not functional. It has 1,161 Instagram followers, and its GooglePlus account was created in 2013 but has not been active since 2014. Telephone numbers are listed for the agency and hours are 24/7.

Conclusions

The Nigerian Emergency Management Agency has evolved and is striving to improve its services; however, findings show that the agency is more response oriented than any of the other phases of disaster management. The agency is focused on staff development but has not really incorporated public involvement in its planning process. Contrary to claims by NEMA, telephone interviews to randomly selected citizens in various areas of the country also show little or no knowledge of disaster management activities in their area. A search of the agency on social media shows that the methods, tools, and format are not standardized, so the various levels of government are free to structure the process.

As a bureaucracy, NEMAs command system is clearly top down. Orders are issued from NEMA to the regional and local offices. Telephone interviews with staff show problems within the agency such as getting all units to agree on which methods and how to do them, and staff turnover – heads of units could be political appointees or are reassigned because some are in the military. Each unit has very different roles to fulfill the agency's goals. The staff agrees there is need for improved collaboration with the public.

There is no public input in any of the agency's dealings and no warning on impending hazards, no forecast or early warning found. A retired NEMA official who tried to stay connected with the agency mentioned that disaster management is controlled by the government and highly political. The relationship between the agency and the public sector is clearly problematic.

Although NEMA states that local governments are empowered to lead disaster risk reduction activities and involve local communities in the decision-making process, findings show that the agency is underfunded and there are differences in emergency management structures from the national level to the state level. There is a lack of collaboration among the different levels of government. The partnership with the telephone companies is for response so that the public can inform the agency of occurrences but not to provide early warning or invite the public for participation in the planning process.

Recommendation

Based on the findings of this study, NEMA needs to take advantage of the telephones and Internet subscribers and use those to improve local citizens' involvement in disaster risk. The agency should reach out to the various local traditional groups such as women's and youth associations and Nollywood – the Nigerian movie industry. These groups all have representation in social media. Religious organizations are numerous and powerful in Nigeria, and NEMA could partner with these groups to disseminate disaster risk information through their social media networks. Most citizens have access to telephones and social media, and NEMA should allow citizens to access data and view the extent and location of hazard events. People can access real time information on disasters on their phones. NEMA can develop an app and make it available free for people by advertising the importance of this on national TV and radio stations. NEMA should widen the means and scope of communication so they can reach more individuals. The agency should also involve the public sector. Businesses are impacted by disasters, and they have presence in social media. Not only will their customers be aware of disaster risk through them, but so will their employees.

Additionally, NEMA should liaise and collaborate with community-based organizations, faith-based organizations, and nongovernmental organizations at all phases of emergency management. These groups could promote public trust and enlightenment of not only their members but others. They already are identified by the agency as first responders, thus expanding their roles. Given that all actions in NEMA are taken at the federal level, the agency could use social media and the telephones, as identified in this chapter, to reach out to all levels of government and consequently involve the general citizens. This study also finds that the SEMAs and LEMAs have no link with one another. NEMA should promote a relationship among these two entities to enhance coordination and collaboration of activities.

References

Brody, S. D. 2003. Are We Learning to Make Better Plans? A Longitudinal Analysis of Plan Quality Associated with Natural Hazards. *Journal of Planning Education and Research*, 23: 191–201.

Brody, S. D., Godschalk, D. R., and Burby, R. J. 2003. Mandating Citizen Participation in Plan Making: Six Strategic Planning Choices. *Journal of the American Planning Association*, 69(3): 245–264.

Central Intelligence Agency (CIA). 2017. *The World Factbook*. Accessed on March 9, 2017 at www.cia.gov/library/publications/the-world-factbook/geos/ni.html.

Cottrell, A., Cunliffe, S., King, D., and Anderson-Berry, L. 2001. *Awareness and Preparedness for Natural Hazards in Remote Communities: Bloomfield River Region and Rossville*. Center for Disaster Studies. Townsville, Australia: James Cook University.

Driscoll, P., and Salween, M. B. 1996. Riding Out the Storm: Public Evaluation of News Coverage of Hurricane Andrew. *International Journal of Mass Emergencies and Disasters*, 14(3): 293–303.

Ephraim, P. E. 2013. African Youths and the Dangers of Social Networking: A Culture-Centered Approach to Using Social Media. *Ethics and Information Technology*, 15(4): 275–284.

Fabiyi, O. O., and Oloukoi, J. 2013. Indigenous Knowledge System and Local Adaptation Strategies to Flooding in Coastal Rural Communities of Nigeria. *Journal of Indigenous Social Development*, 1(2): 1–19.

Fasona, M. J., and Omojola, A. S. 2005. *Climate Change, Human Security and Communal Clashes in Nigeria*. Paper at International Workshop in Human Security and Climate Change, Holmen Fjord Hotel, Oslo, October 21–23.

Fischer, F. 2000. *Citizens, Experts and the Environment: The Politics of Local Knowledge*. Durham: Duke University Press.

Glass, J. J. 1979. Citizen Participation in Planning: The Relationship Between Objectives and Techniques. *Journal of the American Planning Association*, 45(2): 180–189.

Godschalk, D. R., Brody, S. D., and Burby, R. J. 2003. Public Participation in Natural Hazard Mitigation Policy Formation: Challenges for Comprehensive Planning. *Journal of Environmental Planning and Management*, 46(5): 733–754.

Kartez, J. D. 1984. Crisis Response Planning: Toward a Contingent Analysis. *Journal of the American Planning Association*, 50: 9–21.

Mileti, D. 1999. *Disasters by Design: A Reassessment of Natural Hazards in the United States; Natural Hazards and Disasters*. Washington, DC: National Academies Press.

Mileti, D., and O'Brien, P. 1992. *Warning During Disasters: Normalizing Communication Risk*. Emmitsburg, MD: National Emergency Training Center.

Nigerian Emergency Management Agency (NEMA). 2017. Accessed at http://nema.gov.ng/.

Ologunorisa, T. E., and Adeyemo, A. 2005. Public Perception of Flood Hazard in the Niger Delta, Nigeria. *The Environmentalist*, 25: 39–45.

Olonilua, O. 2016. State Mandate Influences on FEMA-Approved Hazard-Mitigation Plans Under the Disaster Management Act of 2000. *World Medical and Health Policy*, 8: 27–45.

Olonilua, O., and Ibitayo, O. 2011. Towards Multi-Hazard Mitigation: An Evaluation of FEMA-approved Hazard Mitigation Under the Disaster Mitigation Act of 2000 (DMA2K). *Journal of Emergency Management*, 9(1): 37–49.

———. 2014. An In-Depth Analysis of the Houston-Galveston Area Council Regional Hazard Mitigation Plan Under the Disaster Mitigation Act of 2000 (DMA2K). *Journal of Risks, Hazards, Crisis, and Public Policy*, 5(3): 316–341.

Perry, R., and Nelson, L. 1991. Ethnicity and Hazard Information Dissemination. *Environmental Management*, 15(4): 581–587.

Prater, C. S., and Lindell, M. K. 2000. Politics of Hazard Mitigation. *Natural Hazards Review*, 1(2): 73–82.

Scanlon, T. J. 1991. Reaching Out: Getting the Community Involved in Preparedness. In *Emergency Management: Principles and practice for Local Government*. (eds.) Thomas, E. Drabek, and Gerard, J. Hoetmer (eds.) Washington, DC: ICMA.

Soneye, A. 2014. An Overview of Humanitarian Relief Supply Chains for Victims of Perennial Flood Disasters in Lagos, Nigeria 2010–2012. *Journal of Humanitarian Logistics and Supply Chain Management*, 4(2): 179–197.

van Niekerk, D. 2015. Disaster Risk Governance in Africa: A Retrospective Assessment of Progress in Against the Hyogo Framework for Action 2000–2012. *Disaster Prevention and Management*, 24(3): 397–416.

Vatsa, K. S. 2004. Risk, Vulnerability, and Asset-Based Approach to Disaster Risk Management. *The International Journal of Sociology and Social Policy*, 24(10–11): 1–48.

Young, I. M. 2000. *Inclusion and Democracy*. Oxford: Oxford University Press.

Part 3

Role of risk communication in resilience

The *Sendai Framework for Disaster Risk Reduction 2015–2030* identified the need to develop and maintain a multi-hazard, multicultural, and people-centered forecasting and early warning system for disaster risk communication and community resilience (UN 2015). While traditional communication approaches are successful in enhancing individual resilience, their role in fostering resilience at the community scale is less clear cut. There remains a great deal of work to be done regarding the factors that affect community resilience before comprehensive strategies can be developed that incorporate communication into resilience building approaches.

Resilience, simply put, refers to bouncing back to an original state. Hazards and disaster research describe it as a process of increasing the adaptive capacity of individuals or communities so that they can return to a new normal after a disaster (McCubbin 2001; Klein, Nicholls, and Thomalla 2003; Paton and Johnston 2006). Community resilience is defined as the "capability of a community to anticipate risk, limit impact, and bounce back rapidly through survival, adaptability, evolution, and growth in the face of turbulent change" (Community and Regional Resilience Institute 2013: 10).

Given that a community can never be impervious to hazards, it is essential for communities to increase their resilience by (1) increasing public awareness of risk and the public's role in risk reduction; (2) assessing and communicating risk; (3) increasing stakeholder participation in policy preparation and implementation; and (4) sharing knowledge/information/lessons learned within a community and among different communities (UN 2004; Duval-Diopa, Curtis, and Clark 2010; National Research Council 2012). To create a truly resilient society, risk communication and resilience cannot be practiced in isolation but must be components of a single comprehensive system of mitigation and recovery.

From a systems perspective, the five components of resilience are: (1) redundancy – the availability of excess capacity and back-up systems to ensure the maintenance of core functionalities in the event of a disturbance; (2) robustness – the ability to absorb and withstand crisis and the presence of adaptive decision-making models to respond to changing conditions; (3) resourcefulness – the ability to adapt to a crisis by having the capacity of self-organization and innovation; (4) response – the ability to respond quickly during a crisis through effective communication and mechanisms that enable stakeholder participation to strengthen trust and ensure information sharing; and (5) recovery – the ability to adapt to new changes and to achieve a new *normal* after a crisis (Howell 2013). From a social science perspective, resilience is dependent on the following four interrelated components: (1) resourcefulness of a community, including its members, businesses, and social institutions; (2) ability of the community to mobilize sources to respond to a problem; (3) availability of mechanisms to integrate resources and adapt to the changes to recover from the crisis; and (4) the presence of strategies to ensure availability of resources and competency to address future crisis (Paton and Johnston 2006).

From these two views of resilience, it is evident that a community's resilience requires understanding the interdependencies among individuals, the community itself, and societal institutions to ensure adaptive capacity and resilience. It is also evident that communication is crucial to mobilizing the resources and undertaking actions to respond and recover from a disaster event. Without communication and access to information, stakeholders will not be involved in the resilience process. Without the real participation of stakeholders, it is not possible to quickly respond to a crisis or to ensure that risk reduction approaches are being implemented.

An effective risk communication requires development of a warning system that accurately detects and disseminates the information about the location and time of a hazard, potential risks, and implications. In addition to ensuring stakeholder participation, risk communication should also focus on designing warning messages, specifically, on message content and style, message delivery methods, and the socio-psychological characteristics of members of the public, such as risk awareness, risk perception, and prior experience, which eventually influence their decision to respond to warnings (Mileti and Peek 2000; NRC 2012; Kar et al. 2016).

This third section of this book highlights the current challenges in developing effective risk communication needed to develop community resilience. Chapter 8 focuses on an earthquake early warning system and the challenges of providing the necessary information to prepare communities to take risk reduction actions. In the event of such uncertainties, it is crucial to develop messages that can reach the broader community and to provide appropriate information through multiple channels to stakeholders. Chapter 9 further develops the issue of message preparation and presents solutions that might be implemented to overcome uncertainty in the decision-making process. Chapter 10 highlights the role of stakeholder participation in determining resilience for the purpose of communication and to increase risk awareness of impacted population in the context of sea ports along the Gulf of Mexico that are at risk from coastal hazards. Chapter 11 takes a different stance by focusing on the need for communication among stakeholders during the reconstruction process following an earthquake in China in order to expedite recovery and enhance stakeholder capacity to deal with future events.

References

Community and Regional Resilience Institute. 2013. *Definitions of Community Resilience: An Analysis*. A CARRI Report. Accessed on November 30, 2018 at www.resilientus.org/wp-content/uploads/2013/08/definitions-of-community-resilience.pdf.

Duval-Diopa, D., Curtis, A., and Clark, A. 2010. Enhancing Equity with Public Participatory GIS in Hurricane Rebuilding: Faith Based Organizations, Community Mapping, and Policy Advocacy. *Community Development*, 41(1): 32–49.

Howell, Lee. 2013. *Resilience: What It Is and Why It's Needed*. Accessed on 20 December 2018 at www.pwc.com/gx/en/governance-risk-compliance-consulting-services/resilience/publications/pdfs/ issue3/what_it_is_and_why_its_needed.pdf.

Kar, B., Cochran, D., Zale, J., Dickens, J., Liu, X., Callais, N., Gillespie, L., Knuth, C., and Bandi, V. 2016. Final Report: An Integrated Approach to Geo-Target At-Risk Communities and Deploy Effective Crisis Communication Approaches. Department of Homeland Security – Science and Technology Directorate. Accessed on 30 March 2019 at https://www.dhs.gov/publication/integrated-approach-geo-target-risk-communities-deploy-effective-crisis-communication.

Klein, R., Nicholls, R., and Thomalla, F. 2003. The Resilience of Coastal Megacities to Weather-Related Hazards. In *Building Safer Cities: The Future of Disaster Risk*. (eds.) A. Kreimer, M. Arnold, and A. Carlin. Washington, DC: The World Bank Disaster Management Facility.

McCubbin, L. 2001. *Challenges to the Definition of Resilience*. Paper Presented at the Annual Meeting of the American Psychological Association, San Francisco, CA.

Mileti, D. S., and Peek, L. 2000. The Social Psychology of Public Response to Warnings of a Nuclear Power Plant Accident. *Journal of Hazardous Materials*, 181–194.

National Research Council (NRC). 2012. *Disaster Resilience: A National Imperative*. Washington, DC: The National Academies Press.

Paton, D., and Johnston, D. 2006. *Disaster Resilience: An Integrated Approach*. Springfield, IL: Charles C. Thomas.

United Nations Inter-Agency Secretariat of the International Strategy for Disaster Reduction. 2004. *Living with Risk: A Global Review of Disaster Reduction Initiatives*. Geneva, Switzerland: UN Sales Publication.

United Nations Office for Disaster Reduction. Sendai Framework for Disaster Risk Reduction 2015–2030. 2015. In *Proceedings of the Third United Nations World Conference; United Nations Office for Disaster Reduction*. Geneva, Switzerland.

8 Earthquake early warning systems

International experience

Frances L. Edwards, Daniel C. Goodrich,
Margaret Hellweg, and Jennifer A. Strauss

Introduction

Earthquakes have long been considered instantaneous, self-notifying events, inca-pable of advanced warnings. Increasingly accurate sensors and faster computers, however, have facilitated the development of effective earthquake early warning systems (EEW) that provide warning information minutes or even seconds before an event. The technology is based on the speed difference between the P-waves and the S-waves created by fault ruptures (Ammon 2001). Japan Railway East (JR East) has been using this technology since the 1960s to stop bullet trains (*Shinkansen*) during earthquakes to prevent derailments. More recently, Japan has developed a public warning system using media broadcasts, computers, and cell phones to warn at-risk populations of impending seismic shaking (JR East 2009). The seismically active Palm Springs, California, area adopted a location-specific earthquake early warning (EEW) technology (SEWS) to speed fire department response in the 1980s (SWS 2015). Following the destructive and deadly Mexico City earthquake of 1985, Mexico developed a public earthquake early warning system (SASMEX) to give populations enough time to duck and cover safely (Fimrite 2017). Its benefits were demonstrated in the two earthquakes in 2017. Other seismically active nations, such as Taiwan and Turkey, have developed pub-lic warning systems based on similar technologies (Nakamura and Saita 2007a).

The U.S. Geological Survey (USGS), California Institute of Technology at Pas-adena (Caltech), University of California Berkeley (UC Berkeley), University of Oregon, University of Washington, California Office of Emergency Services, and other actors are partnering to create a public warning network (ShakeAlert) for the heavily populated, earthquake-prone metropolitan regions of Los Angeles and San Francisco, as well as adjacent areas along the West Coast of the United States (Allen 2013). EEW enhances resilience by developing public risk communication strategies that educate the mainstream public about the meaning of warnings and appropriate responses to them. Automated systems stop BART trains and can be used to warn the affected population to duck and cover or take other immediate protective measures.

EEW has proven to be effective for stopping bullet trains in Japan and opening fire station doors in Palm Springs. Challenges remain, however, in developing effective public warning systems near the epicenter of an earthquake (USGS 2016) and the high cost of developing and maintaining public warning systems in general (Fimrite 2017). These challenges mirror the public policy debate regarding the purpose of EEW as primarily for real-time earthquake engineering (RTEE), necessary for immediate response after P-wave arrival or real-time seismology (RTS), which provides highly accurate but not immediate information about earthquakes (Nakamura and Saita 2007a). This tension affects the design of EEW systems and the level of investment in their construction. Resilience depends on both.

The science of earthquakes[1]

In the mid-20th century, scientists determined that the Earth is made up of more than a dozen separate tectonic plates. The movement and collision of these plates leads to the build-up of pressure and fault lines, or ruptures within the plates, which cause earthquakes (Kious and Tilling 2008). The bigger the earthquake is, the larger the area of a fault line that ruptures, the greater the shift between the sides of the fault line, and the longer the earthquake takes to happen. Like waves in a pond, the seismic waves spread out through the Earth.

There are two types of body waves that make earthquake early warning systems possible. Primary, or P-waves, travel through rock near the earth's surface at about 6 kilometers per second (km/s). Secondary, or S-waves, travel at about 3 km/s, or half the speed of the P-waves. Buildings are designed to withstand the vertical force of gravity and are relatively insensitive to P-waves, while the S-waves cause significant damage. Given that the P-waves travel more quickly, they arrive at a seismic sensor in advance of the damaging S-waves (Ammon 2001). For example, during the September 7, 2017, magnitude 8.1 earthquake that occurred 75 miles off the Pacific coast of Mexico near the state of Chiapas, the EEW system gave people in Mexico City about 90 seconds warning, allowing them to duck and cover (Fimrite 2017). Table 8.1 shows the impact of distance on the time between the arrival of the P-wave and the S-wave (warning time).

Earthquakes vary greatly in size and intensity. The Richter scale is used to describe the amount of energy that is released at the earthquake's point of rupture,

Table 8.1 September 7, 2017, Chiapas, Mexico, SASMEX warnings

City	Distance from epicenter (kilometers)	Warning time
Oaxaca	160 km	13 seconds
Puebla	429 km	63 seconds
Acapulco	458 km	70 seconds
Mexico City	525 km	88 seconds
Guadalajara	960 km	190 seconds

Source: SASMEX 2017

called the magnitude (M). For example, the 2017 earthquake near Chiapas, Mexico, was a Richter magnitude 8.1. Each time an earthquake's magnitude goes up by one unit (M 3.0 to M 4.0) the scaled quantity gets larger. It is now known that while the amplitude of the record from one earthquake is 10 times larger than that of another, the energy released by the first earthquake is about 32 times greater, so the energy released by an M 4.0 is 32 times greater than the amount of energy released by an M 3.0 earthquake. Seismologists now prefer to use the moment magnitude scale (Mw), particularly for larger earthquakes. A quake's moment increases with the area of the rupture zone and the amount of offset, and scales approximately with the energy. For example, the rupture of the M 9.1 earthquake in the Indian Ocean on December 26, 2004, covered 199,947 square kilometers (77,200 square miles). The moment can be determined by estimating the size of the rupture zone from the locations of aftershocks, or it can be modeled using seismic or global positioning system (GPS) recordings (Exploratorium 2013) of the earthquake.

While an earthquake has a single moment magnitude, local shaking intensity in the same earthquake varies, as shown in Table 8.2. The Modified Mercalli scale is used to describe the impact of the earthquake in a particular area. The intensity

Table 8.2 Modified Mercalli intensity scale

Intensity	Effect on People and Property
I	Rarely felt by people except in special circumstances.
II	Felt by a few at rest, especially on upper floors of buildings.
III	Felt by people indoors and on upper floors; vibrations similar to a passing truck.
IV	Felt indoors and sometimes outdoors; cars rock; dishes, windows, and doors disturbed; walls make cracking sound.
V	Felt by everyone; dishes and windows may break, unstable objects may overturn, pendulum clocks may stop.
VI	Felt by all; heavy furniture moves, plaster may fall, slight damage.
VII	Damage negligible in buildings of good design and construction; slight to moderate in well-built ordinary structures; considerable damage in poorly built or badly designed structures; some chimneys broken.
VIII	Damage slight in specially designed structures; considerable damage in ordinary substantial buildings with partial collapse. Damage great in poorly built structures. Fall of chimneys, factory stacks, columns, monuments, walls. Heavy furniture overturned.
IX	Damage considerable in specially designed structures; well-designed frame structures thrown out of plumb. Damage great in substantial buildings, with partial collapse. Buildings shifted off foundations.
X	Some well-built wooden structures destroyed; most masonry and frame structures destroyed with foundations. Rails bent.
XI	Few, if any (masonry) structures remain standing. Bridges destroyed. Rails bent greatly.
XII	Damage total. Lines of sight and level are distorted. Objects thrown into the air.

Source: USGS 2013b

changes depending on distance from the fault and the geology and surface conditions at the site. For example, mud will amplify the shaking, while bedrock near the surface will dampen shaking (USGS 2013b).

Scientists at the U.S. Geological Survey's (USGS) National Earthquake Information Center (NEIC) have asked the public to join them in collecting information about earthquakes. The Did You Feel It? website allows anyone to register how much shaking they felt for a specific event. The information is sometimes added to the Shake Map, which shows intensity and extent of shaking. These observations contribute information to guide the Federal Emergency Management Agency's (FEMAs) response to earthquake disaster events (Welch 2013).

Monitoring earthquakes

Historical seismographs and warning systems

The earliest mention of a seismic sensor comes from China, where Chang Heng developed the first seismoscope in AD 132. European interest in seismoscopes increased in the late 1700s due to a series of earthquakes around the Mediterranean Sea. These primitive instruments were pendulum systems that could etch recordings but provided no time information. Early attempts at incorporating temporal information involved basins of mercury, such as those in use by Cavalli in 1784 and Mallet in 1851. In the late 1800s, seismographs, which provide a written record of shaking as a function of time in one form or another, were invented. The earliest seismographs employed pendulums and were built in Italy by Filippo Cecchi in 1875. Soon after, large advances in damping and recording resulted in improved instrumentation, developed by Milne, Ewing, Gray, Omori, and Wiechert. The modern seismometers in use today have digital output, recording relative motion with respect to the Earth as a function of time (Lay and Wallace 1995). Dr. J.D. Cooper of San Francisco purportedly first proposed the idea of an earthquake early warning system. On November 3, 1868, he wrote a letter to the editor of the *San Francisco Daily Evening Bulletin* suggesting the development of an automatic electrical sensor system, using the city's existing telegraph lines to warn the public of an impending earthquake through the use of an alarm bell to be triggered by electrical current over the telegraph wires (Nakamura and Saita 2007b). He proposed such a system after the 1868 earthquake on the Hayward fault as a means to protect the population of San Francisco during future earthquakes. Although the technology of the time did not permit development of the envisioned telegraph-based system, the first seismic network in the Western Hemisphere was installed less than 10 years later by UC Berkeley, with two stations, one on the Berkeley campus and one at the Mt. Hamilton Observatory near San Jose (Berkeley Seismic Laboratory 2017).

Seismology through international networks

The next major step in earthquake monitoring came when the United States and Russia (then the Union of Soviet Socialist Republics) concluded the Test Ban

Treaty of 1963. Verification of treaty compliance required the installation of sensors that could distinguish between earthquakes smaller than M 4.75 and nuclear tests. The Worldwide Standardized Seismographic Network (WWSSN) was created in 1963, with 75 stations in 40 countries and in 20 U.S. states (Powell and Fries 1964), and could accurately map earthquakes as well.

The National Earthquake Information Center (NEIC) was created in 1966 in Rockville, Maryland. It merged with the USGS and moved to Golden, Colorado, at the Front Range of the Rocky Mountains, where there is a lower seismic hazard than other areas of the west, making for a more resilient location (Welch 2013). The focus of NEIC is to collect and disseminate information to scientists, first responders, Red Cross, USAID and other governmental and nongovernmental bodies, the media, and the public. The seismic networks from which the NEIC collects information are worldwide and rely upon international agreements for data sharing (Welch 2013).

The Global Seismographic Network (GSN) was established in 1984. This partnership between the USGS, the National Science Foundation, and the Incorporated Research Institutions for Seismology (IRIS) provides a permanent digital network of global instruments for monitoring and research. Currently, the GSN includes over 150 modern seismic stations around the world. In 1997, the U.S. Congress authorized the development of a "real-time seismic warning system" for the United States (USGS 2013a). In the summer of 2000, strong motion instruments for the Advanced National Seismic System (ANSS) were installed in San Francisco, Salt Lake City, and Seattle. More than 100 additional instruments were installed in other locations over the next two years (USGS 2013a).

Placement of the sensors is determined by the goal of the system. General monitoring of nuclear tests, or of earthquakes in general, does not require a specific location to be successful. Knowing that the event occurred and its magnitude is the goal, with speed of reporting an incidental factor. In order to create an EEW that triggers a meaningful alarm for the population, however, the sensors have to be placed as near to the fault as possible to allow the maximum time between P-wave detection and the arrival of the damaging S-waves. In areas where the major faults are under the ocean, such as Japan, placing the sensors on the coastline allows for the earliest detection of the arriving P-wave and rapid warning dissemination. For example, in 2011 the fault rupture occurred 200 miles from the coast, creating a significant difference between the arrival of the P-wave at 6 km/h and the S-wave at 3 km/h. However, when cities are built on top or close to the fault lines, as in California's major metropolitan areas, the distance between the rupture and the population center is relatively small, shrinking the time difference between the arrival of the P-wave at 6 km/h and the S-wave at 3 km/h. This different in warning times was demonstrated during the Chiapas Earthquake of 2017 (see Table 8.1).

California's earthquake monitoring projects

California developed a strong motion instrumentation program (SB 1374) following the 1971 Sylmar earthquake. Additional funding (SB 593) was provided after the Whittier Narrows Earthquake of 1987. The goal was to collect data on build-ing performance during earthquake-induced shaking to enable engineers to design more earthquake-resistant structures. Accelerographs were installed in 650 loca-tions representing various types of soil, and earthquake monitoring devices were installed in 170 buildings (including hospitals and essential services buildings) and on 20 dams and 60 bridges. The California Strong Motion Instrumentation Program (CSMIP) is based at the California Geological Survey (CGS). It uses real-time telemetry as well as dial-up modems and, at a few sites still, the collec-tion of paper records, to aggregate data after an earthquake. For example, data collected on shaking near the fault during the Northridge Earthquake was used to improve the Uniform Building Code for structures in near-fault zones and to guide the development of more earthquake-resistant building design (California Geological Survey 2013).

The California Integrated Seismic Network (CISN) was formed in 2000 by the USGS offices in Menlo Park and Pasadena; Caltech Seismological Labora-tory; Berkeley Seismological Laboratory; the California Geological Survey; and the Governor of California's Office of Emergency Services (CalOES) to monitor earthquakes as one of the eight regional networks making up the ANSS. The CISN provides earthquake information as well as dedicated software for receiving and viewing earthquake information: CISN Display and ShakeCast. CISN Display provides software-based rapid maps of earthquake information for emergency response including ShakeMap, special reports, and links to external products, such as HAZUS, which overlays information on community infrastructure and construction (Welch 2013). ShakeCast distributes ShakeMaps and includes post-earthquake automatic notification to users about the event and its relationship to their infrastructure. For example, the California Department of Transportation (Caltrans) uses ShakeCast maps overlaid on Caltrans' infrastructure inventory to help engineers select which overpasses and bridges should be inspected first after an earthquake (Lissade 2010).

Recent USGS advances: PAGER and EEW

NEIC has recently developed PAGER (Prompt Assessment of Global Earthquakes Response) to provide a rapid estimation of possible fatalities and economic losses due to an event. This has greatly added to the available information for post-event hazard analysis and response. The suite of available earthquake information products was rounded out by the addition of the USGS Earthquake Notification System (ENS). This alert service has more than 350,000 subscribers who receive post-event notice of an earthquake in areas they select, using email, text mes-sages, and Twitter. ENS gives the magnitude, location, and depth of earthquakes anywhere in the world (Welch 2013).

In 2006, the USGS supported Phase I of the development and testing of real-time algorithms for EEW in California in partnership with Berkeley and Caltech, the Southern California Earthquake Center and the Federal Technical Institute in Zurich, Switzerland. The *proof of concept* event for the system was the magnitude

5.4 Alum Rock earthquake on October 30, 2007, at 8:04 p.m. local time. The earthquake's epicenter was near San Jose, and the system sent a warning to the scientists 5 seconds before peak shaking was felt in San Francisco, about 50 miles away.

Phase II of the project began in 2009 with the implementation of an end-to-end test or *demonstration* system, which integrated the previously tested methods into a single prototype warning system called ShakeAlert. (Burkett, Given, Douglas, and Jones 2014). ShakeAlert became fully operational in 2011 based on data from 400 seismic sensors throughout the state operated by the CISN and its partners. Alerts are sent out in real time to beta users running the UserDisplay. The beta users include scientists, emergency managers, and the Bay Area Rapid Transit system (BART), among others. The UserDisplay is a Java applet that runs on a computer desktop. It provides information about the magnitude, location, and estimated shaking intensity at a user-configured location and a countdown of the time until the S-wave arrives at that location.

Phase III of ShakeAlert

Phase III commenced in January of 2012 with the support of a $6 million grant from the Gordon and Betty Moore Foundation awarded jointly to USGS, Caltech, UC Berkeley, and the University of Washington. This grant enabled the expansion of the California demonstration system into a prototype for the entire West Coast (USGS 2011). Many algorithm improvements, speed enhancements, and UserDisplay updates were implemented during the ongoing Phase III. One of ShakeAlert's three algorithms, ElarmS, now only requires 100 milliseconds of P-wave data to start the calculations. As a result, for the La Habra earthquake, on March 28, 2014, scientists only 30 kilometers (18.64 miles) from the epicenter in Pasadena received 4 seconds of warning before the arrival of the shaking from the S-wave. BART uses EEW so that trains automatically decelerate once an alert from ShakeAlert is received. "Within 24 seconds we can get the train to a complete stop" (Witze 2014). During the past few years, several small earthquakes (~M 3) that occurred close to the epicenter of the 1989 Loma Prieta rupture were detected by ShakeAlert. "[A]lerts were provided around 20 seconds before peak ground motion arrived in San Francisco, Oakland and Berkeley – illustrating what would be possible in a repeat of the devastating 1989 quake" (Allen 2013). Thus, ample time would be available to slow or stop most trains in the areas where BART operates and prevent catastrophic derailments.

Figure 8.1 shows a simulation of the Loma Prieta earthquake. The house is the user's location, the dot represents the epicenter and the outer and inner circles are the P-wave and S-wave fronts, respectively. It displays the calculated 23 seconds until the S-wave reaches the user's location, the expected moderate shaking intensity V, and the estimated magnitude of 6.9.

Recently, ShakeAlert developers have begun to incorporate data from GPS to measure the gross movement of the Earth's plates as the rupture unfolds. The satellites are part of the U.S. Department of Defense's Nav Star System, which

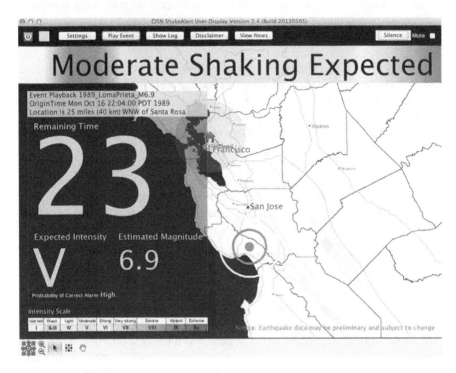

Figure 8.1 ShakeAlert's user display

consists of 21 satellites orbiting 20,000 kilometers (12,427 miles) above the Earth (USGS 2010). For EEW, real-time analysis of plate motion allows for better magnitude estimations for the largest earthquakes, which is important for ensuring that all affected municipalities receive appropriate early warning.

Quake Catcher Network

Elizabeth Cochran, a seismologist with USGS, and Lawrence Jesse of Stanford University operate the Quake Catcher Network (QCN) to broaden the range of earthquake data collection. People are invited to voluntarily join the distributed computing network by purchasing a sensor for $50, plugging it into the USB ports on their computers, and orienting their computers to magnetic North so that data describing the full movement of the Earth at the site can be collected (QCN 2014). Mobile devices can also be part of the network, although the data collection is more limited. The data is communicated from each volunteer's computer to Stanford's server using the user's existing Internet connection.

People in 67 countries are members of QCN (Smolan and Erwitt 2012). Stanford's servers analyze the shaking information from multiple sites to better understand the distribution of shaking intensities (Cochran 2014). This system helped to detect and warn of Chile's M 8.8 earthquake in 2010; the M 6.3 earthquake in Christchurch, New Zealand, in 2011; and an M 4.0 earthquake near Berkeley in 2012 (Smolar and Erwitt 2012).

Cochran plans to add smartphones to the QCN to better serve poor countries and to harden the wireless connections in more developed nations (Smolan and Erwitt 2012). A UNESCO report from 2014 estimates that 6 billion people, out of a global population of 7 billion, have access to mobile phones (UNESCO 2014). While not as precise as the seismological accelerometers, QCN's value is in gathering data from areas without one of the 400 CISN sensors. QCN sensors can also be used to blanket an area after an earthquake to collect data on aftershocks. For example, after the Christchurch earthquake in New Zealand, 180 of these sensors were deployed in the epicentral region (Ransom 2011).

History of earthquake early warning systems in Japan

High-speed rail and EEW

The first strong motion seismograph was developed in Japan in 1953, 80 years after J.D. Cooper wrote a letter to the editor in the *San Francisco Daily Evening Bulletin* outlining his vision for an earthquake early warning system. Following the 1964 Niigata earthquake (M 7.5), the need for a comprehensive warning system for the *Shinkansen* (bullet trains) was recognized. The earthquake of Shizuoka (M 6.1) in 1965 caused some damage to the newly completed railway structures, so a proto-earthquake warning system was put into place "with ordinary alarm seismometers and waveform recording seismometers" (Nakamura and Saita 2007a). Sensors were placed at 20 to 25 kilometer (12.4 to 15.5 mile) intervals along the railroad track to monitor ground acceleration in real time. The seismometers were set to alarm if the horizontal ground acceleration exceeded 40 Gals (1 Gal = 1 cm/s^2, or one thousandth the acceleration of gravity) (Ghasemi et al. 1996). This level was chosen to avoid false alarms from small quakes and passing trains.

Public alerting

This on-site warning system served the rail lines well, but a true early warning system for the population of Japan (such as that envisioned by Dr. Cooper for San Francisco in 1868) required a coastline detection system and public alerts. The Japan Meteorological Agency (JMA) installed a coastline system that began operation in 1982 using a triggered S-wave detection system similar to the on-site warning system used for the *Shinkansen* (Nakamura and Saita 2007a). A similar triggered warning system was created in Mexico in 1991 to alert citizens of Mexico City to expected shaking from earthquakes in the Pacific Ocean along the southern and southwestern coastlines. A similar system was implemented in Istanbul, Turkey, on the bridge over the Straits of Bosporus (Nakamura and Saita 2007a).

P-wave detection methods provide earthquake early warning because they do not require strong ground shaking to trigger. They can provide warning information based on the compressional P-wave alone. Called UrEDAS (Urgent Earthquake Detection and Alarm System) in Japan, the system could issue a warning three seconds after a P-wave was detected. Tests of the front-facing P-wave detector prototype began in 1984. It was operational on the Tokaido Shinkansen line in 1992 and the Sanyo Shinkansen in 1996. Its installation included an automatic train control system, which cut off electricity to the trains and applied the brake. Installation along the various *Shinkansen* routes continued through 1998 (Smith 2003; Nakamura and Saita 2007a).

EEW in the Kobe Quake

The Great Hanshin Awaji Earthquake of 1995, also known as the Kobe earthquake, resulted in significant damage to the region's transportation infrastructure. The UrEDAS and the on-site alarm system both issued alarms, but the UrEDAS warning "did not arrive at the target area due to transmission failure . . . showing the difficulty of controlling" messages to the trains from remote locations (Nakamura and Saita 2007b). The on-site combined S-wave and P-wave alarm system, known as the Compact UrEDAS, was developed soon after with the goal of increasing early warning times for trains. The system combined a new estimation algorithm with a system that included a velocity meter, an accelerometer, and a computer processing unit (Odaka et al. 2006). The Compact UrEDAS was designed to "issue the alarm within one second of P-wave arrival" (Nakamura and Saita 2007b). In 1997, JR East installed 56 sets of the Compact UrEDAS for the *Shinkansen* lines but with only the S-wave alarm actively used. In 1998, the system was adjusted to be an "along-the-railroad, on-site, P-wave detection system" (Nakamura and Saita 2007b: 308). By combining the P-wave and S-wave detectors the Compact UrEDAS "achieves both rapidity and reliability" (Nakamura and Saita 2007a: 266). The new Compact UrEDAS was installed on the Tohoku, Joetsu, and Nagano Shinkansen Lines and eventually also on the Tokyo subway system (2001) (Nakamura and Saita 2007a).

Japan EEW test cases

On May 26, 2003, the Sanriku-Minami (M 7.0) earthquake, also called Miyagiken-Oki, occurred in the northern part of Miyagi Prefecture. The Tohoku Shinkansen line received warning from the Coastline Compact UrEDAS front detection system using a P-wave alarm, which was issued within 3 seconds, and the alarm reached the line before the P-wave's arrival. Two high-speed trains in operation at the time received the warnings. The warning system performed as expected, with the Coastline UrEDAS issuing the first P-wave alarm, followed by the three Compact UrEDAS sensors along the *Shinkansen* line (Nakamura and Saita 2007b).

On Sunday, October 23, 2004, the Niigata-ken Chuetsu earthquake (M 6.8) occurred at 5:56 p.m., with the epicenter almost under the *Shinkansen* tracks. This reduced the available early warning time due to the proximity of the fault rupture. The earthquake caused 35 deaths and 3,183 injuries. In addition, 6,000 buildings were damaged or destroyed and 1,300 landslides occurred (ABS Consulting 2004). It caused "the most extensive structural damage that JR East has suffered" (East Japan Railway Company 2005: 44) up to that time. Damage occurred at 86 locations on five conventional train lines, but the worst event was the first-ever derailment of a *Shinkansen* train, which occurred between Muikamachi and Nagaoka. While none of the 154 passengers was injured, eight of the ten cars derailed, and 900 meters (984 yards) of rail line were damaged (East Japan Railway Company 2005).

The P-wave sensor cut power to the train at 3.9 seconds after the fault rupture began, which caused the brakes to be applied automatically. The driver also put on the emergency brake when he recognized the Compact UrEDAS alarm that states, "emergency braking resulting from power disruption" (Iwamura 2014). "The S-wave hit the train 2.5 seconds after the alarm, and one second later strong shaking hit the train, which continued for about 5 seconds" (Nakamura and Saita 2007b: 244). Because the train was already slowing for a station stop, the 2.5 seconds warning from the alarm allowed for additional slowing and was enough to avoid a catastrophic derailment (Railway Gazette International 2007) when the train encountered the section of track that had been displaced by the rupture. This demonstrated the value of even a brief warning period (Nakamura and Saita 2007b: 275). Regardless of the relative success of the Compact UrEDAS warnings, JR East "invested 1 billion yen ($9.5 million) to upgrade its earthquake detection systems as part of its 2009–2013 Safety Vision program" (East Japan Railway Company 2013, 15). The Early Earthquake Detection System (EEDS), shown in Figure 8.2 (Hiraoka 2011), was the result of this investment: "the fastest early warning system in the world to detect P-waves" (Ono 2014).

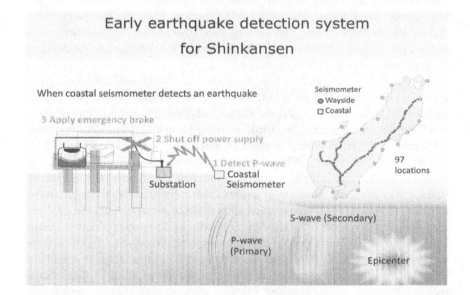

Figure 8.2 Early earthquake detection system for *Shinkansen*

Case study of EEW: the Great East Japan earthquake

Triple disaster: earthquake, tsunami, nuclear reactor

In March 2011, the Tohoku region of Japan suffered a triple disaster: the largest earthquake in recent Japanese history at moment magnitude (M_w) 9.0, (Kobayashi, Mizuno, and Ishibashi 2012), the catastrophic tsunami, and the flooding of the Fukushima Nuclear Power Plant, which led to the release of radioactive materials (Okada and Comfort 2011; Coleman et al. 2012). The JR East system served the disaster area with both its famous high-speed rail system (Tohoku Shinkansen) and a coastal rail line that connected the farmers and fishermen of the region with the markets of metropolitan Tokyo. While the mitigation and preparedness measures taken by the government were very successful in withstanding the shaking of the earthquake, flooding from the tsunami overwhelmed both mitigation measures and community preparedness activities and led to the catastrophic failure of the nuclear power plant reactor (Birmingham and McNeill 2012).

Among all the destruction, one success stood out: the JR East system's mitigation measures, including the earthquake early detection system (EEDS). Although the tsunami damaged most of the coastal rail line and washed five unoccupied trains off the tracks (Iwamura 2013), its flooding did not extend inland to the high-speed rail line (Kobayashi et al. 2012), which suffered no loss of life or rolling stock and relatively little damage (Tenemura 2012), considering the size of the earthquake. This success was built on a combination of robust mitigation and preparedness activities that included the automatic shut-off of electricity and braking for the *Shinkansen* trains, triggered by the EEDS.

Earthquakes are a daily threat in Japan, which sits at the junction of four tectonic plates: The Eurasian Plate, the North American Plate, the Philippine Plate, and the Pacific Plate. In the 20th century alone, there were 13 significant earthquakes, resulting in more than 150,000 deaths and the collapse of "hundreds of thousands of buildings" (Bressan 2011).

On March 11, 2011, at 2:46 p.m. local time, an M 9.0 earthquake occurred about 70 kilometers (43.5 miles) off the east coast of Japan beneath the floor of the Pacific Ocean, where the Pacific Plate is subducting under the North American Plate, setting off a cascading triple disaster (Table 8.3). The JMA's upgraded $600 million EEW, in operation since October 2007, (Alfred E. Alquist Seismic Safety Commission 2008) informed residents of the impending shaking, using cell phones and computer screens as well as TV and radio. The immediate shaking was felt over hundreds of square kilometers, with buildings in Tokyo swaying. Residents of Tokyo received 30 seconds or more warning through text messages sent to cell phones, factories received emails to stop production, (Smolan and Erwitt 2012) and people near the earthquake received 5 to 10 seconds warning (Nyquist 2012). When sensors detect a P-wave, the computer calculates its size then sends out the appropriate warnings. On March 11, 2011, that process took 8.6 seconds, which provided valuable warning time (Smolan and Erwitt 2012).

Table 8.3 Great East Japan earthquake facts

Origin time:	March 11, 2011, 2:46 p.m. local time
Magnitude	M 9.0
Tsunami height:	9.3 meters (over 31 feet)
Major damage:	Fukushima Power Plant inundated, lost power, led to radioactive material leaks
Casualties:	18,000 people dead or missing
Damage area:	500 km² (193 square miles) damage to Tohoku area
Damage cost:	16.9 trillion yen in damage (US $188 billion) = 3% GDP or 18% annual government budget
Global effects:	Balance of trade impact limited, as area accounts for only 2.5% of Japanese economy

Source: Kanno 2013

Because the earthquake occurred at a relatively shallow depth, it created a tsunami with a run-up of almost 38 meters (124 feet). It devastated coastal communities, ports, and transportation systems, including the coastline trains and tracks of JR East, with four trains being unaccounted for at one time (Findlay 2011). The *Shinkansen* was too far inland to be reached by the tsunami (Kobayashi et al. 2012). The third disaster was the inundation of the Fukushima Daiichi power plant by the tsunami wave, which damaged the reactors.

Earthquake early warning in the triple disaster

When the earthquake occurred on March 11, 2011, there were 239 seismometers in the EEDS (Kanno 2013). It "combined the functions of UrEDAS and Compact UrEDAS . . . after the P-wave detection, [EEDS] can issue the alarm within one second and estimate the earthquake parameters in one second" (Nakamura and Saita 2007a: 307). It integrates UrEDAS, Compact UrEDAS, and AcCo functions, and has replaced the earlier sensor systems (Iwamura 2014). In the first second after the P-wave detection, it can "estimate the earthquake parameters . . . can judge the dangerousness of the earthquake motion . . . and can disseminate information and alarms based on acceleration and RI ["realtime intensity"] in real-time" (Nakamura and Saita 2007a: 322). The system cuts the electricity to the *Shinkansen*'s overhead wire, and the ATC (automatic train control) unit aboard the train applies the emergency brake when the power is disrupted. To prevent false positives, four sensors must be triggered for the power to be cut (Ono 2014).

On March 11, 2011, a *Shinkansen* train running through the Sendai area was traveling at 270 km/h (168 mph) when the P-wave reached the sensor. In 3 seconds, while the train traveled 225 meters (246 yards), the power supply was stopped and the emergency brakes deployed. In 70 seconds, when the largest vibration occurred, the train had traveled 4 kilometers (2.5 miles) total since the arrival of the P-wave and had dropped its speed to 100 km/h (63 mph). In 100 seconds after the brake was applied, it had traveled a total of 4.4 kilometers (2.7

miles) and stopped safely. This rapid deceleration prevented a derailment (Kanno 2013).

For local use in specific facilities, AcCo, a palmtop seismometer, was developed. It "can indicate not only acceleration, but also the world's first real-time intensity" (Nakamura and Saita 2007a: 318). It is recommended for use in schools and factories. Because of its ease of use and portability, the AcCo earthquake detection system is used by the Tokyo fire department to detect aftershocks during post-earthquake rescue operations (Nakamura and Saita 2007a: 323). Its first practical use by the Tokyo Fire Department was in rescue operations after the 2005 Pakistan earthquake. It has now been adopted in Japan, the Philippines, and Taiwan, as well as by the Tokyo subway system (Nakamura and Saita 2007a).

Earthquake early warning system: success and challenges

Efforts to create EEW

Japan's greatest earthquakes occur off its east coast in a subduction zone. Oregon, Washington, and northern California share a similar hazard with the Cascadia Subduction Zone off their western shores. The heavily populated areas around the San Francisco Bay and Los Angeles are more directly threatened by the San Andreas Fault system, which can generate great earthquakes with magnitudes of 8.0 and above, and with associated high shaking intensities (Bose and Heaton 2010). The Alfred E. Alquist Seismic Safety Commission has issued a report suggesting that "the [s]tate (California) should make a detailed and interdisciplinary evaluation of Japan's Earthquake Early Warning System, track its progress on how effectively it provides warnings to the public in Japan, and then evaluate the feasibility of implementation in California" (Alfred E. Alquist Seismic Safety Commission 2008). The success of the system in Japan's largest earthquake demonstrates the effectiveness of both the JMA EEW public warning system (RTS) and the JR East EEDS (RTEE) *Shinkansen* protection system. JR East's trains had 70 seconds to slow down before the damaging S-waves arrived; trains slowed down from 270 km/hour (168 mph) to 100 km/hour (63 mph), and there was no derailment (Kanno 2013). The combination of accelerometers to provide the P- and S-wave information and operational emergency braking logic have served the Japanese system well, and their history of almost 50 years of continuous operation without a single fatality is commendable.

Bose and Heaton (2010) of Caltech noted that most EEW systems in operation today use an algorithm with "a fixed time window of a couple of seconds of the seismic P-wave for a rapid estimate of the earthquake magnitude" (2010: 1015). This is what triggers the alarm used by JR East to interrupt the power to trains and apply the brake. Their concern with this approach is that it does not characterize the length of the fault rupture, which is an important predictor of the ultimate size of the earthquake and associated length of time of the shaking. The length of shaking, the intensity of the shaking, and the size of the impacted area are all critical factors for response and recovery operations. As Bose and Heaton (2010) state, "the decision on [how] the EEW system [should be designed] is clearly user specific, and depends on (1) the vulnerability of the considered facility, and (2) the costs of the case of over- or under-estimated ground shaking" (Bose and Heaton 2010: 1028).

According to Kuyuk and others (2014), the latest generation of ShakeAlert ElarmS (E2) uses improved algorithms that "maximize the current seismic network's configuration, hardware and software . . . improving both the speed of the early warning processing and the accuracy of the warnings" (Kuyuk et al. 2014: 1). The improved speed allows an alert to be issued in as little as 3.73 seconds after the first P-wave detection and can be shorter in areas with a denser array of monitoring stations. E2 is using the existing ShakeAlert system to distribute the warnings to test users (Kuyuk et al. 2014).

RTEE and RTS in JAPAN

Based on their experience, the Japanese have separated their earthquake warning systems into two categories: Real-time seismology (RTS) and real-time earthquake engineering (RTEE), each with a distinct application. Nakamura and Saita (2007a) suggest that RTS is needed to give the public and first responders information on "rational action after the earthquake has terminated," while RTEE "is necessary for immediate response after the earthquake occurrence or earthquake motion arrival" (Nakamura and Saita 2007a: 310). They further differentiate the quality of information that is needed for each application, with RTS focusing on "highly accurate but not immediate information," (310) while RTEE needs a rapid alarm and intervention to prevent secondary disasters, like train derailments (Nakamura and Saita 2007a). Therefore, the Japanese have two systems for earthquake monitoring. The large network operated by the JMA EEW collects data over a wide area to enable complete characterization of the seismic event while offering warning to the public and information for emergency responders for post-quake countermeasures. Furthermore, RTS is essential for the greater understanding of the parameters of seismic events, which leads to more rapid seismic detection in the long run, leading in turn to further enhancements of the RTEE system.

For RTEE, JR East operates its own EEDS with along-the-railroad sensors, for example, to ensure rapid engagement of the electricity shut-off and braking application for the *Shinkansen* trains to prevent derailments. Nakamura and Saita (2007b) generalize the requirements of RTEE systems, listing six essential characteristics. They must be "fully automated," "quick and reliable," "small and cheap," "independent of other systems," and "easy to connect to network," and accuracy is desirable but not essential for an alarm (Nakamura and Saita 2007b: 278).

RTS and RTEE in the U.S.: government-sponsored RTS and RTEE development

RTS systems are in use in countries with active seismic hazards, including Turkey, Mexico, Italy, Romania, Taiwan, and as a production prototype system in the

United States (Nakamura and Saita 2007a). The American system, a joint RTS and RTEE system called West Coast ShakeAlert, is operated through the collaboration of several organizations with both academic and seismological expertise, including UC Berkeley, Caltech, USGS, with the recent addition of the University of Washington. Their efforts are focused on furthering scientific understanding of earthquakes and accurately estimating their magnitudes, locations, and levels of damage.

The West Coast ShakeAlert prototype production early warning system is currently in Phase IV and involves the USGS, the California Office of Emergency Services, UC Berkeley, Caltech, the University of Washington, and more than 80 individual corporations and public emergency management organizations in California, Oregon, and Washington. ShakeAlert uses the CISN and PNSN networks as a backbone and will issue alerts to the public, government, and private sector with no subscription fee required. One of the early adopters was BART, which now automatically slows and stops its trains when alerted by ShakeAlert. Google has integrated ShakeAlert into its emergency operations center. San Francisco Department of Emergency Management (DEM) is working with city agencies to facilitate integration of alerts, in particular with the San Francisco Fire Department (to open the bay doors), with the police department, and with public works to enable workers on projects near heavy machinery to take safe action. San Francisco hospitals, data centers, hazardous materials facilities, and the local airports are also developing automated procedures based on ShakeAlert warnings. These actions can be tailored to particular uses to enhance disaster warning and facilitate response efforts.

More sensors will be needed to provide adequate monitoring for the entire West Coast. In California, an EEDS would have to be aligned with California's fault lines, which are primarily not off the coast, with the accelerometers placed to detect fault movement at the earliest possible instant. In addition, some sensors must be more broadly distributed to detect earthquake sources from more broadly spread or unknown faults, like those that ruptured in the Sylmar (1971), Coalinga (1983), and Northridge (1994) earthquakes.

The ShakeAlert early warning system, based on the 200 stations of the CISN and another 540 installed for ShakeAlert, (Fimrite 2017) has demonstrated the capabilities of such a system in both densely and less densely instrumented regions. In earthquakes in the Greater Los Angeles area in the spring of 2014, alerts were produced within 3.3 seconds of the quakes' nucleation. More recently, in the August 2014 M6.0 South Napa earthquake, ShakeAlert produced alerts in 5.2 seconds, allowing actions 5 seconds before the S-wave arrived in Berkeley, 8 seconds before the shaking hit the BART operations center, and 9 seconds before the S-waves reached the San Francisco DEM, as shown in Figure 8.3. BART trains would have automatically begun braking based on the alert; however, the system does not operate on Sundays at 3:20 a.m. PDT. The existing ShakeAlert system applications include elevators stopping at the next floor and the doors opening; operating room alerts to warn surgeons to stop surgery; and stopping the movement of natural gas through pipes to prevent leaks and fires (Grad and Lin II 2017).

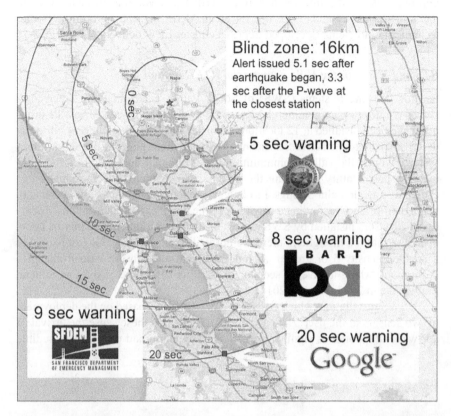

Figure 8.3 Warning contours for real-time ShakeAlert performance during the 2014 Napa earthquake

Studies exist to determine optimum spacing and technical specifications for new stations for a California EEDS (Kuyuk and Allen 2013). California would need 1,675 seismic stations to cover the whole state, Oregon, and Washington, but only 740 had been installed in 2017. Another $38 million is needed to finish building the system, and then $16 million will be needed each year to maintain it (Fimrite 2017).

One challenge to the delivery of information to the public is the blind zone. Because the sensor is triggered by the difference in travel time between the P-wave and the S-wave, locations close to the epicenter may get little to no advanced warning, thus being blind to the imminent shaking. A denser array of sensors would enhance the warning times to the seismic network. In an earthquake greater than magnitude 7, there could be warning times of a few seconds to a minute or more as the distance from the epicenter increases. Another challenge is the delivery of the message to residents and businesses in the affected area. While most *mass messaging technologies* are not quick enough to deliver warning messages, improvements to the Integrated Public Alerting and Warning System (IPAWS) make it a prime candidate for use by ShakeAlert. Smartphone apps and other technologies are being developed to provide faster EEW delivery (USGS 2016).

RTS and RTEE in the U.S.: commercial RTEE in the U.S.

Seismic Warning Systems (SWS) of Scotts Valley, California, and other companies are developing commercial RTEE systems in the United States. Its products have been installed at 12 locations (Housley 2011) in the southern California desert adjacent to the active San Jacinto Fault and other faults of the San Andreas system. Coachella Valley communities have experienced several earthquakes over the past century, including the M 6.6 1986 Painted Hills earthquake that caused damage in Palm Springs. Firefighters responding to damage reports had to begin their rescues by finding a way to open the doors of their fire stations. Today, seismic sensors installed by SWS at each of the fire stations ensure that its doors open and that the firefighters there are notified of expected shaking of Modified Mercalli Intensity 5 or greater. A unit is also installed in the Paso Robles fire department, where it gave 10 seconds of warning before the M 6.5 San Simeon Earthquake in 2003 (Becerra 2014).

An SWS installation, which costs $25,000 per unit, is based on the deployment of two sensors at the user's site (Mulvey 2011). When these sense the arrival of a P-wave that portends significant shaking, they alarm and can activate audible

Figure 8.4 SWS QuakeGuard at SunLine Transit

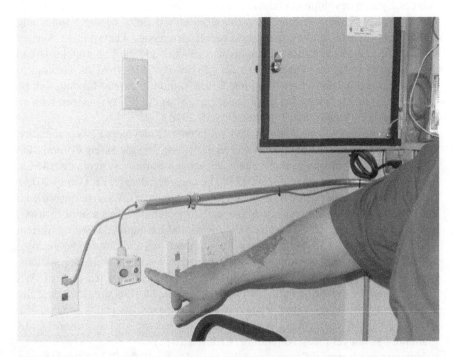

Figure 8.5 SWS P-wave Sensor and Internet line at SunLine Transit

warnings and flashing lights, as well as open garage doors or interrupt industrial activities. The alarm at SunLine Transit in Palm Springs (see Figures 8.4 and 8.5), for example, warns drivers of impending shaking so they can safely stop their buses (Edwards 2013).

SWS' product, QuakeGuard 300, has also been installed at 40 locations other than fire stations in California, including "the Department of Energy's Lawrence Berkeley National Laboratory, NASA's Dryden Flight Research Center and the day care center at Cisco's California headquarters" (Mulvey 2011). The company is proposing to network local sensors for a quicker response time at locations that are more distant from the earthquake's hypocenter – about 1 additional second for every 8 kilometers (5 miles). They also plan to provide a $1,200 per year subscription service for schools and $2,500 per year for hospitals (Becerra 2014).

Public policy and government activities

In 2013 California State Senator Alex Padilla sponsored a bill "to create a state-wide early warning system for earthquakes... [using] technology to outrun shock waves [and] . . . using existing communications infrastructure" (Hoppin 2013). This legislation provides support for the development of the ShakeAlert system, relying on the Governor's Office of Emergency Services to identify funding sources. System development funds have come from a variety of sources: $10 million from USGS; $6.5 million from the Gordon and Betty Moore Foundation; and $5.6 million in funding from the Federal Emergency Management Agency through the California Office of Emergency Services and the Los Angeles Urban Area Security Initiative (UASI) (Pounders 2013). By 2016, the U.S. Geological Survey had estimated that an additional $38.3 million in capital funding will be needed to complete a working earthquake early warning (EEW) system, with an annual operating cost of $16.1 million (USGS 2016).

Local governments have also taken initiatives to develop EEW capability. According to a report to California's Alfred E. Alquist Seismic Safety Commission on September 12, 2012, the stand-alone earthquake warning systems installed in the Coachella Valley starting in 2000 could be considered an RTEE (James 2013). In 2009 the Coachella Valley Association of Governments (CVAG) partnered with the Coachella Valley Emergency Managers' Association, three school districts, and SWS to propose the Coachella Valley Regional Earthquake Warning System (CREWS). Warnings are to be based on existing sensors and those to be installed at additional proposed locations. There are currently sensors in 15 fire stations, four public safety dispatch centers and at the Sun Transit dispatch center (SWS 2015). When the system is built, alerts could be issued to 136 sites including fire stations, schools, health care sites and tribal emergency operations centers. The Riverside County Operational Area has also applied for a $1.5 million FEMA grant but has not yet received funding (CREWS 2012).

Neighboring Imperial County used this model to apply for FEMA funds to create a similar regional earthquake warning system called Imperial County Regional Earthquake Warning System (ICREWS), which will partner with the neighboring CREWS (CREWS 2012). On April 4, 2010, the M 7.2 El Mayor-Cucapah Earthquake in Baja California caused "a seismic movement on multiple faults extending throughout the Salton Trough. The triggered surface movements were at distances up to 172 km (107 miles) from the epicenter" (Garcia and Drysdale 2012). The earthquake caused the strongest shaking in the Imperial Valley since 1892, resulting in liquefaction and permanent ground deformation, leading to long-term damage to fields (Exponent 2010). Damaged buildings and infrastructure included irrigation canals, schools, and downtown businesses. Fire Station 1 in Calexico was damaged by the shaking. Fire Chief Pete Mercado reported that it took the fire station's three-person staff 15 minutes to open the damaged bay doors and move the fire engine. Meanwhile, they were receiving calls for service for gas leaks, power outages, and structure fires (CREWS 2012).

The Imperial County Operational Area, with help from CVAG, successfully applied for a $225,000 hazard mitigation grant under FEMA's DR 1911, the El Mayor-Cucapah earthquake event, to fund the ICREWS. On April 25, 2014, Imperial County awarded a $250,000 contract to SWS, which will install sensors and warning devices to "deploy and maintain this, the nation's first regional earthquake warning system. . . . ICREWS' initial partners include Imperial Co. Fire, Imperial Co. Sheriff's Office, Cities of Brawley, El Centro and Calexico Fire and Police Dispatch Centers, Calipatria Fire, El Centro Medical Center and Pioneers

Memorial Hospital" (Imperial County Emergency Operations Center 2014). The ICREWS system will place P-wave monitors at 6 to 12 kilometer (3.7 to 7.5 mile) intervals along selected faults. Notifications will issue audible alerts, open fire station doors, turn on lights, and display warnings on monitors in public safety and utility dispatch centers. User locations can add activities like starting emergency generators or system shutdowns (CREWS 2012). The system is awaiting FEMA's approval of the hazard mitigation grant.

Conclusion: rapid risk communication and resilience building

The JR East experience in the Great East Japan Earthquake offers a series of useful lessons on EEW, as depicted in Table 8.4. JR East has operated for over 50 years without an earthquake-related casualty because it has learned from each seismic event and continued to invest in improved systems and strategies. There is no quick fix or perfect design for seismic safety, just a path of thoughtful investment and proactive initiatives, and the experience of JR East can be instructive in how best to invest time and money for success.

Collaboration within the California earthquake research community at USGS, UC Berkeley, Caltech, and the private sector could lead to the installation of both useful RTS and critical RTEE earthquake early warning systems. The BART experience of faster computers and more effective algorithms like ShakeAlert's ElarmS shows the practical benefit of RTEE.

Table 8.4 Lessons learned from JR East EEW experiences

EARTHQUAKE EARLY WARNING SYSTEM
EEW prevents derailments
Automatic electricity shut-off and brake application are critical to success – seconds count.
Location of sensors in relation to the fault determines the length of the warning period.
Direct delivery of warnings to the public through cell phones and computer screens enhances the value of EEW beyond the benefits of media-based notices.
EEW can be used for immediate protective measures as well as for understanding the event to manage the response most effectively.
Faster computers and more effective algorithms enhance the speed and accuracy of the EEW system.
Note: A fundamental limitation on EEW is the physics of seismic wave propagation. P-waves must arrive at the instruments enough in advance of the S-waves to permit characterization. The quake in LA provided an alert after 3.3 s, which is about as short a characterization time as possible.

EEW encourages resilience building within the community and the population. Investment in sensors and warning systems allows for a community's critical infrastructure to take defensive actions against earthquake damage. The successful implementation of EEW for the *Shinkansen* clearly shows the benefits through the mitigation of derailments, thus limiting infrastructure damage and injuries and loss of life. This rapid communication is machine-based, requiring no human action, as the P-wave sensor triggers the computer to shut down power to the train and apply the brake. An audible alarm in the trains and stations permits passengers and crew to take further appropriate protective action.

Public notification systems like Mexico's provide an audible alarm, and Japan's uses cell phones, computers, and media broadcasts to display a warning of an impending earthquake. These systems enable the population to take protective actions that they have learned through public education campaigns and practiced during national exercises. In many cases, they also trigger computer-enabled responses like shutting down natural gas transmissions or providing alarms to stop surgery. In each case, the alarm enhances resilience by limiting loss of life and injury by giving time for people to take protective action and infrastructure to be shut down before the damaging shaking commences. As computers are able to process data faster and algorithms become more efficient, the lag time between first P-wave detection and issuing of the public warning is shrinking, enhancing the time for protective measures to be taken.

Note

1 Some material in this chapter was originally published in *Great East Japan Earthquake, JR East Mitigation Successes, and Lessons for California High-Speed Rail*, Report. 12–37, Mineta Transportation Institute, April 2015 http://transweb.sjsu.edu/project/1225.html, and is used by permission of the Institute.

References

ABS Consulting. 2004. *Flash Report on the Niigata Chuetsu Earthquake*. Accessed on June 13, 2014 at www.absconsulting.com/resources/Catastrophe_Reports/Niigata%20Earthquake%2004%20Report.pdf.

Alfred, E. Alquist Seismic Safety Commission. 2008. *Niigata Chuetsu-oki, Japan Earthquake and Disaster Preparedness in Shizuoka Prefecture: Lessons for California*. Accessed on April 12, 2013 at www.seismic.ca.gov/pub/CSSC_08-02_JapanEarthquake2007FINALv5.pdf.

Allen, Richard, M. 2013. Seconds Count. *Nature*, 502: 29–31.

Ammon, Charles J. 2001. *Seismic Waves and Earth's Interior*. Public Lecture. Department of Geosciences. Pennsylvania State University, State College, PA.

Becerra, Hector. 2014. Scientists, Private Firms Wrangle Over Quake Alert System for California. *Los Angeles Times*, March 23. Accessed on April 20, 2014 at www.redding.com/news/2014/mar/23/scientists-private-firms-wrangle-over-quake-alert/.

Berkeley Seismic Laboratory. 2017. *Detailed History of the BSL*. Accessed on January 31, 2017 at http://seismo.berkeley.edu/history/.

Birmingham, Lucy, and McNeill, David. 2012. *Strong in the Rain: Surviving Japan's Earthquake, Tsunami, and Fukushima Nuclear Disaster*. New York: Palgrave Macmillan.

Bose, Maren, and Heaton, Thomas. 2010. Probabilistic Predictions of Rupture Length, Slip and Seismic Ground Motions for an On-Going Rupture: Implications for Early Warnings for Large Earthquakes. *Geophysical Journal International*, 183: 1014–1030.

Bressan, David. 2011. *Historic Earthquakes in Japan*. Accessed on April 3, 2013 at http://historyofgeology.fieldofscience.com/2011/03/historic-earthquakes-in-japan.html.

Burkett, Erin R., Given, Douglas D., and Jones, Lucille. 2014. *ShakeAlert – An Earthquake Early Warning System for the United States West Coast*. Accessed on November 10, 2018 at https://pubs.er.usgs.gov/publication/fs20143083. US Department of the Interior and US Geological Survey.

California Geological Survey. 2013. *Strong Motion Instrumentation Program*. Accessed on November 3, 2013 at www.conservation.ca.gov/cgs/smip/Pages/about.aspx.

Centro de instrumentacion y registro sismico, a.c., Sistema de Alerta Sismico Mexicano (SASMEX). 2017. *Current Information*, September 7. Accessed on September 10, 2017 at www.cires.org.mx/docs_info/Reporte_008.pdf.

Cochran, Elizabeth. 2014. *USGS*. Interview by Frances Edwards and Daniel Goodrich, January 14.

Coleman, Norman C., Whitcomb Jr., Robert, C., Miller, Charles W., and Noska, Michael A. 2012. Commentary on the Combined Disaster in Japan. *Radiation Research*, 177: 15–17. doi:10.1667/RRXX40.1 (Accessed April 2, 2013).

CREWS. 2012. *Coachella Valley (CREWS) and Imperial Valley (ICREWS) Report to the Alfred E. Alquist Seismic Safety Commission*, September 12. Accessed on April 30, 2013 at www.seismic.ca.gov/meeting_info/Sept12_2012/12-Item%20XII%20CREWS.pdf.

East Japan Railway Company. 2005. Report on Niigata Chuetsu Earthquake. *Investor Relations Annual Report*, p. 44.

———. 2009. *Safety Vision: Challenging Safety by Thinking and Acting for Ourselves. FY 2009–2013*. East Japan Railway Company.

Edwards, Thomas. 2013. *SunLine Transit Manager*. Interview by Frances Edwards and Daniel Goodrich, April 12.

Exploratorium. 2013. Accessed on November 5, 2013 at www.exploratorium.edu/faultline/.

Exponent. 2010. *El Mayor-Cucapah Earthquake Reconnaissance*. Accessed on June 30, 2013 at www.exponent.com/files/Uploads/Documents/news%20and%20features/earthquake.pdf.

Fimrite, Peter. 2017. Earthquake Early Warning in Mexico Reminds California What It Still Lacks. *San Francisco Chronicle*, September 8. Accessed on September 8, 2017 at www.sfchronicle.com/bayarea/article/Earthquake-early-warning-in-Mexico-reminds-12184393.php.

Findlay, Russell. 2011. They Didn't Stand A Chance: Horror in Japan 10,000 Missing in Just One Town as Destruction Left by Quake and Tsunami Is Revealed. *Glasgow Sunday Mail*, March 13.

Garcia, Susan, and Drysdale, Don. 2012. Triggered Fault Movement from Baja Quake Reveals Previously Unknown Faults in Southern California. *USGS*, March 8. Accessed on April 30, 2013 at www.usgs.gov/newsroom/article.asp?ID=3141#.U6yDp_ldXdI.

Ghasemi, Hamid, Otsuka, Hisanori, Cooper, James D., and Nakajima, Hiroyuki. 1996. Aftermath of the Kobe Earthquake. *Public Roads*, 60(2). www.fhwa.dot.gov/publications/publicroads/96fall/p96au17.cfm (Accessed November 1, 2013).

Grad, S., and Lin II, R. G. 2017. Mexico Got Early Warning Before Deadly Earthquake Struck. When Will California Get That System? *Los Angeles Times*, September 8. Accessed on September 8, 2017 at www.latimes.com/world/la-me-mexico-quake-earth-warning-20170908-htmlstory.html.

Hiraoka, Shigenori. 2011. *The Effects of the Recent Earthquake and Tsunami on Rail and Bus Operations in Japan.* Presentation, APTA Public Education Embassy Roundtable, June 24.

Hoppin, Jason. 2013. Brown Signs Bill for Early Warning System. *San Jose Mercury News*, September 27, p. A-1.

Housley, Adam. 2011. Earthquake Early Warning System a Reality in California. *Fox News*, February 23. Accessed on January 24, 2013 at www.foxnews.com/scitech/2011/02/23/quake-early-warning-reality-california.

Imperial County Emergency Operations Center. 2014. *ICRWS: Imperial County Regional Earthquake Warning System*, April 25, p. 1. Accessed on June 1, 2014 at www.linkedin.com/today/post/article/20140424005507-43921746-icrews-imperial-county-regional-earthquake-warning-system.

Iwamura, Yasuhiro. 2013. About the Measures Against Earthquake Disaster of JR East. In *Safety Research Laboratory, East Japan Railway Company.* Tokyo, Japan: JR East Railway Company.

———. 2014. Personal Communication. February 18.

James, Ian 2013. Earthquake Early Warning: Public, Private Systems Seek to Provide Critical Seconds. *Desert Sun*, May 5. Accessed on June 30, 2013 at www.mydesert.com/article/20130504/NEWS0805/305040047/Earthquake-early-warning-Public-private-systems-seek-provide-critical-seconds?nclick_check=1.

Kanno, Masao. 2013. *Japanese Transportation Systems after the Great East Japan Earthquake.* San Francisco: Consulate of Japan.

Kious, W. Jacquelyne, and Tilling, Robert I. 2008. *This Dynamic Earth.* Washington, DC: USGS. Accessed on November 1, 2013 at http://pubs.usgs.gov/gip/dynamic/dynamic.pdf.

Kobayashi, Masahu, Mizuno, Koichiro, and Ishibashi, Tadayoshi. 2012. Damage Caused to Shinkansen Structures by the Great East Japan Earthquake and Early Restoration. In *Proceedings of the International Symposium on Engineering Lessons Learned from the 2011 Great East Japan Earthquake*, Tokyo, Japan, March 1–4.

Kuyuk, H. Serdar and Allen, Richard M. 2013. Optimal Seismic Network Density for Earthquake Early Warning: A Case Study from California. *Seismological Research Letters*, 84(6): 946–954.

Kuyuk, H. Serdar, Allen, Richard M., Brown, Holly, Hellweg, Margaret, Henson, Ivan and Neuhauser, Douglas. 2014. Designing a Network-Based Earthquake Early Warning Algorithm for California: Elarm S-2. *Bulletin of the Seismological Society of America*, 104(1): 1–12.

Lay, Thomas, and Wallace, Terry C. 1995. *Modern Seismology. International Geophysics Series, Volume 58.* San Diego: Academic Press.

Lissade, P. E., Herby. 2010. *Chief, Caltrans Office of Emergency Management.* Interview by Frances Edwards and Daniel Goodrich, April 3.

Mulvey, Jeanette. 2011. After Japan Earthquake, U.S. Detection Firm in Spotlight. *Business News Daily*, March 14.

Nakamura, Yutaka, and Saita, Jun. 2007a. FREQL and AcCo for a Quick Response to Earthquakes. In *Earthquake Early Warning Systems*. (eds.) Paolo Gasparini, Gaetano Manfredi, and Jochen Zschua. Berlin, Germany: Springer-Verlag, pp. 307–324.

————. 2007b. UrEDAS, the Earthquake Warning System: Today and Tomorrow. In *Earthquake Early Warning Systems*. (eds.) Paolo Gasparini, Gaetano Manfredi, and Jochen Zschua. Berlin, Germany: Springer-Verlag, pp. 249–282.

Nyquist, Charles. 2012. The USGS and Partners Work to Develop an Earthquake Early Warning System for California. *USGS* (Blog), April 17. Accessed on April 12, 2013 at www.usgs.gov/blogs/features/usgs_top_story/the-usgs-brings-an-earthquake-early-warning-system-to-california/.

Odaka, Tosjukazu, Ashiya, Kimitoshi, Tsukada, Shin'ya and Miyauchi, Toru. 2006. New Stand Alone and Advanced Earthquake Early Warning Systems Designed to Protect Railways. *Transportation Research Record*, 1943: 20–24.

Okada, Aya, and Comfort, Louise. 2011. *"Black swan" in Northeastern Japan: Interdependent Systems, Escalating Disaster on March 11, 2011*. Working Paper 1105. Pittsburgh, PA: Center for Disaster Management, University of Pittsburgh. Accessed on April 21, 2013 at www.cdm.pitt.edu/AboutCDM/CDMWPS/tabid/1346/Default.aspx.

Ono, Seiichiro. 2014. *Director, Japan Railways Group*. Interview by Frances Edwards and Daniel Goodrich, January 29.

Pounders, Erik. 2009. Earthquake Early Warning System Possible. *USGS*, December 14. Accessed on November 3, 2013 at http://yubanet.com/california/Earthquake-Early-Warning-System-Possible.php#.Utx4JRDTmM8.

Powell, Tom, and Fries, Donald. 1964. *Handbook: World-Wide Standard Seismograph Network*. Ann Arbor: Institute of Science and Technology, University of Michigan.

QCN. 2014. *Introduction to the Network*. Accessed on June 14, 2014 at http://qcn.stanford.edu/about-qcn/about-network.

Railway Gazette International. 2007. Joetsu Shinkansen Fully Restored After Earthquake Damage. *Railway Gazette International*, June 1. Accessed on November 3, 2013 at www.railwaygazette.com/news/single-view/view/joetsu-shinkansen-fully-restored-after-earthquake-damage.html.

Ransom, Clarice N. 2011. President Obama Honors Quake-Catcher Network Inventor Elizabeth Cochran. *USGS Newsroom*, October 4. Accessed on January 14, 2014 at www.usgs.gov/newsroom/article.asp?ID=2969#.U50o7_ldXdI.

Smith, Roderick A. 2003. The Japanese Shinkansen: The Catalyst for the Renaissance of Rail. *Journal of Transport History* 24(2): 222–237.

Smolan, Rick, and Erwitt, Jennifer. 2012. *The Human Face of Big Data*. Sausalito, CA: Against All Odds Productions.

SWS. 2015. *Earthquake Warning for the Coachella Valley: Existing Technology, Public-Private Partnering*. Accessed on March 1, 2017 at www.seismicwarning.com/sws-CREWS.html.

Tanemura, Masayuki. 2012. *The Great East Japan Earthquake*. Final Report of the US-China Disaster Assistance Working Group Workshop, January 5–8. San Jose, CA: Mineta Transportation Institute.

UNESCO. 2014. *Reading in the Mobile Era*. Paris, France: UNESCO. Accessed on June 12, 2014 at www.unesco.org/new/en/unesco/themes/icts/m4ed/mobile-reading/reading-in-the-mobile-era/.

USGS. 2010. *Earthquake Hazards Program. About GPS*, April 29. Accessed on March 31, 2014 at http://earthquake.usgs.gov/monitoring/gps/about.php.

————. 2011. *Earthquake Hazards Program*, April 7. Accessed on November 3, 2013 at https://sslearthquake.usgs.gov/ens/.

————. 2013a. *Advanced National Seismic System*. Accessed on April 13, 2013 at https://earthquake.usgs.gov/monitoring/anss/.

————. 2013b. *The Modified Mercalli Intensity Scale*. Accessed on November 3, 2013 at http://earthquake.usgs.gov/learn/topics/mercalli.php.

————. 2016. *ShakeAlert*. Accessed on March 1, 2017 at www.shakealert.org/faq/#how work.

Welch, Randy. 2013. All Shook Up: Colorado Earthquake Center tracks "What's Rocking". *FEMA Region VIII*. Accessed on November 1, 2013 at www.fema.gov/about-fema/employee-news-and-announcements/all-shook-colorado-earthquake-center-tracks-whats-rocking.

Witze, Alexandra. 2014. Buying Time When Quakes Hit. *Science News*, April 4. Accessed on June 6, 2014 at www.sciencenews.org/article/buying-time-when-quakes-hit?mode=magazine&context=721.

9 The role of social media in enhancing risk communication and promoting community resilience in the midst of a disaster

Kathryn E. Anthony, Steven J. Venette,
Andrew S. Pyle, Brandon C. Boatwright, and
Carrie E. Reif-Stice

Introduction

Early on January 15, 2017, the roiling skies over Hattiesburg, Mississippi, were visible by a constant procession of lightning flashing above waving pine trees. The ominous cacophony was interrupted by blaring weather alert radios announcing a tornado warning. Community sirens sprung to life as push notifications lit cell phone screens and other electronic devices. Social media posts indicated people were scared. Surprisingly, they also hinted that some people did not know what to do. Over the next few minutes, a tornado touched down and tore a path through the small city. Vehicles were tossed, structures were destroyed, and tragically, four lives were lost. Confusion and concern dominated communication as calls for information transitioned to pleas for help. But where was help most urgently needed? What resources were required? Should citizens try to render assistance or stay out of the way?

A community's resilience to tragedies strongly depends on the communication surrounding them before, during, and after crises. Some scholars and practitioners see risk communication as the process of letting people know about hazards that have been identified by experts. Understanding of this process, however, is limited, and efforts to improve public awareness of hazards and removing people from harm's way have proven ineffective. Our chapter explains why the unidirectional, *single-shot* model, or deficit approach, of risk communication is insufficient. Next, the impact social media has had on contemporary conceptualization of risk communication will be articulated as an impetus for change. Finally, a dynamic model of communication that promotes message convergence while supporting community resilience will be presented.

As this book is intended for a diverse audience, some terms should be clarified simply because concepts may be used differently in various fields. Risk can be understood in a number of ways. The most prevalent definition, from a scholarly perspective, states that risk is equal to the likelihood of a negative event multiplied by that event's consequences (Aven 2007). For a risk to manifest, a threat must be present. A threat must have the capability of adversely affecting a system by changing its state. For example, pandemic influenza is a risk to the health care system because hospitals can quickly become overwhelmed by an influx of patients seeking urgent care. Beyond the technical definition of risk, Slovic and others (2004) describe the role of affect in risk perception. They argue that in addition to employing reason and logic, individuals form perceptions of risk based on their emotions and experiences. In fact, experiences and emotions inevitably affect whether or not people perceive certain situations to be inherently risky.

From a communication perspective, risk communication is the exchange of messages that create or modify the perception of the likelihood of a negative event (Venette 2008). This definition highlights that risk communication is not unidirectional (where one entity sends a message to an audience) but rather is a dynamic, ongoing exchange of thoughts and feelings to promote understanding about a hazard. In times of uncertainty and heightened risk, there is often much incomplete or inconsistent information available. In making sense of the uncertainty, individuals often seek available information and construe risk messages or "infer meaning by assessing the importance and accuracy of the information and the authenticity of the source" (Sellnow et al. 2009). "Listeners construe risk by noting the ways in which the arguments within the greater narrative reinforce or contradict and by comparing this unity or disparity to their previously held belief on the issue" (Perelman and Olbrechts-Tyteca 1969: 348). When facing risk and uncertainty, Mileti (1999) argues that individuals assess and observe the information they can obtain to determine the best course of action for protecting themselves. Therefore, creating dialogue with stakeholders and providing all available information is imperative for an effective crisis response.

Resilience has been defined by U.S. federal agencies as the ability to recover the state of a system after it has been disrupted. This conceptualization is primarily borrowed from science and engineering vocabulary and is parallel to elasticity. An airplane wing is resilient insofar as it can snap back to its original shape after deflection caused by a perturbation, such as air turbulence. Thus, resilience can be seen as "a community's ability to strengthen its response to deal with crises or disruptions" (Veil and Bishop 2014: 723). In fact, a resilient community "is able to bounce back from an event, not necessarily to return to normal, but to return to a new normal in the initial days, weeks, and months depending on the size and scope of the disaster" (Veil and Bishop 2014: 723).

Resilience is also a function of efficacy. Three major types of efficacy help explain people's understanding of the existence and viability of responses to negative events. Self-efficacy is a person's perception that she has some course of action to mitigate a risk to protect herself or her loved ones (Witte, Meyer, and Martell 2001). Telling a person to *stop, drop, and roll* if his clothing catches on fire promotes self-efficacy. System efficacy is a person's belief that a solution exists within the system that will protect that person or his interests (Macpherson et al. 2014). Most citizens do not know how to fight house fires or battle organized crime; knowledge that fire departments and law enforcement agencies exist to protect people is sufficient for most to perceive system efficacy. Finally, response efficacy is the degree to which a person views a particular response as likely to solve the problem or reduce damage (Witte, Meyer, and Martell 2001). A person might recognize that law enforcement exists to protect people from home invasion (system efficacy), but he might not believe that the policy will be able to respond in time to save him and his family from a criminal attack (indicating a lack of response efficacy). That person therefore might purchase a weapon for home defense (self-efficacy).

Organizations respond to hazards in much the same way that individuals do. Human-based systems, such as organizations and networks, strongly depend on communication as a means of promoting resilience. Actors cannot respond to a negative event without accurate information processing and effective coordination of activities, both of which are impossible without information exchange. In fact, one theoretical perspective, the communicative constitution of organizations (Putnam and Mcphee 2009), explains that communication is the substance of organizations. In other words, organizations cannot exist without the exchange of ideas. Through this exchange of ideas, priorities and goals are established, resources are identified, rules and norms are negotiated, and activities are conducted. Both individuals and organizations rely on communication to identify valuable parts of a system that ought to be preserved, to establish strategies for mitigating threats to those valued elements, and to respond to important system disruptions when they manifest. Thus, coordinated action to create and maintain resilience cannot occur without effective communication.

Additionally, to promote an efficient response and recovery during and after a disaster, organizations and agencies tasked with responding must be prepared to communicate with key stakeholders and manage a variety of potentially conflicting needs and goals. And because of that, risk communicators should ensure that they are providing messages that not only address the informational needs of a community but must also address the efficacy needs of the community. The following section will detail the various approaches to risk communication message design, including *one-shot* and dialogic approaches.

Risk communication models

Traditional notions of disseminating risk messages to the public were predicated on the practice of merely transmitting information from expert to layperson. This model is referred to as the "deficit" model, in which experts communicate in a "one-way, top-down" approach in an attempt to fill the public's knowledge gap concerning risk (Trench 2008: 119). In this model, message designers created risk messages for the public based scientifically on what they believed the public needed to hear and not necessarily what community members perceived their needs to be (Sauer 2003). This approach, however, has routinely proved to be unsuccessful in effectively reaching stakeholders (Trench 2008). The deficit model has continued because scientists are rarely trained to communicate effectively with diverse publics, and as a result, the practice persists (Simis et al. 2016).

Additionally, risk message design according to this approach does not usually yield the dissemination of useful information people need. For instance, simply telling citizens that they must evacuate does not necessarily answer the specifics of the concerns or needs they may have. Emergency managers must focus on improving both the awareness and understanding of the public of terminologies and procedures in the wake of an impending disaster (Rowan et al. 2009). Unfortunately, organizations that engaged in this early *top-down* type of risk communication tended to cite their efforts as successful or unsuccessful based on the sheer number of people who encountered them, regardless of whether or not those messages resonated with the actual needs of the community members or their cultural understandings of risk.

The far more accepted model for risk message design is a participatory, two-way model for communicating with the public. Emergency managers and organizations responding to a crisis must plan in advance to engage members of the public both in the precrisis and crisis stage (Coombs 2014). Emergency managers must engage in dialogue with publics before disaster strikes to understand more fully the specific material and communicative needs of the communities they serve (Rowan et al. 2009). Similarly, Houston and others (2015) argue that dialogue between publics and government organizations during and after a disaster enables individuals to obtain the help necessary for recovery. Similarly, Veil and Anthony (2017) argue that if an organization does not have established lines of communication between practitioners and stakeholders before a disaster, they must strive to create a way for practitioners and the members of the public to communicate.

Much literature reveals the importance of promoting dialogue between practitioners and stakeholders. And given the rise of social media, the ability to promote communication between all parties has become increasingly common. The following section will consider the ways in which social media can enhance risk communication between practitioners and affected publics.

Social media in risk communication

According to the Federal Emergency Management Agency (FEMA), disaster events have been on the rise over the past few decades (FEMA 2017). This is supported by NASA research suggesting a recent increase in natural disasters, including catastrophic weather events (Reibeek 2005). As disaster events become more common, social media usage is also becoming more prevalent. Whereas in the past, individuals may have solely relied on radio or television reports during and after a disaster, individuals now have the option to seek (and share) disaster information online.

Social media platforms such as Facebook, Twitter, and Instagram allow users to develop personalized profiles, create and manage a list of users with whom they interact, and explore interconnected relationships in a networked system. Of the

86 percent of Americans who are Internet users, more than 80 percent use at least one social media platform (Greenwood, Perrin, and Duggan 2016). A majority of Americans (62 percent) get at least some news from social media (Gottfried and Shearer 2016). In fact, disaster events drive publics to online sources for information seeking, and in some instances, audiences view social media as more credible than traditional mass media (Procopio and Procopio 2007). Procopio and Procopio (2007) found that during Hurricane Katrina, 75 percent of respondents utilized social media platforms to both seek and share information. This study was conducted before the boom in social media platforms we have seen over the past decade, suggesting that – with an increase in social media presence – people may be more likely today than in the past to seek out these platforms for information during and after a disaster.

According to a 2009 study of more than 400 management, marketing, and human resources executives, however, only 13 percent of companies represented have any sort of reference to social media in their crisis communication plans (Russell and Ethos Business 2009). Additionally, according to Liu, Faustino, and Jin (2015), while 75 percent of Americans surveyed in a 2010 study by the American Red Cross expect to have a response within one hour of posting to a social media page, few emergency managers have personnel tasked with the responsibility of engaging with publics on social media during a disaster. This is a clear and troubling gap between apparent social media expectations of the general public and actual social media practice of corporations and agencies.

Scholars have only recently begun to study the use of social media platforms during and after disaster events (see Freberg, Palenchar, and Veil 2013; Lachlan et al. 2016). These studies have provided valuable insight into how publics engage with social media messages during and after a crisis. Veil, Buehner, and Palenchar (2011) argued that the National Center for Food Protection and Defense (NCFPD) best practices in risk and crisis communication (Seeger 2006; Venette 2006, 2007), ranging from "establish risk and crisis management policies and process approaches" to "acknowledge and account for cultural differences" (Sellnow and Vidoloff 2009), must also be considered when facilitating participation and dialogue with stakeholders through social media platforms. The scholars suggest "using social media to educate the public regarding risks, encourage visible support of an organization or cause, and establish a venue for open dialogue online . . . all approaches to incorporating social media in risk and crisis communication" (Veil, Buehner, and Palenchar 2011: 113).

As technologically advanced audiences increasingly rely on social media for the exchange of information, a significant opportunity exists for risk communicators. Traditional, unidirectional models of risk communication prove ineffective in this environment (Trench 2008; Simis et al. 2016); however, when new strategies and tactics are enacted, the positive influence of communication efforts become multiplied. Beyond actively dialoguing with stakeholders, this multiplicative impact is realized through the use of artistically coordinated multi-messages (Sellnow et al. 2009). Because single messages are likely to be ineffective, message designers should construct multiple messages that are tied together artistically. Geico advertising perfectly exemplifies this approach. For just a few examples, one message uses cave people ("so easy a caveman can do it"); another uses a gecko as a spokesperson; yet another says that if you do not know about Geico's services, then you must have been living under a rock. Each message is tied together through the use of a common logo and a consistent slogan (15 minutes will save you 15 percent). A viewer may not like cave dwellers or lizards, but may like the humor of people living under rocks. With a multi-message approach, members of the audience are allowed the freedom to select the message that most appeals to them. We argue, however, that in a multi-message approach, each variation in the presentation should reflect the same core message. Geico's marketing is effective only if the various advertisements are in fact reiterating the same message. Attentiveness to any of the messages means that the information campaign was successful for that audience. Organizations should ensure that the messages they develop are coordinated, both in terms of their content and their design. The more similarities in information people encounter, the more likely they are to follow the suggested recommendations (Anthony, Sellnow, and Millner 2013). Social media is a channel that encourages brutal honesty about what audiences think are strengths and weaknesses of the different messages. The organizations, in turn, must be attentive to that feedback.

Additionally, social media messages should not only be designed to ensure that content is consistent across multiple messages but that messages should also be disseminated across multiple social media channels (Anthony, Sellnow, and Millner 2013). For instance, in the midst of a food contamination crisis, parents responsible for making nutritional decisions for their families felt more confident managing their uncertainty in the midst of heightened risk if they perceived that the Centers for Disease Control and Prevention's (CDC) Facebook page and the Food and Drug Administration's (FDA) home page were reporting similar things (Anthony, Sellnow, and Millner 2013). Organizations more fully understand the messages' reception and influence when audiences exchange information with each other and with the senders of the messages dynamically, which is the inherent strength of social media. Organizations must be willing to engage in active dialogue with stakeholders through social media (Lin et al. 2016). Specifically, social media enables community members to pose questions and concerns to public health experts on digital platforms, and this technology facilitates the capability for response organizations to directly reply to their stakeholders.

Social media, location information, and hazard response

Social media outlets such as Facebook, Snapchat, YouTube, and Twitter have altered how information is accessed and shared. To construct an effective crisis communication response, practitioners need to integrate best social media practices within the precrisis, crisis, and postcrisis phases of a crisis management plan (Coombs 2014). During the precrisis stage, social media helps practitioners conduct environmental monitoring for crisis signals, identify target audiences, and build community partnerships. Once a crisis occurs, social media can create an opportunity for sharing information between organizations and stakeholders (Briones et al. 2011; Veil, Buehner, and Palenchar 2011). For example, to manage crisis events, stakeholders and practitioners can share pictures, stories, and videos of their experiences and crowdsource for additional help or information. Finally, social media helps practitioners and stakeholders co-construct postcrisis narratives (e.g., Facebook memorial pages, YouTube videos), facilitate coordinate/rebuilding efforts, and build trust (Coombs 2014). Therefore, at all stages of the crisis cycle, social media can assist in communication between organizations and their stakeholders. A September 2013 report published by Pew Research revealed that the role of *location* among online platforms is changing "as growing numbers of Internet users are adding a new layer of location information to their posts, and a majority of smartphone users opt in to their phones' location-based services" (Zickuhr 2013: 2). This finding underscores the premise that social data can influence communication and action during a crisis scenario. Not only are people able to share their thoughts and observations through online platforms, but also their physical locations – information that is critical when facing disasters. Location-based services of social media also promote community resilience following a disaster event. The ability to engage in community mapping, whereby responders are able to assess more clearly the areas of the community most negatively affected by a disaster, is of paramount importance for promoting community resilience following a disaster (Wells et al. 2013). Social media platforms can assist responders in this endeavor, particularly in risk management, emergency management, and disaster response (Palen et al. 2009).

The increasing prevalence and versatility of social media platforms such as Twitter and Instagram have allowed for emergency responders, community members, and organizational leaders to have a greater sense of how crises unfold in real time (Liu et al. 2008; Palen and Liu 2007). Additionally, social media platforms are necessary for disaster response plans because "risk communication and other public health messages are most effective when they are delivered through trusted channels that are understandable and culturally appropriate" (Chandra et al. 2011: 22). The advent of social media platforms and the potential for messages, images, or videos to become viral, or to rapidly gain widespread viewership, has created both opportunities and risks for organizations and communities. Specifically, hashtags (keywords preceded by "#") serve as potential focal points for support, encouragement, and recovery during and after a crisis event. For example, after the 2011 London riots, hashtags related to cleaning up the city and seeking recovery were focal points, and they lasted longer than hashtags with emotional reactions to the event (Glasgow and Fink 2013). After the 2015 shooting of a professor at the University of South Carolina, the hashtag #PrayforUSC became a hub for information seeking, information sharing, and social support (Boatwright and Pyle 2015). By engaging with the hashtag, community members were able to establish or reestablish connections with friends and family and to look for ways to promote community recovery. Concerning disasters, Lin and others (2016) argue that response organizations should be vigilant to employ disaster-related hashtags to continually update the public on what is occurring in the midst of a disaster. Doing so both keeps them informed and allows stakeholders to dialogue with them (Lin et al. 2016). However, hashtags have also served as focal points for self-inflicted social media and public relations crises for organizations and for people who use them inappropriately (Pyle 2016).

A fascinating example of social media platforms being employed to mitigate risk, respond to a crisis, and develop community resilience (both at a micro-level in communities and a macro-level in national contexts) is the Ushahidi platform. Ushahidi, which means "testimony" in Kiswahili, was built as a website that would collect and organize reports of violence, allowing every citizen to become a journalist reporting on the frontlines of a political warzone. Ushahidi has been developed and enhanced as a more versatile platform and has been employed in Haiti, Indonesia, and Nepal, to name a few places (Morrow et al. 2011). This platform has created the capacity for community members to rally together and provide contextual information that has enabled responders to reach people long before official communication channels would have been able to connect responders to those in need. It also promotes the opportunity for community mapping to better understand areas affected by the disaster.

For example, Ushahidi has been employed in Semarang, Indonesia, following a series of devastating floods. The implementation of Ushahidi in Semarang enabled aid organizations to understand more clearly the areas most affected by the flooding. Similarly, following the earthquake in Nepal in 2015, Ushahidi allowed for the open mapping of the area to assess the damage and understand the needs of individuals affected (Roberts 2015). While the initial Ushahidi platform had challenges with establishing credibility and confirmation of sources (Okolloh 2009), it has continued to develop, and the system has become more reliable over time.

Additionally, Facebook has made strides in creating location-based tools to simplify users' seeking and sharing of information following a disaster. In 2014, the company launched Safety Check, a geographical feature that enables individuals to *check in* and let others know they are safe. Facebook has initiated safety check for several disasters, including Hurricane Matthew, wildfires in California and Tennessee, and flooding in Louisiana. Since its inception, the safety check notification has appeared in the feeds of over a billion people worldwide (Metz 2016). Facebook also plans to pair Safety Check with a *Community Help* feature for users' to ask for help or offer aid to those in need (O'Brien 2016). More recently, Facebook announced it is developing *crisis hub*, which will systematically organize information into a single stream, including the identification of false or inaccurate information, to create an accurate portrayal of a disaster event (Metz 2016).

While there are a variety of ways that social media can be employed as a function of risk management to enhance communication efforts and community resilience, it is important to note that social media should be viewed as complementing traditional media, not as operating in opposition to traditional media (Jin and Liu 2010). This partnership becomes more important when working with certain populations, as there are some publics that still do not trust messages from social media sources (Seo, Kim, and Yang 2009). Additionally, it is useful to seek opportunities for partnerships with bloggers. Many blogs are viewed with a level of credibility today previously reserved for traditional media sources, and it will serve communities and organizations well to seek out bloggers as allies for risk management and crisis mitigation (Veil, Buehner, and Palenchar 2011).

Social media outlets such as Facebook, Snapchat, YouTube, and Twitter have altered how information is accessed and shared. To construct an effective crisis communication response, practitioners should integrate best social media practices within the precrisis, crisis, and postcrisis phases of a crisis management plan (Coombs 2014). During the precrisis stage, social media helps practitioners conduct environmental monitoring for crisis signals, identify target audiences, and build community partnerships. Once a crisis occurs, social media can create an opportunity for sharing a wealth of information between organizations and stakeholders (Briones et al. 2011; Veil, Buehner, and Palenchar 2011). For example, stakeholders and practitioners can share pictures, stories, and videos of their experiences; organizations and individuals can also crowdsource additional help or information. Finally, social media helps practitioners and stakeholders co-construct postcrisis narratives (e.g., Facebook memorial pages, YouTube videos), facilitate and coordinate rebuilding efforts, and build trust (Coombs 2014). Therefore, at all stages of the crisis cycle, social media should promote communication between organizations and their stakeholders.

Social media analytics as a risk communication tool

Data analytics are beneficial before, during, and after a crisis. Qadir and others found that big data analytics can be used to "respond in emergencies in ways that can mitigate or even avoid a crisis" (Qadir et al. 2016: 2). Social analytics can afford communities additional avenues for building resilience following a disaster. Identifiers afford insight into how information is processed, disseminated, and received by communities engulfed in crises. MacEachren and others, for instance, examined how social media (particularly Twitter) can be used to "leverage explicit and implicit geographic information for tweets . . . to enable understanding of place, time, and theme components of evolving situations" (MacEachren et al. 2011: 1).

Further, location data and mapping programs can assist scholars in understanding what people are discussing and the accuracy of that information. Active monitoring of social media allows response organizations to make inferences about the informational needs of the public, and it allows them to assist the public with emergent message-need incongruities. Additionally, monitoring social media also allows organizational leaders and response agencies to identify incorrect information while disseminating credible information through recognizable social media accounts (Lin et al. 2016).

Given the wide range of platforms that contribute to what constitutes *big data*, a wide array of analytic tools are available to provide insight into data during crises. Many programs are able to measure and identify variables such as volume, sentiment, trends, key influencers, and key words or phrases. Free, open-source analytics tools are available (Hootsuite, Tweetdeck, and Quintly, to name a few) that primarily focus on measuring social media conversation from users' managed profiles. Paid platforms generally provide more robust social analytic services. SocialStudio, Crimson Hexagon, and Geofeedia are all platforms that provide rich, archivable data that can be used to examine the crisis life-cycle in greater depth. However, no analytic tools are exhaustive, as they cannot capture *all* of the conversations around a particular topic. The volume of data gathered is often contingent on characteristics of the data being gathered such as privacy settings, location services, and other variables.

Nevertheless, social analytic platforms can provide practitioners unique avenues for data analysis. For example, in researching the murder of the University of South Carolina professor, two of the authors of this chapter began tracking the #PrayforUSC tag that was trending on social media through Radian6 software. By measuring the volume of data using that hashtag, the authors identified several characteristics of emergent digital citizen groups that formed to provide information and social support to users affected by the crisis.

Social media and mobile technology have fundamentally altered the communicative landscape associated with crisis events. There are hundreds of smartphone applications that users simply download to predict, monitor, and respond to crisis events ranging from natural disasters to active shooters. Many of those applications also incorporate social media functions that allow users to mark themselves safe during a crisis or provide real-time developments as the crisis unfolds. Additionally, visually-based social media platforms (such as Instagram and Snapchat) provide avenues for eyewitnesses of disasters to transmit firsthand accounts of events as they transpire.

Conclusion

Ultimately, risk planning and message design before, during, and after a disaster is paramount for promoting an effective community response and engendering community resilience. Social media have proven to be incredibly effective in not only providing community members with the opportunity to dialogue with government agencies and response organizations, helping correct and clarify misinformation in real time during a disaster, but also in helping responders understand the location-based areas of greatest need, which is critical for distributing aid. Additionally, social media have facilitated recovery and resilience efforts by connecting concerned citizens to rally around a common cause through hashtags that not only bring awareness to recovery efforts but also facilitate grouping and ordering messages connected to the same concern.

Given the potential for social media to facilitate response and resilience, emergency managers must abandon any notions of a *top-down* approach as their sole strategy of disaster and risk communication and incorporate social media into their response plan to encourage dialogue with stakeholders. Response organizations should employ social media strategists who are actively scanning platforms, with the assistance of software listed above, in an effort to keep the public informed.

Additionally, the creation of messages that complement one another, both in content and in design, are necessary when attempting to promote convergence for stakeholders following a crisis. Doing these things may allow practitioners to promote an improved community response and resilience following a disaster event.

References

Anthony, Kathryn E., Sellnow, Timothy L., and Millner, Alyssa G. 2013. Message Convergence as a Message-Centered Approach to Analyzing and Improving Risk Communication. *Journal of Applied Communication Research*, 41(4): 346–364.

Aven, Terje. 2007. On the Ethical Justification for the Use of Risk Acceptance Criteria. *Risk Analysis*, 27(2): 303–312.

Boatwright, Brandon C., and Pyle, Andrew S. 2015. *Coming Together Around Hashtags: Exploring the Formation of Digital Emergent Citizen Groups*. Paper Presented at the National Communication Association, Las Vegas.

Briones, Rowena L., Kuch, Beth, Liu, Brooke Fisher, and Jin, Yan. 2011. Keeping Up with the Digital Age: How the American Red Cross Uses Social Media to Build Relationships. *Public Relations Review*, 37(1): 37–43.

Chandra, Anita, Acosta, Joie, How, Stefanie, Uscher-Pines, Lori, Williams, Malcolm V., Yeung, Douglas, Garrnett, Jeffery, and Meredith, Lisa S. 2011. *Building Community Resilience to Disasters: A Way Forward to Enhance National Health Security*. Washington, DC: Rand Corporation Technical Support. US Department of Health and Human Services.

Coombs, W. Timothy. 2014. *Ongoing Crisis Communication: Planning, Managing, and Responding*. Thousand Oaks, CA: Sage Publications.

Federal Emergency Management Association. 2017. Disasters. *FEMA*. Accessed on August 7, 2017 at www.fema.gov/disasters.

Freberg, Karen, Palenchar, Michael J., and Veil, Shari R. 2013. Managing and Sharing H1N1 Crisis Information Using Social Media Bookmarking Services. *Public Relations Review*, 39(3): 178–184.

Glasgow, Kimberly, and Fink, Clayton. 2013. Hashtag Lifespan and Social Networks During the London Riots. In the *Social Computer, Behavioral-Cultural Modeling and Prediction*. (eds.) Ariel M. Greenberg, William G. Kennedy, and Nathan D. Bos. Washington, DC: Springer, pp. 311–320.

Gottfried, Jeffrey, and Shearer, Elisa. 2016. News Use Across Social Media Platforms 2016. *Pew Research Center's Journalism Project* (Blog). Accessed on November 11, 2017, www.journalism.org/2016/05/26/news-use-across-social-media-platforms-2016/.

Greenwood, Shannon, Perrin, Rew, and Duggan, Maeve. 2016. Social Media Update 2016. *Pew Research Center: Internet, Science & Tech* (Blog). Accessed on November 11, 2017 at www.pewinternet.org/2016/11/11/social-media-update-2016/.

Houston, J. Brian, Hawthorne, Joshua, Perreault, Mildred F., Park, Eun Hae, Hode, Marlo Goldstein, Halliwell, Michael R., McGowen, Sarah E. Turner, Davis, Rachel, Vaid, Shivani, McElderry, Jonathan, and Griffith, Sandford A. 2015. Social Media and Disasters: A Functional Framework for Social Media Use in Disaster Planning, Response, and Research. *Disasters*, 39(1): 1–22.

Jin, Yan, and Liu, Brooke Fisher. 2010. The Blog-Mediated Crisis Communication Model: Recommendations for Responding to Influential External Blogs. *Journal of Public Relations Research*, 22(4): 429–455.

Lachlan, Kenneth A., Spence, Patric R., Lin, Xialing, Najarian, Kristy, and Del Greco, Maria. 2016. Social Media and Crisis Management: CERC, Search Strategies, and Twitter Content. *Computers in Human Behavior*, 54: 647–652.

Lin, Xialing, Spence, Patric R., Sellnow, Timothy L., and Lachlan, Kenneth A. 2016. Crisis Communication, Learning and Responding: Best Practices in Social Media. *Computers in Human Behavior*, 65: 601–605.

Liu, Brooke, Faustino, Julia, and Jin, Yan. 2015. How Disaster Information Form, Source, Type, and Prior Disaster Exposure Affect Public Outcomes: Jumping on the Social Media Bandwagon? *Journal of Applied Communication Research*, 43(1): 44–65.

Liu, Sophia, Palen, Leysia, Sutton, Jeannette, Hughes, Amanda, and Vieweg, Sarah. 2008. In Search of the Bigger Picture: The Emergent Role of Online Photo Sharing in Times of Disaster. In *Proceedings of the 5th International ISCRAM Conference*. Washington, DC, pp. 140–149.

MacEachren, Alan M., Jaiswal, Anuj, Robinson, Anthony C., Pezanowski, Scott, Savelyev, Alexander, Mitra, Prasenjit, Zhang, Xiao, and Blanford, Justine. 2011. SensePlace2: Geotwitter Analytics Support for Situational Awareness. In *IEEE Conference on Visual Analytics Science and Technology*, pp. 181–190.

Macpherson, Linda, Snyder, Shane, Venette, Steven, J., Calloway, and Slovic, Paul. 2014. *Context and Core Messages for Chromium, Medicines and Personal Care, NDMA, and VOCs (Project #4457)*. Denver, CO: Water Research Foundation. Accessed on November 11, 2017 at www.waterrf.org/Pages/Projects.aspx?PID=4457.

Metz, Cade. 2016. How Facebook Is Transforming Disaster Response. *WIRED*. Accessed on November 11, 2017 at www.wired.com/2016/11/facebook-disaster-response/.

Mileti, Dennis. 1999. *Disasters by Design: A Reassessment of Natural Hazards in the United States*. Washington, DC: Joseph Henry Press.

Morrow, Nathan, Mock, Nancy, Papendieck, Adam, and Kocmich, Nicholas. 2011. Independent Evaluation of the Ushahidi Hatie Project. *Development Information Systems International*. Accessed on November 11, 2017 at http://api.ning.com/files/HX-j3*PqLLSgdkf8w5RVQwTyx-8GN*wEGnr3zb-aZoeXYGoOLSBhU5nFC5-qTSj4C7m7StA0yHmGmHWgdDuDtu48CJRnwW8Q/Ushahidi_Haiti_Eval_final.pdf.

O'Brien, Sara Ashley. 2016. Facebook Ramps Up Its Crisis Response Features. *CNNMoney*. Accessed on November 17, 2017 at http://money.cnn.com/2016/11/17/techno logy/facebook-community-help/index.html.

Okolloh, Ory. 2009. Ushahidi or "Testimony": Web 2.0 Tools for Crowdsourcing Crisis Information (PLA 59). *Participatory Learning and Action*, 59(1): 65–70.

Palen, Leysia, Vieweg, Sarah, Liu, Sophia B., and Hughes, Amanda Lee. 2009. Crisis in a Networked World: Features of Computer-Mediated Communication in the April 16, 2007, Virginia Tech Event. *Social Science Computer Review*, 27(4): 467–480.

Palen, Leysia, and Liu, Sophia B. 2007. Citizen Communications in Crisis: Anticipating a Future of ICT-Supported Public Participation. In *Proceedings of the Sigchi Conference on Human Factors in Computing Systems, San Jose, 2007*, New York: Association for Computing Machinery, pp. 727–736.

Perelman, Chaïm, and Olbrechts-Tyteca, Lucie. 1969. *The New Rhetoric. (La Nouvelle Rhétorique): A Treatise on Argumentation*. Notre Dame: Notre Dame Press.

Procopio, Claire H., and Procopio, Steven T. 2007. Do You Know What It Means to Miss New Orleans? Internet Communication, Geographic Community, and Social Capital in Crisis. *Journal of Applied Communication Research*, 35(1): 67–87.

Putnam, Linda, and Mcphee, David. 2009. Building Theories of Organization: The Constitutive Role of Communication. In *Building Theories of Organization: The Constitutive*

Role of Communication. (eds.) Linda Putnam and Anne Nicotera. New York: Routledge, pp. 187–205.

Pyle, Andrew S. 2016. Surviving the Conflict of Self-Inflicted Organizational Crises. In *Handbook of Research on Effective Communication, Leadership, and Conflict*. (eds.) Anthony Normore, Larry Long, and Mitch Javidi. Hershey: IGI Global.

Qadir, Junaid, Ali, Anwaar, Rasool, Raihan ur, Zwitter, Andrej, Sathiaseelan, Arjuna, and Crowcroft, Jon. 2016. Crisis Analytics: Big Data-Driven Crisis Response. *Journal of International Humanitarian Action*, 1(1): 1–21.

Reibeek, Holli. 2005. *The Rising Cost of Natural Hazards: Feature Articles*. Accessed on August 7, 2017 at https://earthobservatory.nasa.gov/Features/RisingCost/rising_cost5.php.

Roberts, Shadrock. 2015. *Kathmandu & Semarang: Community Mapping and Open Data in Two Cities*. The Rockefeller Foundation. Accessed on August 7, 2017 at www.rockefeller foundation.org/blog/kathmandu-semarang-community-mapping-and-open-data-in-two-cities/.

Rowan, Katherine E., Botan, Carl H., Kreps, Gary L., Samoilenko, Sergei, and Fansworth, Karen. 2009. Risk Communication Education for Local Emergency Managers: Using the CAUSE Model for Research, Education, and Outreach. In *Handbook of Crisis and Risk Communication*. (eds.) Robert L. Heath, and H. Dan O'Hair. New York: Routledge, pp. 168–191.

Russell, Herder, and Ethos Business Law. 2009. *Social Media: Embracing the Opportunities, Averting the Risk*. Accessed on August 7, 2017 at http://russellherder.com/wp-content/uploads/2014/01/socialmedia_whitepaper.pdf.

Sauer, Beverly A. 2003. *The Rhetoric of Risk: Technical Documentation in Hazardous Environments*. New York: Taylor and Francis.

Seeger, Matthew W. 2006. Best Practices in Crisis Communication: An Expert Panel Process. *Journal of Applied Communication Research*, 34(3): 232–244.

Sellnow, Timothy L., Ulmer, R. R., Seeger, M. W., and Littlefield, R. S. 2009. *Effective Risk Communication: A Message-Centered Approach*. New York: Springer.

Sellnow, Timothy L., and Vidoloff, K. G. 2009. Getting Crisis Communication Right: Eleven Best Practices for Effective Risk Communication Can Help an Organization Navigate the Slippery Path through a Crisis Situation. *Food Technology*, 63(9). Accessed at https://works.bepress.com/tim_sellnow/43/.

Seo, Hyunjin, Kim, Ji Young, and Yang, Sung-Un. 2009. Global Activism and New Media: A Study of Transnational NGOs' Online Public Relations. *Public Relations Review*, 35(2): 123–126.

Simis, Molly J., Madden, Haley, Cacciatore, Michael A., and Yeo, Sara K. 2016. The Lure of Rationality: Why Does the Deficit Model Persist in Science Communication? *Public Understanding of Science*, 25(4): 400–414.

Slovic, Paul, Finucane, Melissa L., Peters, Ellen, and MacGregor, Donald G. 2004. Risk as Analysis and Risk as Feelings: Some Thoughts About Affect, Reason, Risk, and Rationality. *Risk Analysis*, 24(2): 311–322.

Trench, Brian. 2008. Towards an Analytical Framework of Science Communication Models. In *Communicating Science in Social Contexts*. (eds.) Donghong Cheng, Michel Claessens, Toss Gascoigne, Jenni Metcalfe, Bernard Schiele, and Shunke Shi. Dordrecht: Springer Publications, pp. 119–135.

Veil, Shari R., and Anthony, Kathryn K. 2017. Exploring Public Relations Challenges in Compounding Crises: The Pariah Effect of Toxic Trailers. *Journal of Public Relations Research*, 29(4): 1–17.

Veil, Shari R., and Bishop, Bradley Wade. 2014. Opportunities and Challenges for Public Libraries to Enhance Community Resilience. *Risk Analysis: An Official Publication of the Society for Risk Analysis*, 34(4): 721–734.

Veil, Shari R., Buehner, Tara, and Palenchar, Michael J. 2011. A Work-in-Process Literature Review: Incorporating Social Media in Risk and Crisis Communication. *Journal of Contingencies and Crisis Management*, 19(2): 110–122.

Venette, Steven J. 2006. Special Section Introduction: Best Practices in Risk and Crisis Communication. *Journal of Applied Communication Research*, 34(3): 229–231.

———. 2007. *Risk Communication as an Intervention/Mediation Strategy*. Paper Presented at the Los Alamos National Laboratory Risk Symposium, Santa Fe, New Mexico.

———. 2008. Risk as an Inherent Element in the Study of Crisis Communication. *Southern Communication Journal*, 73(3): 197–210.

Wells, Kenneth B., Tang, Jennifer, Lizaola, Elizabeth, Jones, Felica, Brown, Arleen, Stayton, Alix, Williams, Malcolm, Anita Chandra, David Eisenman, Stella Fogleman, Alonzo Plough. 2013. Applying Community Engagement to Disaster Planning: Developing the Vision and Design for the Los Angeles County Community Disaster Resilience Initiative. *American Journal of Public Health*, 103(7): 1172–1180.

Witte, Kim, Meyer, Gary, and Martell, Dennis P. 2001. *Effective Health Risk Messages: A Step-By-Step Guide*. Thousand Oaks: Sage Publications.

Zickuhr, Kathryn. 2013. Location-Based Services. *Pew Research Center: Internet, Science & Tech* (Blog). Accessed on November 11, 2017 at www.pewinternet.org/2013/09/12/location-based-services/.

10 The Ports Resilience Index

A participatory approach to building resilience

Lauren L. Morris and Tracie Sempier

Introduction

Coastal ports connect users of land and sea transport in an environment exposed to coastal hazards and climate change impacts, including flooding, storm surge, and sea level rise (Mileti 1999; The Heinz Center 2009; Becker et al. 2012, 2014; Becker and Caldwell 2015). Ports also experience risk through organizational challenges, technological interruptions, worker safety issues, and public health threats (PIANC 2016). Port authorities represent management organizations with unique governance structures and variability in operations. Recent international efforts propose the use of participation and collaboration between policy makers, researchers, practitioners, and residents to develop climate-resilient infrastructure frameworks (Kreft et al. 2014; Vallejo and Mullan 2017).

Academia, government agencies, and private sector companies offer many definitions of resilience. Most are centered around the idea of the capacity or ability of a system, whether physical or human, to prepare for disruption, absorb or resist stress from disturbance, recover from impact in a timely manner, and adapt for future disruptive events (Holling 2001; Cox, Prager, and Rose 2011; The National Academies 2012; Rosati, Touzinsky, and Lillycrop 2015; PIANC 2016). The primary difference between human systems and ecological systems rests on the cognitive ability and adaptive capacity of humans to learn from past experiences, exercise flexibility in decision-making and problem solving, and adapt to new circumstances, sometimes catalyzed by disturbance (Adger 2000; Carpenter et al. 2001; Adger et al. 2005; Folke 2006).

To build community resilience requires progress toward anticipation, response, recovery, and reduced vulnerability (Colten, Kates, and Laska 2008; Wilbanks 2008). Anticipation, defined as when a community understands the possibilities of hazards and takes action to prepare, requires risk communication as a first step. Understanding mechanisms of risk communication and community resilience requires understanding community processes and how social interaction plays a role at various institutional levels and spatial-temporal scales. A process that builds resilience involves multiple stakeholders, recognizes local citizen input and knowledge, addresses the needs of the target community, and seeks resources to implement strategies that promote resilience (Cote and Nightingale

2012; MacKinnon and Derickson 2013; Weichselgartner and Kelman 2015). Such a process implies interactive discussion about how to anticipate, adapt, and transform action to work toward resilience.

In the United States, no specific federal requirements exist for disaster planning at ports. Instead, time and resources get devoted to legislatively mandated security planning for terrorist threats, and any existing disaster preparedness plans show wide variation from port to port (U.S. GAO 2007). By evaluating assets and capabilities before a hazard event strikes, port management can identify the resources needed to increase efficiency of hazard mitigation, response, and recovery, thereby increasing organizational resilience. With the number of potential threats and increasing frequency of hazardous events, port authorities should be more concerned with improving resilience to protect their vital role in facilitating global, national, and regional commerce.

Literature review

In an effort to know whether communities have increased their resilience, academic institutions and government agencies have sought a baseline reference measurement. Some scholars approach resilience assessment by measuring vulnerability. For example, the Disaster Resilience of Place (DROP) model presents a conceptual framework for quantifying resilience to natural hazards at the community level (Cutter et al. 2008). Cutter's team has established baseline disaster resilience indicators (BRIC) as a way to operationalize and test the DROP model at the local level. The material used to identify BRICs comes from publicly available quantitative and demographic data, such as the U.S. Census, County Business Patterns, and data sets from FEMA, NOAA, U.S.G.S., and the American Hospital Directory (Cutter, Burton, and Emrich 2010). In another example, the Spatially Explicit Resilience-Vulnerability (SERV) model uses place and scale-specific weighted indicators to assess vulnerability at the county level (Frazier, Thompson, and Dezzani 2014). Limitations still exist, however, with the quantitative and statistical approach of the SERV model due to inaccuracies generated from statistical conversions. Qualitative methods, particularly surveys, interviews, and meetings, have been used with quantitative methods in studies of resilience indicators (Fontalvo-Herazo, Glaser, and Lobato-Ribeiro 2007; Xu et al. 2015). In addition, a few community resilience frameworks have been developed with quantitative and qualitative methods (Peacock et al. 2010; Renschler et al. 2010). In these frameworks, however, researchers gave priority to readily available quantitative data to develop resilience indicators, with qualitative elements providing ancillary support instead of informing indicators.

Quantitative methods and tools result in quick assessments of *resilience* at broad spatial scales and rely on proxies that may not adequately represent resilience. Furthermore, efforts geared toward resilience indicators focus on governments and communities and do not translate well to ports. Ports themselves represent a unique industrial sector, and within that group, each port authority represents a unique organization in terms of geographic location, exposure to hazards, commodity flow, and management and operation. Quantitative measures for ports focus on structural engineering and infrastructure, but human communication and interpersonal relationships necessarily influence the way a port operates, functions, and achieves resilience. Given the dynamic nature of resilience and the importance of social relationships at local scales, purely quantitative approaches do not adequately address place-based, community resilience and cannot account for variations in social relationships and social networks. Researchers cannot understand the process of place-based resilience at ports without engaging port practitioners in a conversation about resilience.

Qualitative resilience assessment tools offer a way to provide insight into social interactions, organizational process, and risk communication without relying upon quantitative metrics. As an example of a qualitative tool to assess resilience and communicate risk, the Coastal Resilience Index (CRI) focuses on community resilience to natural hazards. The CRI aims to help a community understand its level of resilience through yes-or-no questions under six different categories, including but not limited to critical infrastructure, transportation, community plans, mitigation measures, and social systems (Sempier et al. 2010). The participatory approach of the CRI focuses on facilitating a discussion of local community resilience in order to establish a list of steps to take in order to enhance resilience. Index elements are not weighted or aggregated into a single composite index. The focus of the CRI is not the *score* but rather the conversation that takes place. After several years of implementation of the CRI along the Gulf of Mexico Coast, participating communities often commented on the absence of ports in the discussion of community resilience.

Participatory methods can provide the bridge between building capacity for resilience and measuring or assessing resilience. In some cases, the participatory process of engaging stakeholders to develop measures of resilience facilitates a conversation about resilience that may actually increase community capacity for resilience (Gibbon, Labonte, and Laverack 2002; Wisner 2006). Through participatory and qualitative approaches, the scale of analysis can be highly local and can focus on groups of people with hazard experience. For this project, the collaboration of larger groups of port professionals was necessary to achieve the objective of developing a useful resilience assessment tool that would be widely applicable to a variety of ports but specific enough to be useful to a single port. This chapter offers an answer to the question of how the participatory process can be used to identify the factors that ports consider important in building resilience to hazards.

The Delphi method represents one example of a participatory research technique to collect experience and expert opinion on challenging concepts through multiple rounds of expert consultation (Dalkey and Helmer 1963; Dalkey 1967; Pill 1971; Linstone and Turoff 1975; Okoli and Pawlowski 2004). This chapter describes the use of the Delphi method in the development of a qualitative resilience assessment tool, the Ports Resilience Index (PRI), which functions as a conversation starter to identify and discuss actions that contribute to and develop port resilience. The Delphi method provides a structure to understand the concept of resilience and to build capacity for and promote resilience in a manner more responsible than quantitative diagnoses or proxies of resilience. In this chapter, we represent the project team for the PRI development, which was funded by an NOAA grant to the Gulf of Mexico Alliance, a nonprofit organization that works toward a plan for environmental health and community resilience in the states bordering the Gulf of Mexico: Texas, Louisiana, Mississippi, Alabama, and Florida. This project also served as the foundation and data collection for the dissertation research of the first author.

Over a period of two years, the PRI project team engaged port practitioners through several rounds of consultation to develop a self-assessment tool for port authority personnel that provides a simple and inexpensive method of predicting their ability to reach and maintain an acceptable level of functionality during and after disasters caused by coastal hazards, specifically hurricanes. Such an assessment helps port authorities communicate and discuss risk, identify operational strengths and weaknesses, and identify action items to work toward ensuring maximum functionality during and after a disaster. We describe the phases of the Delphi method and how we used the process to engage port practitioners in defining the *indicators* that contribute to port resilience and therefore make up the Ports Resilience Index. We also provide a few examples of how the participatory process of completing the PRI encourages communication about risk and preparedness beyond existing hurricane plans. We must acknowledge that the PRI is not a theoretical model but a communication tool to predict readiness and to encourage behavioral change. The PRI does not aim to replace more academically stringent exercises that focus on quantitative measures of resilience. Rather, the PRI can be used as a starting point for conversations about resilience with port authorities and in the surrounding communities.

The Delphi method

In the 1950s, the RAND Corporation developed the Delphi method as a way to solicit expert opinion and reach consensus on matters of defense and military strategy. RAND used successive rounds of intense questioning with experts to refine their opinions and reach statistically sound numbers to predict and quantify potential outcomes of threats against national security (Dalkey and Helmer 1963). After the Delphi method became public, researchers applied it to many problems and questions that used expert opinion to quantify uncertain or unknown variables. Over the years, the Delphi method has become recognized as a structured communication process that helps organize information lacking strong conceptual or theoretical form. While initially a method used for quantitative problems, researchers also use the Delphi method to deal with non-concrete concepts and to gather multiple opinions and varieties of experience (Pill 1971). A structured process led by a good facilitator ensures effective communication to stimulate conversation and stakeholder inclusion to show participants how their comments contribute to the knowledge being generated.

In their 1975 book, *The Delphi Method: Techniques and Applications*, Linstone and Turoff describe four distinct phases of the Delphi method. First, the researchers explore the subject under discussion by conducting literature reviews or distributing a preliminary survey to the selected experts. During this phase of the Delphi method, researchers do not aim for statistical significance or robustness but instead seek to gather information from the expert group in order to establish a baseline of knowledge from which to work (Linstone and Turoff 1975). In the second phase, researchers learn how the group of experts views the topic or issue, either through individual surveys or group interaction. The third phase involves highlighting and evaluating any disagreements on how members of the group view the issue through additional surveys to refine expert opinion. In the final phase, all the information generated up to that point has been analyzed, evaluated, and sent back to the experts for their consideration and approval.

Over the decades, researchers using the Delphi method have assembled groups of experts through various techniques, from distributing formal invitations to selecting top-cited and peer-reviewed academic experts. The suggested number of people to include in a Delphi expert group ranges anywhere from three to 18 (Okoli and Pawlowski 2004; Alshehri, Rezgui, and Li 2015; Vidal, Carvalho, and Cruz-Machado 2014). To help researchers understand and develop resilience frameworks, the Delphi process has been used in combination with other qualitative methods, including case-study analysis and textual content analysis (Jordan and Javernick-Will 2013; Alshehri, Rezgui, and Li 2015; Labaka et al. 2014). In these studies, researchers effectively collected expert input and knowledge to inform their research; however, little evidence exists to show ground-truthing or pilot testing of these tools and frameworks beyond their development, to see if they make sense in a real-world application.

Based on the literature review of both the Delphi method and resilience indicators, we felt that traditional Delphi processes rarely included ground-truthing for research products with actual practitioners during development. Therefore, we wanted to conduct pilot tests as a way to ensure the effectiveness of the PRI tool for the end user and to develop a type of *local* knowledge with port practitioners. Through iterative rounds of expert consultation, the Delphi method combined with the use of focus groups provided a robust method to give structure to the loosely defined topic of port resilience assessment.

Phases of the participatory approach used to develop the Ports Resilience Index

Port authorities function as a community, with stakeholders internal to the port authority and external to the port's physical boundaries. Port stakeholders include the port authority management structure; tenants who lease port property; federal agencies with regulatory authority over some function of the port; importers and exporters; shipping lines and shipping agencies; and commercial and recreational users of port property (Becker and Caldwell 2015). From the beginning, we wanted to ensure stakeholder input to the research process and diverse representation on our expert committee (Figure 10.1).

Given the wide variety of stakeholders involved in marine transportation systems and port networks, full representation of every possible port stakeholder on the expert committee would have yielded a group too large to facilitate effectively. For the purpose of developing a tool to be used by port management organizations, we targeted stakeholders internal to the port management structure, such as port authority staff members involved in port operations and individuals who work closely with port authority personnel. The Ports Resilience Expert Committee (PREC) included 13 members, mostly with representation from port authorities across the Gulf of Mexico in Texas, Louisiana, Mississippi, and Florida (Table 10.1).

Recruitment for the PREC began with contacting port representatives met through local and regional meetings, followed by calling their recommended contacts to inquire about willingness to participate. To ensure geographic diversity, the PREC included representation from deep-draft and shallow-draft ports from Texas to Florida with operations including agricultural imports and exports, military shipbuilding, and petrochemical refining and shipping. These ports function

Figure 10.1 Phases of the participatory approach used to develop the Ports Resilience Index; each arrow indicates a period of work by the lead facilitator, in preparation for the next cycle of engagement with port practitioners

Table 10.1 Members of the Ports Resilience Expert Committee

State	# of representatives	Internal to Port Authority	External to Port Authority	Deep-draft	Shallow-draft	Primary commodities
Texas	2	1	1	1	-	Petrochemical
Louisiana*	5	5	-	2	3	Petrochemical; agriculture import/ export; offshore supply service
Mississippi	1	1	-	1	-	Petrochemical; agriculture import/ export; military shipbuilding
Florida	1	1	-	-	-	Cargo shipping and storage
Gulf Coast	4	N/A	4	N/A	N/A	N/A

Note: *Due to the location of the researcher at LSU, many representatives came from Louisiana.

as public agencies in their respective states and act as landlords by leasing facilities and property to tenants. The PREC also included individuals with port-specific expertise including insurance, engineering, and maritime administration.

Following the assembly of the expert committee, the next phase included background research of the academic literature on port resilience and distribution of an online survey to the PREC (Figure 10.1). Sources from the literature review informed a list of survey questions to gather baseline information and begin identifying the factors that are important for port authorities to consider in order to build resilience to disasters and unexpected events. For example, in a report by the U.S. Government Accountability Office (GAO), stakeholders from 17 major U.S. ports that experienced earthquakes and hurricanes reported challenges with damage to port infrastructure, debris clogging the waterways, and delivery of utility services such as electricity and water (U.S. GAO 2007). The most reported challenges, however, included problems with communication, personnel management, and coordination with local, state, and federal stakeholders, both in the response phase and for days to weeks after an event. In 2012, Hurricane Sandy proved challenges still exist for the ports and maritime industry in terms of disaster response and recovery, including hazard mitigation for waterfront buildings (Smythe 2013). Recent studies have looked at the influence of Hurricane Katrina on perception of risk and how ports should incorporate resilience (particularly to sea level change) into planning for the future (Becker and Caldwell 2015). Additionally, a key step in port planning includes understanding assets available for response (Berle, Asbjørnslett, and Rice 2011; Berle, Rice, and Asbjørnslett 2011; U.S. GAO 2007; Mansouri, Nilchiani, and Mostashari 2010; Mileski and Honeycutt 2013). By understanding assets ahead of time and assembling a preparedness plan, maritime industry members and governments with maritime interests will know the availability of resources to deploy after an event in the effort to increase efficiency of disaster response and aid (Mileski and Honeycutt 2013). A recent study in the U.K. concluded that all stakeholders have different types of information, but planning the flow of that information, from suppliers to users, is crucial for port resilience planning (Shaw, Grainger, and Achuthan 2017).

In the survey to the PREC, 15 questions addressed topics such as size and management structure of ports; previous experience with natural hazards; specific activities during planning and response phases; and general preparedness and planning efforts at ports. The survey results provided an initial glimpse of the PREC's priorities for resilience, including the benefits of increased preparedness and communication.

In the next phase, the project team gathered participants together for an in-person meeting to signal the official start of the PRI project (Figure 10.1). As a group, we looked at Mileti's four stages of disaster management (1999) – preparedness, response, recovery, and mitigation – and agreed that our working definition of resilience described the ability of ports to return to an acceptable level of functioning after a disaster and to bounce forward in preparation for the next event. Members of the PREC agreed about the importance of long-term resilience planning for ports and agreed that a resilience tool for port authorities must include questions broad enough to be widely applicable to ports but also specific enough to be useful to individual port authorities. Furthermore, the final product could be something for a new port authority staff member, without previous disaster experience, to use when planning for disasters and resilience.

The PREC recommended starting with the American Association of Port Authorities *Emergency Preparedness and Continuity of Operations Planning Manual for Best Practices* for developing indicators for port resilience (Saathoff 2006). To encourage port authorities to think about long-term planning for resilience, we also developed questions from sources such as NOAA's prototype *Port Tomorrow: Resilience Planning Tool* and Becker and Caldwell's paper on resilient planning strategies for ports (Becker and Caldwell 2015). The first draft PRI included 251 indicator questions, which the PREC reviewed and critiqued during two days of small group work sessions in round one of consultation (Figure 10.1). Over the next few months, comments from each small group were incorporated, and the questions were revised to reflect the input of the PREC, resulting in a list of 146 indicator questions, with many questions having been consolidated to avoid repetition.

The PREC recommended the indicator questions be tested with a few port authorities to gather more feedback and further refine the tool. Three members of the PREC volunteered their port organizations to serve as PRI pilot tests but expressed concerns that 146 questions were too many to discuss with their staff. Sometimes in a Delphi process, the researcher or facilitator must trim down the questions to keep the group engaged (Landeta 2006). To further refine the number of questions, only the broadly worded questions targeting long-range resilience planning or actions that might require year-round effort were kept, resulting in a tool that encourages anticipatory thinking. We held Port Resiliency Pilot Meetings at a port in Texas, in Mississippi, and in Louisiana, with a total of 39 participants representing port authority staff, federal agencies, and private tenants in order to collect on-the-ground expertise to improve the tool and to ensure the effectiveness of the PRI for the end user.

During the pilot test phase, we used a focus group discussion format, facilitated by the lead researcher, to discuss 46 questions in the PRI. Participants provided feedback on the wording and substantive content of the questions, the format of the PRI, and the participatory process as a whole. Each focus group lasted two and a half hours and yielded approximately 75 pages of transcribed discussion. After the pilot tests, the lead researcher incorporated all the comments from the focus group discussions and developed another iteration of the PRI to send to the PREC for final review (Table 10.2). Some of the comments referred to indicator questions that were not explicitly asked in the pilot PRI but were in the longer checklist of 146 questions, and many questions from that list were included in the final version of the PRI.

Due to time and budget constraints, PREC members agreed to a webinar as the most achievable and acceptable format for the last round of discussion and comments (Figure 10.1). Members of the PREC generally agreed with the final wording of the questions and supported the final format of the PRI, which includes

Table 10.2 Examples of how focus group participant feedback (in italics) changed the wording of the questions from the pilot test version to the final Ports Resilience Index

Pilot test PRI question	Final version of PRI question
Does your Port consider historical trends and past events (i.e., climatic data and hurricane paths) to identify information related to hazard risks in long-term planning (i.e., 20 years) for disasters?	Does your Port consider historical trends and past events (e.g., climatic data, *weather records, incidents on-site, economic trends*) for *future chronic events (e.g., sea level rise, shoreline erosion, economic recession)*?
Does the Port conduct regular hazard risk assessments of infrastructure to determine what level of damage and repair can be expected based on the size of an event?	*Has your Port determined an acceptable level of risk (or risk tolerance) for various hazards?*
Does your Port have pre-event contracts in place to allow for fast-track procurement of emergency response and recovery services?	Does your Port have *a list of vendors and contact information to allow for quick scheduling* of emergency response and recovery services *(e.g., equipment, supplies, damage assessment, facility control, channel maintenance)*?

87 questions, divided into eight sections that respondents can answer with a yes, no, or non-applicable (N/A) (Morris 2016) (Table 10.3). Despite the inclination to write very specific indicator questions and reach a consensus on *yes* or *no*, researchers intended for the assessment tool to provide a stimulant for conversation about resilience and to help port authority staff identify action items to improve resilience. To accommodate all types of ports (i.e., large or small; public or private; part of municipality or independent), we added an N/A column to each question. For example, questions about which personnel get sent to the alternative emergency operations location may not apply if the port authority does not evacuate or use a physical location.

For each section of the PRI, the ratio of questions answered *yes* to total questions answered yields a percentage, which corresponds to a resilience range decided by the project team (i.e., 0–49% = low; 50–75% = medium; and 76–100% = high). The project team considers the questions within each section to be directional indicators of port resilience. While the scoring rubric does not yield a numerical value that can be supported by existing engineering, economic, or social indicators, the *yes* or *no* answers to the questions do indicate progress toward a higher range of resilience to coastal hazard impacts on port operations.

Summary of content of the Ports Resilience Index

The substantive content of the PRI addresses structural and organizational resilience, exposing operational policies and procedures that depend on communication

Table 10.3 Example indicator questions from the final version of the Ports Resilience Index

---

Example indicator questions from the Ports Resilience Index

Planning Documents for Hazards and Threats

Has your Port identified and prioritized the critical facilities and services to be restored in order for the Port to resume normal operations (e.g., berths and wharves, roadways, rail, terminal equipment, storage facilities)?

Hazard Assessment: Infrastructure and Assets

Has your Port performed an assessment to identify infrastructure and facility upgrades necessary to limit damage due to flooding, wave and wind action for various storm scenarios?

Insurance and Risk Management

Does your Port have pre-event video or photo documentation of its assets and infrastructure and the supplies to document damages to provide for FEMA and other insurance claims after an event?

Continuity of Operations Planning for Infrastructure and Facilities

Do other government entities in the area have master service agreements for emergency response and restoration that could benefit the Port (e.g., highway cleaning equipment to clear debris from roads leading into and out of the port facility)?

Internal Port Authority Communications

Are recall instructions clear in communicating to Port employees how they will find out when they are to return to work after an event?

Tenant and External Stakeholder Communications

Is there a mechanism in place for your Port to conduct emergency preparedness and hurricane readiness meetings to review the Port's policies and procedures with customers and tenants?

Emergency Operations Location (Physical or Virtual)

Does your Port have an offsite evacuation haven or alternative operations location site, based on the type of event, where it can continue basic operations?

Critical Records and Finance

Does your Port have the ability to process payroll from an alternate location?

---

and partnership, which depend on risk awareness and communication within and outside of the port authority. The first section of the PRI, *Planning Documents for Hazards and Threats*, examines if port authorities have emergency plans that address the procedures of preparing for oncoming threats and if those plans include inventories of critical facilities and business processes that have been prioritized for restoration after a disruption.

The second section, *Hazard Assessment: Infrastructure and Assets*, examines how to assess infrastructure and facilities for safety issues and how to identify necessary upgrades to reduce damage from wind and flood hazards. Port authorities have maintenance and engineering staff that continually patrol port property and assess whether or not infrastructure upgrades need to be made. When considered alongside insurance strategies, however, the decision to undertake construction and implement upgrades depends on cost-benefit analysis. Two questions ask if the port authority considers historic trends and past events to identify information for hazard risks and probabilities that might occur in the future, either for episodic storm events or for long-term environmental change due to sea level rise or shoreline erosion. Pilot test participants also wanted to include consideration of additional threats, such as technological hazards, port-specific hazards (like vessel collisions), and cyber threats. These types of questions encourage port authorities to identify and communicate future risks.

The third section, *Insurance and Risk Management*, provides tools that help port authorities decide if they have the right property insurance strategy based on its identified risks, loss exposure, and economic tolerance. Pilot test participants recommended that questions related to hazard insurance indicate the level of risk a port authority is willing to accept rather than trying to predict the amount of money that might be required for repair and reconstruction from different storm scenarios. Expected damage will change based on the type of event, which requires that a risk management expert understand the type of threat and expected impacts. Other questions ask if port authorities have the materials to document and file insurance claims immediately after an event and if port authorities have formal mutual aid agreements with neighboring ports to provide emergency support operations.

Questions in the fourth section, *Continuity of Operations Planning for Infrastructure and Facilities*, ask port authorities to consider certain pre-storm measures to enhance response and recovery. For example, port authorities should have a pre-identified damage assessment team to conduct quick assessments after an event in compliance with FEMA regulations and procedures for official damage assessment. The PREC originally suggested port authorities establish master service agreements or pre-event contracts with recovery companies to enable faster service after an event. During the pilot test phase, participating port authorities referred to pre-event contracts as nearly impossible to arrange because port staff do not know which companies will be present and available after an event. They suggested rewording the question to emphasize having a list of potential vendors and their contact information to ensure quick contact after an event.

The next two sections of the PRI specifically address communication. Pilot test participants spent considerable time discussing the distinctions between port authority (i.e., the management structure) and port users (i.e., customers utilizing the port facilities), emphasizing the distinction between communications internal to the port authority and communications with tenants and stakeholders external to the port authority. For *Internal Port Authority Communications*, the questions help a port authority determine if it has a sustainable communications plan for port authority employees during times of crisis, including emergency notification, communication during evacuation, recall instructions, and reentry policies. For *Tenant and External Stakeholder Communications*, the questions ask about mechanisms in place to establish long-term communication between the port authority and port users, including harbor safety committee meetings, annual port-wide reminders to review preparedness plans, incident-driven Port Coordination Team conference calls, and daily briefings with the media.

Questions in the *Emergency Operations Location* section help a port authority evaluate if it has the time and resources to manage and maintain a physical emergency operations location. In general, the alternate operations location may not be a physically designated location because the identification of meeting points or muster points depends on the specific characteristics of the hazard event. Having access to several locations and being able to pick up and move quickly is desirable because each event will have a different trajectory and impact area. Similarly, the supplies needed to resume some level of operation will be different for each event and location. In terms of surviving and operating without any external assistance, any port authority has to balance the efficiency of a skeleton crew versus maintaining the supplies required to support a larger staff.

The final section, *Critical Records and Finance*, helps a port authority determine if it has the materials and equipment to access vital records, continue payroll, authorize emergency spending, and conduct banking during an emergency situation. Discussion on electronic data storage and access to that data resulted in a list of examples of important documents to back up electronically, either to the cloud or to a backup server in an offsite physical location.

Participatory process reveals risk communication practices

The participatory process of discussing the PRI questions goes beyond the *what* of hurricane plans to the *how* of resilient practices and allows a look at the mechanisms of port resilience through the eyes of port practitioners. By visiting three different port authorities with three different perspectives, the project team gathered practitioner input to revise the questions of the PRI and suggested additional questions (Table 10.4). In this section, we provide a brief example of how the participatory process of completing the PRI assessment encourages risk communication beyond existing hurricane preparedness plans. Even though the example is a small subset of the PRI, the discussion stimulated by the questions about communication with tenants and customers provides support for the participatory process as a method to facilitate a conversation to promote adaptive capacity and to build resilience.

Academic and government efforts to evaluate resilience might include analysis of written documents, including hazard mitigation or emergency response plans (Cutter, Burton, and Emrich 2010; Renschler et al. 2010; Frazier et al. 2013). In general, port hurricane plans emphasize the *response* element of resilience and focus on ensuring operational fluidity and access to the resources needed in the 72 hours before and after hurricane landfall. Consequently, hurricane plans might be a tool to *help* port authorities implement resilient practices, but understanding *actual* implementation requires communication and discussion with port authorities.

While no standard format exists for writing or updating port hurricane plans, the pilot test port authorities usually incorporate lessons learned after each hurricane season in order to improve their ability to respond to the next event. The Texas port's plan addresses communication and preparation within the port authority to great detail, including many pages devoted to identifying essential personnel and their duties before, during, and after a storm event. In contrast, the plans for

Table 10.4 Pilot test and final version of questions related to communication with tenants and external stakeholders, revised with feedback from focus group participants (in italics)

Pilot test PRI question	Final version of PRI question
Does your Port conduct routine emergency preparedness and hurricane readiness meetings to review policies and procedures with customers and tenants?	*Is there a mechanism in place for* your Port to conduct emergency preparedness and hurricane readiness meetings to review *the Port's* policies and procedures with customers and tenants?
Does your Port remind tenants and customers to review their company's storm plans for storm preparation activities (e.g., coordinating vessel activity; moving barges; securing cargo)?	*Is there a mechanism in place* to remind customers and tenants to review their company's storm plans for storm preparation activities?
–	*Does your Port require its tenants to provide a copy of their business continuity plan?*
–	*Does your Port rebroadcast internal and external advisories (e.g., U.S. Coast Guard Marine Safety Information Bulletin) to communicate with tenants as needed during the crisis?*

the Mississippi port and the Louisiana port provide direction for communicating with port authority personnel before a hurricane makes landfall but also for communicating with federal and state agencies. The reference to communication with external entities may be a result of recent experience with hurricanes, especially in 2005. Forums for cross-communication between port authorities, agency partners, and marine industries have been established as a way to share storm information, mitigate damages, spur recovery, and access post-storm resources. The hurricane plans reflect this difference in experience, with references by the Mississippi and Louisiana ports to incident-driven groups like the Port Coordination Team and Port Emergency Action Team.

As mentioned previously, one of the challenges for port authorities in communicating with tenants involves distinguishing between port authority responsibility and port user responsibility. Communicating with port tenants and port users represents a way to improve resilience by reaching out to other members of the port community and increasing awareness of potential risks and readiness policies and procedures. The PRI helped stimulate a discussion of this topic by including questions that required the port authority to consider activities that might broaden the reach of port communications beyond the port authority staff. For example, two pilot test questions specifically asked about port authority efforts to communicate risk by raising awareness of port policies to customers and tenants in order to minimize property damage and ensure personal survival during and after an event. To reflect participant input on these questions, the wording was changed to read "is there a mechanism in place . . ." to conduct these efforts (Table 10.4).

This nuance in wording demonstrated the port authority is not necessarily responsible for explaining preparedness strategies to tenants and customers but can offer opportunities for tenants and customers to learn about and be aware of the policies and procedures.

At the port in Texas, participants initially responded that the port authority does not conduct routine emergency preparedness meetings to review procedures with customers and tenants. Four participants discussed with each other why the port authority *should* actively remind tenants to assume responsibility for their property and facilities. One participant justified why the port authority should remind port users to review company preparedness plans: "kind of almost a moral obligation, I mean, we [the port authority] have to recognize that we have lots of tenants that are coming in here that are not from this area, that are not climatized to . . . our situations . . . we have . . . stakeholders now that may need a little assistance." Another participant offered that it is professional courtesy to remind tenants of the port tariff, especially as it relates to company responsibility after an event: "[T]here's due diligence on both parts required. . . . We can advise them . . . as a professional courtesy." With high traffic flow from customers representing all parts of the world, the act of raising situational awareness with port users enables the broader port community to prepare for hazardous events. Participants agreed that the port authority can send media broadcasts to customers to remind them of hurricane season and to encourage them to review the updated port tariff. Another participant suggests that involvement by customers and tenants in port-wide groups would enable information to be shared with port users.

For the port in Mississippi, the hurricane plan indicates that the port authority reaches out to marine interests and port users to remind them of the start of hurricane season, provide them with the plan, and keep communication open during the 96 hours before hurricane landfall. Similarly, at the port in Louisiana, port authority staff members distribute the hurricane plan to their customers and tenants and remind them to review their own company's readiness plans. However, the discussion reveals that the port staff does not actively review the policies and procedures in a meeting format with customers and tenants; such an active review only happens with other port authority staff.

During the discussion at the port in Louisiana, one of the participants who represented private industry offered his past experience of having to submit a hurricane preparedness plan to the property landlord. He describes how the preparedness plan needed to replicate the landlord's preparedness plan and suggests that the port authority might consider something similar: "[W]e [the tenants] just would mirror yours [hurricane plan], but at least we'd sign off on it and say 'we're buying into what you're selling.' That we'd pick up all our stuff, that we'd be responsible for all our equipment." Another participant mentions that when the port closes, all the tenants have to leave anyway, which elicits a response from a third participant, who says "But it may not be a bad idea to have the tenants . . . everybody's got the plan . . . if you have a plan that mirrors ours and we say we're at Whiskey [U.S. Coast Guard Condition Whiskey is reached when tropical storm force winds are expected in 96 hours], you know what to do." Even though the port in Louisiana distributes its hurricane plan to port users, the port authority staff could take more active steps in making sure that port tenants understand preparedness actions.

Discussion and conclusion

Participatory research methodologies can help facilitate the development of useful tools that are informed by expert input, address social interactions and process, and help communicate risk to hazards. The participatory approach used for the PRI successfully resulted in a qualitative resilience assessment tool that functions as a decision-support tool useful to port authorities and their stakeholders. By using the input and expertise of the PREC members, the project team developed a draft list of indicator questions. Through the pilot test phase, we were able to ground-truth these questions with entire port authority staffs to adjust the specific wording and content of the indicator questions. Based on input from each round of expert consultation, we adjusted the format of the tool and improved the utility of the tool in stimulating a conversation on resilience.

For the PRI, we began with an already established document to develop indicator questions. However, the participatory approach ensured we took a critical approach to those original questions and modified them to reflect reality but also to encourage new ways of thinking and discussing resilience. We emphasized practitioner input rather than academic expertise to ensure the final product would be useful to the end user group of port authorities. In a way, our expert committee helped to build "local" expert knowledge. The pilot tests proved an essential step to ground-truth indicator questions, which became evident in each port's critique of the questions and suggestions for improvement.

The benefits of face-to-face interaction become more evident during the pilot test phase. As an organizational self-assessment, the PRI should not be completed by individuals at their desks but as a group sitting together in one room and having a conversation. During the pilot tests, members within a single port authority sometimes disagreed with each other on the answer to a question. Upon further discussion, the disagreement stemmed from different interpretations of the question, which merited some editing, or from unclear understanding of how individual departments operate within a port authority.

After incorporating feedback gathered during the pilot test phase, the PREC agreed that the PRI is a tool that encourages port authority staff members to engage in critical conversation about resilience. One PREC member suggested that port authorities complete the PRI each year as a way to record trends and progress in resilience planning. By establishing a record, any new staff member or executive leader will have the ability to look back and see how operations and planning procedures have changed, which helps to establish an internal accountability process and to codify institutional memory. Several PREC members agreed that if port authority leadership buys into the PRI process and encourages it each year, then port personnel will have the incentive to sit down with each other to discuss potential hazard risks and areas of operation and planning where they might improve.

All data sets have limitations, and the process of discussing individual perspective creates a situation where data cannot be standardized or normalized. Challenges exist in taking the extracts of nuanced discussion from a few ports and generalizing it to the maritime industry, but this challenge justifies the participatory process as an appropriate method for the purpose of assessing organizational resilience. Since individual staff members and port tenants bring unique perspective to the collective whole of a port authority and port community, a process to assess resilience that revolves around discussion and interaction is an appropriate way to communicate risk and make decisions, inherently building capacity for resilience.

The process of completing the PRI questions in a participatory setting allows researchers to understand how port practitioners perceive anticipatory actions, which is often different from how researchers and policy makers perceive them. Researchers and policy makers maintain a position of being removed from ports in a physical and operational sense. From the practitioner's side, the realities of the job put anticipatory actions in a different light. While academic researchers might experience frustration with audiences that do not readily implement anticipatory actions, the participatory process of discussing questions within the self-assessment requires further discussion in a setting where individuals' jobs are not on the line and budget pressures are minimized. International and national frameworks for action often imply or assume money will be available to implement anticipatory or climate-resilient strategies. In a time when budgets for these activities are constantly streamlined, the PRI provides a way to have a conversation about feasible actions or the low-hanging fruit that might be implemented at an organizational level to improve resilience. For example, low-hanging fruit may include communication with tenants and port users. As vessels move through the maritime transportation network, high fluidity across port users and tenants requires proactive measures by the port authority to promote readiness.

Both researchers and participants benefited from the participatory nature of the project. For the PRI, the process benefited participants by stimulating a conversation on resilience and by formalizing collective experiences to inform other port authorities. The PRI project benefited the researchers by contributing to the concept of port resilience, providing insight into place-based resilience at the port authority level, and providing structure to a methodology to develop resilience assessment tools. Through pilot tests and face-to-face interaction, the participatory approach helped develop a tool that stimulates conversation and aids in decision-making, to move beyond written plans and to encourage action.

References

Adger, W. N. 2000. Social and Ecological Resilience: Are They Related? *Progress in Human Geography*, 24(3): 347–364.

Adger, W. N., Hughes, T. P., Folke, C., Carpenter, S. R., and Rockström, J. 2005. Social-Ecological Resilience to Coastal Disasters. *Science*, 309(5737): 1036–1039.

Alshehri, S. A., Rezgui, Y., and Li, H. 2015. Delphi-Based Consensus Study into a Framework of Community Resilience to Disaster. *Natural Hazards*, 75(3): 2221–2245.

Becker, A. H., and Caldwell, M. R. 2015. Stakeholder Perceptions of Seaport Resilience Strategies: A Case Study of Gulfport (Mississippi) and Providence (Rhode Island). *Coastal Management*, 43(1): 1–34.

Becker, A. H., Inoue, S., Fischer, M., and Schwegler, B. 2012. Climate Change Impacts on International Seaports: Knowledge, Perceptions, and Planning Efforts among Port Administrators. *Climatic Change*, 110(1): 5–29.

Becker, A. H., Matson, P., Fischer, M., and Mastrandrea, M. D. 2014. Towards Seaport Resilience for Climate Change Adaptation: Stakeholder Perceptions of Hurricane Impacts in Gulfport (MS) and Providence (RI). *Progress in Planning*, 99(1): 1–49.

Berle, Ø., Asbjørnslett, B. E., and Rice, J. B. 2011. Formal Vulnerability Assessment of a Maritime Transportation System. *Reliability Engineering and System Safety*, 96(6): 696–705.

Berle, Ø., Rice Jr, J. B., and Asbjørnslett, B. E. 2011. Failure Modes in the Maritime Transportation System: A Functional Approach to Throughput Vulnerability. *Maritime Policy and Management*, 38(6): 605–632.

Carpenter, S., Walker, B., Anderies, M. J., and Abel, N. 2001. From Metaphor to Measurement: Resilience of What to What? *Ecosystems*, 4(8): 765–781.

Colten, C. E., Kates, R. W., and Laska, S. B. 2008. Three Years After Katrina: Lessons for Community Resilience. *Environment: Science and Policy for Sustainable Development*, 50(5): 36–47.

Cote, M., and Nightingale, A. J. 2012. Resilience Thinking Meets Social Theory: Situating Social Change in Socio-Ecological Systems (SES) Research. *Progress in Human Geography*, 36(4): 475–489.

Cox, A., Prager, F., and Rose, A. 2011. Transportation Security and the Role of Resilience: A Foundation for Operational Metrics. *Transport Policy*, 18(2): 307–317.

Cutter, S. L., Barnes, L., Berry, M., Burton, C., Evans, E., Tate, E., and Webb, J. 2008. A Place-Based Model for Understanding Community Resilience to Natural Disasters. *Global Environmental Change*, 18(4): 598–606.

Cutter, S. L., Burton, C. G., and Emrich, C. T. 2010. Disaster Resilience Indicators for Benchmarking Baseline Conditions. *Journal of Homeland Security and Emergency Management*, 7(1): 1–22.

Dalkey, N. C. 1967. *Delphi*. Santa Monica, CA: RAND Corporation.

Dalkey, N. C., and Helmer, O. 1963. An Experimental Application of the Delphi Method to the Use of Experts. *Management Science*, 9(3): 458–467.

Folke, C. 2006. Resilience: The Emergence of a Perspective for Social-Ecological Systems Analyses. *Global Environmental Change*, 16(3): 253–267.

Fontalvo-Herazo, M. L., Glaser, M., and Lobato-Ribeiro, A. 2007. A Method for the Participatory Design of an Indicator System as a Tool for Local Coastal Management. *Ocean & Coastal Management*, 50(10): 779–795.

Frazier, T. G., Thompson, C. M., and Dezzani, R. J. 2014. A Framework for the Development of the SERV Model: A Spatially Explicit Resilience-Vulnerability Model. *Applied Geography*, 51: 158–172.

Frazier, T. G., Thompson, C. M., Dezzani, R. J., and Butsick, D. 2013. Spatial and Temporal Quantification of Resilience at the Community Scale. *Applied Geography*, 42: 95–107.

Gibbon, M., Labonte, R., and Laverack, G. 2002. Evaluating Community Capacity. *Health & Social Care in the Community*, 10(6): 485–491.

The H. John Heinz III Center for Science, Economics and the Environment. 2009. *The Hidden Cost of Coastal Hazards: Implications for Risk Assessment and Mitigation*. Washington, DC: The Heinz Center.

Holling, C. S. 2001. Understanding the Complexity of Economic, Ecological and Social Systems. *Ecosystems*, 4(5): 390–405.

Jordan, E., and Javernick-Will, A. 2013. Indicators of Community Recovery: Content Analysis and Delphi Approach. *Natural Hazards Review*, 14(1): 21–28.

Kreft, S., Eckstein, D., Junghans, L., Kerestan, C., and Hagen, U. 2014. *Global Climate Risk Index 2015: Who Suffers Most from Extreme Weather Events? Weather-Related Loss Events in 2013 and 1994 to 2013*. Berlin: Germanwatch. Accessed at https://hazdoc.colorado.edu/handle/10590/2924.

Labaka, L., Comes, T., Hernantes, J., Sarriegi, J. M., and Gonzalez, J. J. 2014. *Implementation Methodology of the Resilience Framework*. Paper Presented at the 47th Hawaii International Conference on System Sciences, Waikoloa, HI.

Landeta, J. 2006. Current Validity of the Delphi Method in Social Sciences. *Technological Forecasting and Social Change*, 73(5): 467–482.

Linstone, H. A., and Turoff, M. 1975. *The Delphi Method: Techniques and Applications*. Reading, MA: Addison-Wesley.

MacKinnon, D., and Derickson, K. D. 2013. From Resilience to Resourcefulness: A Critique of Resilience Policy and Activism. *Progress in Human Geography*, 37(2): 253–270.

Mansouri, M., Nilchiani, R., and Mostashari, A. 2010. A Policy Making Framework for Resilient Port Infrastructure Systems. *Marine Policy*, 34(6): 1125–1134.

Mileski, J. P., and Honeycutt, J. 2013. Flexibility in Maritime Assets and Pooling Strategies: A Viable Response to Disaster. *Marine Policy*, 40: 111–116.

Mileti, D. 1999. *Disasters by Design: A Reassessment of Natural Hazards in the United States*. Washington, DC: Joseph Henry Press.

Morris, L. L. 2016. *A Port Management Self-Assessment: Understanding How Prepared Your Port Organization Is for a Disaster*. Accessed on November 11, 2018 at www.gulfofmexicoalliance.org/documents/pits/ccr/ports_resilience_index.pdf.

The National Academies. 2012. *Disaster Resilience: A National Imperative*. Prepared by the Committee on Increasing National Resilience to Hazards and Disasters, Committee on Science, Engineering, and Public Policy. Washington, DC: National Academies Press.

Okoli, C., and Pawlowski, S. D. 2004. The Delphi Method as a Research Tool: An Example, Design Considerations and Applications. *Information & Management*, 42(1): 15–29.

Peacock, W. G., Brody, S. D., Seitz, W. A., Merrell, W. J., Vedlitz, A., Zahran, S., Harriss, R. C., and Stickney, R. 2010. *Advancing Resilience of Coastal Localities: Developing, Implementing, and Sustaining the Use of Coastal Resilience Indicators: A Final Report*. Texas A&M University, Hazard Reduction and Recovery Center. Accessed on November 11, 2018 at www.researchgate.net/profile/Walter_Peacock/publication/254862206_Final_Report_Advancing_the_Resilience_of_Coastal_Localities.pdf.

PIANC Cross-Commission Task Group 193. 2016. *Background: Resilience of the Maritime and Inland Waterborne Transport System*. Accessed on November 11, 2018 at www.pianc.org/envicomactivewg.php.

Pill, J. 1971. The Delphi Method: Substance, Context, a Critique and an Annotated Bibliography. *Socio-Economic Planning Sciences*, 5(1): 57–71.

Renschler, C., Fraizer, A. E., Reinhorn, A. M., Arendt, L., and Cimellaro, G. P. 2010. *A Framework for Defining and Measuring Resilience at the Community Scale: The PEOPLES Resilience Framework*. Buffalo, NY: University of Buffalo, Multidisciplinary Center for Earthquake Engineering Research.

Rosati, J. D., Touzinsky, K. F., and Lillycrop, W. J. 2015. Quantifying Coastal System Resilience for the U.S. Army Corps of Engineers. *Environment Systems and Decisions*, 35(2): 196–208.

Saathoff, P. 2006. *Emergency Preparedness and Continuity of Operations Planning: Manual for Best Practices*. Alexandria, VA: American Association of Port Authorities.

Sempier, T. T., Swann, L. D., Emmer, R., Sempier, S. H., and Schneider, M. 2010. *Coastal Community Resilience Index: A Community Self-Assessment*. Accessed on November 11, 2018 at www.masgc.org/pdf/masgp/08-014.pdf.

Shaw, D. R., Grainger, A., and Achuthan, K. 2017. Multi-level Port Resilience Planning in the UK: How Can Information Sharing Be Made Easier? *Technological Forecasting and Social Change*, 121: 126–138.

Smythe, T. C. 2013. *Assessing the Impacts of Hurricane Sandy on the Port of New York and New Jersey's Maritime Responders and Response Infrastructure*. Quick Response Report No. 238. University of Colorado, Natural Hazards Center.

U.S. Government Accountability Office (U.S. GAO). 2007. *Port Risk Management: Additional Federal Guidance Would Aid Ports in Disaster Planning and Recovery*. Washington, DC: U.S. GAO.

Vallejo, L., and Mullan, M. 2017. *Climate-Resilient Infrastructure: Getting the Policies Right*. OECD Environment Working Papers, 121. Paris: OECD Publishing.

Vidal, R., Carvalho, H., and Cruz-Machado, V. A. 2014. *Strategic Resilience Development: A Study Using Delphi*. Paper Presented at the Proceedings of the Eighth International Conference on Management Science and Engineering Management, Lisbon, Portugal.

Weichselgartner, J., and Kelman, I. 2015. Geographies of Resilience: Challenges and Opportunities of a Descriptive Concept. *Progress in Human Geography*, 39(3): 249–267.

Wilbanks, T. J. 2008. Enhancing the Resilience of Communities to Natural and Other Hazards: What We Know and What We Can Do. *Natural Hazards Observer*, 32(5): 10–11.

Wisner, B. 2006. Self-Assessment of Coping Capacity: Participatory, Proactive and Qualitative Engagement of Communities in Their Own Risk Management. In *Measuring Vulnerability to Natural Hazards: Towards Disaster Resilient Societies*, (ed.) J. Birkmann. Tokyo: United Nations University Press, pp. 316–327.

Xu, L., Marinova, D., Xin, P., and Guo, X. 2015. Resilience-Based Sustainability Indicators for Freshwater Lakes with Application for Dongting Lake, China. *Environment and Natural Resources Research*, 5(2): 165.

11 Advancing resilience post-disaster

Improving designer–user communication in the post-Lushan earthquake reconstruction and recovery

Haorui Wu

Introduction and background

On April 20, 2013, an earthquake with a magnitude of 7.0 earthquake hit Lushan County, Ya'an, Sichuan (Geoscience Australia Earthquake 2013). As the epicenter was in Lushan County, the earthquake was named for it. This was the second most deadly earthquake to happen in Sichuan, taking place only five years after the Wenchuan Earthquake, which occurred on May 12, 2008. The Seismological Society of America reported that the Lushan earthquake resulted in 203 deaths and 11,492 injuries, with over 1.5 million people affected (RedOrbit 2014). On April 21, 2013, Chinanews listed on its website that at the epicenter and in its vicinity, local infrastructure, including power, water, and gas, was utterly destroyed, as was residential housing in nine towns and townships and in the metropolitan area of neighboring Ya'an City.

After the earthquake, drawing from lessons learned from the Wenchuan case, the national Post-Lushan Earthquake Reconstruction and Recovery Committee was highly motivated to improve the quality of the built environment in the earthquake-hit areas of Lushan to better support future community resilience (Wu and Hou 2016). This required synchronizing the social, economic, and ecological dimensions of long-term recovery. This aim aligned with the priorities of the United Nations' 2015 Sendai Framework on Disaster Risk Reduction, which states, "it is urgent and critical to anticipate, plan for and reduce disaster risk in order to more effectively protect persons, communities, and countries, their livelihoods, health, cultural heritage, socioeconomic assets and ecosystems, and thus strengthen their resilience" (United Nations 2015, 10).

Post-disaster civic participation and resilience

According to Ungar (2013), resilience indicates two types of individual and collective capacities. The first involves obtaining and managing various resources (including social, physical, and cultural) to support residents' well-being (Ungar 2013). Good civic participation in post-disaster reconstruction and recovery has proven to be the best way to guarantee disaster survivors' access to different community-based resources so that their basic living requirements could be fulfilled (Kennedy et al. 2008). With regard to different types of support and resource, local residents are often the best judges in determining how their lives and livelihoods should be reconstructed (Asian Development Bank 2006). The process of facilitating various supports and resources in the community reconstruction and recovery empowers local dwellers' leadership and builds the resilience at individual, family, and community levels (Wu and Drolet 2016).

Community-based civic participation is a community-driven civic engagement strategy, the objective being the improvement of livelihoods and social life and the advancement of holistic resilience (Kyamusugulwa 2013). The participatory approach has been broadly utilized after disasters for a variety of purposes, from emergency response to reconstruction and long-term recovery (World Bank 2006). The participatory approach involves as many stakeholders as possible, especially local residents, in making democratic decisions and contributing to shared community development goals. This participatory approach has come to be accepted as an effective strategy that builds social connections among all the inhabitants, strengthens social cohesion, and supports community diversity and residents' livelihood recovery (International Rescue Committee 2007).

Chandrasekhar (2012) argues that all stakeholders affected by a particular disaster should be involved in all stages of that region's post-disaster reconstruction and recovery. After the Lushan earthquake, the top-bottom design of the governmental system produced a powerful governance and information dissemination pathway from decision makers to users in the form of informing and consultation (Sanoff 2000). It only superficially examined the needs of the end users and ineffectively conveyed grassroots input to inform upper level decision making (Sanoff 2000). The centralized, authoritarian Chinese government exemplifies the limitations of top-down political governance. A two-way approach to communication and participatory collaboration is required to promote risk communication and address the grassroots level's urgent requirements during post-disaster reconstruction and recovery. Such an approach is much more effective in creating solutions that effectively rebuild the lives and livelihoods of survivors. Since civic participation can be very limited in the post-disaster scenario, when it comes to the planning of the new community and architectural design of the new housing, few local residents are able to becoming involved.

Within the survivors' original communities, the local inhabitants' long-term engagement in navigating and utilizing different resources within both the natural and built environments supports their social connections and social networks, which influences their livelihood and holistic well-being (Halilovich 2011). Lo and Cheung (2016: 874) argue that spatial change after post-disaster reconstruction "facilitates neighborly interaction and risk communication across a neighborhood" and enhances household and community resilience. Hence, both physical reconstruction and social recovery play significant roles in the long-term post-disaster recovery (Wu 2014). Architects, urban planners, and urban designers should focus on how the planning and design of the new built environment could stimulate the people's engagement with that environment so that their daily routine activities may be conducted in such a meaningful way that social relatedness is reestablished, holistic wellness is supported, and eventually, resilience capacity is built and even advanced (Wu 2014). Social recovery interventions should emphasize human dignity and social capacity in community development and should aim to empower local residents' leadership toward accessing community-based resources and utilizing them in culturally meaningful ways (Dominelli 2012). Synthesizing both physical reconstruction and social recovery will accelerate the recovery process and help the disaster survivors rebuild their lives (Tierney and Oliver-Smith 2012). Hence, it is important to determine, at the beginning of reconstruction, an approach that synthesizes the human-place relationship and to stay with that approach during the entire recovery stage (Wu 2018). The designer–user partnership developed under this scenario.

Designer–user partnerships in community planning and architectural design

The post-Lushan earthquake reconstruction and recovery was conducted by three levels of government, the Central Government, the Sichuan Provincial Government, and the Ya'an Municipal Government. The Provincial Post-Earthquake Reconstruction and Recovery Committee (PPERRC), which formed immediately after the earthquake, consisted of multiple levels of government officials, scholars, researchers, practitioners, and other professionals from various fields, including architecture, civil engineering, urban planning and design, commerce and finance, geography, geology, and other disciplines from the social sciences and humanities. Architects were appointed by the central and provincial governments to lead the committee. The committee established the guidelines, policies, and plans that supervised the overall planning and reconstruction and recovery activities.

Sichuan Agricultural University (SAU) is the only comprehensive university located in the city of Ya'an. It is also the nearest comprehensive university to the epicenter of the earthquake. Immediately after the Lushan earthquake, faculty (architects, urban planners, and urban designers) and students (who served as research assistants) from the Department of Architecture and the Department of Urban Planning, College of Architecture and Urban-Rural Planning (CAURP) of SAU, served on PPERRC, and some led the sub-committees, as well. As an architect and adjunct faculty member affiliated with CAURP, collaborating with other faculty members, the author conducted several reconstruction-related research projects and took charge of several villages' reconstruction (community planning and architectural design) in the worst-hit areas. Following the PPERRC's instruction, the author and some of the other faculty members co-led research teams and conducted field research in the quake-hit areas in order to decipher the best reconstruction strategies that would support the villages' long-term recovery and resilience.

Wide-ranging knowledge of the local physical, social, and cultural landscapes plays an essential role in any successful planning and architectural design project (Lyles-Chockley 2008). Architects are required to have a thorough understanding of these landscapes and need to be able to reflect them into the design work (Lawson 2005). Plenty of internal and external factors, such as very short design processes and unavailable background information and related data, however, increase the difficulty in accessing this information and data (Cairns and Jacobs 2014). On the other hand, local residents have rich place-making knowledge from their long-term engagement with the local built and natural environments of a place (Wu 2014). They are *architects by nature* and provide reliable reference sources for place-making related skills for designers (Brook 2013). Architects were encouraged to directly communicate with local residents. Since architects used to represent the government in China, the historically unhappy relationship between the government and residents made the Chinese architect rarely facilitate this type of cooperation with local residents (Wu 2014).

After the Lushan earthquake, the author, faculty members, students, and other professionals conducted field trips to appointed villages and communities and lived with the local inhabitants for several days at a time (based on family units) in order to better understand the survivors' wishes and requirements regarding their new homes. This team cooperated with local governments, taking advantage of the reconstruction opportunity to achieve long-term recovery and improving community resilience goals in accordance with each village or community's unique characteristics and needs. In order for the committee to understand the local residents' immediate and long-term requirements, each student directly communicated with one family and collected information that he or she then conveyed to the professional designers (faculty members). Each faculty member supervised about 5–8 students. The faculty-student teams worked together to use the information they collected to communicate with the local governmental decision makers in order to facilitate the overall reconstruction and recovery plan. The faculty members and students kept in constant dialogue with local families to establish their reconstruction plan. This collaboration during the entire process, including fieldwork, planning, and the design process, eventually produced a very special designer–user partnership and communication approach among the faculty members, students, governmental officials, local dwellers, and other stakeholders. Furthermore, this partnership stimulated the local residents' engagement in their own community's reconstruction, contributing to their resilience building by allowing them to facilitate various community-based resources.

Ultimately, the designer–user partnership successfully promoted communication post-disaster by contributing to a number of very positive reconstruction achievements of the high-quality built environment. With these recovery outcomes, the local inhabitants were able to resume their daily lives and rebuild their livelihood by taking advantage of their new environment and related resources. The local government officials illustrated that the reconstruction of their villages opened a new door for their village's long-term recovery and redevelopment and dramatically advanced these communities' post-disaster resilience capacities.

Methodology

During the fieldwork in the earthquake-hit areas of the Lushan earthquake, the author conducted qualitative research, organizing four focus groups and

Table 11.1 Participants in research

Research activities	Focus groups				Personal interview
	User I	*User II*	*Designer I*	*Designer II*	
Participants	8 residents from Guchengping Village	6 residents from Tianquan Town	8 students from CAURP at SAU	4 faculty members from CAURP at SAU	3 local government officials and 1 community planner

conducting four personal interviews and analyzing the resulting responses (see Table 11.1). The focus groups and interviews were completed over the course of two years after the Lushan earthquake. They were designed for the two main groups that made up the designer–user partnership: two designer focus groups and two user focus groups (local inhabitants). One designer focus group recruited eight students from SAU, and the other designer focus group consisted of four faculty members from the CAURP at SAU. Eight residents from Guchengping Village and six from Tianquan Town respectively were in the two user focus groups. Both the village and the town were located in the worst-hit area affected by the Lushan earthquake. The personal interviewees included three local government officials and one community planner. All those taking part in both the focus groups and the individual interviews were directly involved in the entire reconstruction effort.

All of the focus groups and personal interviews were audiotaped. The analysis of transcriptions was supported by the qualitative data analysis software NVivo 10. The author coded all the transcriptions and grouped related codes into appropriate themes. The main findings, supported by related themes, are reported in the following section.

Contribution of the designer–user partnership

Findings regarding the influence of designer–user partnerships on post-disaster reconstruction and recovery will focus on the three stages: planning, reconstruction, and recovery. The planning stage focused on foundations of reconstruction and recovery within the villages and communities. This set the basic tone and defined the orientation of the project under the central government's general master plan of reconstruction and recovery. This stage was completed within three months. The reconstruction stage concentrated on short-term physical reconstruction of the built environment, with the predominant focus on rebuilding housing and village- and community-level infrastructure (this included reconnecting local infrastructure with that of the surrounding areas). The cases involved in this research include mostly the residential housing, along with local infrastructure. Most reconstruction was finished within one year after the earthquake. Long-term recovery usually begins immediately after the completion of physical reconstruction and is always interlaced with the reconstruction stage (Johnson and Hayashi

2012). This stage could last anywhere from three to five years or even longer, as international studies have shown (Kamel and Loukaitou-Sideris 2004). The recovery stage reported by this research illustrates the completion of short-term recovery within two years after the earthquake.

During the planning stage, understand local residents' practical needs and reduce their anxiety

As mentioned before, governmental reconstruction plans need to fundamentally reflect the local residents' requirements. Due to the historically strained relationship between residents and the government, however, direct interventions by the government regarding the collection of information from the residents was extremely difficult (Wu 2014). This section will demonstrate that the designer–user partnership narrowed this gap by building trust and bridging communication among the faculty members, students, and local residents.

An elderly woman described her experience of her first meeting with a faculty member and a student:

> I clearly remember the first time they came to my old wooden house, a teacher and a student from SAU. The teacher praised how excellent my carpentry work is. I thought they were tourists. Then he (the teacher) introduced them and wanted to talk about how we wanted our new house to be built. . . . [At that point], I believed that they were just asking but wouldn't be serious. My husband just kept silent. He heard from somewhere that these people only ask but did nothing after that. He felt that it's a waste of time to talk with them at all. We didn't talk a lot the first time. They just looked around my house, my storage room, the garden . . . I told them that this house was built by my family and neighbors. The teacher also asked some questions, such as how many years did [it take to complete the house]? Who helped us? How did we prepare the construction materials? . . . I saw they were very serious, because the student was carefully taking notes all the way. . . . Several days later, I saw the teacher again in our village meeting. Almost all my neighbors came to hear the announcement regarding the reconstruction plan for our village. My village leader told us that the teachers from SAU would help us to rebuild our new village and then they talked about the plan. . . . I was astonished that the teacher, who came to my house, said some of my thoughts during our talk. I told my neighbors that this time they were very serious. My neighbors agreed; they felt the same.

This case illustrates how the designers began to build trust with local residents through communication. Initially, trust was built with individuals or a family in the village, and gradually it spread through word of mouth to reach the entire village. As the initial and primary step for successful civic participation in the governmental decision-making process, the trust establishes the basic communication foundation so that the dwellers can be able to diminish their concerns and eliminate their prejudices (Uslaner and Brown 2004). This also stimulated the residents to open their hearts, explain their concerns, and actively offer more information to be further involved in the later stages.

An elderly man recalled how the good communication dispelled the family worries:

> We thought that our house was OK. It survived after the Wenchuan earthquake, which was 10 times stronger than this one [Lunshan earthquake]. But the teacher told us that the inner structure might be damaged although the outside might still look good. It was livable, but for long-term, rebuilding it would be the best choice. Meanwhile, the government has invested certain funding to support the reconstruction. . . . My wife told them [a faculty member and several students] that her sister, who live in Wenchuan, was moved to the residential community [which had been built by the government]. She [the sister] always complained about the new condo, very small and no place to put their farming tools. My wife was very worried about if we would have to move to the same one [as her sister]. We wanted our house because we had gotten used to it and we were too old to move into a condo. . . . The teacher told us that they were not planning to build the smaller residential communities like the ones in the big cities. Small houses with gardens is good for us and our environment. After that, we felt a little bit easy.

This gentleman's words not only reflect the positive influence of the designer–user partnership on addressing their concerns but also display an eagerness to pursue an open communication with the decision makers in order to build the influence of the residents' leadership capacity upon the decision-making process of the building of their new communities Previously, these people's stressed relationship with the government officials, to some extent, had weakened their motivation to relate helpful information and even undermined their pursuance of their right-to-know and right-to-control. However, the designer–user partnership repaired the trust connections and reopened their hearts. The increased positive affect of the partnership on the inhabitants' well-being and resilience capacity was demonstrated by the gentleman's words, "*we felt a little bit easy*" after hearing the designer's clarification.

During the reconstruction stage, the designer–user partnership encourages local innovation for practical and educational goals

In the most devastated rural areas hit by the Lushan earthquake, most residential housing had been constructed by the local residents. The elderly woman's words above demonstrate that and further indicate that the dwellers collaborated together to build their houses. This historical collaboration has enabled the accumulation of practical and useful experience and increased the capacity of utilizing different resources regarding how the built environment adapts to the natural environment. The experience is understood as sociocultural heritage, which would help the nonlocal professionals to better understand the local-based knowledge and skills so that ultimately, their design could be improved. The capacity directly contributes to the community resilience.

A local carpenter proudly described his contributions during the reconstruction:

> All of my family members are carpenters for generations. I am not showing off, but they [construction crew from outside] really did not know how to use the local materials. The teachers from SAU asked me to show them how to use the wood. Frankly, at the beginning I did not want to do that [because] they were my own professional skills, [but after thinking about it], I realized this would be good for everyone because the new community was built for all my neighbors. So I agreed with that. I also persuaded my neighbor, a very famous mason, to train the construction crews. We just gave them some small tips, and they worked very well. This also made us very famous. To this day, I still receive calls sometimes from them [members or managers of construction crews]. They asked me some questions and also suggested that I should have a company! [laughing]

Several students were astonished about local residents' construction knowledge and skills and learned tremendously from them:

> I only heard that they [local residents] were talented designers by nature but had not seen it. . . . They did not use computers or drawings, but their design and construction were perfect for the natural surrounding and their daily lives. . . .
>
> They utilized the grain shells and straws to mix with mud to produce the bricks, without any chemical ingredients, which was way better than the industrial products. They also had the tradition of planting and collecting trees from the mountains for construction materials. . . .
>
> I also saw how they collaborated during the construction process: men built the house, women did light labor and took care of the farmlands, and elders cooked and took care of the children. What good teamwork!

A faculty member in the architect program, serving as a designer, shared some ideas about how the designer–user partnership contributed to the students' disaster architecture and urban planning education.

> My students told me that they used to be very proud that they were professionals with modern training and technologies obtained from university. They said that they formerly "looked down" upon the local "skilled constructors." They had believed that the local masons' and carpenters' skills were out of date and that the local Fengshui masters just know blind worship (superstition) skills. However, these incorrect attitudes completely changed when they were involved in the real reconstruction work. [After that], they became very humble and always wanted to learn from these "local, uneducated skilled

constructors." Some students even suggested that these people should be invited to present in our class and their internship should be conducted with them, in the countryside, rather than in the architecture firms. Some students even suggested that we should move our design studio to the local communities and engage all the local residents into the design projects.

The words above are from three respondents: a local resident, a student, and a faculty member. Collectively, they illustrate the three functions of the designer–user partnership. The partnership stimulated conversation between nonlocal supporters and local residents. Nonlocal supporters had the opportunity to utilize the local expertise to improve their design to be more compatible and adaptive to the various local environments. Meanwhile, the partnership also provided an approach to protect the local place-making and construction knowledge and skills, which contributes to community resilience. Furthermore, the protection of local expertise was also reflected in education through students' participatory learning experience.

Through communication with local residents, it became apparent that the primary outcome was that the students learned knowledge and skills that they would utilize as part of their education and their future careers. From the perspective of education in the fields of built environment as well as emergency and risk management (post-disaster reconstruction and recovery), students developed the capacity to become qualified architects in the field of post-disaster reconstruction and recovery by facilitating risk communication with local professionals. The partnership enabled students to understand the importance of respecting their clients and engaging them into the planning, design, and construction process for a better product, as well as to protect local expertise. This would contribute to the improvement of the quality of built environment in order to specifically support the disaster survivors' various requirements and stimulate the long-term recovery process. This communication also positively influenced the students' career development.

During the recovery stage, designer–user partnership facilitated sustainable development

During the recovery stage, the built environment is supposed to offer a solid physical platform to support social, economic, and ecological development, which is the requirement of community sustainability (Oliver-Smith 2005). The following cases illustrate the ways in which the designer–user partnership can contribute to long-term community sustainability.

An elderly woman portrayed her story regarding her family's new life in their new house:

> I used to operate a family hotel with my husband and my daughter-in-law. The old concrete building was OK, but we wanted to rebuild it in the traditional wood-stone style because my previous tourists said that they wanted to see here what they were not able to see in their cities. [We thought] the

traditional style would attract more tourists so that our business would be better. . . [before the reconstruction], my neighbor said that the government was planning to build the brick-concrete one because it would be safer [than the wooden one]. We did not agree. You can see that most of the collapsed buildings [after the earthquake] were brick-concrete ones and the wooden ones were OK . . . I could not believe that they did accept our opinions and built the wooden house. . . . Of course, the business has become better [than before]. My daughter-in-law said that she needs to hire some helpers. My husband is also considering adding more local dishes [into the menu] to attract more tourists.

A young mother portrayed her life change in the new community:

The plaza was rebuilt and was at least doubled in size [compared to the old one]. In the daytime, my kids can play with their friends over there. The old men play chess over there. In the early evening, several older women dance over there. The teachers really considered everybody's idea of having a plaza. These types of activities are much more than before.

A local government official commented on how the teachers and students combined the village's reconstruction with the long-term development:

The village attracted a lot of tourists every year [before the earthquake]; tourism used to be a very important [nonagricultural] income for these residents. The earthquake partially destroyed the tourist spots. For quite some time, only a few travelers came here. . . . Of course, all the inhabitants wanted to redevelop these tourist spots so they could increase their income again. The local residents had a lot of ideas. . . . The students from the SAU visited all the families in the village, collecting their opinions, house by house, and consulted with their teachers about the potential plan. Finally, we worked together to complete the master plan. This plan focused on the protection of the traditional architectural characteristics and the local natural environment. The tourists now can visit the tourism spots, stay in the wood-stone houses, participate in the farming activities, and eat the local fresh fruit and vegetables (very fresh and organic!). These would be hard to find and buy (and expensive) [in the urban area]. On their way out, the tourists can buy local produce and also embroidery, made by the ladies. I heard a lot of complaints [regarding the new housing] from other villages. However, I dare not say all, but most of my villagers are very satisfied with the new village because the residents can feel the changes of their life becoming better and better than before.

The ultimate aim of post-disaster reconstruction and recovery is to rebuild disaster survivors' lives and advance their resilience, at least to the point of reaching the equivalence of the pre-disaster living circumstances (Drolet et al. 2015). The planning and design of the built environment needs to fundamentally support the recovery and resilience as it develops. The two residents' cases above convey that the designer–user partnership supported the long-term economic and social recovery by supporting the local residents' livelihoods and creating a common open space for traditional activities and their daily social lives. The local government official's comments further demonstrate the partnership's contribution toward the long-term recovery by protecting the unique, local cultural heritage (tourist spots, farming, and handicraft) and by utilizing local resources to stimulate the residents' income.

Discussion

The designer–user partnership promotes the human-centered participatory approach in the community planning and architectural design process by facilitating multi-stakeholder communication. In the post-Lushan earthquake case, during the planning stage, the partnership assisted the professional designers to create an atmosphere of equality and inclusion by requesting the local residents' input, addressing their practical requirements, reducing their anxiety, and increasing their influence in the decision-making process. During the reconstruction stage, the partnership stimulated civic participation by involving and protecting local traditional expertise and including the expertise of the locals into the reconstruction of their built environment. It also acted as a participatory pedagogic instrument to train future professionals in the field of risk and disaster management. During the recovery stage, the outcomes of the partnership accelerated the disaster survivors' long-term rehabilitation by enriching their daily social and cultural lives and increasing their income.

This case study documents the designer–user partnership in the post-Lushan earthquake reconstruction and recovery process within small rural communities. There would certainly be challenges to this approach on a broader scale. Despite this limitation, this community-based partnership method allowed stakeholders (most of whom were local residents) to directly communicate with the architects and planners about their unique knowledge of community-based place-making and construction in order to improve the quality of the built environment. With greater communication, both short-term and long-term needs of local residents were heard and addressed by project leaders. More importantly, the communication approach allowed the residents to access different community-based resources and use these resources to improve their community's reconstruction and long-term recovery. The quality enhancement of the built environment accelerated the disaster survivors' holistic recovery process. The process augmented individual and family's resilience capacity and furthered the ultimate goal of community resilience and sustainability.

Conclusion

The designer–user partnership model helped to promote civic participation in the post-earthquake recovery and reconstruction of Lushan, but it is essential to note that the government tightly controlled the entire reconstruction process. Local residents had only a certain amount of freedom in steering the partnership, which might have had a somewhat negative influence on their holistic resilience. Even so, the positive outcomes were obvious. Moving from the Lushan case to the international perspective, there are still many countries worldwide, including China, whose authoritarian governments do not offer their citizens complete freedom to participate. This illustrates the fact that, for at least some time to come, civic participation under strongly held central government-led initiatives will remain, to some degree, limited. Regardless, this type of partnership is an effective and practical approach, and it helps to stimulate better communication between professionals and local residents during post-disaster reconstruction and recovery. Better communication increases the chances that the views of all stakeholders, especially the local inhabitants, are protected, and in turn, their leadership was enhanced in the reconstruction of their homes, thus contributing to their resilience. Consequently, the designer–user partnership could be considered a worthwhile reference, contributing to the improvement of lives and to the resilience of communities affected by disasters, climate change, and other crises worldwide.

References

Asian Development Bank. 2006. *A Review of Community-Driven Development and Its Application to the Asian Development Bank*. Accessed on December 21, 2016 at https://brownschool.wustl.edu/sites/DevPractice/Reports%20of%20Development%20Agencies/A%20review%20of%20CDD%20to%20ADB.pdf.

Brook, Daniel. 2013. *A History of Future Cities*. New York: W.W. Norton & Company.

Cairns, Stephen, and Jacobs, Jane. 2014. *Buildings Must Die: A Perverse View of Architecture*. Cambridge: MIT Press.

Chandrasekhar, Divya. 2012. Digging Deeper: Participation and Non-Participation in Post-Disaster Community Recovery. *Community Development*, 43(5): 614–629.

Chinanews. 2013. *Residential Housing 100% Damaged in 9 Towns and Townships, and Lushan County*. Accessed on January 15, 2017 at www.chinanews.com/gn/2013/04-21/4750370.shtml.

Dominelli, Lena. 2012. *Green Social Work: From Environmental Crises to Environmental Justice*. Cambridge: Polity.

Drolet, Julie, Dominelli, Lena, Alston, Margaret, Ersing, Robin, Mathbor, Golam, and Wu, Haorui. 2015. Women Rebuilding Lives Post-Disaster: Innovative Community Practices for Building Resilience and Promoting Sustainable Development. *Gender and Development*, 23(3): 433–448.

Geoscience Australia Earthquake. 2013. *Earthquake Details*. April 22. Accessed on November 11, 2018 at www.ga.gov.au/earthquakes//getQuakeDetails.do?quakeId=3352536.

Halilovich, Hariz. 2011. Beyond the Sadness: Memories and Homecomings Among Survivors of "ethnic cleansing" in a Bosnian Village. *Memory Studies*, 4(1): 42–52.

Haorui Wu. 2014. *Post-Wenchuan Earthquake Rural Reconstruction and Recovery, in Sichuan China: Memory, Civic Participation, and Government Intervention*. 2018. Ph.D. Dissertation. University of British Columbia.

International Rescue Committee. 2007. *IRC's Approach to Community-Driven Reconstruction. A Basic Primer for First Generation Programming. Designed for Contextual*

Adaptation. Accessed on December 1, 2010 at www.theirc.org/resources/IRC-CDR-Manual-FINAL.pdf.

Johnson, Laurie A., and Hayashi, Haruo. 2012. Synthesis Efforts in Disaster Recovery Research. *International Journal of Mass Emergencies and Disasters*, 30: 212–238.

Kamel, Nabil M. O., and Loukaitou-Sideris, Anastasia. 2004. Residential Assistance and Recovery Following the Northridge Earthquake. *Urban Studies*, 41: 533–562.

Kennedy, Jim, Ashmore, Joseph, Babister, Elizabeth, and Kelman, Ilan. 2008. The Meaning of "build back better": Evidence from Post鈥? Tsunami Aceh and Sri Lanka. *Journal of Contingencies and Crisis Management*, 16(1): 24–36.

Kyamusugulwa, Patrick Milabyo. 2013. Participatory Development and Reconstruction: A Literature Review. *Third World Quarterly*, 34(7): 1265–1278.

Lawson, Bryon. 2005. *How Designers Think: The Design Process Demystified.* London: Elsevier.

Lo, Alex Y., and Lewis To Cheung. 2016. Geographies of Social Capital: Catastrophe Experience, Risk Perception, and the Transformation of Social Space in Post-Earthquake Resettlements in Sichuan, China. *Annals of the American Association of Geographers*, 106(4): 874–890.

Lyles-Chockley, Adrienne. 2008. Building Livable Places: The Importance of Landscape in Urban Land Use, Planning, and Development. *Buffalo Environmental Law Journal*, 16: 95–136.

Oliver-Smith, Anthony. 2005. Communities After Catastrophe: Reconstructing the Material, Reconstituting the Social. In *Community Building in the Twenty-First Century.* (ed.) Stanley Hyland. Santa Fe: School of American Research Press, pp. 25–44.

RedOrbit. 2014. *Multi-Study Focuses on Link Between Lushan, Wenchuan Earthquakes*, January 3. Accessed on November 11, 2018 at www.redorbit.com/news/science/1113038422/china-lushan-wenchuan-earthquakes-linked-010314/.

Sanoff, Henry. 2000. *Community Participation Methods in Design and Planning.* Hoboken: John Wiley and Sons.

Tierney, Kathleen, and Oliver-Smith, Anthony. 2012. Social Dimensions of Disaster Recovery. *International Journal of Mass Emergencies and Disasters*, 30(2): 123–146.

Ungar, Michael. 2013. Social Ecologies and Their Contribution to Resilience. In *The Social Ecology of Resilience: A Handbook of Theory and Practice.* (ed.) Michael Ungar. New York: Springer, pp. 13–31.

The World Bank. 2006. *World Bank- Civil Society Engagement Review of Fiscal Years 2005 and 2006.* Accessed on December 21, 2016 at http://siteresources.worldbank.org/CSO/Materials/21063337/CSEngagement06Final.pdf.

Wu, Haorui, and Hou, Chaoping. 2016. Community Social Planning: The Social Worker's Role in Post-Earthquake Reconstruction and Recovery Planning, Sichuan China. *Social Dialogue*, 13(4): 26–29.

United Nations. 2015. Sendai Framework for Disaster Risk Reduction (2015–2030). Accessed at https://www.unisdr.org/files/43291_sendaiframeworkfordrren.pdf.

Uslaner, Eric, and Brown, Mitchell. 2004. Inequality, Trust, and Civic Engagement. *American Politics Research*, 31(x): 1–28.

Wu, Haorui, and Drolet, Julie. 2016. Adaptive Social Protection: Climate Change Adaptation and Disaster Risk Reduction. In *Social Development and Social Work Perspectives on Social Protection.* (ed.) Julie Drolet. Abingdon: Routledge, pp. 96–119.

Wu, Haorui. 2018. Promoting Public Interest Design: Transformative Change Toward Green Social Work During Post-Lushan Earthquake Reconstruction and Recovery in Sichuan, China. In *Handbook of Green Social Work.* (eds.) Lena Dominelli, Hok Bun Ku, and Bala Raju Nikku. Abingdon: Routledge, pp. 87–98.

Part 4

Challenges and future direction of risk communication

Community resilience requires citizens to build partnerships that improve their capacity to respond to and recover from disasters and provide them the means to adapt their communities and their lives to become more resilient to future disasters. The Sendai Framework calls for "all-of-society engagement and partnership" with a focus on "the improvement of organized voluntary work of citizens" (UN 2015). The United Nations International Strategy for Disaster Reduction (UNISDR) and the Rockefeller 100 Resilient Cities Initiative have emphasized the importance of public-private partnerships to improve resilience. How such partnerships should be created and nurtured is a critical challenge to all community leaders and stakeholders today.

As with community resilience, risk communication must also be the result of reciprocal partnerships among all actors and stakeholders. Despite recent technological advancements, risk communication tends to be hierarchical in nature and characterized by insufficient input from the communities and citizens who are actually at risk. The following three areas need to be explored to enhance the effectiveness of risk communication practices and to increase overall community resilience.

1 Citizen participation – Current risk communication practices fail to account for local expertise and knowledge when it comes to providing risk information after a disaster. This is often due to a lack of motivation on the part of public institutions and government agencies involved in communication. It is also due to the absence of institutional mechanisms that might facilitate greater participation or to the lack of access to technologies that might enable incorporating citizen expertise into the risk information stream. The expansion of social media, however, has made it possible for a public-oriented, participatory and collaborative solution to the challenge of risk communication. Given that social media allows real-time situational awareness and improves risk communication, it provides citizens the means to participate during emergencies as knowledge brokers who can share, gather, critique, and disseminate risk information. The PetaJakarta project is a good example of the successful involvement of citizens in risk communication and the

potentially important role citizens can play in promoting resilience (Holderness and Turpin 2016). This project also highlights the importance of citizen participation in risk communication, which subsequently contributes to citizens' responses to alert and warning messages.

2   Contextualize communication practices – Alert and warning messages are often disseminated in the language of the demographic majority of a nation (e.g., risk information is normally communicated in English in the United States), but the communities impacted by disasters are home to individuals from diverse ethnic and cultural backgrounds. The lack of coherent policies regarding the language of risk communication for populations that are culturally and ethnically diverse has been found to be a major drawback of contemporary communication practices (Kar et al. 2016). Specifically, existing practices often fail to reach specific demographic groups, and those groups must rely on other information sources, including social media, to get updated and geotargeted information. While citizen participation would promote resilience and potentially increase public response to communication, contextualizing communication to meet the needs of impacted communities would enable more citizen engagement and sharing of unfolding stories on the ground that are focused, updated, and timely.

3   Technological adaptation – While traditional communication channels such as TV, radio, and printed materials are still used for disseminating alerts and warnings, social media is increasingly found to be more accessible to more people. Furthermore, virtually every demographic group now has access to smartphones and mobile technologies that enable them to participate in risk communication and access information in real time. Greater use of social media by government agencies might increase their relevance with younger generations and might help facilitate more sharing of reliable and accurate information (Cool et al. 2015). What is really needed, however, is for government actors to promote more bidirectional communication practices that would enhance citizen participation and contextualized communication and would reduce the effect of rumor mongering, thereby increasing the value and relevance of social media content.

This final section of the book includes four chapters that highlight a variety of issues that impact contemporary risk communication and will likely be challenges for decades to come. Chapters 12 and 13 explore risk communication associated with coastal and tourism communities that attract diverse populations that need context specific communication practices. Chapter 14 discusses the challenges faced by public K-12 schools to devise risk communication strategies that prepare students, parents, and school personnel to increase their participation during preparation and response phases of emergency management. Chapter 15 explores the use of social media as an added and sometimes alternative channel to communication among impacted communities, and sheds light on issues that should be addressed to improve communication in the future.

References

Cool, C., Claravall, M., Hall, J., Taketani, K., Zepeda, J., Gehner, M., and Lawe-Davies, O. 2015. Social Media as a Communication Tool Following Typhoon Haiyan. *Western Pacific Surveillance and Response Journal*, 6(1): 86–90.

Holderness, T., and Turpin, E. 2016. From Social Media to Geosocial Intelligence: Crowdsourcing Civic Co-Management for Flood Response in Jakarta, Indonesia. In *Social Media for Government Services*, Springer (preprint version).

Kar B., Cochran, D., Zale, J., Dickens, J., Liu, X., Callais, N., Gillespie, L., Knuth, C., and Bandi, V. 2016. Final Report: An Integrated Approach to Geo-Target At-Risk Communities and Deploy Effective Crisis Communication Approaches. Department of Homeland Security – Science and Technology Directorate. https://www.dhs.gov/publication/integrated-approach-geo-target-risk-communities-deploy-effective-crisis-communication

United Nations Office for Disaster Reduction (UN). 2015. Sendai Framework for Disaster Risk Reduction 2015–2030. In *Proceedings of the Third United Nations World Conference*, United Nations Office for Disaster Reduction. Geneva, Switzerland.

12 A case study of climate change, extreme weather events, and risk communication in a coastal community

Christopher A. Craig, Elizabeth L. Petrun Sayers, and Song Feng

Introduction

Businesses and local communities in the southeastern United States are increasingly facing challenges related to climate change-induced extreme weather events (Feng et al. 2017; Ingram et al. 2013; Preston 2013). Businesses must adapt to this change and share risk communication to relevant stakeholder groups. This is particularly true for businesses in the tourism industry located in vulnerable coastal regions of the United States. Over the past 15 years, the American Southeast has been more exposed than any other region in the United States to extreme events and has experienced the highest frequency of billion-dollar disasters (NCEI 2018). Coastal regions already account for 39 percent of the population of the United States, and estimates suggest population growth will continue for the foreseeable future (NOAA 2017; United States Census Bureau 2017). Individuals in this region will experience adverse consequences from extreme events, including negative health, economic, and safety outcomes (Allen and Craig 2016). A clearer understanding of the impacts of extreme events is needed to enhance preparedness, response, and recovery.

The tourism industry is a driver of local economies around the world. Tourism is the second largest economic sector after health care, and coastal tourism remains the largest segment of tourism as a whole (Bigano, Hamilton, and Tol 2007; Rutty and Scott 2016). This trend is salient in the American Southeast, where beaches and other outdoor activities are located along the Gulf of Mexico and the Atlantic seaboard. Climate and extreme weather events are important determinants of tourism activities (Bigano, Hamilton, and Tol 2007; Craig and Feng 2018; Yu, Schwartz, and Walsh 2009), and tourist destinations in coastal areas are influenced by current and future weather conditions, extreme weather events, and persistent climate change. For businesses that embrace all aspects of sustainability, including economic, environmental, and social communication strategies can be used to engage both internal and external stakeholder groups

(Allen 2016). As climate change and extreme weather events become more prominent, analyses of climate change communication and its impact on the public have proliferated (Nerlich, Koteyko, and Brown 2009). Due to the complexity of the topic and the myriad of prescribed actions, however, specific communication strategies related to climate change and extreme weather events are still being developed.

Given the susceptible nature of coastal tourism locations, by including the business location this research provides a unique perspective by linking climate change and weather events to business outcomes. The goal of this chapter is to inform economic decisions and offer guidance on how communication can be leveraged to help mitigate community health and safety concerns. It presents a case study of a privately owned business located in the coastal community of Virginia Beach, Virginia, and analyzes relationships between climate change, extreme weather events, and economic activity. The findings of this study are used to develop actionable communication strategies for businesses and salient stakeholder groups, including business units, customers, and community members. In the next section, we provide an overview of the business that is the focus of this study, followed by a review of relevant literature as well as well as the methodology, results, analysis, and implications.

Business overview

This study focused on a privately owned company that operates private campsites and outdoor entertainment around the United States. The estimated revenues of the company are over $100 million, with percentage sales growth over double the average of the tourism industry in the United States. Camping options include tents, recreational vehicles (RV), and cabins. Examples of outdoor entertainment include popular outdoor tourist attractions, swimming, miniature golf, play areas for children, and outdoor social events. The parent company and local business are not named to protect sensitive and confidential information. The focal business location in Virginia constitutes a robust single case study with findings relevant to other businesses throughout the southeast United States. This study also provides a blueprint for other businesses and communities in other regions of the United States and around the world for how to analyze complex climatic relationships.

The parent company's businesses located in the region have already experienced severe damages from extreme weather events in recent years. In response to these events, the parent company has deployed additional human and financial assets to maintain operations, but to date, neither the parent company nor the local case study site have a long-term climate change strategy in place. Leadership from the parent company supported this study, recognizing the possibility of and susceptibility to extreme events including hurricanes, thunderstorms, flooding, drought, and heat. Ideally, they hoped to learn how the findings could be applied to other locations to reduce impacts.

Literature review

Climate change and extreme weather in the southeast

Climatic and extreme weather trends pose economic, health, and safety challenges for local businesses and surrounding communities. While climate change and extreme weather events are related, there is a distinction between the two. Climate change occurs over a longer span of time, such as an observed increase in long-term averages of daily weather, whereas weather has a short-term orientation and can be more easily experienced and understood by individuals (National Aeronautics and Space Administration 2005). Weather generally includes "sunshine, rain, hail, snow, sleet, freezing rain, flooding, blizzards, ice storms, thunderstorms, steady rains from a cold front or warm front, excessive heat, heat waves, and more" (National Aeronautics and Space Administration 2017). Extreme events result from unusual and dangerous changes in weather conditions.

Extreme weather events in the American Southeast have become more noticeable due to climate trends in recent years. For instance, global sea surface temperature (SST) has increased at an unprecedented, exponential rate along the Gulf of Mexico and the Atlantic Ocean over the past 30 years. This has resulted in increased intensity and duration of thunderstorms and hurricanes (Ingram et al. 2013; EPA 2017; Wang et al. 2010). Events in the region are further intensified because "the sharp contrast in temperature and humidity in the vicinity of the jet stream can promote the development of severe thunderstorms, damaging winds, large hail, and tornados" (Ingram et al. 2013: 11). Climate models generally agree that climate change will contribute to increase in heavy precipitation, decrease in moderate or light precipitation, higher temperatures, and severe drought (Feng et al. 2017; Ingram et al. 2013; Wang et al. 2010). Over the past 20 years, the southeastern United States has also observed a decrease in colder days during the winter (Craig and Feng 2017), a potential economic opportunity for coastal businesses. Based on these findings, the climatic and weather variables of interest in this case study are related to precipitation and temperature.

Over the past 15 years, the frequency and intensity of billion-dollar disasters from extreme weather remain greater in the southeast than in any other region in the United States (NOAA 2017). The economic loss potential in the region is magnified by increased intensity and frequency of events, socioeconomic change, number of people, shift in population, increased infrastructure, and the subsequent amount of wealth and economic value (NOAA 2017; Preston 2013; United States Census Bureau 2017). In addition to economic loss, mortality, health, and safety risks are also magnified (Allen 2016; Craig and Feng 2018). For areas that are at risk from disasters and change, including the American Southeast, planning and adaptation strategies are essential (Hyman 2013).

For businesses and community members in this study, a clearer understanding of the historical climatic trends and extreme weather events can help with the capacity to profile past events, plan for future events, and then respond when necessary (Linnenluecke and Griffiths 2012). The nine variables of interest in the study include precipitation, extreme precipitation over 10 millimeters (mm) and 20 mm, maximum temperature, maximum temperature above 34° and under 25°, minimum temperature under 24° and under 0°. The focal variables are described in greater detail below in the methods section. To help inform communication strategies for preparedness and response to future change and events, the first research question asks:

RQ1: What trends in weather conditions, climate change, adverse weather, and extreme weather events are present in the community?

Outdoor tourism

The business in this study focuses on outdoor tourism. Camping is a fast-growing segment of outdoor tourism, with some areas of camping experiencing faster growth rates than the industry average (Fjelstul and Fyall 2015; Recreational Vehicle Industry Association 2017). Considering the sensitivity of tourism activities to climate change, "the anticipated change in climate patterns . . . are expected to influence tourist destination selection, tourism activity participation, tourism demand, and tourism seasonality" (Yu, Schwartz, and Walsh 2009: 552). Extremes and persistent adverse conditions are related to the economic well-being of tourism businesses as well as the safety and health of tourists and local community members. In 2016 alone, travel and tourism contributed $1,509 billion, or 8.1 percent, to the GDP in the United States (WTTC2017). According to the WTTC (2017), this sector is the fourth largest in the United States and is projected to grow by over 3.3 percent over the next ten years. In addition to the economic vulnerability for businesses, health and safety risks are further magnified by population growth in coastal regions of the American Southeast.

Shifts in weather events and seasonality have been attributed to climate change across the United States. Recent studies that examined 276 locations in U.S. national parks provide evidence of long-term change for temperature and precipitation across the country (Monahan et al. 2016; Monahan and Fisichelli 2014). Monahan and others (2016) found historically high temperatures in camping and outdoor-centric locations. In addition to extreme warm conditions, there has been a shift in seasonality, where 76 percent of the locations examined experienced an early spring, 53 percent of which experienced an extremely early spring. These changes demonstrate a shift in timing of when warmer and cooler days occur, which might ultimately change when and how tourists visit the locations. In terms of precipitation, rising SSTs are attributed to trends in precipitation such as less persistent, soaking rains, and an increased frequency of high intensity severe thunderstorms and downpours (Ingram et al. 2013). Yet the attention to the connection between climate change and extreme weather events has been limited, particularly studies that match high-resolution climatic and business data in modelling (Bigano et al. 2005; Bigano, Hamilton, and Tol 2007).

Business sustainability and resilience

Businesses tend to enact sustainability initiatives using expected economic benefits as justification (Allen 2016). Sustainability initiatives can enhance economic, environmental, and social well-being both within and outside an organization. External stakeholders increasingly hold businesses accountable for acting in a socially responsible manner (Allen and Craig 2016). In other words, businesses are beholden to actors whose interests may not be economic, while also to those who have clearly defined economic interests such as shareholders or employees.

Business have taken the lead on sustainability initiatives that are community or society focused in the past on issues such as public health and carbon emissions (Allen 2016; Cox 2009). Risks associated with climate change and extreme weather events are not only economic in nature; they also have societal consequences (i.e. safety, health, and income) for both internal (e.g. employees) and external stakeholders (e.g. community members). Businesses with a clear understanding of how climatic conditions and extreme events affect them are uniquely positioned to address two key pillars of sustainability by: (1) using the knowledge to serve internal economic interests and (2) assisting local members to enhance their preparedness and response capacity.

While many business leaders understand the utility of integrating climate change and its consequences into strategic planning, in practice, businesses have struggled to create a clear roadmap for doing so (Allen 2016). When climate change or extreme weather events are outside the coping capacity of a business, the susceptibility of the business and those associated with it are brought into question (Linnenluecke and Griffiths 2012). To enhance the resiliency of businesses to climate change and extreme weather events, Linnenluecke and Griffiths (2012) provided guidance on four mechanisms that businesses use, including: historical profiling, expert analysis, case study comparison, and model explorations. Each method yields strengths and weaknesses. We integrate components of each method to explore the complex interactions between climate, weather, and important business outcomes. Historical business profiling is accomplished through the longitudinal analysis of business outcomes and climatic variables using the following research question (RQ2). The use of time series methodology in the study allows production of a robust model for the focal business. The resultant model will provide a case comparison for businesses and communities in the climate region, and the methodology (i.e., expert analysis) will provide a blueprint for future analysis for other regions.

> RQ2: What is the longitudinal relationship between past business trends, seasonality, weather conditions, climate change, adverse weather, and extreme weather events for the Virginia business?

Climate, risk, and weather communication

In this section, we will review the relevant literature related to climate, risk, and weather communication. We will use the review as a basis for discussing the communication implications that take into consideration the findings from RQ1 and RQ2.

Businesses affected by climate change can apply various coping mechanisms, including information dissemination, appeals to influence consumer attitudes, and ultimately efforts to influence consumer behaviors. For example, businesses may choose to inform consumers how they are adapting to climate change (e.g., adapting building structures, controlling pollution, saving energy) or inform consumers about topics that can help curb climate change (e.g., suggesting ways that consumers can offset their carbon footprint). As discussed above, due to variable temporal proximity of climate change (long term) versus extreme weather events (short term), business responses may differ depending on the stakeholder (e.g., business unit, employee, customer, community members). For example, Aspen Skiing Company in western Colorado communicates about the potential impact of climate change on skiing in Aspen (Allen 2016). Aspen Skiing Company partnered with an advocacy organization to reduce the effects of climate change on winter sports and local economics. Other general types of informational communication include the science behind climate change, causes, potential impacts, and possible solutions (Moser 2009).

Moser (2009) specifically calls out two more categories of communication efforts related to climate change, including social engagement or social action and enacting changes in social norms and cultural values. Social engagement includes behavioral (e.g., consumption-related action) or political action spanning support for candidates, policies, or programs (Moser 2009). Ockwell, Whitmarsh, and O'Neill (2009) suggest that this approach is particularly important and encourage climate communication to stimulate social demand for regulation. This recommendation stems from the fact that individual behavior changes can be difficult, and regulation or policy changes can often yield swifter changes for curbing carbon behaviors.

Changing social norms through educational interventions for young people and adults can influence deeply rooted values and behavioral norms (Moser 2009). Communicating about social norms and values is important considering recent work suggesting that science literacy and technical reasoning alone do not ensure whether individuals will be concerned about climate change (Kahan et al. 2012). Rather, beliefs about climate change are likely to align with an individual's peer groups (Kahan et al. 2012). Prior to beginning communication planning, businesses need to consider what type of strategy is desired and carefully scope subsequent plans.

Weather communication differs from climate change communication in that it is more tangible and actionable. Businesses with emergency plans may include plans for expected natural disasters, particularly if a business is in a geographic region prone to flooding, hurricanes, extreme heat, or other climate-change-related scenarios. Emergency alerts, however, may also come from the government. For example, the United States. Federal Emergency Management Agency (FEMA) authorized emergency management officials to broadcast Wireless Emergency Alerts (WEAs) to cellular and mobile phone providers to notify individuals of imminent hazards (Bean et al. 2015). WEAs deliver short messages to people who are physically located in an area under threat. This type of technology, however, might be less helpful for individuals traveling to or from a location facing imminent hazards, as traveling may interfere with the ability to receive warning messages.

Risk messages contain information about impending threats, including details about a hazard and suggested protective actions. Risk communication constitutes a two-way flow of information among individuals, groups, or organizations. Risk communication can involve messages about the characteristics, concerns, opinions, reactions, and/or management of risks (National Research Council 1989). For example, during a heat emergency, warning messages might call for those without access to air conditioning to seek a cooling shelter. During a flash flood, warning messages might advise travelers to avoid certain areas. Warning research over the years suggests a variety of best practices for effective warning messages, such as including information about the nature, location, guidance, time, and source or hazard of the risk (Sorensen 2000). Other stylistic aspects encompass message specificity, consistency, accuracy, certainty, and clarity (Sorensen 2000; Bean et al. 2015).

Institutions and communities may also have their own systems for disseminating warnings to extreme weather. For example, many universities now have their own emergency alert systems. One large university tested emergency alerts during a tornado warning. Research based on the event documented the communication system used by students, staff, and faculty and if people followed prescribed actions (e.g., sheltering in place) (Sherman-Morris 2010). Sherman-Morris (2010) found that the alerts were successful and individuals who received the warning took the prescribed action. It is important to remember, however, that not all communication about extreme weather is successful. Poor communication in the face of imminent threats is also a possibility, which can lead to losses of life and property. A striking example remains the communication failure during Hurricane Katrina in the Gulf Coast region. The evacuation language at both pre-Katrina levels and in the hours preceding landfall were vague, uncertain, and poorly articulated (Cole and Fellows 2008).

Businesses have an opportunity to communicate about climate change and extreme weather events. Government agencies "for a variety of reasons yet to be determined," are more likely to face "lingering crises when compared to their corporate counterparts" (Avery and Lariscy 2010: 326). In other words, corporate organizations may be able to craft, implement, and deliver communication strategies more effectively than strategies currently in place by government entities. Specific recommendations for communication practices will be made in the discussion section of this chapter.

Methods

Procedure and measures

This study used a single case design to address the research gap in longitudinal analysis of the relationship between climatic conditions and important business outcomes in the at-risk outdoor tourism industry. The "longitudinal examination [of a single case] provides a systematic way of observing the events, collecting data, analyzing information, and reporting the results over a long period of time"

(Zainal 2007: 2), and the single case design has been successfully deployed in a variety of contexts when exploring tourism (Beerli and Martin 2004). One of the criticisms for the use of a single location as a case study is the lack of generalization arising from the inability to pattern match (Zainal 2007). As Karl and Koss (1984) noted, however, through extensive historical climate analysis dating back to the 1890s, scientists have identified nine unique climate regions that help position local anomalies within a larger geographic and historic perspective (Karl and Koss 1984). The focal location shares a climate zone with the at-risk coastal states of Alabama, Georgia, Florida, South Carolina, and North Carolina.

Daily occupancy data for cabins, RVs, and tents was obtained for the Virginia-based outdoor business. Financial staff of the parent company provided authors with the daily occupancy data for each of the categories from January 1, 2007, to July 31, 2016. Daily precipitation, minimum temperature, and maximum temperature were obtained by authors from January 1, 2007, to July 31, 2016, from the high-resolution PRISM dataset developed by the University of Oregon (DiLuzio et al. 2008). The data were available at the 2.5-minute (approximately 4 kilometer) resolution during the study period for the focal location.

Six additional variables were used to capture adverse and extreme weather events related to precipitation and temperature, and two categories were used to capture daily variation: (1) days that exceeded an extreme or adverse threshold and (2) days that did not exceed the threshold. The climatic data was nominally recoded to capture adverse weather conditions and extreme weather events where days that exceeded the threshold were coded 1 and days that did not were coded 0. When analyzing time series, this coding allows for the inclusion of adverse or extreme events, where 1 signifies an event occurred. The study included two variables for extreme precipitation, including days in which more than 10 millimeters (mm) of precipitation and days in which 20 mm of precipitation occurred. The threshold for what is considered extreme precipitation is 10 mm per day (Frich et al. 2002). The study also included the 20 mm measure to capture precipitation in a day that exceeded double the threshold. Two additional variables each were included for minimum and maximum temperature. The minimum temperature variables included days below 24° and days below 0°. The threshold for minimum temperature considered adverse by a coastal tourist is 24° (Rutty and Scott 2016). The commonly used measure to capture extreme cold weather is a frost day, or days below the 0° threshold (Frich et al. 2002). The maximum temperature variables included days when the maximum temperature was above 34° and days when the maximum temperature was below 25°. Research has demonstrated that tourism is unacceptably hot at 34°, and at 25° outdoor destinations experience decreases in occupancy (Rutty and Scott 2016).

Statistical analysis

Descriptive statistics, frequencies, and graphs were used to assess the trends in weather conditions, change, and extreme events. Mean values and frequencies are included for the climatic variables of interest in Table 12.1. Descriptive statistics

Table 12.1 Descriptives and frequencies for climatic variables

Year	Mean PPT	Max PPT	>10 mm	>20 mm	Mean Tmin	Tmin < 24°C	Tmin < 0°C	Mean Tmax	Tmax > 34°C	Tmax < 25°C
2007	2.12	57.23	6.0%	2.7%	12.10	89.6%	11.5%	21.14	5.5%	58.4%
2008	3.62	91.70	12.3%	4.1%	11.89	96.2%	10.4%	20.48	3.0%	63.4%
2009	4.19	123.26	12.3%	5.2%	11.65	97.3%	13.2%	19.91	3.0%	64.1%
2010	3.49	93.58	10.7%	4.7%	11.50	90.7%	17.8%	20.15	6.8%	60.3%
2011	2.89	207.53	7.9%	2.7%	12.11	94.2%	10.1%	20.97	5.2%	60.3%
2012	3.85	136.01	11.7%	4.4%	12.57	92.9%	5.5%	21.10	4.6%	63.7%
2013	3.47	74.13	12.6%	5.8%	11.63	95.9%	12.1%	19.84	1.9%	66.0%
2014	3.96	148.71	11.5%	6.6%	11.35	94.8%	13.2%	19.85	2.7%	62.2%
2015	3.25	61.91	9.9%	4.9%	13.10	89.0%	11.5%	21.37	5.2%	57.0%
2016	5.33	295.73	13.0%	5.4%	14.85	82.6%	6.6%	22.95	10.8%	52.2%

Notes: PPT = precipitation and is measured in millimeters; Tmin = minimum temperature and is measured in degrees Celsius (C); Tmax = maximum temperature and is measured in degrees Celsius (C); % values measure frequency percentage that a temperature is within the defined range; 2016 values only include 311 days and do not represent an entire year

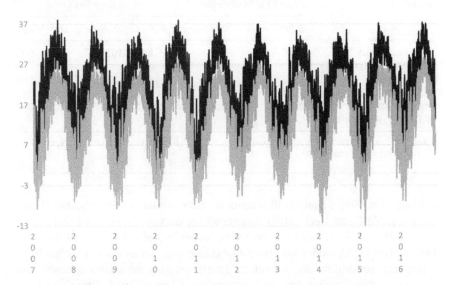

Figure 12.1 Virginia Beach, Virginia, minimum and maximum temperatures from January 2007 through November 2016 (black shading represents daily maximum temperature and is measured in degrees Celsius (°); light gray shading represents daily minimum temperature is measured in degrees Celsius (°))

about the actual daily occupancy at the focal business are not provided to ensure privacy and confidentiality. Graphs of daily values for precipitation, minimum temperature, maximum temperature, and occupancy by category are provided in Figures 12.1 and 12.2 and in Table 12.2. For nonstationary data where seasonality is inherent, such as business occupancy or climatic studies, it is appropriate to

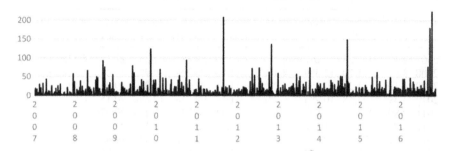

Figure 12.2 Virginia Beach, Virginia, daily precipitation from January 2007 through November 2016 (precipitation is measured in millimeters)

Table 12.2 Time series ARIMA models

Variable	Model Fit Statistics			Ljung-box Q (18)		
	# Predictors	Stationary R²	R²	Statistic	DF	Sig.
Cabin Occupancy ARIMA (2, 0, 5) (0, 1, 1)	3	.515	.866	105.78	12	.000
RV Occupancy ARIMA (0, 1, 6) (0, 1, 1)	1	.517	.920	53.19	11	.000
Tent Occupancy ARIMA (1, 0, 4) (0, 1, 1)	2	.639	.722	63.09	13	.000

Notes: Virginia Beach overall model: stationary r² = .557, SE .071, min = .515, max = .639; r² = .836, SE .102, min = .722, max = .920

conduct a time series analysis to account for autocorrelations with the data (Craig and Feng 2018; van Heck 2010). Nonstationary data series are those that do not resemble the long-term mean of the series. An autoregressive integrated weighted average (ARIMA) model was used to explore time series data. This model is appropriate for differencing as well as determining lag days, autoregressive and moving average components, and seasonality (Clement 2014; Craig and Feng 2016, 2018; van Heck 2010).

The goodness-of-fit statistics of stationary R^2 and R^2 are provided for the overall model in addition to the models created for each category. As the default goodness-of-fit statistic for ARIMA modeling, stationary r^2 is the primary goodness-of-fit statistic used, as it is more appropriate than R^2 when trends and seasonal patterns are present, which is the case here. Ljung-box statistics are used as a diagnostic check for ARIMA models (Clement 2014) and were included for each model. Table 12.2 provides an overview of these goodness-of-fit and diagnostic statistics.

Results and analysis

RQ1 asked about the trends in weather conditions, climate change, adverse weather, and extreme weather events in the focal community of Virginia Beach, Virginia. Based on Table 12.1, it appears as though Virginia Beach, Virginia, has had no discernible change in mean minimum temperature or mean maximum temperature. However, based on Figure 12.1, there is a salient trend related to temperature where a decrease in minimum temperatures was observed during the study period. This indicates the occurrence of fewer cold days.

As shown in Table 12.1, mean values for precipitation vary from year to year with no discernible pattern. Upon examining Figure 12.2, however, extreme precipitation events appear to increase throughout the study period. While average daily precipitation remained relatively steady, maximum precipitation amounts increased throughout the study period, demonstrating extreme weather events (i.e., hurricanes or tropical storms). The increase in extreme events highlights the occurrence of less frequent but more intense precipitation events in the region. In 2007 and 2011 there was a lower percentage of extreme precipitation days, suggesting that fewer intense rain events occurred during these two years. These two years also had lower average precipitations, suggesting that extreme events may in fact be more salient drivers of overall precipitation, as suggested by previous studies (EPA 2017; Ingram et al. 2013).

RQ2 asked about the longitudinal relationships between past business trends, seasonality, weather conditions, climate change, adverse weather, and extreme weather events. See Table 12.2 for the overall model fit by category for the focal location. Table 12.3 shows the result of analysis of the time series regression analysis by camping type (cabin, RV, and tent).

The overall model fit explained 55.5 percent of the variability (stationary $R^2 = .555, p < .001$). Cabin camping explained 51.5 percent of variability (stationary $R^2 = .515, p < .001, p < .001$) with a model that consisted of three predictors in addition to the previous auto-regressive and moving average variable for cabin occupancy. The three predictors captured extreme temperature daily events and included minimum temperature less than 24°, maximum temperature less than 25°, and maximum temperature greater than 34°. The auto-regressive term captures the correlation of current occupancy to past occupancy, while the moving average is an error term related to past occupancy. For each of the four variables there was a difference in seasonality by one season. The relationships with previous occupancy demonstrated that future occupancy is positively related to past occupancy one and two days previously, as well as an error term both in the current season for previous third and fifth days, and the previous season. The relationship with minimum temperature less than 24° was negative ($t = -2.30, p < .01$) with a six-day delay, suggesting that lower temperatures six days out in the future adversely impact occupancy for cabin camping. Both maximum extreme values (i.e., < 25°, > 34°) were positive with delays of seven days and five days, respectively. These relationships suggest that lower maximum temperatures seven

Table 12.3 Virginia Beach model

Model	Coefficients	Estimates	S.E.	t-value	Sig.
Cabin Model					
Cabin Occupancy	AR Lag 1	.694	.017	41.44	.000
	AR Lag 2	.273	.018	15.10	.000
	MA Lag 2	.397	.019	21.42	.000
	MA Lag 3	.228	.018	12.84	.000
	MA Lag 5	.082	.018	4.66	.000
	Seasonal Difference	1			
	MA Seasonal Lag 1	.666	.014	48.70	.000
Tmin < 24°C	Delay	6			
	Numerator Lag 0	−.921	.338	−2.30	.006
	Seasonal Difference	1			
Tmax < 25°C	Delay	7			
	Numerator Lag 0	.492	.231	2.13	.033
	Seasonal Difference	1			
Tmax >34°C	Delay	5			
	Numerator Lag 0	.882	.366	2.41	.016
	Seasonal Difference	1			
RV Model					
RV Occupancy	Difference	1			
	MA Lag 1	−.113	.017	−6.75	.000
	MA Lag 2	.117	.017	6.98	.000
	MA Lag 3	.387	.017	22.96	.000
	MA Lag 4	.071	.017	4.17	.000
	MA Lag 5	.045	.017	2.66	.008
	MA Lag 6	.055	.017	3.31	.001
	MA Seasonal Difference	1			
	MA Seasonal Lag 1	.838	.009	89.21	.000
PPT > 20 mm	Delay	5			
	Numerator Lag 0	−2.061	.773	−2.67	.008
	Difference	1			
	Seasonal Difference	1			
Tent Model					
Tent Occupancy	AR Lag 1	.558	.020	89.17	.000
	MA Lag 1	−.225	.023	−9.86	.000
	MA Lag 4	−.068	.017	−4.119	.000
	AR Seasonal	−.055	.023	−2.40	.017
	Seasonal Difference	1			
	MA Seasonal	.706	.016	42.89	.000
Tmin < 24°C	Delay	6			
	Numerator Lag 0	−.759	.293	−2.59	.010
	Denominator Lag 2	.634	.191	3.33	.001
	Seasonal Difference	1			
Tmax < 25°C	Delay	4			
	Numerator Lag 0	−.462	.145	−3.18	.001
	Denominator Lag 2	.877	.050	17.70	.000
	Seasonal Difference	1			

days in the future and that higher maximum temperature five days in the future are positively related to cabin occupancy.

For RV camping, the model explained 51.7 percent of the variability (stationary $R^2 = .517$, $p < .001$) and included one extreme weather predictor: daily precipitation over 20 mm five days in the future. There was a seasonal difference for both previous occupancy and extreme precipitation over 20 mm. For occupancy, only the error terms were significant for the previous first through sixth day, as well as the error term from the previous season. Precipitation over 20 mm was negatively related to RV camping occupancy ($t = -2.30$, $p < .01$) with a five-day delay, suggesting that extreme precipitation events will adversely impact RV occupancy five days in the future.

For tent camping, 63.9 percent of the variability (stationary $R^2 = .639$, $p < .001$) was explained by a model that included two extreme weather predictors in addition to previous occupancy. There was a seasonal difference for previous occupancy, minimum temperature less than 24°C, and maximum temperature less than 25°. For previous occupancy, auto-regression to the previous day was positively related to current occupancy ($t = 89.17$, $p < .001$), yet negatively related to the error terms for days one and four prior to the current occupancy day. There was a negative auto-regressive relationship with the previous season, demonstrating that current occupancy is negatively related to occupancy from the previous season. The positive season relationship with the moving average, or the error term, was positive. The relationship with minimum temperature less than 24° was negative ($t = -2.59$, $p < .01$) with a six-day delay, suggesting that lower temperatures six days in the future adversely impact occupancy for tent camping. The maximum extreme values of less than 25° was negative related with a delay of four days, suggesting that lower maximum temperatures four days in the future are negatively related to tent occupancy. The error term (i.e., the denominator in Table 12.3) suggests a positive relationship lagged two days for both of the extreme weather variables.

Discussion and conclusion

Relatively little is known about the economic impact, both long term and short term, of climate change and extreme weather events on the outdoor tourism industry. This has led to a continued interest in the tourism industry among researchers, practitioners, governmental agencies, and nonprofit organizations (Craig and Feng 2016; de Freitas 2003; Bigano, Hamilton, and Tol 2007; WTTC 2017). Chen and others (2017) echoed the sentiment of researchers from the past 15 years (Bigano et al. 2005; Bigano, Hamilton, and Tol 2007; de Freitas 2003) in noting that the knowledge gap in the understanding of climate change, weather conditions, and business outcomes in the tourism industry persists. The gap is further compounded by increasing weather uncertainty and the subsequent adverse impacts on businesses, particularly those related to tourism in at-risk regions (Chen et al. 2017; Ingram et al. 2013; Preston 2013). This case study takes steps to address this knowledge gap by examining the interactions between prevailing change, extreme events, and an important, economic business outcome for a single, at-risk community. By longitudinally exploring high-resolution business outcomes and climatic data, this research provides a template for studying the relationships as well as guidance on how to use the findings to address risks through communication.

The most important finding of this study is the presence of increased frequency of extreme precipitation events in the southeast United States and the associated risks in coastal communities. Consistent with previous research (EPA 2017; Ingram et al. 2013), the study demonstrated that extreme precipitation is the most salient event influencing average and yearly rainfall in the focal community. Despite the increased frequency and intensity of precipitation events in the region, however, the relationship between occupancy and precipitation was only significant for RV campers. For those camping in cabins and in tents, the lack of a significant relationship with extreme precipitation and occupancy signals a potential danger when extreme weather events occur. This finding is not overly surprising for cabins because there is some degree of protection from outside weather conditions. For tent campers, it may be that individuals are able to make or alter plans to avoid heightened weather risks. Regardless, the lack of a significant relationship between occupancy and an extreme event suggests that these two categories of campers may be more at-risk to immediate weather-related threats. For coastal regions, the risk is magnified further by the possibility of flooding associated with a rise in sea level. Bloetscher, Heimlich, and Meeroff (2011) noted that rising sea levels in coastal regions result in increasing groundwater table levels, making the areas more susceptible to flooding during the intense precipitation events.

The significance of precipitation in the study suggests that both short-term and long-term strategies for communicating the risk of extreme precipitation and flooding are needed. A challenge for this case is the difficulty for short-term warning messages to reach transient individuals (i.e., tourists or visitors) in time to influence their behavior. First, individuals may not have access to typical information sources. This could include print (e.g., newspapers, magazines), radio, television, or online outlets. While mobile devices provide an opportunity to communicate with individuals on the go, more information is needed to assess cellular and Internet connectivity surrounding the business location. In times of emergency such as the aftermath of hurricanes, when communication is needed most, network congestion and availability of communication infrastructure can make it difficult for individuals to obtain information (FCC 2017). The FCC (2017) offers tips for communication including the use of SMS texting, brevity of phone calls, and the trial of various communication services.

Ideally, WEA messages could reach individuals in the face of forthcoming extreme precipitation. Given the fact that visitors might not be familiar with the threat (e.g., extreme precipitation and flood), however, message convergence (i.e., receiving information from more than one source) could be important in persuading individuals to take prescribed actions (Anthony, Sellnow, and Millner 2013). In this instance, the business should consider the best practices noted by Sorensen (2000) and include information about the nature, location, guidance, time, and source or hazard of the risk when communicating about extreme precipitation and flooding. Additional research is needed to fully understand the opportunities and barriers to deliver warnings to customers.

The focal outdoor tourism business has a unique opportunity to use communication to mitigate internal financial risks and external risks to the community. For instance, one of the metrics that FEMA relies upon in local communities to assess the severity of weather disasters is based on a three-prong scale (red, yellow, green) used by the Waffle House restaurant chain. The *Waffle House Index* can be used to assess the severity of an extreme weather event or disaster where red indicates lack of access to utilities (e.g., water, electricity) and green indicates full functionality (Bauerlein 2011, par. 2). Similarly, Facebook has a safety check feature that allows friends on the social media site to let each other know they are safe after a disaster occurs (Broida 2017). Unlike these two services that are responsive to disasters, the Virginia business has an opportunity to communicate *before* an event with all customers (including cabin, RV, and tent) and employees to provide potential risk levels. One option could be to couple warning information with visit reminders and welcome messages typically emailed to customers prior to their arrival. A similar update could be provided to employees. The research methods used in this study that integrated climatic and weather conditions with sales forecasting can serve as a blueprint for businesses to understand these complex relationships regardless of location and engage local communities based on the findings. Businesses and communities located in the southeast climate zone can use the findings to understand local relationships based on the historic and geographic consistencies in the region (Karl and Koss 1984).

None of the weather indices were significant past seven days in the study, demonstrating that consumers are not regularly altering destination plans more than a week in advance. The outdoor business has another opportunity to communicate prior to weather events to both reduce safety risks during camping due to extreme precipitation and flooding and to accommodate a change in location to avoid economic losses from events. With enhancement of predictions by NOAA to two weeks or further into the future, this capability can be leveraged (see: www.cpc.ncep.noaa.gov/products/predictions/814day). By extending the warning time, individuals who have reserved camping gear and space may be more likely to engage in mitigation strategies to avoid locations with a high probability of weather-related risks. The business also has an opportunity to use weather prediction information to redirect customers and assets to other locations to mitigate the financial risks of cancellations. For example, when faced with a high probability of a natural disaster such as a hurricane, the business can use risk communication strategies to attempt to rebook a reservation at a later date, to rebook a reservation at another company owned location, or to redirect marketing budgets to offset or recoup losses. The business may also extend their communication, via email or website, to broader distribution to other community channels. Other studies suggest that including elements of locality in messaging can be important to maintain credibility. Individuals are more likely to trust local community members over state or federal spokespersons (Pollard 2013).

This case study also provides invaluable information about how outdoor locations and temperature are related. The relation of temperature to persistent climate change documented in this study highlights the need to examine how subtle changes or events can impact business outcomes. For cabin campers, consistent with previous research (Rutty and Scott 2016), traditionally undesirably low temperatures are adversely related to occupancy. However, when maximum temperatures are below 25° or above 34°, there is a positive relationship with cabin occupancy. The positive association with high temperatures below 25° occurs seven days in advance, indicating that customers are making the decision a week in advance. Because cabins are equipped with campfire rings and can be heated, this finding provides evidence that individuals are not deterred by cooler temperatures. While not indicative of the other events customers engage in while visiting, the positive correlation between hotter temperatures (i.e., greater than 34°) suggest that customers are more likely to book cabin camping five days prior to extremely warm days. As shown in the tent model, however, this is not the case, where low minimum temperatures adversely impact occupancy six days prior to the cool event and maximum temperatures below 25° adversely impact occupancy four days prior to the arrival date. Lower maximum temperatures are more closely associated with colder nights than minimum temperatures, which suggest that tent campers are waiting even longer to decide whether or not the colder nights are acceptable.

As noted by Perch-Nielsen, Amelun, and Knutti (2010), tourists can become accustomed to climatic conditions. For temperature, this very well may be the case, and communication can be used to help encourage camping behaviors during historically less than ideal conditions. Another business that uses temperature to inform indices for outdoor activities is the Weather Channel. Based on local real-time conditions, the Weather Channel provides a one to ten ranking of how desirable it is to engage in outdoor activities such as jogging or snow skiing that is linked to the hourly forecast. With the full knowledge of the interaction between temperature and occupancy for cabin and tent campers, the outdoor company has the capability to create a metric based on temperature and precipitation to gauge the desirability to camp. The company may also have the capability to communicate with consumers prior to typically camping decisions being made via website, email, and/or other marketing channels to promote favorable conditions or to shift assets to counter negative conditions.

Limitations and future research

This chapter described a case study of an outdoor business located in Virginia Beach, Virginia, to analyze relationships between climate change, extreme weather events, and economic outcomes. The findings highlight resilience and communication strategies to increase preparedness of businesses and communities located in volatile coastal regions. Results address the understudied intersection of climate change, weather, economic outcomes, and risk communication. This work, however, has several limitations, beginning with the use of a single location in the United States. More specifically, adding other locations of the outdoor business to our data and expanding our focus from Virginia Beach, Virginia, to other coastal communities would augment the generalizability of our findings. As mentioned previously, the longitudinal nature of the study provides a blueprint for replicability within and outside the region. While not absolute, the historic and geographic consistency of conditions in the southeast climate zone can help inform relationships between business outcomes, climate change, and weather events in the region as well. We also only capture camping as an outcome variable, instead of other indicators such as sales. Finally, we are missing other extreme weather variables such as wind, hail, and thunderstorms.

Future research could explore the impact of a communication intervention on camping outcomes over time, ultimately contributing to improved individual safety and organizational and community resilience. Future research should also expand on the number of locations included, the number of climate zones represented, the number of climatic variables and extreme event variables included, and the number of non-climatic variables included. Specific to businesses, future research has the potential to draw from the growing environmental management accounting (EMA) literature (Christ, Burritt, and Varsei 2016) to accomplish these research goals. For instance, researchers drawing from the EMA literature could explore the economic impact among multiple locations by analyzing location-specific weather conditions, extremes, and communication variables such as media market, social-media engagement, and internal organizational communication. Future research encompassing communication interventions might pose a unique opportunity to monitor the impact on camping and other business outcomes. For example, advance warnings to individuals about extreme precipitation and flooding could contribute to better preparedness and response strategies. Additional work could explore how tourists or visitors receive warning messages and how likely they are to respond. Other variables including timing (i.e., sending messages more than a week in advance) and locality (i.e., message received from local businesses instead of state of national spokespersons) could also be integrated into new messaging. The outdoor business could also explore adaptation strategies to encourage individuals to frequent the business during the times when the temperature is desirable.

References

Allen, Myria W. 2016. *Strategic Communication for Sustainable Organizations Theory and Practice*. New York: Springer.

Allen, Myria W., and Craig, Christopher A. 2016. Rethinking Corporate Social Responsibility in the Age of Climate Change: A Communication Perspective. *International Journal of Corporate Social Responsibility*, 1(1): 1–11.

Anthony, Kathryn E., Sellnow, Timothy L., and Millner, Alyssa G. 2013. Message Convergence as a Message-Centered Approach to Analyzing and Improving Risk Communication. *Journal of Applied Communication Research*, 41: 346–364.

Avery, Elizabeth Johnson, and Lariscy, Ruthann W. 2010. FEMA and the Rhetoric of Redemption: New Directions in Crisis Communication Models for Government

Agencies. In *The Handbook of Crisis Communication*. (eds.). W. Timothy Coombs and Sherry J. Holladay. Chichester: Wiley-Blackwell.

Bauerlein, Valerie. 2011. How to Measure a Storm's Fury One Breakfast at a Time. *Wall Street Journal*. September 1. Accessed at www.wsj.com/articles/SB10001424053111 90471660457654246073605364.

Bean, Hamilton, Sutton, Jeanette, Liu, Brooke F., Madden, Stephanie, Wood, Michele M., and Mileti, Dennis S. 2015. The Study of Mobile Public Warning Messages: A Research Review and Agenda. *Review of Communication*, 15(1): 60–80.

Beerli, Asuncion, and Martin, Josefa D. 2004. Tourists' Characteristics and the Perceived Image of Tourist Destinations: A Quantitative Analysis – A Case Study of Lanzarote, Spain. *Tourism Management*, 25: 623–636.

Bigano, Andrea, Goria, Alessandra, Hamilton, Jacqueline M., and Tol, Richard S. J. 2005. The Effect of Climate Change and Extreme Weather Events on Tourism. In *Nota di Lavoro, Fondazione Eni Enrico Mattei*. Milano: Foundazione Eni Enrico Mattei (FEEM), p. 30.

Bigano, Andrea, Hamilton, Jacqueline M., and Tol, Richard S. J. 2007. The Impact of Climate Change on Domestic and International Tourism: A Simulation Study. *The Integrated Assessment Journal*, 7(1): 25–49.

Bloetscher, Frederick, Heimlich, Barry, and Meeroff, Daniel E. 2011. Development of an Adaptation Toolbox to Protect Southeast Florida Water Supplies from Climate Change. *Environmental Reviews*, 19: 397–417.

Broida, Rick. 2017. Find Facebook's Hidden Safety Check Feature. *CNET*. Accessed on October 12, 2017 at www.cnet.com/how-to/find-facebooks-hidden-safety-check-feature/.

Chen, Chiang-Ming, Yu-Chen Lin, Eldon Y. Li, Chia-Change Liu, Chiang-Ming Chen, Yu-Chen Lin, Ledon Y. Li, and Chia-Chang Liu. 2017. Weather Uncertainty Effect on Tourism Demand. *Tourism Economics*, 23(2): 469–474.

Christ, Katherine Leanne, Burritt, Roger, and Versei, Mohsen. 2016. Towards Environment Management Accounting for Trade-Offs. *Sustainability Account, Management and Policy Journal*, 7(1): 428–448.

Clement, Etonbong P. 2014. Using Normalized Bayesian Information Criterion (Bic) to Improve Box-Jenkins Model Building. *American Journal of Mathematics and Statistics*, 4(5): 214–221.

Cole, Terry W., and Fellows, Kelli L. 2008. Risk Communication Failure: A Case Study of New Orleans and Hurricane Katrina. *Southern Communication Journal*, 73(3): 211–228.

Cox, Robert. 2009. *Environmental Communication and the Public Sphere*, Second Edition. Thousand Oaks, CA: Sage Publications.

Craig, Christopher A., and Feng, Song. 2016. An Examination of Electricity Generation by Utility Organizations in the Southeast United States. *Energy*, 116: 601–608.

Craig, Christopher A., and Feng, Song. 2018. A Temporal and Spatial Analysis of Climate Change, Weather Events, and Tourism Businesses. *Tourism Management*, 67: 351–361.

de Freitas, C. R. 2003. Tourism Climatology: Evaluating Environmental Information for Decision Making and Business Planning in the Recreation and Tourism Sector. *International Journal of Biometereology*, 48(1): 45–54.

DiLuzio, Mauro, Johnson, Gregory L., Daly, Christopher, Eischeid, Jon K., and Arnold, Jeffrey G. 2008. Constructing Retrospective Gridded Daily Precipitation and Temperature Datasets for the Conterminous United States. *Journal of Applied Meteorology and Climatology*, 47: 475–497.

Federal Communication Commission (FCC). 2017. *Emergency Communication*. Accessed on October 11, 2017 www.fcc.gov/consumers/guides/emergency-communications.

Feng, Song, Trnka, Miroslav, Hayes, Michael, and Zhang, Yongjun. 2017. Why Do Different Drought Indices Show Distinct Future Drought Risk Outcomes in the U.S. Great Plains? *Journal of Climate*, 30: 265–278.

Fjelstul, Jill, and Fyall, Alan. 2015. Sustainable Drive Tourism: A Catalyst for Change. *International Journal of Tourism Research*, 17: 460–470.

Frich, P., Alexander, L. V., Della-Marta, P., Gleason, B., Haylock, M., Klein Tank, A. M., and Peterson, T. 2002. Observed Coherent Changes in Climatic Extremes During the Second Half of the Twentieth Century. *Climate Research*, 19: 193–212.

Hyman, Tracy-Ann. 2013. Assessing the Vulnerability of Beach Tourism and Non-Beach Tourism to Climate Change: A Case Study from Jamaica. *Journal of Sustainable Tourism*, 22(8): 1197–1215.

Ingram, K., Dow, K., Carter, L., and Anderson, J. (eds.). 2013. *Climate of the Southeast United States: Variability, Change, Impacts, and Vulnerability*. Washington, DC: Island Press.

Kahan, Dan M., Peters, Ellen, Wittlin, Maggie, Slovic, Paul, Oullette, Lisa Larrimore, Braman, Donald, and Mandel, Gregory. 2012. The Polarizing Impact of Science Literacy and Numeracy on Perceived Climate Change Risks. *Nature Climate Change*, 2(10): 732–735.

Karl, Thomas, and Koss, Walter James. 1984. Regional and National Monthly, Seasonal, and Annual Temperature Weighted by Area, 1895–1983. *Historical Climatology Series*, 4, no. 3. Asheville: National Climate Data Center.

Linnenluecke, Martina K., and Griffiths, Andrew. 2012. Assessing Organizational Resilience to Climate and Weather Extremes: Complexities and Methodological Pathways. *Climate Change*, 113: 933–947.

Monahan, William B., and Fisichelli, Nicholas A. 2014. Climate Exposure of U.S. National Parks in a New Era of Change. *PloS One*, 9(7): e101302.

Monahan, William B., Rosemartin, Alyssa, Gerst, Katharine L., Fisichelli, Nicholas A., Ault, Toby, Schwartz, Mark D., Gross, John E., and Weltzin, Jake F. 2016. Climate Change Is Advancing Spring Onset Across the US National Park System. *Ecosphere*, 7(10): 1–17.

Moser, Susanne C. 2009. Communicating Climate Change: History, Challenges, Process and Future Directions. *Wiley Interdisciplinary Reviews: Climate Change*, 1(1): 31–53.

National Aeronautics and Space Administration (NASA). 2005. *NASA – What's the Difference Between Weather and Climate?* August 7. Accessed at www.nasa.gov/mission_pages/noaa-n/climate/climate_weather.html.

National Oceanic and Atmospheric Administration (NOAA). 2017. *What Percentage of the American Population Lives Near the Coast?* October 10. Accessed at http://ocean service.noaa.gov/facts/population.html.

National Research Council (NRC). 1989. *Improving Risk Communication*. Washington, DC: National Academy Press.

Nerlich, Brigitte, Koteyko, Nelya, and Brown, Brian. 2009. Theory and Language of Climate Change Communication. *Wiley Interdisciplinary Reviews: Climate Change*, 1(1): 97–110.

NOAA National Centers for Environmental Information (NCEI). 2018. *U.S. Billion-Dollar Weather and Climate Disasters*. Accessed at www.ncdc.noaa.gov/billions/.

Ockwell, David, Whitmarsh, Lorraine, and O'Neill, Saffron. 2009. Reorienting Climate Change Communication for Effective Mitigation: Forcing People to Be Green or Fostering Grass-Roots Engagement? *Science Communication*, 30(3): 305–327.

Perch-Nielsen, Sabine L., Amelung, Bas, and Knutti, Reto. 2010. Future Climate Change Resources for Tourism in Europe Based on the Daily Tourism Climate Index. *Climate Change*, 103(3–4): 363–381.

Pollard, William E. 2013. Public Perceptions of Information Sources Concerning Bioterrorism Before and After Anthrax Attacks: An Analysis of National Survey Data. *Journal of Health Communication*, 8(1): 93–103.

Preston, Benjamin L. 2013. Local Path Dependence of U.S. Socioeconomic Exposure to Climate Extremes and the Vulnerability Commitment. *Global Environmental Change*, 23: 719–732.

Recreational Vehicle Industry Association. 2017. *RV Ownership Trends*. Accessed on October 2, 2017 at www.rvia.org/?esid=trends.

Rutty, Michelle, and Scott, Daniel. 2016. Comparison of Climate Preferences for Domestic and International Beach Holidays: A Case Study of Canadian Travelers. *Atmosphere*, 7(2): 30.

Sherman-Morris, Kathleen. 2010. Tornado Warning Dissemination and Response at a University Campus. *Natural Hazards*, 52(3): 623–638.

Sorensen, John H. 2000. Hazard Warning Systems: Review of 20 Years of Progress. *Natural Hazards Review*, 1(2): 119–125.

United States Census Bureau. 2017. *Maps and Data*. Accessed on July 1, 2017 at www.census.gov/geo/maps-data/.

United States Environmental Protection Agency (EPA). 2017. *Climate Change Indicators: Sea Surface Temperature*. Accessed on July 1, 2017 at www.epa.gov/climate-indicators/climate-change-indicators-sea-surface-temperature.

van Heck, Tanja. 2010. Time Series Analysis to Forecast Temperature Change. *Mathematical Scientist*, 35: 63–69.

Wang, Hui, Fu, Rong, Kumar, Arun, and Li, Wenhong. 2010. Intensification of Summer Rainfall Variability in the Southeastern United States During Recent Decades. *Journal of Hydrometeorology*, 11(4): 1007–1018.

World Travel and Tourism Council (WTTC). 2017. *Travel & Tourism Economic Impact 2017 United States*. Accessed on July 6, 2017 at www.wttc.org//media/files/reports/economic-impact-research/countries-2017/unitedstates2017.pdf.

Yu, Gongmei, Schwartz, Zvi, and Walsh, John E. 2009. A Weather-Resolving Index for Assessing the Impact of Climate Change on Tourism Related Climate Resources. *Climate Change*, 95(3–4): 551–573.

Zainal, Zaidah. 2007. Case Study as a Research Method. *Jurnal Kemanusiaan*, 5(1): 1–6.

13 Waves of change

Coastal hazards, tourism development, and risk communication along the Pacific coast of Nicaragua

Matthew L. Fahrenbruch

Introduction

Effective risk communication systems are essential components of risk reduction and resilience building efforts in communities (Mileti and Peek 2002; Morgan et al. 2002; Hooke and Rogers 2005; Fischhoff 2009). Defined broadly, a risk communication system provides accurate and timely information about risk to impacted stakeholders so that they may adjust their behaviors to mitigate their exposure (Plough and Krimsky 1987). Common examples include inclement weather forecasting (tornados, hurricanes, flooding), hazard maps (flood plain, forest fire, avalanche, and tsunami zones), and for human crises, embassy alerts and media reports.

In this chapter, I discuss risk communication within the specific context of tourism communities. While all communities are vulnerable to crises, tourism destinations are particularly sensitive and need special consideration in terms of risk communication. This sensitivity is especially acute in historically crisis-prone locations such as Nicaragua. In this chapter, I describe recent advances in risk communication that have been made in the tourism community of San Juan del Sur, Nicaragua, and I discuss the need to reconceptualize the traditional narrative of risk communication to further build resilience in the community (Figure 13.1).

Worldwide, tourism has been growing rapidly in recent decades. In 2017, the number of international tourism arrivals reached 1.3 billion worldwide, a movement equal to 17.5 percent of the world population (UNWTO 2018). Tourism is increasingly viewed and promoted by development organizations and governments as a viable and sustainable option for economic growth and diversification in developing countries (USAID 2005; Hawkins and Mann 2007; Mitchell and Ashley 2010). The growth of tourism, however, is challenging risk management systems, especially in smaller tourism destinations that have limited resources, like San Juan del Sur.

On September 2, 1992, San Juan del Sur, along with numerous other communities along Nicaragua's Pacific coast, was devastated by a large tsunami. The tsunami, generated by a magnitude 7.6 earthquake off the coast of Nicaragua, ranged in height from 2 meters in the north and south to just over 11 meters along the

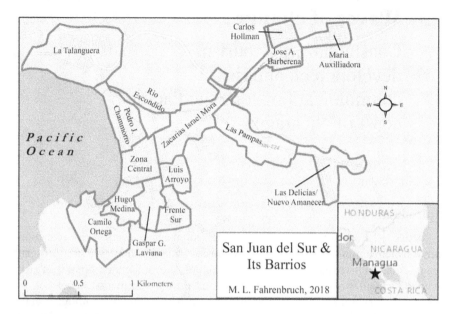

Figure 13.1 San Juan del Sur, Nicaragua, and its barrios

central coast; the run-up in San Juan del Sur was approximately 5 meters (Satake et al. 1993; Baptista, Priest, and Murty 1993). United Nations reports made in the days after the event estimated that 60 percent of the homes in San Juan del Sur were destroyed and more than 800 people displaced (UNDHA 1992). In total, the tsunami claimed 170 lives, left 13,000 homeless, and destroyed 1,500 homes in Nicaragua (Satake et al. 1993).

Since 1992, tourism has grown significantly in Nicaragua as a whole and around San Juan del Sur in particular (Fahrenbruch and Cochran 2014; Alvarado and Taylor 2014). Annual international arrivals have grown from under a million in 2008 to over 1.7 million in 2018 (INTUR 2012, 2018). Nicaragua bills itself as a cheaper alternative to neighboring Costa Rica, and San Juan del Sur is now a top destination for cruise ship traffic, ground-based *sun, sea, and beach* tourism, and a growing contingent of North American and European expatriates.[1]

In light of the 1992 event and the growth of tourism, the Nicaraguan government has been working to increase its crisis response capability and develop an effective risk communication strategy. The country has made great strides since 1992, but challenges remain in terms of developing a risk communication strategy that is sensitive to both the needs of impacted residents and the tourism industry on which they increasingly rely. In the following sections, I describe the nature of the tsunami risk in the region, the evolution of the Nicaragua risk communication system[2], and some of the challenges that communities like San Juan del Sur still face.

Tsunami risk in the region

The geologic environment of Central America is affected by the interactions of four tectonic plates: North American, Caribbean, Cocos, and Nazca (Rojas, Bungum, and Lindholm 1993; Coates 1997) (Figure 13.2). The major tectonic feature of Pacific Central America is the Middle American Trench (MAT), which marks the subduction of the Cocos plate beneath the Caribbean plate and runs parallel to the coast from approximately Puerto Vallarta, Mexico, to the Osa Peninsula of Costa Rica. In their 1996 study, Ambraseys and Adams cataloged 51 historical seismic events with magnitudes of 7 or greater occurring in Central America between 1898 and 1994. The authors found that 93 percent of the events originated along the MAT (Ambraseys and Adams 1996); an earlier study by Rojas, Bungum, and Lindholm (1993) came to a similar conclusion. In addition to being a geologically active area prone to earthquakes, the region is also active in terms

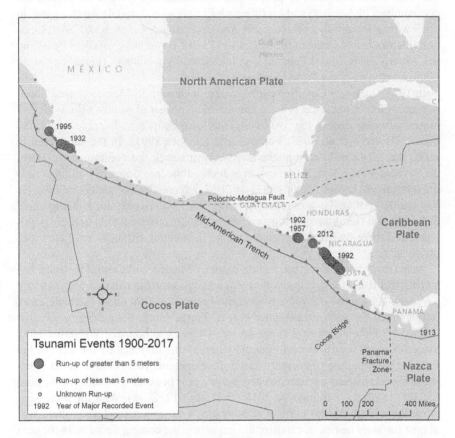

Figure 13.2 The Middle American Trench Region with tectonic features and tsunami events between 1900 and 2017

Source: The Global Historical Tsunami Database (NOAA) and Lindholm, Strauch, and Fernández 2017

of tsunamis (Fernández et al. 2000; Fernández, Ortiz-Figueroa, and Mora 2004; Lindholm, Strauch, and Fernández 2017).

The National Oceanic and Atmospheric Administration (NOAA), which operates the Pacific Tsunami Warning System and the Global Historical Tsunami Database, estimates that 37 tsunami events with validity ratings of 3–4 (probable-to-definite occurrence) impacted the MAT region between 1900 and 2017 (NGDC/WDC 2018). Of these, 32 had reported wave heights that range between 0.09 and 11 meters. An additional three, 1902 and 1957 in El Salvador and 1913 in Panama, had no wave height estimates but are reported to have been damaging events (Fernández et al. 2000; Lindholm, Strauch, and Fernández 2017).

Tsunamis with wave heights similar to the 1992 event in San Juan del Sur are quite common along the Pacific coast of Central America. Seven events with estimated wave heights of 5 meters or more have struck the region since 1900. Several of these events are documented in the literature. The 1902 Guatemala-El Salvador tsunami killed 185 people and devastated low-lying areas around the communities of Acajuela and La Libertad, El Salvador. Acajuela was hit again in 1957 with a tsunami that originated in Alaska (Fernandez et al. 2000, 2004; Lindholm, Strauch, and Fernández 2017). In 1913, the community of Villas Pedasi on the Azuero Peninsula of Panama was inundated by a tsunami (Fernandez et al. 2000; Lindholm, Strauch, and Fernández 2017).

In 1932, the Great Cuyutlán earthquake and tsunami in Mexico caused flooding in the low-lying areas around Cuyutlán, southeast of Manzanillo, with 2–3 meters of water destroying five hotels, the local church, and approximately 80 houses (Borrero et al. 1997; Farreras and Sanchez 1991). In the same area in 1995, the Manzanillo earthquake and tsunami struck the community of Barra de Navidad with a 5-meter wave that inundated the first floors of buildings near the waterfront (Borrero et al. 1997). In 2012, a 6 meter wave generated by a 7.4 magnitude earthquake was reported along the Pacific coasts of Nicaragua, El Salvador, and Honduras. Fortunately, the areas impacted were not densely populated, and there was little reported damage (Lindholm, Strauch, and Fernández 2017).

Based on existing data, the Pacific coast of Mexico and Central America has a statistical risk of a tsunami with a wave height of greater than 5 meters every 17 years. With only 117 years of data, however, it is difficult to calculate exact return times for such catastrophic events. Furthermore, a catastrophe is often defined by the amount of damage an event causes to humans. While the 2012 event impacted a still sparsely populated area, this may not be the case in the future, given the rate of current coastal development. Tourism arrivals in Nicaragua have grown on average 8.6 percent per year between 2008 and 2018, from 850,000 to over 1.7 million by 2018 (INTUR 2012, 2018). With the increasing attractiveness of coastal tourism and prospects for rising sea levels, there will almost certainly be risk of catastrophic impacts in the coming decades. In the next section, I discuss actions taken in Nicaragua and San Juan del Sur following the 1992 Nicaraguan Tsunami to improve risk communication.

1992 Nicaraguan tsunami: shocked into action

An early warning system is an essential component of any risk communication strategy. It is also an important tool for crisis-prone tourism destinations to help assuage fears about *no-escape* disaster scenarios (Huan, Beaman, and Shelby et al. 2004). Unfortunately, in 1992 such a system was beyond the reach of the Nicaraguan government (Strauch 2005). San Juan del Sur residents interviewed in 2012 about the 1992 tsunami recounted that the government issued no warning about the wave, nor was there any perceptible shaking from the earthquake to alert them[3]. One resident, a young man at the time, was watching a movie at a local school near the waterfront when the wave hit. He remembered the wave rising slowly enough that he and his friends were able to wade to safety. He and others recounted severe damage to businesses and homes along the waterfront and penetration of the wave at least 2.5 blocks inland into the Zona Central. A restaurant owner who operates in the same area of the waterfront remembered finding her refrigerator a block and a half inland, and a housekeeper in the La Talanguera neighborhood remembered finding beach chairs lodged in the second story balcony of the beachfront home where she worked (Fahrenbruch and Cochran 2014).

Official estimates of the 1992 tsunami in San Juan del Sur put the run-up of water at 5 meters and its maximum penetration approximately 250 meters inland from the beach in the Zona Central neighborhood (Abe et al. 1993; Baptista, Priest, and Murty 1993; Satake et al. 1993). Affected residents, lacking information and afraid they would be caught in another wave, remained in the hills surrounding the town for three days after the event (Preuss 1994). Despite the absence of any warning, only 170 people across Nicaragua lost their lives, and only two of those were in San Juan del Sur (Baptista, Priest, and Murty 1993; Satake et al. 1993).

At the time of the 1992 tsunami there was no institutional awareness of tsunami risk in Nicaragua and no risk communication strategy. There was also no seismic network in the country to detect tsunami events, nor was Nicaragua a member of the Pacific Tsunami Warning System (Strauch 2005; Strauch et al. 2018). Even if these detection capabilities were in place, there was no communication infrastructure to get warnings to endangered communities nor trained personnel on the ground to facilitate evacuation (Strauch 2005; Strauch et al. 2018).

Following the 1992 event, Nicaragua embarked on a process of developing a national tsunami warning infrastructure. The nation joined the Pacific Tsunami Warning System, installed digital seismic equipment and a 24-hour seismic warning center, and in 1996 installed radio-based communication systems in coastal municipalities (Strauch 2005; Strauch et al. 2018).

The Nicaraguan tsunami warning system functioned in the following manner. Upon detection of the occurrence of a major seismic event, automatic warnings were generated by the National Institute for Territorial Studies (INETER), under which the tsunami warning center is based. The warning then was sent automatically to the National System for the Prevention, Mitigation, and Attention of Disasters (SINAPRED), the Nicaraguan Emergency Management Agency.

SINAPRED would relay the warning to mass media outlets (primarily local radio stations) for distribution and to local authorities via radio. Radios were installed in the homes of local government officials who were/are responsible for alerting their communities. Within each municipality, a municipal emergency response committee would convene at the *alcaldia* (city hall) and work with volunteer *barrio* (neighborhood) and municipal brigades to evacuate low-lying areas.[4] Before the installation of sirens in 2013, alerts were slow and rudimentary and consisted of bells, loudspeakers, car horns, and word of mouth (Strauch 2005; Strauch et al. 2018).

While the Nicaraguan system in 2012 was more advanced than other Central American nations in terms of crisis preparation and communication, the system was still fundamentally flawed by its slow speed of information dissemination that followed the issuance of a warning (GFDRR 2011; Fahrenbruch and Cochran 2014). A major challenge to the system was the proximity of the MAT and the time it took for the affected residents to be alerted and evacuated. In 2012, the local SINAPRED director stated that in San Juan del Sur, approximately 2,500 residents would need to be evacuated within 20 to 45 minutes depending on the source area of the tsunami. In the tourist season, however, its population has been known to rise as high as 13,000 (Fahrenbruch and Cochran 2014). The SINAP-RED director did not consider an evacuation of those numbers to be realistic.

Another challenge to the system was a general level of mistrust toward government officials. The SINAPRED officer lamented about the fatalistic attitudes of local residents. In a survey conducted by the author in 2012, respondents in 145 of 146 households reported being aware of tsunami risk, but the SINAPRED director related his experience of being ridiculed by residents for highlighting the risk: "only God knows when a tsunami will hit" they told him (Fahrenbruch and Cochran 2014).

The official recounted one situation in the community following the 2011 Japanese tsunami. The event triggered an evacuation warning for San Juan del Sur. While many of the tourists reluctantly evacuated, few residents heeded the warning. Several American expats I interviewed even recounted taking a case of beer and their surfboards down to the beach to *wait for the wave*. They highlighted their lack of confidence in the Nicaraguan authorities despite the fact that, unbeknownst to them, the warning was likely issued by U.S. authorities at the Pacific Tsunami Warning Center in Hawaii (Fahrenbruch and Cochran 2014). In the end, fortunately, there was no wave.

In 2012, Nicaragua was working with the Japanese International Cooperation Agency (JICA) and the Center for Coordination for the Prevention of Natural Disasters in Central America (CEPREDENAC) on a six-year project, nicknamed *BOSAI* (JICA 2011). The goal of the project was to develop capacity within communities, municipalities, and crisis management agencies across Central America to better respond to natural disasters (JICA 2011). In Nicaragua, the goal of the project was to increase the capacity of coastal residents to respond to tsunamis by increasing the speed of crisis communication and public confidence in the warning system. The pilot project in the Department of León on the central coast included the development of hazard maps, the establishment of a tsunami early warning siren system, community evacuation drills, and first responder training in organization, search and rescue, and evacuation. The program also sought to facilitate a regional tsunami alert system for Central America based in Managua (JICA 2011; Lindholm, Strauch, and Fernández 2017; Strauch et al. 2018).

In early 2013, two early warning sirens were installed in the municipality of San Juan del Sur. This new system has fundamentally changed risk communication in the municipality. Now when INETER generates a tsunami warning, the alarm system is activated from Managua and the warning reaches those at risk near instantaneously. As in León, with the installation has come increased training in the community, including capacity-building workshops, evacuation drills, and several actual warnings. The new system has not been without its faults or critics, but participation in tsunami preparation has increased significantly since 2012.

In addition to the above measures for local residents and officials, by 2015, the city had also installed informational signboards near the waterfront with maps of evacuation routes, safety zones, and assembly areas to assist and reassure visitors and locals. According to local informants, public attitudes have also changed with the installation of the sirens. The local residents are now more proactive, attending workshops and taking part in community-wide evacuation drills. One informant suggested that the sirens hold a certain faceless authority that local officials do not. On the other hand, perhaps with the alarms, people think they actually have a chance to escape in time, thus helping them to move beyond their previously fatalistic perspectives.

San Juan del Sur and Nicaragua as a whole have made great strides in increasing capacity for risk communication with the tsunami early warning and evacuation system. There is, however, a great deal more work to be done. San Juan del Sur is highly dependent on tourism activity, and there is still a need in the community for a risk communication strategy that takes tourism into account (Fahrenbruch and Cochran 2014). In the next section, I shift the focus away from early warning risk communication systems that save lives to postcrisis risk communication strategies that can save livelihoods. I ask readers to consider the nature of tourism communities and to expand their perceptions of risk communication from the precrisis preparation and warning narratives that dominate the risk communication literature to postcrisis rebuilding, where risk communication is essential for rebuilding confidence and assuaging fears in the minds of potential tourists.

Challenges: risk communication in tourism recovery

All communities are vulnerable to crises, but tourism destinations are particularly sensitive to secondary *reputational* crises that can hinder long-term economic recovery (Beirman 2003; Ritchie 2004; Ichinosawa 2006). A reputational crisis can result from a variety of primary crises including natural disasters, terrorism, crime, economic downturn, and social and political unrest (Slovic et al. 1991; Kasperson 1992; Sönmez and Graefe 1998; Sönmez, Apostopoulos, and Tarlow 1999; Faulkner and Vikulov 2001; Slovic 2002; Beirman 2003; Ichinosawa 2006).

While the media is a strong partner in communicating risk information during and after a primary crisis, media coverage can create reputational crises through the persistent distortion of risk that is communicated to potential visitors. Media organizations tend to focus on a limited number of key elements that determine the newsworthiness of an issue. Most notable are the stories that fit the *if it bleeds, it leads* model (Beirman 2003). The rapid destruction of a destination is more newsworthy than its slow recovery. The result is that everyone knows when a destination has been ravaged, but few know when it has recovered.

The perception of risk is deeply psychological, especially in terms of foreign travel. Tourists already experience a heightened sense of risk when traveling abroad due to language barriers and cultural differences. The tourism industry is designed to overcome these barriers in the form of guidebooks, travel blogs, translation apps, tourism offices, and all-inclusive travel packages. These *tools*, however, are often not controlled by local communities but by international travel agencies, cruise ship companies, publishers, and national tourism agencies. In the event of a crisis, publishers may advise against travel to crisis areas, travel agencies and cruise ship operators may drop the impacted destinations, and national tourism agencies may avoid promoting the impacted areas to save the national image (Slovic 2002; Beirman 2003; Ichinosawa 2006; Calgaro and Lloyd 2008). This all serves to heighten the perception of risk and uncertainty among potential visitors.

A well-documented case study is the coastal tourism industry of Thailand after the 2004 Indian Ocean Tsunami. After the tsunami, over 7,000 people were dead or missing in Thailand, of which 2,000 were foreigners; many thousands more were injured[5] (Ichinosawa 2006). Twenty-four-hour global media coverage of the tsunami and its aftermath quickly stigmatized Thailand in the eyes of tourists. The area was hit by a *reputational* crisis that continued to affect the area long after the physical damage was cleaned up (Ichinosawa 2006: 112; Calgaro and Lloyd 2008). A year after the event, much of the tourism infrastructure was rebuilt, but sales were only 10–30 percent of what they were before the tsunami, and international arrivals were down by 68 percent from the year before (Ichinosawa 2006).

In a second case, the Australian tourism destination community of Katherine, Northern Territory, was destroyed by a large flood in 1998. The media portrayed the community as literally being "washed off the map" (Faulkner and Vikulov 2001: 335). In response, local tourism authorities hired publicists to specifically emphasize to potential visitors that the community still indeed existed and was recovering. Despite a lack of insurance coverage, the following year infrastructure had been largely rebuilt and arrivals were up 15 percent over the year prior to the flood. While the scales and cultural contexts of the Thailand and Katherine events differed greatly, corruption and tepid support for postcrisis marketing by the Thailand Tourism Authority have been cited as reasons for the weak recovery, while the successful recovery of Katherine was largely credited to a strategy that effectively communicated risk to potential visitors and let them know when Katherine was back (Faulkner and Vikulov 2001; Ichinosawa 2006; Calgaro and Lloyd 2008).

There are many additional examples of risk communication in the tourism industry (see, Slovic 2002; Beirman 2003; Sönmez and Graefe 1998; Sönmez, Apostopoulos, and Tarlow 1999; Faulkner and Vikulov 2001; Ritchie 2004). In virtually all cases, the researchers' conclusions can be boiled down to two main needs. First is the need for unified and directed representation of the local tourism industry to emergency managers and aid agencies to facilitate the quick rebuilding of cash-generating infrastructure. Second is the simultaneous need for a risk communication strategy that focuses on potential visitors and counters misleading and damaging press coverage, referred to in the tourism industry as *crisis marketing* (Beirman 2003).

In 2012, I discussed these needs with the local director of the Nicaraguan Institute of Tourism (INTUR) in San Juan del Sur and the local president of the National Chamber of Tourism of Nicaragua (CANTUR), a national trade organization that supports Nicaraguan-owned tourism businesses. The INTUR director explained that in the event of a tsunami, his office would represent the local industry as part of INTUR's larger collaboration within the SINAPRED system. However, INTUR is not an official part of SINAPRED, nor is the tourism industry included in the municipal crisis management plans (SINAPRED 2008; Sánchez 2009).

I asked the director about the current marketing strategy for the community and questioned whether it would change after a crisis. The director explained that INTUR promotes the community as part of its national marketing strategy. The strategy includes promotion to domestic markets and internationally through their website, in media advertisements, through tourism offices in Nicaragua's foreign embassies, and through their negotiations with cruise ship operators and, most recently, foreign television producers[6]. He highlighted however, that the community still relies heavily on decentralized word-of-mouth marketing through individual business websites, social media, and third-party sites like TripAdvisor. In terms of crisis marketing, the INTUR director did not suggest any special strategy beyond the normal marketing channels highlighted above, nor did he indicate how INTUR would counter negative media.

Conversations with the local CANTUR president yielded more concerning results. The president related that in the event of a crisis, his organization would represent their members to the government and other organizations when lobbying for recovery funds; however, he highlighted that his organization only represents Nicaraguan-owned businesses. He highlighted growing animosity in the community between nonlocal and local residents. Many local residents blame tourism for the rise in drug and alcohol use, illegal activity, and rampant inflation that has impacted the community (Fahrenbruch and Cochran 2014).

The CANTUR president related his sense that foreign/nonlocal tourism development is paving over the old to make way for the new and is leaving local livelihoods, history, and values in the wake (Fahrenbruch and Cochran 2014; Alvarado and Taylor 2014). He was doubtful about the prospects for collaboration between nonlocals and locals, and it appeared likely that in the event of a crisis, tourism businesses could end up fighting each other. The CANTUR president, like the

INTUR director, related that when it comes to marketing, it really comes down to every business for itself. This would likely be the risk communication *strategy* as well in the event of a crisis and represents a major challenge to any postcrisis risk communication strategy.

Conclusion

In a 2011 report from the Global Facility for Disaster Reduction and Recovery (GFDRR), Nicaragua is lauded as a leader in Central America for its comprehensive approach to crisis management and the emphasis on crisis management as a part of the country's overall development plan (GFDRR 2011). The growing importance of tourism in Nicaragua and in communities like San Juan del Sur, however, necessitates a greater focus on tourism-sensitive postcrisis risk communication strategies within the traditional sphere of crisis management. Early warning systems such as what I have discussed here go a long way to assuage the fears of tourists about potential no-escape disaster scenarios and can be a valuable selling point after a crisis, but this, along with recovery information, needs to be more effectively communicated to the public.

Destination communities need risk communication strategies to communicate with potential visitors and counter misleading and damaging media representations. San Juan del Sur and other communities likely have a limited capability to implement such initiatives. There is at present no mention of the role of INTUR in either the national or municipal crisis management plans, nor does there appear to be a crisis marketing strategy for San Juan del Sur beyond the individual promotion of businesses via personal and third-party websites and social media. Furthermore, there is a lack of cohesion within the tourism industry as locals struggle with the dramatic changes brought by the rapid metamorphosis of their community into a tourism destination.

Several actions, however, could be implemented that would create the foundations for a tourism-sensitive risk communication strategy. First, INTUR could be included as a part of municipal crisis response strategies and the national strategy. Tourism is quickly growing in economic importance across Nicaragua, and it already dominates the economy of San Juan del Sur and surrounding coastal communities. The quick recovery of the tourism industry will be essential to the overall resilience of these communities in the event of a tsunami or other crisis. Second, a local risk communication strategy, including a locally controlled website, needs to be developed to promote the community, counter negative media representations, and provide strong, unified leadership that can overcome local divisions and attract tourists as soon as infrastructure is rebuilt. The community cannot base its crisis marketing on the websites and social media of individual businesses and third parties. The majority of tourism businesses in San Juan del Sur are located near the waterfront. As in 1992, these businesses will be occupied with rebuilding, not with marketing.

This chapter highlighted the advances made in Nicaragua toward improving its crisis communication capacity, specifically its early warning tsunami system.

The study indicates that in tourism communities, such as San Juan del Sur, there is a need to consider postcrisis communication needs. Historically, risk communication has been a top-down centralized effort to mitigate the exposure of stakeholders at direct risk. This is evidenced by the early warning system highlighted above. The system has one goal: to warn stakeholders and get them out of harm's way. The resilience of tourism communities, however, requires not only saving lives but also livelihoods. This means effectively communicating risk to far-away potential tourists to help counter negative media, assuage fears and uncertainty and get them back into the community so recovery can occur.

Notes

1 San Juan del Sur, with a population of about 10,000 residents, hosted 42 cruise ships in 2017 and 31,625 disembarking passengers (INTUR 2018). Additionally, the community is a prime holiday destination for Nicaraguans and other Central Americans. During the Christmas and Easter seasons, its population can reach 13,000 (Fahrenbruch and Cochran 2014).
2 Risk communication in this chapter refers to the timely transfer of information from experts to a general audience of stakeholders so that those stakeholders are aware of the risk and can adequately judge what actions they should take to safeguard their lives and possessions (Plough and Krimsky 1987). In the case of the tourism industry, stakeholders include local residents and business owners in the destination community, as well as potential tourists and the private and public organizations that facilitate and promote tourism.
3 The 1992 tsunami, and the recent 2012 tsunami were caused by *slow* earthquakes, which are relatively common along the MAT and are characterized by large magnitudes, but low frequencies. The result is that they can cause large tsunami events with little, if any, perceptible shaking on land (Kanamori and Kikuchi 1993; Lindholm, Strauch, and Fernández 2017).
4 In Latin America, the term *municipio* translates as municipality. In the United States, a municipality is considered to be the jurisdiction of a city. In Latin America, a municipality is a county-level jurisdiction. The municipality of San Juan del Sur covers an area of 411.05 km², and includes 33 communities. Barrio brigades are used within the city proper, while municipal brigades are used in the outlying areas.
5 The 2004 Indian Ocean tsunami killed over 220,000 people across 14 countries with Indonesia, Sri Lanka, India, and Thailand experiencing the highest casualty rates. The single city of Banda Aceh, on the Indonesian island of Sumatra, suffered approximately 160,000 deaths.
6 In the last several years, San Juan de Sur has become a reality TV and retirement darling in the United States. In addition to being featured in numerous newspaper and magazine articles, HGTVs *House Hunters International* has featured the community at least five times, and CBS's Emmy award winning show *Survivor* has used the community as a base for four seasons including the aptly named season 29, *Survivor: San Juan del Sur*. These shows have served to raise the profile of the community in international markets.

References

Abe, Kuniaki, Abe, Katsuyuki, Tsuji, Y., Imamura, F., Katao, H., Iio, Y., Satake, K., Bourgeois, J., Noguera, E., and Estrada, F. 1993. Field Survey of the Nicaraguan Earthquake and Tsunami of September 2, 1992. *Bulletin Earthquake Research Institute of the University of Tokyo*, 68: 23–70.

Alvarado, N. A., and Taylor, M. J. 2014. Del mar quien es dueno? Artisanal Fisheries, Tourism Development and the Struggles Over Access to Marine Resources in Gigante, Nicaragua. *Journal of Latin American Geography*, 13(3): 37–62.

Ambraseys, N., and Adams, R. 1996. Large Magnitude Central American Earthquakes: 1898–1994. *Geophysical Journal International*, 127(3): 665–692.

Baptista, A. M., Priest, G. R., and Murty, T. S. 1993. Field Survey of the 1992 Nicaraguan Tsunami. *Marine Geodesy*, 16: 169–203.

Beirman, D. 2003. *Restoring Tourism Destinations in Crisis. A Strategic Marketing Approach*. Oxen: CABI Publishing.

Borrero, J., Ortiz, M., Titov, V., and Synolakis, C. 1997. Field Survey of Mexican Tsunami Produces New Data, Unusual Photos. *EOS*, 78(8): 85–92.

Calgaro, E., and Lloyd, K. 2008. Sun, Sea, Sand and Tsunami: Examining Disaster Vulnerability in the Tourism Community of Khao Lak, Thailand. *Singapore Journal of Tropical Geography*, 29: 288–306.

Coates, A. G. 1997. *Central America: A Natural and Cultural History*. New Haven, CT: Yale University Press.

Fahrenbruch, M. L., and Cochran Jr., D. M. 2014. Waiting for the Wave: Assessing the Vulnerability of Tourism in San Juan del Sur, Nicaragua to Tsunamis. *Journal of Latin American Geography*, 13(3): 11–35.

Farreras, S. F., and Sanchez, A. J. 1991. The Tsunami Threat on the Mexican West Coast: A Historical Analysis and Recommendations for Hazard Mitigation. *Natural Hazards*, 4: 301–316.

Faulkner, B., and Vikulov, S. 2001. Katherine, Washed Out One Day, Back on Track the Next: A Post-Mortem of a Tourism Disaster. *Tourism Management*, 22: 331–344.

Fernández, M., Molina, E., Havskov, J., and Atakan, K. 2000. Tsunamis and Tsunami Hazards in Central America. *Natural Hazards*, 22: 91–116.

Fernández, M., Ortiz-Figueroa, M., and Mora, R. 2004. Tsunami Hazards in El Salvador. In *Natural Hazards in El Salvador*. (eds.) W. I. Rose, J. J. Bommer, D. L. López, M. J. Carr, and J. J. Major. Boulder, CO: Geological Society of America, pp. 435–444.

Fischhoff, B. 2009. Risk Perception and Communication. In *Oxford Textbook of Public Health*. (eds.) R. Detels, R. Beaglehole, M. Lansang, and M. Gulliford. Oxford: Oxford University Press, pp. 940–952.

Global Facility for Disaster Reduction and Recovery (GFDRR). 2011. *Disaster Risk Management in Central America: GFDRR Country Notes, Nicaragua*. Washington, DC: GFDRR. Accessed on January 23, 2013 at www.gfdrr.org/sites/gfdrr.org/files/Nicaragua_DRM.pdf.

Hawkins, D. E., and Mann, S. 2007. The World Bank's Role in Tourism Development. *Annals of Tourism Research*, 34: 348–363.

Hooke, W. H., and Rogers, P. G. 2005. *Public Health Risks of Disasters: Communication, Infrastructure, and Preparedness: Workshop Summary*. Washington, DC: National Academies Press.

Huan, T-C., Beaman, J., and Shelby, L. 2004. No-Escape Natural Disasters: Mitigating Impacts on Tourism. *Annals of Tourism Research*, 31: 255–273.

Ichinosawa, J. 2006. Reputational Disaster in Phuket: The Secondary Impact of the Tsunami on Inbound Tourism. *Disaster Prevention and Management*, 15: 111–123.

Instituto Nicaragüense de Turismo (INTUR). 2012. *Boletín de Estadísticas de Turismo: Año 2000*. INTUR, Managua, Nicaragua. Accessed on July 7, 2018 at www.intur.gob.ni/estadisticas-de-turismo/#tab-5b3c043b0c7bc-.

————. 2018. *Boletín de Estadísticas de Turismo: Año 2015*. INTUR, Managua, Nicaragua. Accessed on July 7, 2018 at www.intur.gob.ni/estadisticas-de-turismo/#tab-5b3c043b0 c7bc-1.

Japan International Cooperation Agency (JICA). 2011. *20 Años de Cooperación en Nicaragua: Memoria*. JICA Nicaragua Office, Managua, Nicaragua. Accessed on July 7, 2017 at www.jica.go.jp/nicaragua/office/others/ku57pq00001wj1es-att/memoria.pdf.

Kanamori, H., and Kikuchi, M. 1993. The 1992 Nicaragua Earthquake: A Slow Tsunami Earthquake Associated with Subducted Sediments. *Nature*, 361: 714–716.

Kasperson, R. E. 1992. The Social Amplification of Risk: Progress in Developing and Integrative Framework. In *Social Theories of Risk*. (eds.) S. Krimsky, and D. Golding. Westport, CT: Praeger Press, pp. 153–178.

Lindholm, C., Strauch, W., and Fernández, M. 2017. Tsunami Hazard in Central America: History and Future. In *Tsunamis: Geology, Hazards and Risks*. (eds.) E. M. Scourse, N. A. Chapman, D. R. Tappin, and S. R. Wallis. London: Geological Society of London, Special Publication 456, pp. 90–104.

Mileti, D. S., and Peek, L. 2002. Understanding Individual and Social Characteristics in the Promotion of Household Disaster Preparedness. In *New Tools for Environmental Protection: Education, Information, and Voluntary Measures*. (eds.) T. Dietz, and P.C. Stern. Washington, DC: The National Academies Press, pp. 125–139.

Mitchell, J., and Ashley, C. 2010. *Tourism and Poverty Reduction: Pathways to Prosperity*. London: Earthscan.

Morgan, M. G., Fischhoff, B., Bostrom, A., and Atman, C. J. 2002. *Risk Communication: A Mental Models Approach*. Cambridge: Cambridge University Press.

National Geophysical Data Center/World Data Center (NGDC/WDC) Global Historical Tsunami Database. Accessed on July 22, 2018 at www.ngdc.noaa.gov/hazard/tsu_db.shtml.

Plough, A., and Krimsky, S. 1987. The Emergence of Risk Communication Studies: Social and Political Context. *Science, Technology, & Human Values*, 12(3–4): 4–10.

Preuss, J. 1994. *Field Report: Investigation of September 2, 1992 Nicaragua Tsunami*. FMHI Paper 21, Florida Institute for Mental Health, Tampa, Florida. Accessed on February 4, 2014 at http://scholarcommons.usf.edu/fmhi_pub/21.

Ritchie, B. W. 2004. Chaos, Crises and Disasters: A Strategic Approach to Crisis Management in the Tourism Industry. *Tourism Management*, 25: 66983.

Rojas, W. H. Bungum, and Lindholm, C. 1993. Historical and Recent Earthquakes in Central America. *Revista Geológica de América Central*, 16: 5–22.

Sánchez, J. 2009. *Plan de Respuesta Municipal con Enfoque de Gestión del Riesgo Municipio de San Juan del Sur*. San Juan del Sur, Nicaragua: Alcalde de San Juan del Sur.

Satake, K., Bourgeois, J., Abe, K., Abe, K., Tsuji, Y., Imamura, F., Iio, Y., Katao, H., Noguera, E., and Estrada, F. 1993. Tsunami Field Survey of the 1992 Nicaragua Earthquake. *EOS*, 74: 145–160.

Sistema Nacional para la Prevención, Mitigación y Atención de Desastres (SINAPRED). 2008. Plan Nacional de Respuesta del SINAPRED. *SINAPRED*, Managua, Nicaragua.

Slovic, P. 2002. Terrorism as Hazard: A New Species of Trouble. *Risk Analysis*, 22(3): 425–426.

Slovic, P., Layman, M., Kraus, N., Flynn, J., Chalmers, J., and Gesell, G. 1991. Perceived Risk, Stigma, and Potential Economic Impacts of a High-Level Nuclear Waste Repository in Nevada. *Risk Analysis*, 11(4): 683–696.

Sönmez, S. F., Apostopoulos, Y., and Tarlow, P. 1999. Tourism in Crisis: Managing the Effects of Terrorism. *Journal of Travel Research*, 38: 3–8.

Sönmez, S. F., and Graefe, A.R. 1998. Influence of Terrorism Risk on Foreign Tourism Decisions. *Annals of Tourism Research*, 25: 112–144.

Strauch, W. 2005. *Experience in Nicaragua on the Development of a Tsunami Warning System. Instituto Nicaragüense de Estudios Territoriales*. Accessed on April 10, 2017 at http://webserver2.ineter.gob.ni/tsunami/experience.htm.

Strauch, W., Talavera, E., Tenorio, V., Ramírez, J., Arguello, G., Herrera, M., Acosta, A., and Morales, A. 2018. Toward an Earthquake and Tsunami Monitoring and Early Warning System for Nicaragua and Central America. *Seismological Research Letters*, 89(2A): 399–406.

United Nations Department of Humanitarian Affairs (UNDHA). 1992. *Nicaragua Earthquake/Tsunami Sep 1992 UN DHA Situation Reports 1–7*. Undha, Geneva, Switzerland. Accessed on July 22, 2018 at www.reliefweb.int/rw/rwb.nsf/db900SID/ACOS-64BHCW?OpenDocument.

United Nations World Tourism Organization (UNWTO). 2018. *UNWTO World Tourism Barometer*. UNWTO, Madrid, Spain. Accessed on April 30, 2018 at http://mkt.unwto.org/en/barometer.

United States Agency for International Development (USAID). 2005. *USAID and Sustainable Tourism: Meeting Development Objectives*. USAID, Washington, DC. Accessed on April 4, 2011 at http://pdf.usaid.gov/pdf_docs/PNADE710.pdf.

14 Risk and crisis communication in schools

Understanding current challenges and opportunities

Tyler G. Page, Brooke Fisher Liu, Holly Ann Roberts, and Michael Egnoto

Introduction

Risks are "probabilistic occurrences that can have positive or negative outcomes of various magnitudes" (Proutheau and Heath 2009: 576). These risks can result in crises. A crisis is "a specific, unexpected, non-routine event or series of events that creates high levels of uncertainty and a significant or perceived threat to high priority goals" (Sellnow and Seeger 2013: 7). Schools often serve as community lifelines before, during, and after crises (Kingshot and McKenzie 2013). They help establish balance and continuity within their communities (Lerner, Volpe, and Lindell 2003), they play integral roles in local crisis response systems, and they can improve or hinder crisis response and recovery. Researchers have just begun to identify the role that communication can have in helping communities *bounce forward* after crises and other adverse events (Manyena et al. 2011; Houston et al. 2015). That said, a school's traditional function as an educational institution can be impacted by crises. This study examines how schools prepare for such incidents.

Schools and crisis planning

K-12 schools are often harmed by crises. All but five of the 126 public schools in New Orleans were destroyed during 2005's Hurricane Katrina (Harvard Educational Review 2005). During 2012's Superstorm Sandy, thousands of schools along the East Coast closed (Dunabeitia 2012). From the Columbine massacre until April 2018, the United States experienced 85 attempted mass murders in schools, which took the lives of over 223 people (San Diego Union-Tribune Editorial Board 2018). Such incidents are especially tense because parents are separated from their children. When a crisis occurs, teachers and administrators are the first responders (Kingshot and McKenzie 2013) and are charged with communicating to children what they should do to protect themselves. Indeed, schools have a "high-priority goal of ensuring student safety at all times" (Barker and Yoder 2012: 79), especially during crisis situations.

School crisis planning has been the focus of academic research (Seeger et al. 2001; Gower 2013; Crockett-Lohr 2015), professional associations (National Education Association Health Information Network 2007), and government agencies (U.S. Department of Education n.d.). As a whole, this body of knowledge provides insights into effective school crisis communication plans and procedures. Recent experience has shown that preparation is not complete (Stein 2006; Regan 2013), and some have begun to find holes within existing school preparation. For example, the incorporation of social media into planning is a recent development for many schools (Agozzino and Kaiser 2014; Crockett-Lohr 2015). Other literature has demonstrated that schools lack preparation for specific crisis types, such as emerging infectious diseases, bioterrorism, and pandemics (Sapien and Allen 2001; Rebmann et al. 2012, 2015).

Key communication components of school crisis plans include creating necessary templates and messages and establishing important protocols (National Education Association Health Information Network 2007; Gower 2013). The literature suggests nine different templates for communication that should be prepared in advance of an emergency. These templates and messages include an email listserv for stakeholders who must be contacted regularly, such as staff, media, parents, and elected officials, and call logs to track media. The literature also suggests protocols to have in place prior to crises, such as identifying who will provide guidance to teachers about media interviews, establishing policies about media presence on school grounds and in buildings, and outlining notification procedures for parents (National Education Association Health Information Network 2007; Gower 2013; Agozzino and Kaiser 2014). To address school crisis planning, we asked two primary questions:

Q1a: How prepared are schools to respond to crisis events?
Q1b: What templates have schools prepared in the event of a crisis?

Media coverage of school crises

Most people rely on the media as their first source of information about school crises (Walsh-Childers and Lewis 2011; Hincker and Holloway 2015). Media coverage of school crises can be high volume and extensive in duration (Chyi and McCombs 2004; Muschert and Carr 2006).

This extraordinary media coverage can directly impact students' well-being. For example, a student who had witnessed the Virginia Tech shootings described how after the shootings he went home to take a nap, and when he woke up two hours later he had 250 missed calls with 70 voicemails from journalists who wanted to interview him (Walsh-Childers and Lewis 2011). In addition, public information officers have reported journalists arriving on the scene after shootings at a high school and "waving $50 bills in the air, offering to buy yearbooks from students so they could obtain instant photos of those who had been shot" (Stein 2006: 115).

Due to the potential high volume and long duration of media crisis coverage, researchers and practitioners recommend deciding in advance whether to provide media relations guidelines for members of school communities who may want to talk with the media. School officials need to decide in advance whether they will facilitate such interviews (Gower 2013; Hincker and Holloway 2015). Likewise, it is important to consider whether media should be banned from parts of campus to shield affected stakeholders, especially children, from unwelcome attention (Hincker and Holloway 2015). Faculty and staff need to know their legal rights when interacting with media, including what information they can and should withhold (Agozzino and Kaiser 2014). For instance, the Family Educational Rights and Privacy Act (FERPA) should guide communication about any affected students. State laws about planning requirements and school district policies should also be considered and shared with teachers and staff who may interact with media (National Education Association Health Information Network 2007). With regard to media coverage of school crises, we asked the following question:

Q2: How prepared are schools to respond to media inquiries in the event of a crisis?

Social and mobile media use during crises

How and why to effectively integrate social and mobile media into school crisis communication receives scant attention in academic literature and government policy (Gower 2013; Hincker and Holloway 2015; Mazer et al. 2015). Yet the limited studies of social media in schools demonstrate that stakeholders will actively use social and mobile media to communicate during crises (Wigley and Fontenot 2010; Barker and Yoder 2012). For example, one study found that people actively used social media to share details about the incidents, emotional reactions, personal connections, thoughts and prayers, and calls for change and calls for action during a school shooting (Mazer et al. 2015). Importantly, not all the information shared was accurate, including information about the location of the shootings, number of victims, and reunification points for parents.

Some schools may be reticent to use social media given that there are age restrictions on many sites (e.g., Facebook restricts users to 13 years and older) (U.S. Department of Education n.d.). The literature reveals, however, that during school-based crises, parents can be active information seekers and sharers online (Mazer et al. 2015). They may even receive initial crisis information from phone calls or text messages from their children (Mazer et al. 2015). There is evidence that students' mobile phone use can significantly contribute to information sharing during crises (Wigley and Fontenot 2010; Barker and Yoder 2012).

There are many examples of this in the literature. Virginia Tech students turned to social media to correctly identify who the victims were well before the school released the names (Vieweg et al. 2008). Multiple incidents document parents of high school students turning to social media to determine the location of active shooters, the number of fatalities, and reunification points – and in the process sharing misinformation (Mazer et al. 2015).

Less frequent, but also present in the literature, are examples of schools effectively using social media after crises. For example, after the 2011 tornadoes in Tuscaloosa, Alabama, one school system posted a request for volunteers to help clean up schools, and within 30 minutes almost 80 people showed up to help (Stephens 2011).

While few studies combine the concepts of schools and social media, a substantial amount of research exists regarding social media and crisis, as well as social media generally. In terms of crisis, the social-mediated crisis communication model explains how messages impact organizations, social media, and traditional media, with influence from social media content creators, followers, and inactives (Liu et al. 2012). The model provides a guide for how messages can be created by one source (e.g., an influential content creator) and then eventually influence traditional media or an organization's statements. Other literature has also found the circumstances under which people will share messages online during crises as opposed to other channels (Liu, Fraustino, and Jin 2015, 2016). In addition, social media literature demonstrates that posts that contain imagery, videos, or other graphic content have higher share rates and greater impact on their audiences (Xiong et al. 2012; Can, Oktay, and Manmatha 2013; Feng et al. 2015). In addition, hashtags are encouraged, as they help share information to involved stakeholders during crises (Gupta, Joshi, and Kumaraguru 2012; Starbird et al. 2012). They also build a sense of community (Moorley and Chinn 2014). In total, the literature shows that messages sent from one source can impact other sources. It further provides some limited guidance (e.g., hashtags, imagery) for how to create an impactful message. Accordingly, we ask the following question to understand the use of social media in schools preparing for and responding to crisis situations:

Q3: How do schools use social media to prepare for and respond to crisis situations?

It is also important to write in a way that students and parents will be able to read. A common way to test readability is the Flesch-Kincaid Readability Tests: Flesch Reading Ease and Flesch-Kincaid Grade Level (Flesch n.d.; Kincaid et al. 1975). The average reading level in the U.S. is seventh grade, and so that is suggested for writing in order to communicate with parents (National Center for Educational Statistics 2006). Therefore we ask the following question to assess the readability of social media posts by schools:

Q4: How readable and engaging is the crisis content published by schools on social media?

Although the literature on school use of social media for crisis communication is limited, the U.S. Department of Education (n.d.) provided recommendations for how schools might do so: (1) communicate during full-scale exercises; (2) provide notifications for school closures; (3) post and receive status information; (4) disseminate safety information, news alerts, and health alerts; (5) post reunification protocols; (6) add redundancy to current communication networks; (7) allow for more directly and timely information dissemination; (8) establish a system for rapid communication to the media and broader community; (9) eliminate media gatekeeping/filter; (10) share crisis counseling information; (11) share information about how the community can help; (12) communicate temporary relocation information; (13) communicate reopening procedures; and (14) thank volunteers. Therefore, we assess whether schools follow these guidelines:

Q5: Do schools follow the United States Department of Education's guidelines for using social media during crises?

Crisis messages

While researchers and practitioners acknowledge the critical importance of communication in a school crisis response (Seeger et al. 2001; Regan 2013), the treatment of the communication component of school crisis responses is limited. Most literature has emphasized the importance of functioning and redundant communication systems rather than the specific nature and content of the message itself (Regan 2013; Perry 2015). There are powerful examples of what happens when schools do not actively and effectively provide information during crises. For example, families trying to reach loved ones after the 2007 Virginia Tech shootings overwhelmed regional cellular capacity (Hincker and Holloway 2015).

This, however, does not address how schools should communicate and which channels are most effective. The new media landscape has opened up a variety of channels that schools can use. In this environment, some literature has even found that the medium itself is more important than the message (Schultz, Utz, and Goritz 2011). Some literature has begun to document these channels and the redundant use of them. Perry (2015) noted that more than three-quarters of college campuses use at least three methods for communicating directly with the campus community during an emergency, and some use as many as 37 methods. Agozzino and Kaiser (2014) examined a new channel in the form of emergency outcall systems that create a voicemail that then goes to every parent, teacher, and staff via phone calls, emails, text messages, Facebook posts, and tweets. This evaluation sought to understand which channels schools use in order to communicate in the wake of a crisis:

Q6: Which channels do schools use to disseminate messages in the event of a crisis?

Methods

Social media analysis method

We developed a coding protocol based on a review of academic literature and of best practices outlined in crisis communication plans (Fearn-Banks 2010; Coombs

2015). These focused on suggested best practices in social media literature as well as suggestions from the U.S. Department of Education. The social media coding protocol contained two categories (background and message content), with 30 items coded. This coding protocol was applied to all school system-level posts about crises on Facebook, Twitter, and Instagram from October 2014 through September 2015. In total, we examined 611 social media posts: 498 tweets, 102 Facebook posts, and 11 Instagram posts. Of the 24 local school systems in the state, 22 posted crisis information on Twitter, 13 on Facebook, and one on Instagram. Two coders cross-coded 15 percent of the data across all categories, achieving reliabilities via Cronbach's alpha between .742 and 1.0, which ranges from acceptable to excellent (George and Mallery 2003).

Survey method

A 30-minute survey on school crisis planning, crisis communication protocols, and crisis experiences was distributed through superintendents and supporting state agencies in the state's school system to principals, teachers, nurses, safety officers, communication officers, health officers, and other staff members. Participation was entirely voluntary, and state regulations did not allow participants to be compensated for their time completing the survey. Participants were not required to answer any individual question. Rather, they were given the opportunity to skip questions they felt unqualified or unwilling to answer. In total, 132 participants answered multiple questions, and 93 completed the entire survey. All survey responses are reported here.

Scales measuring media preparation, crisis planning, and general preparedness were used to assess the current state of preparation in the sample. The media preparedness scale consisted of three items drawn from Cloudman and Hallahan (2006) asking how well the school has done key activities to prepare for media interest (e.g., "identified organizational spokesperson") scaled 1–7, where 1 was not well at all and 7 was extremely well. This scale has been used to assess how well organizations are prepared to deal with media in the event of a crisis. The scale was considered reliable ($\alpha = .872$), and so it was combined into a single item.

The crisis planning scale consisted of four items also drawn from Cloudman and Hallahan (2006) focused on the degree of preparation for a crisis situation (e.g., "My school district leadership is dedicated to crisis communications planning"), where 1 was strongly disagree and 7 was strongly agree. This scale has been used to assess comfort of stakeholders with crisis preparation. The scale was considered reliable ($\alpha = .962$) and was combined into a single item.

The general preparedness scale consisted of 13 items drawn from Fowler, Kling, and Larson (2007) asking if participants agreed with statements regarding general preparation (e.g., "I am very familiar with our building's evacuation plan"), where 1 was strongly disagree and 7 was strongly agree. This scale described the specific knowledge employees should have in the event of a crisis, attitudes toward the organization's preparation, and actions the organization has taken. The scale was considered reliable ($\alpha = .858$) and was combined into a single item. Each of these scales had previously been recommended to assess the level of preparation for their unique subjects.

The remainder of the questions asked participants for their demographics, their school's social media platforms, their experiences with crises, and whether their schools performed specific actions suggested by the literature. The specific actions included asking how they were trained on crisis plans (Regan 2013), what training exists for dealing with media requests (National Education Association Health Information Network 2007; Gower 2013; Hincker and Holloway 2015), how they use social media to communicate about crises (Crockett-Lohr 2015; U.S. Department of Education n.d.), and what templates they had already created in advance of sending messages (Gower 2013).

Results

Crisis preparation

Preparation level

The survey revealed schools are more prepared for some crises than others (Q1a). Over 80 percent of the sample knew of plans for active shooter situations, bomb threats, building issues necessitating evacuation, fires, and natural disasters. However, fewer than half knew of plans to address public health issues, social media threats, or other types of crises (Table 14.1). If participants reported that their school had a crisis communication plan, they were asked how they were trained to understand the plan. The most likely form of training was in a team meeting, though some participants had been trained individually or only through a manual (Table 14.2).

Table 14.1 Crisis experienced and plan in place

Crisis	Active shooter	Bomb threat	Building issue	Fire	Natural disaster	Public health	Social media	Other
Experienced	5.3%	40.9%	47.7%	28.8%	20.5%	11.4%	15.2%	11.4%
Plan	82.6%	89.4%	82.6%	90.2%	84.1%	49.2%	11.4%	12.9%

Table 14.2 Crisis plan training

Crisis	Active shooter	Bomb threat	Building issue	Fire	Natural disaster	Public health	Social media	Other	Total average
Trained individually	13.8%	13.5%	9.4%	11.3%	10.3%	8.6%	20.0%	14.3%	12.7%
Trained in team	55.3%	47.1%	61.5%	63.2%	58.8%	60.3%	53.3%	57.1%	57.1%
Manual only	30.9%	39.4%	29.2%	25.5%	30.9%	31.0%	26.7%	28.6%	30.3%

Templates created

Analysis revealed a gap in the number of school jurisdictions that are creating the templates suggested in the literature (Q1b) (National Education Association Health Information Network 2007; Gower 2013; Agozzino and Kaiser 2014). Indeed, less than half of all jurisdictions had created any of the suggested templates (Table 14.3).

Scales

Scales assessing crisis planning and general preparedness were used to evaluate the current state of preparation in the sample. The crisis planning scale consisted of four questions scaled 1–7, where 7 was best planning. Participants' mean score was 20.33 out of a total possible of 28. That is an average score of 5.08 per scale point, suggesting the planning is above the scale midpoint but could be improved. The general preparation scale consisted of 13 questions scaled 1–7, where 7 was the most ready. Participants' mean score was 64.33 out of a possible 91. That is an average of 4.94 per scale item, suggesting that general preparedness could be improved (Table 14.4).

Media preparation

Participants' mean score on the media preparedness scale was 16.07 out of a possible 21 (Q2). This is an average of 5.36 per scale item, suggesting that general preparedness is good but has significant room to improve (Table 14.4).

Table 14.3 Templates created in advance

Template	Percentage
Call logs	13.9%
Daily FAQ sheet	9.2%
Draft messages for voicemail	27.7%
Email update	24.6%
Email Listserv of stakeholders	40.0%
Email to journalists	10.8%
Emergency website	23.1%
General FAQs	12.3%
Letter or email to parents	44.6%

Table 14.4 Preparedness and readiness

	Media preparedness	Crisis planning	General preparation
N	89	100	90
Mean	16.07	20.33	64.33
Median	17.00	20.00	66.00
Std. deviation	4.57	6.19	13.60
Minimum	3	4	21
Maximum	21	28	91

Just over half (53.2 percent) of participants reported they have a full-time public relations practitioner on hand. Only 6.4 percent did not have a spokesperson of any kind. The rest stated that they have a part-time public relations person or someone designated within the staff. Participants were allowed to select more than one option, as some schools might have multiple staff members. Occasionally, participants reported having both full-time and part-time public relations personnel or a spokesperson independent of the staff (Table 14.5).

According to the survey results, only 77 percent of spokespeople have been trained to deal with media. Fewer (62.2 percent) have been trained about their legal responsibilities, and less than half (44.6 percent) have their contact information published online (Table 14.6). With the exception of notification procedures for parents and managing media coverage, a minority of schools reported having additional crisis protocols (Table 14.7).

Table 14.5 PR person in place

Asset	Percentage
Full-time PR	53.2%
Part-time PR	5.3%
Volunteer PR	3.2%
Spokesperson from existing staff	62.8%
Training for faculty and staff for media interviews	6.4%

Table 14.6 Spokesperson training

Trained on	Percentage
Dealing with media	77.0%
Legal responsibilities (e.g., FERPA)	62.2%
Contact info published online	44.6%

Table 14.7 Crisis protocols

Protocol	Percentage
Identified person to prepare faculty and students for media interviews	29.8%
Media partnerships	48.8%
Notification procedures for parents	71.4%
Plan to prioritize stakeholders	25.0%
Managing media coverage	53.6%
Set up information hotlines	26.2%
Translation service	21.4%
Policy about media presence on school grounds	42.9%
Policy on planning memorial	10.7%

Social media results

The social media content analysis answered the remaining evaluation questions (Q3, Q4, and Q5). With regard to school use of social media (Q3), we found that Facebook is the most used social media tool. The only other social media network with a substantial presence in schools is Twitter (Table 14.8). Survey results also suggested that no single school employee is universally encouraged to scan social media for threats. Rather, the responsibility for scanning social media is given to different groups in different school systems (Table 14.9). By investigating how schools use social media via content analysis, the vast majority of communication sent by districts pertains to delays, early closures, or cancellations, largely due to a stated weather event but quite often without stating the type of incident that is causing the interruption at all (Table 14.10). Very few of the posts used video, images, or hashtags. In addition, few provided links for additional information (Table 14.11).

The readability of school social media posts (Q4) was assessed via the Flesch-Kincaid Readability Tests. Overall, the reading ease was acceptable. The Flesch Reading Ease indicated writing was appropriate for persons age 13 and up (Flesch n.d.) ($M = 71.81$, $SD = 17.59$). The Flesch-Kincaid Grade Level assessment gave a similar result with mean grade level between sixth and seventh grade ($M = 6.18$, $SD = 3.43$). This level is recommended in the United States (National Center for Educational Statistics 2006). However, when comparing district by district,

Table 14.8 School social media presence

Social Media	Percentage
Facebook	72.1%
Google	12.3%
LinkedIn	6.6%
Twitter	46.7%
YouTube	11.5%
Other	15.6%

Table 14.9 Encouraged to report social media threats

Role	Percentage
Administration	59.2%
Faculty	35.2%
Parents	32.4%
Staff	38.0%
Students	25.4%
Other	15.5%
None of the above	26.7%

Table 14.10 Type of notification and purpose of notification

Type	Count	Percentage
Delays	179	29.3%
Early closures	53	8.7%
Cancellations	283	46.3%
Not declared	96	15.7%
Total	611	100%

Purpose	Count	Percentage
Weather	225	36.8%
Other	91	14.9%
Not reported	295	48.3%
TOTAL	611	100%

Table 14.11 Hashtag, video, and images

Content	Percentage
Video	0.3%
Image	0.3%
Hashtag	3.8%
Link	10.8%

Table 14.12 Readability assessment overall

Cluster	Count	Percentage
1 – Too high level	185	30.3%
2 – Easily readable	408	66.8%
Not rated	18	2.9%
Total	611	100.0%

a concerning trend emerged. The data was not normally distributed and actually formed two groups: one slightly too complicated for adults to read and one ideal cluster that was comprehensible by most Americans.

A one-way ANOVA test showed meaningful between district differences for reading levels [$F(22,569) = 5.669$, $p < 0.001$]. Post hoc Brown-Forsythe tests further confirmed these differences [$F(22,348.54) = 5.417$, $p < 0.001$]. Tukey's HSD suggested a two-factor solution with a $p = 0.055$ assuming unequal group size ($M = 21.96$). This two-factor solution was confirmed via two-step cluster analysis and was supported when a two-cluster solution was presented (Cluster 1, $M = 10.23$, Cluster 2, $M = 4.26$) (Table 14.12).

This means that the examined school districts communicate via social media in two clusters of literacy at approximately tenth grade (cluster 1) and fourth grade (cluster 2) levels. Table 14.12 presents the proportion of social media communication that fits into each of the clusters identified in the two-step cluster process.

U.S. Department of Education suggestions on social media use

This study analyzed each school district's social media communication to see which of the U.S. Department of Education's 14 recommendations for social media use they currently implement (Q5) and asked school officials in the survey about their future plans for social media use. Four suggestions could not be analyzed in the content analysis as they concerned intent and off-line communication. These were instead analyzed in the survey.

The results confirm that these suggestions largely are not employed in planning and in practice. Three were observed as happening in substantial numbers: Provide notifications for school closures; post and receive status information; and disseminate safety information, news alerts, and health alerts. No other strategy, however, composed more than 1 percent of observed social media activity. Further, the survey detected limited intention to start implementation of these recommendations anytime soon. Nearly a majority (45.9 percent) have no plan to accomplish *any* suggestions (Table 14.13).

Message dissemination

The survey asked which communication channels schools planned to use in the event of a crisis (Q6). The results make clear that many different channels are used. Automated phone calls are most common, though jurisdiction websites, social media, and text alert systems all are used as well (Table 14.14).

Table 14.13 Plans to do DOE suggestions

Plans	Reported plan	Observed on social media
Communicate during full-scale exercises	24.6%	0.7%
Communicate reopening procedures	24.6%	0.5%
Communicate temporary relocation information	24.6%	0%
Disseminate safety information, news alerts, health alerts	34.4%	100%
Eliminate media gatekeeping	6.6%	N/A
Establish system for rapid communication	19.7%	N/A
Post and receive status information	21.3%	94.4%
Post reunification protocols	19.7%	0%
Provide notifications for school closures	36.1%	84.3%
Repeat communication sent through other channels	27.9%	N/A
Share crisis counseling information	23.0%	0%
Share information about how community can help	23.0%	0%
Thank volunteers	23.0%	0.3%
None of the above	45.9%	0%

Table 14.14 Communication methods

Method	Percentage
Website	74.4%
Email	59.8%
Letter	58.5%
Automated calls	85.4%
Personal calls	29.3%
Social media	62.2%
Text	72.0%
Other	3.7%

Discussion

Schools in this study are at a basic level of preparedness for many crises and, like many organizations, improvements can be made. In this section we review the current state of school crisis preparedness in our sample and provide suggestions for improvement.

Preparation

Schools reported having some plan for dealing with most crisis situations, but their preparations for such events are incomplete. Participants reported that the vast majority of schools have plans for active shooter incidents, bomb threats, building issues, fires, and natural disasters. Fewer have plans for public health emergencies (49.2 percent) and managing social media during crises (11.4 percent). This might explain why, when asked about the level of crisis communication preparedness (Cloudman and Hallahan 2006; Fowler, Kling, and Larson 2007), participants rated their schools as moderately prepared.

One focal element of this future preparation should be developing communication templates suggested by the literature (National Education Association Health Information Network 2007; Gower 2013). A majority of schools in this sample do not have templates. Such templates should certainly include call logs to track media, messages for voicemail, email listservs of stakeholders, an email template for journalists, and letters to parents (National Education Association Health Information Network 2007; Gower 2013). Organizations overseeing schools, such as departments of education at the state and federal level, might even help by providing recommended templates. Likewise, as schools develop templates, they could share them with other schools.

In all of these cases, schools may benefit from improved plans, which may boost confidence regarding the level of preparedness and also equip school employees to more adequately respond to crisis situations.

Media management

Analysis revealed that schools could benefit from providing more training to spokespeople and other individuals to help key internal stakeholders prepare for crises. These trainings should include dealing with the media and school personnel's responsibilities surrounding education privacy law (Agozzino and Kaiser 2014; Hincker and Holloway 2015). Further, schools need to consider creating policies governing the extent to which media will have access to students, teachers, and staff, along with resources for teachers and adult students who may wish to talk with the media (National Education Association Health Information Network 2007; Gower 2013; Hincker and Holloway 2015). In this case, the state's current guidance is that only the public information officer may speak with media. This preparation should also include current policies on dealing with inquiries in the world of social media. For instance, schools should be prepared to take requests and comments from parents hearing stories on social media rather than assuming they can just break the story themselves or only use traditional media to disseminate information (Ashby 2007; Wigley and Fontenot 2010; Barker and Yoder 2012; Mazer et al. 2015).

Social media use

Findings from the social media portion of the survey indicate an absence of social media use in crisis planning. Schools should consider posting more information about crises, especially using imagery, videos, graphics, and links to more information to make messages more powerful and shareable (Xiong et al. 2012; Can, Oktay, and Manmatha 2013; Feng et al. 2015). This should include more information about past crises and about crisis preparation for the future so that stakeholders are more prepared when crises inevitably occur (Gower 2013). Schools also should consider targeting specific stakeholders, including parents, local community members, and prospective volunteers, with information and calls to action. Using hashtags would help them do this by either starting or getting involved in conversations that are easily found (Gupta, Joshi, and Kumaraguru 2012; Starbird et al. 2012; Moorley and Chinn 2014).

One specific area of improvement has to do with encouraging students to report suspicious activities. This is an opportunity for improvement along with increasing the use of social media throughout all phases of crisis response (like sharing information about how the community can help and how to thank volunteers). In addition, schools in our sample have started to implement some of the U.S. Department of Education's (n.d.) suggestions for using social media during a crisis; however, none appear to be widespread, according to this survey.

The vast majority of crisis information sent by districts via social media pertained to school delays (29.3 percent), early closures (8.7 percent), or school day cancellations (46.3 percent), according to the results of the social media content analysis. School districts should consider expanding the crisis topics they communicate about via social media, particularly in the realm of crisis preparedness. For example, they could share crisis preparedness tips in advance of common crises like severe winter weather.

Districts' social media posts could also be improved by including more specific calls to action and guidance to indicate what stakeholders should do with the information provided. Only 16.5 percent of the analyzed posts included calls to action, and only 0.3 percent included guidance on how to perform recommended actions related to crises. When providing specific actions, districts also should consider including specific temporal recommendations in their social media posts, when appropriate, so stakeholders better understand when they need to take action and how much time they have to take action. The posts analyzed in this evaluation inconsistently and predominately referred to time vaguely, if at all.

Finally, districts should work to better craft their crisis messages in order to increase comprehension. Furthermore, understanding any additional audience needs would be beneficial to message construction, thereby increasing readability (e.g., tailoring messages for special needs populations, non-English speaking communities, etc.).

Conclusion

Given the dearth of literature on school crisis communication, there is also ample opportunity for the field to better help schools prepare for, respond to, and recover from crises through effective communication. This study provides an evaluation from only one state, albeit a large and diverse one. While it did not analyze internal communications within school systems, this study nevertheless represents a starting point for future research to consider how well prepared schools are to communicate in the event of a crisis.

Specifically, we found that most schools have plans for crises such as fires, natural disasters, and active shooter incidents, but less than half of our sample had plans for public health emergencies, and fewer had plans for social media threats. Further, we found that few schools have prepared templates to communicate in the event of crisis and that more preparation for working with media in the event of a crisis could be very helpful. Finally, we found that some crisis communication occurs on social media but that communication could benefit from discussing additional suggested topics (e.g., U.S. Department of Education n.d.) and being written at an appropriate reading level for its audience. We hope that this chapter serves as a rallying call for scholars to begin to fill in the gaps we have identified in this chapter.

References

Agozzino, A., and Kaiser, C. 2014. Social Media as a Practical Approach in Engaging Key Stakeholders in School Crisis Communication Plans: A Qualitative Analysis. *Journal of School Public Relations*, 35: 43–62.

Ashby, M. 2007. *Emergency Management: Status of School Districts' Planning and Preparedness*. Statement at United States House of Representatives.

Barker, G., and Yoder, M. 2012. The Virginia Tech Shootings: Implications for Crisis Communication in Educational Settings. *Journal of School Public Relations*, 33: 78–101.

Can, E., Oktay, H., and Manmatha, R. 2013. Predicting Retweet Count Using Visual Cues. In *Proceedings of the 22nd ACM International Conference on Information & Knowledge Management*. San Francisco, CA, pp. 1481–1484.

Chyi, H., and McCombs, M. 2004. Media Salience and the Process of Framing: Coverage of the Columbine School Shootings. *Journalism & Mass Communication Quarterly*, 81(1): 22–35.

Cloudman, R., and Hallahan, K. 2006. Crisis Communications Preparedness Among US Organizations: Activities and Assessments by Public Relations Practitioners. *Public Relations Review*, 32(4): 367–376.

Coombs, W. 2015. *Ongoing Crisis Communication: Planning, Managing and Responding*. Thousand Oaks, CA: Sage Publications.

Crockett-Lohr, A. 2015. *Social Media and Crisis Communication: An Update to the 2000 National Education Association's Crisis Communications Guide and Toolkit*. Master's Creative Project. Ball State University.

Dunabeitia, J. A. 2012. Hurricane Sandy 2012 School Closings: Full List of Closed Schools. *Now Public*. Accessed at www.nowpublic.com/environment/hurricane-sandy-2012-school-closings-full-list-closed-schools.

Fearn-Banks, K. 2010. *Crisis Communication: A Casebook Approach*. New York: Routledge.

Feng, Z., Li, Y., Jin, L., and Feng, L. 2015. A Cluster-Based Epidemic Model for Retweeting Trend Prediction on Micro-Blog. In *Database and Expert Systems Applications*. Springer International Publishing, pp. 558–573.

Flesch, R. n.d. How to Write Plain English. *Management, Marketing, and Entrepreneurship*. Accessed at www.mang.canterbury.ac.nz.

Fowler, K., Kling, N., and Larson, M. 2007. Organizational Preparedness for Coping with a Major Crisis or Disaster. *Business & Society*, 46(1): 88–103.

George, D., and Mallery, P. 2003. *SPSS for Windows Step by Step: A Simple Guide and Reference*. 11.0 update, Fourth Edition. Boston, MA: Allyn & Bacon.

Gower, S. 2013. *The Current Status of School Crisis Communication Plans: A Survey of Indiana Public School Districts*. Master's Research Paper. Ball State University.

Gupta, A., Joshi, A., and Kumaraguru, P. 2012. Identifying and Characterizing User Communities on Twitter During Crisis Events. In *Proceedings of the 2012 Workshop on Data-Driven User Behavioral Modelling and Mining from Social Media*. Maui, HI, pp. 23–26.

Harvard Educational Review. 2005. *What Can the United States Learn International Experiences with Education in Displacement?* Accessed at http://hepg.org/her-home/issues/harvard-educational-review-volume-75-issue-4/herarticle/what-can-the-united-states-learn-from-internationa.

Hincker, L., and Holloway, R. 2015. Learning and Renewal Through Crisis. *Spectra*, 51(3): 8–13.

Houston, J., Spialek, M., Cox, J., Greenwood, M., and First, J. 2015. The Centrality of Communication and Media in Fostering Community Resilience: A Framework for Assessment and Intervention. *American Behavioral Scientist*, 59(2): 270–283.

Kincaid, J., Fishburne, R., Rogers, R., and Chissom, B. 1975. *Derivation of New Readability Formulas (Automated Readability Index, Fog Count, and Flesch Reading Ease Formula) for Navy Enlisted Personnel*. Research Branch Report 8–75. Chief of Naval Technical Training: Naval Air Station. Memphis.

Kingshot, B., and McKenzie, D. 2013. Developing Crisis Management Protocols in the Context of School Safety. *Journal of Applied Security Research*, 8(2): 222–245.

Lerner, M., Volpe, J., and Lindell, B. 2003. *A Practical Guide for Crisis Response in Our Schools*, Fifth Edition. New York: The American Academy of Experts in Traumatic Stress.

Liu, B. F., Fraustino, J. D., and Jin, Y. 2015. How Disaster Information Form, Source, Type, and Prior Disaster Exposure Affect Public Outcomes: Jumping on the Social Media Bandwagon? *Journal of Applied Communication Research*, 43(1): 44–65.

———. 2016. Social Media Use During Disasters: How Information Form and Source Influence Intended Behavioral Responses. *Communication Research*, 43(5): 626–646.

Liu, B. F., Jin, Y., Briones, R., and Kuch, B. 2012. Managing Turbulence in the Blogosphere: Evaluating the Blog-Mediated Crisis Communication Model with the American Red Cross. *Journal of Public Relations Research*, 24(4): 353–370.

Manyena, S., O'Brien, G., O'Keefe, P., and Rose, J. 2011. Disaster Resilience: A Bounce Back or Bounce Forward Ability? *Local Environment: The International Journal of Justice and Sustainability*, 16(5): 417–424.

Mazer, J., Thompson, B., Cherry, J., Russell, M., Payne, H., Kirby, E., and Pfohl, W. 2015. Communication in the Face of a School Crisis: Examining the Volume and Content of Social Media Mentions During Active Shooter Incidents. *Computers in Human Behavior*, 53: 238–248.

Moorley, C., and Chinn, T. 2014. Nursing and Twitter: Creating an Online Community Using Hashtags. *Collegian*, 21(2): 103–109.

Muschert, G., and Carr, D. 2006. Media Salience and Frame Changing Across Events: Coverage of Nine School Shootings, 1997–2001. *Journalism and Mass Communication Quarterly*, 84(4): 747–766.

National Center for Educational Statistics. 2006. *A First Look at the Literacy of America's Adults in the 21st Century*. Accessed at www.nces.ed.gov.

National Education Association Health Information Network. 2007. *School Crisis Guide: Help and Healing in a Time of Crisis*. Accessed at http://neahealthyfutures.org/wpcproduct/school-crisis-guide/.

Perry, D. 2015. Planning: The Key to Campus Emergency Prevention and Response. *Spectra*, 51(3): 8–13.

Proutheau, S., and Heath, R. 2009. Precautionary Principle and Biotechnology: Regulators Are from Mars and Activists Are from Venus. In *Handbook of Risk and Crisis Communication*. (eds.) R.L. Health and H.D. O'Hair. New York, NY: Routledge, pp. 576–589.

Rebmann, T., Elliott, M. B., Artman, D., VanNatta, M., and Wakefield, M. 2015. Missouri k-12 School Disaster and Biological Event Preparedness and Seasonal Influenza Vaccination Among School Nurses. *American Journal of Infection Control*, 43(10): 1028–1034.

Rebmann, T., Elliott, M. B., Reddick, D. D., and Swick, Z. 2012. US School/Academic Institution Disaster and Pandemic Preparedness and Seasonal Influenza Vaccination Among School Nurses. *American Journal of Infection Control*, 40(7): 584–899.

Regan, M. 2013. A False Sense of Security. *School Administrator*, 9(70): 26–29.

San Diego Union Tribune Editorial Board. 2018. All of These People Have Died in School Shootings Since Columbine. Enough. *San Diego Union-Tribune* (San Diego, CA), April 20.

Sapien, R. E., and Allen, A. 2001. Emergency Preparation in Schools: A Snapshot of a Rural State. *Pediatric Emergency Care*, 17(5): 329–333.

Schultz, F., Utz, S., and Göritz, A. 2011. Is the Medium the Message? Perceptions of and Reactions to Crisis Communication Via Twitter, Blogs and Traditional Media. *Public Relations Review*, 37(1): 20–27.

Seeger, M., Heyart, B., Barton, E., and Bultnyck, S. 2001. Crisis Planning and Crisis Communication in Public Schools: Assessing Post Columbine Responses. *Communication Research Reports*, 18(4): 376–383.

Sellnow, T., and Seeger, M. 2013. *Theorizing Crisis Communication*. New York: Wiley-Blackwell.

Starbird, K., Palen, L., Liu, S., Vieweg, S., Hughes, A., Schram, A., and Schenk, C. 2012. Promoting Structured Data in Citizen Communications During Disaster Response: An Account of Strategies for Diffusion of the "tweak the tweet" Syntax. *Crisis Information Management: Communication and Technologies*, 43–63.

Stein, A. 2006. We Thought It Could Never Happen Here: The Crisis Communications Response to the Thurston High School Shootings. *Journal of Promotion Management*, 12(3–4): 99–128.

Stephens, K. 2011. Tuscaloosa City Schools Turn to Social Media After the Storms. *Idisaster 2.0*. Accessed at http://idisaster.wordpress.com/2011/08/18/ tuscaloosa-city-schools-turn-to-social-media-after-the-storms/.

U.S. Department of Education Office of Safe and Healthy Students. n.d. S*ocial Media in School Emergency Management: Using New Technology to Improve Emergency Management Communications*. Accessed at https://rems.ed.gov/docs/Training_SocialMediaInEM.pdf.

Vieweg, S., Palen, L., Liu, S., Hughes, A., and Sutton, J. 2008. Collective Intelligence in Disaster: An Examination of the Phenomenon in the Aftermath of the 2007 Virginia Tech Shooting. In *Proceedings from the 5th International ISCRAM Conference*. Washington, DC.

Walsh-Childers, K., and Lewis, N. 2011. Listeners, Not Leeches: What Virginia Tech Survivors Needed from Journalists. *Journal of Mass Media Ethics*, 26(3): 191–205.

Wigley, S., and Fontenot, M. 2010. Crisis Managers Losing Control of the Message: A Pilot Study of the Virginia Tech Shooting. *Public Relations Review*, 36(2): 187–189.

Xiong, F., Liu, Y., Zhang, Z. J., Zhu, J., and Zhang, Y. 2012. An Information Diffusion Model Based on Retweeting Mechanism for Online Social Media. *Physics Letters A*, 376: 2103–2108.

15 The use of social media in crisis communication

Amber Silver

Introduction

The rapid proliferation of new information and communications technologies (ICTs) has revolutionized the ways that individuals and organizations communicate with each other. This is particularly true in terms of risk and crisis communications, which have seen a marked shift from traditional sender-receiver approaches to increasingly collaborative, participatory, and multidirectional communication during emergencies. The development of the Internet, mobile phones and mobile phone applications, and the Wireless Emergency Alert system (WEA), for example, have fundamentally altered the way that many citizens obtain, interpret, and respond to official and unofficial information. These changes have profound implications – and notable challenges – for emergency management. This chapter explores the use of social media for risk and crisis communication, and thus begins with a discussion of these concepts as well as an introduction to Web 2.0 and social media. Next, the strengths and weaknesses of social media as a communications tool will be presented, and several strategies that have been employed to manage common challenges will be discussed. The chapter will conclude with a discussion about the implications for the use of these new technologies for resilience in the face of disasters and will outline several opportunities for future research.

Risk and crisis communication

Although the terms risk and crisis communication are often used interchangeably, they are distinct in important and practical ways. McComas (2006: 76) defines risk communication as "an iterative exchange of information among individuals, groups, and institutions, related to the assessment, characterization, and management of risk." Risk communication is most often used to describe messaging that intends to inform or persuade the public about potential risks and often aims to enact long-term behavioral or environmental changes (Reynolds and Seeger 2005). Risk communication about flood hazards in a particular community, for example, might try to raise awareness about the probability of flood hazards while also encouraging preventative protective behaviors (such as purchasing flood insurance and installing sump pumps) and discouraging dangerous behaviors (such as driving through flooded roads). The overarching goal of most risk communication messaging is to provide citizens with information about potential risks as well as strategies to reduce or avoid potential harm.

By contrast, crisis communication is often conceptualized as narrower in scope and refers to messaging about an ongoing emergency. It is therefore more urgent in nature. Crisis communication "seeks to explain the specific event, identify likely consequences and outcomes, and provide specific harm-reducing information to affected communities in an honest, candid, prompt, accurate, and complete manner" (Reynolds and Seeger 2005: 45). Crisis communication about a devastating flood might aim to inform citizens about evacuation zones and routes and the location of public shelters and to provide protective recommendations, such as to avoid approaching riverbanks. A substantial portion of the existing literature on crisis communication has been written from an organizational perspective, rather than that of the end user. This body of research tends to focus on the role of crisis communication as a tool to manage public expectations and minimize backlash; repair an organization's image and improve stakeholder confidence; and apologize for or explain why a crisis occurred (Gasco et al. 2017; Jin, Liu, and Austin 2014; Kaplan and Haenlein 2010; Reynolds and Seeger 2005; Stern 2017).

The origins of risk and crisis communication research can be traced to the development of chemical and nuclear technologies in the mid-20th century (Sjöberg 2000; Slovic 1987). During this time, scientists and policy makers were confronted with stark public opposition to these technologies – opposition that frustrated and confounded many experts, who generally perceived these technologies in a favorable light given their presumed positive risk-benefit trade-offs. This opposition also raised questions about the ways that different publics perceive risks. For example, why was there often such opposition to nuclear technologies (which have a low probability of catastrophic failure), while other more common and salient risks (such as smoking cigarettes or drinking alcohol) were generally accepted?

These and other questions spurred research into the domain of public risk perception from the 1970s onward. This early body of research investigated the disparity between public and expert perceptions of risks, with the goal of understanding how best to encourage public acceptance of *risky* technologies (Fischhoff et al. 1978; Slovic, Fischhoff, and Lichtenstein 1982; Slovic 1987). Accordingly, risk communication during this time was predominately sender-to-receiver (expert-to-citizen) oriented, and the goal was largely one of persuasion. Given the information and communications technologies of the time, there was little capacity for citizens to disseminate information about risks themselves and virtually no collaboration between experts and citizens in the development of official warning information. In many respects, citizens were viewed as passive receivers of information rather than active interpreters and creators.

This narrow perception of citizens as end users persisted until the early 2000s, when advances in information and communications technologies began to change the ways that individuals, experts, and organizations interacted with one another.

Following the invention of the Internet, Web 2.0 changed how various end users utilized the World Wide Web (Figure 15.1).

Specifically, Web 2.0 is "a platform whereby content and applications are no longer created and published by individuals, but instead are continuously modified by all users in a participatory and collaborative manner" (Kaplan and Haenlein 2010: 61). Web 2.0 resulted in the rapid proliferation of websites that allowed citizens to create, share, comment on, and like content. These websites were described as social media – as opposed to traditional media – for their ability to empower people outside of the mainstream media realm to create and exchange content. No longer are citizens passive receivers of information – now they are capable of becoming powerful content creators as well.

Although the term "social media" refers to those Internet-based applications that allow users to create and share content, the types of applications vary dramatically. Consider three of the most active social networking websites: Facebook (2.2 billion monthly active users), YouTube (1.5 billion monthly active users), and Instagram (794 million monthly active users) (Statista 2018). All three websites allow users to create a personal profile, upload user-generated content, comment on and share others' content, and follow other users. However, the emphasis of each application is very different. For example, YouTube is primarily intended to share video content, such as news clips, music videos, or video blogs ("vlogs"). Although Instagram also allows video sharing, it is a predominately a photo-sharing service that allows users to filter images, add hashtags, and add location

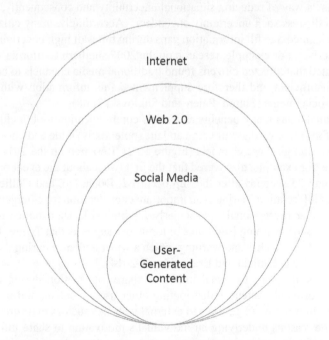

Figure 15.1 Relationship between common terminologies associated with digital applications

tags. Facebook is a platform for users to share information about themselves and their lives. They do so through the creation of status updates, which can exceed 60,000 characters in length and can include pictures, videos, and links to external websites. Accordingly, although all three of these applications fall under the "social media" umbrella, the user interface and the type of content shared through each application can vary dramatically.

Strengths of social media and related applications for crisis communications

The rapid proliferation of social media websites and mobile applications has profound implications for emergency management and response. Citizens utilize social media during disasters for a variety of purposes, including information seeking, information sharing, interpretation and sensemaking, organization of response and recovery efforts, and collective coping. As noted above, however, social media is not a homogenous platform. Different social media applications are used in different ways by different actors across a broad spectrum of hazardous and disastrous events (Eriksson and Olsson 2016; Reuter and Kaufhold 2017).

During crises when crucial information is sparse, individuals experience a high degree of uncertainty. To reduce this uncomfortable sensation, individuals will seek information through alternative channels (Jurgens and Helsloot 2017; Stern 2017). As explained by Jones and others (2017: 11663), information-seeking behavior is "a way of reducing situational uncertainty and consequently, the psychological distress such uncertainty engenders." Accordingly, many citizens will turn to social media to fill information gaps during times of high uncertainty, such as during crises. For example, research on the 2007 southern California wildfires demonstrated that affected citizens found traditional media channels to be important but insufficient and therefore supplemented this information with content found on social media (Sutton, Palen, and Shklovski 2008).

Social media has many benefits as a crisis communication tool, including the rapidity of information dissemination and the (potentially) wide audience that can be reached through these channels (Figure 15.2). Research on the 2011 Tōhoku earthquake, for example, discovered that the first tweet about the event originated 1 minute and 25 seconds after the slip occurred (Doan, Ho, and Collier 2012). Rapidity of information sharing is an important consideration for emergency managers and other professionals, particularly for high-risk, short-notice disasters. Research on short warning lead times of tornadoes suggests that Twitter hashtags can help weather watches and warnings reach a wider audience during the critical pre-impact stage (Chatfield and Brajawidagda 2014).

Individuals also turn to social media to share information during disasters by creating original content, redistributing other users' content, and by sharing third-party information (e.g., links to external websites such as mainstream news media). The reasons underlying an individual's motivation to share information during crises are complex but are often rooted in the desire to assist others and to

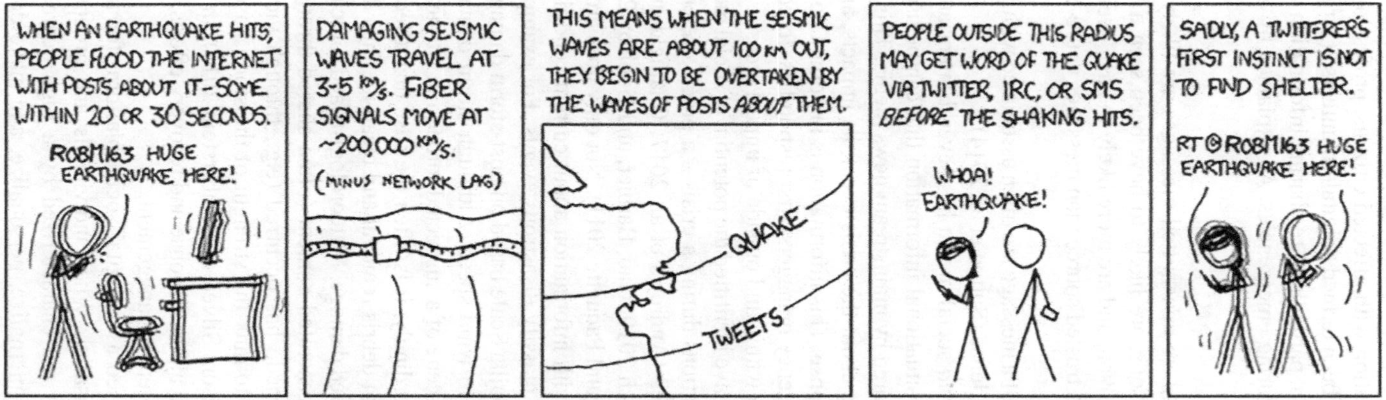

Figure 15.2 "Seismic Waves" comic

Source: xkcd.com

help mitigate the impacts of an event (Sutton, Palen, and Shklovski 2008). Individuals who share information with affected citizens, professionals, or organizations during disaster have been termed "digital volunteers" (Jurgens and Helsloot 2017). Sharing information, particularly re-sharing information created by others, is of crucial importance during emergencies. As explained by Sutton and others (2014: 766):

> All things being equal, re-transmitted messages are likely to be seen by a larger number of persons, are likely to have been seen a larger number of times by any given person, and are more likely to have been received from a personally known and trusted source than messages not re-transmitted.

Thus, multiple exposures of a message are often associated with increased perceptions of veracity and confidence (Sutton et al. 2014).

Content that is shared *via* social media has several important functions. First and foremost, it provides situational information that can be used to supplement and/or confirm content shared by mainstream news media. This situational information can include details about the crisis event, its impacts, and/or appropriate actions to take in the response. This information is important not just for affected citizens but also for emergency managers, first responders, forecasters, and other professionals located both within and outside of impact areas.

Numerous researchers have identified the potential of social media as a platform to gather citizens' observations during a crisis – a process referred to as crowdsourcing or "infoveillance" (Andrews et al. 2017; Chatfield and Brajawidagda 2014; Chew and Eysenbach 2010; Gao, Barbier, and Goolsby 2011; Stern 2017; Vieweg et al. 2010; Yates and Paquette 2011). Not only does crowdsourcing provide crisis professionals with information about current conditions and impacts, but it can also be used to classify disastrous events. For example, tornadoes are ranked on the Enhanced Fujita Scale based on post-storm damage surveys, which correlate on-site damage to wind speed. Although storm damage survey teams endeavor to arrive at the scene of a suspected tornado in a timely fashion, this is not always possible. Accordingly, it is often the case that affected citizens have begun the process of storm debris removal and clean-up, thus destroying important indicators of wind speed damage. Meteorologists and forecasters are increasingly relying on citizen-generated content (often shared through social media) to confirm whether a tornado has occurred (e.g., through videos and pictures of the tornado itself) and to rank the strength of the storm based on pictures of post-storm damage (Harrison, Silver, and Doberstein 2015). In this way, crowdsourcing allows citizens to aid in response and recovery efforts, either directly or indirectly, as part of emergency management.

Social media is also used as a digital social platform for interpretation and sensemaking during a disaster. When individuals and groups are confronted with risky situations that are characterized by a high degree of uncertainty, they seek to understand, internalize, personalize, and make decisions based on constantly evolving information (Sutton et al. 2014). Stern (2017: 4) explains that sensemaking:

> refers to the challenging task of developing an adequate interpretation of what are often complex, dynamic, and ambiguous situations. This entails developing not only a picture of what is happening, but also an understanding of the implications of the situation from one's own vantage point and that of other salient stakeholders.

Social media platforms can be effective at facilitating and accelerating this collaborative process (Gasco et al. 2017; Jurgens and Helsloot 2017; Stieglitz et al. 2017). Importantly, sensemaking acts as an intermediate step between message receipt and action (Sutton et al. 2014).

One example of an action that can result from the collective process of sensemaking is volunteerism. Recent research has demonstrated that social media can act as a powerful and flexible platform to organize volunteers, as well as the donation of physical and financial aid (Muralidharan et al. 2011; DHS 2013; DHS 2014). In a recent study of the use of social media for community response and recovery following an F3 tornado, it was found that Facebook and Facebook groups played a crucial role in rapidly and effectively organizing citizen groups (Silver and Matthews 2017). The citizens in this project indicated that Facebook allowed members of the community to connect with one another, even if they did not share "real life" social circles. In other words, Facebook facilitated strangers helping strangers in the aftermath of a devastating disaster (Silver and Matthews 2017).

In terms of digital volunteerism, an emerging trend can be found within the realm of so-called "SOS" messaging. During crises when traditional communications channels are overwhelmed or have ceased functioning, citizens are increasingly turning to social media for assistance. During Hurricane Sandy, for example, citizens tweeted the New York Fire Department's twitter feed (@fdny) to report people trapped in buildings, to request assistance, and to report flooding. The FDNY responded to many of these requests, thereby assisting citizens who had not been able to contact emergency services via traditional means (DHS 2013). The trend of SOS messaging appears to be gaining traction, particularly on Twitter. For example, when Hurricane Harvey affected Houston, Texas, in August 2017, Twitter was inundated with tweets containing SOS-related hashtags such as #HarveySOS, #HarveyRescue, #peoplewithboats, and #boatrescue.

Taken together, it is clear that social media can be used in a variety of different ways by numerous actors throughout the disaster-response cycle. Social media often acts a digital social environment for information seeking, information sharing, organization, and emotional support and coping processes. Owing to its flexibility, rapidity, and participatory and collaborative nature, as well as its ease of access and broad user base, social media is emerging as a powerful communications tool. This tool is one of a host of resources that emergency managers, first responders, and other professionals tasked with risk and crisis communication may utilize in order to engage with citizens before, during, and after disaster.

Potential weaknesses of social media and related applications for crisis communications

Although the strengths of social media are marked and varied, there also exists several notable challenges – and potential weaknesses – associated with the use of these applications for crisis communication. These challenges include: issues of misinformation and gossip, perishability of information, and compromising safety.

The issue of misinformation and gossip has often been raised as a concern regarding the use of social media, and this is particularly true during crises when uncertainty and urgency are high (Sutton, Palen, and Shklovski 2008). Misinformation can be shared unintentionally (i.e., when a user believes information is credible) or maliciously (i.e., when a user knowingly shares false or misleading information). It is not difficult to imagine how the spread of misinformation or gossip could have profound implications for crisis management, whether the information is related to the event, its impacts, or recommended actions. However, inherent to this line of thinking is the assumption that end users are passive recipients of information rather than active interpreters. Recent research has found that many users tend to question, verify, and correct misinformation received through social media in what is termed misinformation management or collective error correction (Sutton, Palen, and Shklovski 2008). Research across a spectrum of crises, including tornadoes (Silver and Matthews 2017), wildfires (Sutton, Palen, and Shklovski 2008), pandemics (Chew and Eysenbach 2010), floods, and earthquakes (Mendoza, Poblete, and Castillo 2010) have found that false information is often questioned, corrected, and filtered by online communities.

The effectiveness of misinformation management can be improved by using a number of different strategies. One such strategy is the active engagement and involvement of knowledgeable experts and community leaders on social media during crisis events. Research on tsunami hazards, for example, has found that misinformation and rumor proliferate more readily when there is a lack of engagement by officials (Sutton, Hansard, and Hewett 2011). A recent study on tornadoes supports this finding, and suggests that many community members desire and expect their local leadership to engage via social media (Silver and Grek-Martin 2015). Another strategy to improve misinformation management during crises can be found in ongoing risk communication efforts. For example, the National Weather Service frequently shares infographics detailing how to assess the veracity and credibility of information during severe weather (Figure 15.3).

The infographic portrayed in Figure 15.3 also addresses the second concern of using social media for crisis communication, which is the highly perishable nature of certain official warning information. Weather watches and weather warnings, for example, are highly dynamic and can be rapidly issued, upgraded, downgraded, or dropped during a severe weather outbreak. Sharing outdated information, even

Figure 15.3 An example of an infographic shared by the National Weather Service via Twitter, which outlines strategies for misinformation management

Source: @NWSNorman

though it might have been accurate at one point in time, can confound the disaster narrative on social media. Risk communication campaigns, such as those of the National Weather Service described above, are a valuable tool that can be used to educate social media users on best practices during crisis events.

An emerging concern regarding the use of social media for crisis communications involves the potential to compromise the safety of first responders and citizens. After the 2013 Boston Bombing, social media was inundated with posts containing tactical information, such as videos and pictures of SWAT team locations (Figure 15.4). The following tweet from the Boston Police Department urging citizens not to share tactical information was re-tweeted over 10,000 times:

> #MediaAlert: WARNING: Do Not Compromise Officer Safety by Broadcasting Tactical Positions of Homes Being Searched
>
> (Boston Police, April 19. 2013)

A social news aggregation website called Reddit was also involved in compromising the Boston Bombing investigation (Potts and Harrison 2013; Washington Post 2013). A subreddit called r/FindBostonBombers was established immediately

#MediaAlert: WARNING: Do Not Compromise Officer Safety by Broadcasting Tactical Positions of Homes Being Searched.

Figure 15.4 A tweet from the Boston Police Department urging citizens not to share information about officer movements

Source: @Boston_Police

after the bombing, whose goal was for users to investigate and identify potential suspects. One individual who was incorrectly identified was a 22-year-old man named Sunil Tripathi. The subsequent witch hunt resulted in the Tripathi family receiving hundreds of threatening and anti-Islamic messages and a waste of resources as police followed up on numerous leads that turned out to be dead ends (New York Times 2013; Starbird et al. 2014). Although users of numerous social media websites, including Twitter and Reddit, actively engaged in misinformation management during the aftermath of the bombing, the damage was significant (Potts and Harrison 2013; Starbird et al. 2014).

Misinformation and gossip, perishability of information, and potential safety concerns are three notable challenges associated with the use of social media for crisis communication. Citizens and organizations, however, have developed numerous strategies for minimizing the negative aspects of these communication channels. Educational infographics, engagement by experts and community leaders, and misinformation management have all been effective to some degree in minimizing the negative aspects of social media for crisis communication. That is not to say that these issues have been solved – on the contrary, they remain persistent challenges that must continue to be acknowledged and addressed. However, the challenges of social media for crisis communications are not as insurmountable as once believed.

Social media and community resilience

Given the dynamic and evolving nature of resilience as a concept, social-ecological resilience can be defined in many ways. Berkes and Jolly (2001) propose that social-ecological resilience has three characteristics: (1) the amount of change a system can experience and still retain the same controls on function and structure, (2) the degree to which the system is capable of self-organization, and (3) the system's ability to build and increase its capacity for learning and adaptation. Over the last decade, there has been a substantial body of literature published that directly links the resilience of a social-ecological system with its adaptive capacity (Adger 2000; Berkes 2007; Folke 2006; Smit and Wandel 2006). Building on this line of thinking, Manyena (2006) defines disaster resilience as "the intrinsic capacity of a system, community, or society predisposed to a shock or stress to adapt and survive by changing non-essential attributes and rebuild itself."

Social media has the capacity to strengthen community and individual resilience in a number of ways. Jurgens and Helsloot (2017) note that social media facilitate information gathering, information sharing, collaboration and problem solving, and coping. As described above, these attributes can positively influence the ability of individuals and communities with self-organization and adaptation following a crisis. With regard to coping, recent research has demonstrated that social media can be used as a platform for emotional support after a disaster (Jurgens and Helsloot 2017; Qu, Wu, and Wang 2009; Tandoc and Takahashi 2017; Vieweg et al. 2010). Coping refers to the "conscious, purposeful behaviours or cognitions initiated in response to the experience of a chronically stressful situation or following the occurrence of a stressful life event" (Eckenrode 1991: 1). By using social media to share their experiences, provide and obtain support, and/or release their negative emotions, individuals often feel more connected, supported, and optimistic (Jurgens and Helsloot 2017).

Research on tornadic storms, for example, has underscored the usefulness of Facebook and Facebook groups as digital platforms for this type of psychosocial healing (Silver and Grek-Martin 2015; Silver and Matthews 2017). Specifically, Facebook groups allowed members to share their experiences during and after the tornado, ask questions and provide support, vent negative emotions such as guilt, frustration, and anger, and to organize volunteer groups (Silver and Grek-Martin 2015; Silver and Matthews 2017). One volunteer group that was organized through Facebook was the "Goderich Trees Project," a group that assisted private property owners with "re-greening" their property (i.e., replacing bushes, trees, and other flora destroyed by a tornado). The act of coming together to replants trees and restore the town's aesthetic appeal became such a powerful symbol of recovery that the one year monument to the tornado was a broken tree showing signs of new growth (Figure 15.5).

Conclusions and opportunities for future research

The ways that individuals, organizations, and experts interact with and communicate to one another have been revolutionized by the rapid advancements in the development and proliferation of information and communications technology. This has numerous profound implications and challenges for the domain of emergency management. As Jurgens and Helsloot (2017) note, the four aspects of self-resilience are information gathering and dissemination, collaborative

Figure 15.5 The one-year monument to the Goderich, Ontario, tornado
Source: Silver 2015

problem-solving, and coping. Accordingly, social media has a tremendous capacity to positively (and negatively) affect individual resilience during disasters (Jurgens and Helsloot 2017).

It is prudent, therefore, to delve more deeply into the capacity of social media as a crisis communications tool. Although there exists a blooming body of research on this topic, there are several notable areas where further research could benefit our understanding of social media usage during disasters. Firstly, although Twitter is ranked 11th of the most famous social networking sites worldwide, with *only* 330 million active monthly users (Statista 2018), it is the focus of a disproportionately high number of research articles (Acar and Muraki 2011; Chatfield and Brajawidagda 2014; Chew and Eysenbach 2010; Doan, Ho, and Collier 2012; Gasco et al. 2017; Helsloot and Groenendaal 2013; Kryvasheyeu et al. 2016; Mendoza, Poblete, and Castillo 2010; Palen et al. 2010; Murthy and Longwell 2013; Starbird et al. 2014; Sutton, Palen, and Shklovski 2008; Sutton et al. 2014; Vieweg et al. 2010). There is a comparative dearth of research on Facebook, Instagram, YouTube, and other far more popular social networking sites. This is owing in large part to the ease and accessibility of gathering and analyzing tweets compared to the more onerous task of gathering and analyzing content such as pictures and videos. The disproportionate emphasis on Twitter is potentially problematic, however, as insights from these studies are often generalized to social media as a whole and, as discussed previously, social media is not a homogenous entity. There is a pressing need, therefore, to shift scholarly focus to how other social networking sites and mobile applications are being used during crises (Potts and Harrison 2013; Stern 2017; Sutton, Woods, and Vos 2017; Tandoc and Takahashi 2017).

A second area of research that has the potential to improve our understanding of social media and its effects on community and self-resilience involves so-called *digital vigilantes* (Starbird et al. 2014). Digital vigilantism has been seen in terms of online harassment, "doxing" (i.e., publishing private information online), stalking, physical threats, and more (Pew Research Center 2017). However, it is often the case that digital vigilantes begin as digital volunteers and intend for their actions to have positive outcomes – such as the case of the Boston Bombing subreddit. Understanding the divide between digital volunteerism and vigilantism within the context of crises has been largely underemphasized yet has significant implications for issues of misinformation management.

Lastly, there is a small (but growing) emphasis on the ways that mobile phones and other smart devices are utilized during a crisis, both to access social networking sites and as platforms for mobile applications (Stern 2017; Sutton, Woods, and Vos 2017). It seems to be an unspoken assumption within the disaster literature that social networking sites are accessed and utilized in the same ways across platforms, yet we do not know if this is true. Accordingly, additional research on the ways that different types of technologies are utilized in crisis (both as a platform for social media and as independent devices) would be beneficial.

References

Acar, A., and Muraki, Y. 2011. Twitter for Crisis Communication: Lessons Learned from Japan's Tsunami Disaster. *International Journal of Web Based Communities*, 7(3): 392–402.

Adger, W. N. 2000. Social and Ecological Resilience: Are They Related? *Progress in Human Geography*, 24(3): 347–364.

Andrews, S., Day, T., Domdouzis, K., Hirsch, L., Lefticaru, R., and Orphanides, C. 2017. Chapter 6: Analyzing Crowd-Sourced Information and Social Media for Crisis Management. In *Application of Social Media in Crisis Management*. (eds.) B. Akhar, A. Staniforth, and D. Waddington. New York: Springer, pp. 77–96.

Berkes, F. 2007. Understanding Uncertainty and Reducing Vulnerability: Lessons from Resilience Thinking. *Natural Hazards*, 41: 283–295.

Berkes, F., and Jolly, D. 2001. Adapting to Climate Change: Socio-Ecological Resilience in a Canadian West Arctic Community. *Conservation Ecology*, 5(2): 18.

Boston Police Department. 2013. *Boston Police Department Twitter Account*. Accessed at https://twitter.com/bostonpolice/status/325230546928160768.

Chatfield, A. T., and Brajawidagda, U. 2014. Crowdsourcing Hazardous Weather: Weather Reports from Citizens via Twittersphere Under the Short Warning Lead Times of EF5 Intensity Tornado Conditions. In *Proceedings of the 47th Hawaii International Conference on System Science*, pp. 2231–2241.

Chew, C., and Eysenbach, G. 2010. Pandemics in the Age of Twitter: Content Analysis of Tweets During the 2009 H1N1 Outbreak. *PLoS One*, 5(11): 13.

Department of Homeland Security (DHS). 2013. Lessons Learned: Social Media and Hurricane Sandy. *Virtual Social Media Working Group and DHS First Responders Group*, p. 39.

———. 2014. Using Social Media for Enhanced Situational Awareness and Decision Support. *Virtual Social Media Working Group and DHS First Responders Group*, p. 44.

Doan, S., Ho Vo, B-K., and Collier, N. 2012. An Analysis of Twitter Messages in the 2011 Tohoku Earthquake. *Lecture Notes of the Institute of Computer Sciences, Social Informatics and Telecommunications Engineering*, 91(4): 58–66.

Eckenrode, J. 1991. Introduction and Overview. In *The Social Context of Coping*. (ed.) J. Eckenrode. New York: Springer, pp. 1–12.

Eriksson, M., and Olsson, E-K. 2016. Facebook and Twitter in Crisis Communication: A Comparative Study of Crisis Communication Professionals and Citizens. *Journal of Crisis and Contingencies Management*, 24(4): 198–208.

Fischhoff, B., Slovic, P., Lichtenstein, S., Read, S., and Combs, B. 1978. How Safe Is Safe Enough? A Psychometric Study of Attitudes Towards Technological Risks and Benefits. *Policy Science*, 9: 127–152.

Folke, C. 2006. Resilience: The Emergency of a Perspective for Social-Ecological Systems Analyses. *Global Environmental Change*, 16: 253–267.

Gao, H., Barbier, G., and Goolsby, R. 2011. Harnessing the Crowdsourcing Power of Social Media for Disaster Relief. *Intelligent Systems, IEEE*, 26(3): 10–14.

Gasco, M., Bayerl, P. S., Denef, S., and Akhgar, B. 2017. What Do Citizens Communicate About During Crises? Analyzing Twitter Use During the 2011 UK Riots. *Government Information Quarterly*, 34: 635–645.

Harrison, S., Silver, A., and Doberstein, B. 2015. Post-Storm Damage Surveys of Tornado Hazards in Canada: Implications for Mitigation and Policy. *International Journal of Disaster Risk Reduction*, 13: 427–440.

Helsloot, I., and Groenendaal, J. 2013. Twitter: An Underutilized Potential During Sudden Crises? *Journal of Contingencies and Crisis Management*, 21(3): 178–183.

Jin, Y., Liu, B. F., and Austin, L. L. 2014. Examining the Role of Social Media in Effective Crisis Management: The Effects of Crisis Origin, Information Form, and Source on Publics' Crisis Response. *Communication Research*, 41: 74–94.

Jones, N. M., Thompson, R. R., Schetter, C. D., and Silver, R. C. 2017. Distress and Rumor Exposure on Social Media During a Campus Lockdown. *Proceedings of the National Academy of Science*, 114(44): 11663–11668.

Jurgens, M., and Helsloot, I. 2017. The Effect of Social Media on the Dynamics of (self) Resilience During Disasters: A Literature Review. *Journal of Contingencies and Crisis Management*, 1–10.

Kaplan, A. M., and Haenlein, M. 2010. Users of the World, Unite! The Challenges and Opportunities of Social Media. *Business Horizons*, 53: 59–68.

Kryvasheyeu, Y., Chen, H., Obradovich, N., Moro, E., van Hentenryck, P., Fowler, J., and Cebrian, M. 2016. Rapid Assessment of Disaster Damage Using Social Media Activity. *Science Advances*, 2(3): 11.

Manyena, S. B. 2006. The Concept of Resilience Revisited. *Disasters*, 30(4): 433–450.

McComas, K. A. 2006. Defining Moments in Risk Communication Research: 1996–2005. *Journal of Health Communication*, 11: 75–91.

Mendoza, M., Poblete, B., and Castillo, C. 2010. Twitter Under Crisis: Can We Trust What We RT? *1st Workshop on Social Media Analytics*, Washington, DC, pp. 71–79.

Muralidharan, S., Rasmussen, L., Patterson, D., and Shin, J-H. 2011. Hope for Haiti: An Analysis of Facebook and Twitter Usage During the Earthquake Relief Efforts. *Public Relations Review*, 37: 175–177.

Murthy, D., and Longwell, S. A. 2013. Twitter and Disasters: The Uses of Twitter During the 2010 Pakistan Floods. *Information, Communication, and Society*, 16(6): 837–855.

New York Times. 2013. *Should Reddit Be Blamed for the Spreading of a Smear?* Accessed on February 20, 2018 at www.nytimes.com/2013/07/28/magazine/should-reddit-be-blamed-for-the-spreading-of-a-smear.html?partner=rss&emc=rss&_r=0&pagewanted=all.

Palen, L., Starbird, K., Vieweg, S., and Hughes, A. 2010. Twitter-Based Information Distribution During the 2009 Red River Valley Flood Threat. *Bulletin of the American Society for Information Science and Technology*, 36(5): 13–17.

Pew Research Center. 2017. *Online Harassment 2017*. Accessed on February 20, 2018 at www.pewinternet.org/2017/07/11/online-harassment-2017/.

Potts, L., and Harrison, A. 2013. Interfaces as Rhetorical Constructions: Reddit and 4Chan During the Boston Marathon Bombings. In *Proceedings of SIGDOC'13*, Greenville, North Carolina, p. 9.

Qu, Y., Wu, P. F., and Wang, X. 2009. Online Community Response to Major Disaster: A Study of Tianya Forum in the 2008 Sichuan Earthquake. In *Proceedings of Hawaii International Conference on System Science*, pp. 1079–1088.

Reuter, C., and Kaufhold, M-A. 2017. Fifteen Years of Social Media in Emergencies: A Retrospective Review and Future Directions for Crisis Informatics. *Journal of Contingencies and Crisis Management*, 1–17.

Reynolds, B., and Seeger, M. W. 2005. Crisis and Emergency Risk Communication as an Integrative Model. *Journal of Health Communication*, 10: 43–55.

Silver, A., and Grek-Martin, J. 2015. "Now we understand what community really means": Reconceptualizing the Role of Sense of Place in the Disaster Recovery Process. *Journal of Environmental Psychology*, 42: 32–41.

Silver, A., and Matthews, L. 2017. The Use of Facebook for Information Seeking, Decision Support, and Self-Organization Following a Significant Disaster. *Information, Communication, and Society*, 20(11): 1680–1697.

Sjöberg, L. 2000. Factors in Risk Perception. *Risk Analysis*, 20: 1–11.

Slovic, P. 1987. Perception of Risk. *Science*, 236: 280–285.

Slovic, P., Fischhoff, B., and Lichtenstein, S. 1982. Why Study Risk Perception? *Risk Analysis*, 2: 83–93.

Smit, B., and Wandel, J. 2006. Adaptation, Adaptive Capacity and Vulnerability. *Global Environmental Change*, 16: 282–292.

Starbird, K., Maddock, J., Achterman, P., and Mason, R. M. 2014. Rumors, False Flags, and Digital Vigilantes: Misinformation on Twitter After 2013 Boston Marathon Bombings. In *iConference 2014 Proceedings*, pp. 654–662.

Statista. 2018. *Most Famous Social Network Sites Worldwide as of January 2018, Ranked by Number of Active Users (in millions)*. Accessed on 22 February 2018 at www.statista.com/statistics/272014/global-social-networks-ranked-by-number-of-users/.

Stern, E. 2017. Unpacking and Exploring the Relationship Between Crisis Management and Social Media in the Era of "smart devices". *Homeland Security Affairs*, 13(4): 1–15.

Stieglitz, S., Bunker, D., Mirbabaie, M., and Ehnis, C. 2017. Sense-Making in Social Media During Extreme Events. *Journal of Contingencies and Crisis Management*, 1–12.

Sutton, J., Hansard, B., and Hewett, P. 2011. Changing Channels: Communication Tsunami Warning Information in Hawaii. In *Proceedings of the 3rd International Joint Topical Meeting on Emergency Preparedness and Response, Robotics, and Remote Systems*, p. 14.

Sutton, J., Palen, L., and Shklovski, I. 2008. Backchannels on the Front Lines: Emergent Uses of Social Media in the 2007 Southern California Wildfires. In *Proceedings of the 5th International ISCRAM Conference*, Washington, DC.

Sutton, J., Spiro, E. S., Fitzhugh, S., Gibson, B., and Butts, Carter T. 2014. Warning Tweets: Serial Transmission of Messages During the Warning Phase of a Disaster Event. *Information, Communication, and Society*, 17(6): 765–787.

Sutton, J., Woods, C., and Vos, S. C. 2017. Willingness to Click: Risk Information Seeking During Imminent Threats. *Journal of Contingencies and Crisis Management*, 1–12.

Tandoc, E. C., and Takahashi, B. 2017. Log in If You Survived: Collective Coping on Social Media in the Aftermath of Typhoon Haiyan in the Philippines. *New Media and Society*, 19(11): 1778–1793.

Vieweg, S., Hughes, A. L., Starbird, K., and Palen, L. 2010. Microblogging During Two Natural Hazard Events: What Twitter May Contribute to Situational Awareness. In *Proceedings of the SIGCHI Conference on the Human Factors in Computing Systems*. Atlanta, Georgia, pp. 1079–1088.

Washington Post. 2013. *Police, Citizens and Technology Factor into Boston Bombing Probe*. Accessed on February 20, 2018 at www.washingtonpost.com/world/national-security/inside-the-investigation-of-the-boston-marathon-bombing/2013/04/20/19d8c322-a8ff-11e2-b029-8fb7e977ef71_print.html.

xkcd.com. 2018. *Seismic waves (comic)*. Accessed on February 22, 2018 at https://xkcd.com/723/.

Yates, D., and Paquette, S. 2011. Emergency Knowledge Management and Social Media Technologies: A Case Study of the 2010 Haitian Earthquake. *International Journal of Information Management*, 31: 6–13.

Index

Note: Numbers in **bold** indicate a table. Numbers in *italics* indicate a figure.